ANALECTA BIBLICA
INVESTIGATIONES SCIENTIFICAE IN RES BIBLICAS

123

SCARIA KUTHIRAKKATTEL

THE BEGINNING OF JESUS' MINISTRY ACCORDING TO MARK'S GOSPEL (1,14-3,6): A REDACTION CRITICAL STUDY

EDITRICE PONTIFICIO ISTITUTO BIBLICO – ROMA 1990

Vidimus et approbamus ad normam Statutorum

Pontificia Universitas Gregoriana
Romae, die 16 mensis decembris anni 1987

R. P. I. DE LA POTTERIE, S.J.
R. P. J. KILGALLEN, S.J.

ISBN 88-7653-123-8

EDITRICE PONTIFICIA UNIVERSITÀ GREGORIANA
EDITRICE PONTIFICIO ISTITUTO BIBLICO
Piazza della Pilotta, 35 - 00187 Roma

We should show interest in the life and work of each confrere and help and encourage him to bring his life and talents to fuller development.

- SVD Constitutions, n. 303

This work is dedicated to

all those who

by their interest,

their assistance,

and their encouragement

enabled me to

bring to completion

this thesis

on Mark's Gospel.

ACKNOWLEDGEMENTS

The present work is a thoroughly revised edition of a doctoral dissertation defended at the Gregorian University in December 1987. To Prof.
Ignace de la Potterie, S.J., director of the thesis, whose keen interest, constant
encouragement, and judicious criticisms accompanied my research from start
to finish I extend my heartfelt thanks. I am also very grateful to Prof. John
Killgallen, S.J., the reader of my thesis, for his valuable suggestions, ready
availability, and his personal concern.

It was Prof. N. M. Seel (Tübingen) and his family and Mrs. Else Streit
who not only procured for me much needed works on Mark in the German
language but who also encouraged me at each critical stage of my research.
To them I most humbly acknowledge my indebtedness and will ever value
their timely assistance and genuine friendship. I also wish to acknowledge
my indebtedness to Frs. Pietro Sessolo, Peter McHugh, Almiro Werle, Dermot
Walsh, Herman Wijtten and Josef Scheidler — all of the Society of the Divine
Word — for their constant support throughout the duration of this project.

To Fr. Heinrich Heekeren (former superior general) and to the members
of his generalate I am immensely grateful for granting me the opportunity
and allotting me the time to undertake and complete this research and to have
it published in the *Analecta Biblica*. To Fr. Heinrich Barlage (the present
superior general) and the members of his generalate I am grateful for allowing
me to return to Rome to undertake its publication.

This work would not have seen the light of day had not Frs. Roger
Schroeder, SVD, and Ladislav Nemet, SVD, contributed their time and effort
to keyboarding the voluminous text of the dissertation in order to meet my
deadline. It is a pleasure for me to extend my sincerest thanks to Fr. Friedrich
Förster, SVD, Information Systems Manager, for his ever-helpful advice and
computer assistance in the formatting and production of the thesis. It was also
an enriching experience for me to work with Fr. Charles Schoderbek, SVD,
whose editorial skills and varied expertise have made the written text clearly
more readable in its present form. To him I am beholden for his generous
services.

Grafica per la Stampa undertook the task of formating the text for publication. I am immensely gratuful to Mr. Massimo Antonioni, its director, and Mr. Romano Pignani, his assistant, for their services and friendship.

And finally, a special word of thanks is due to Prof. Luis Alonso Schökel, S.J., for accepting this thesis for publication in the *Analecta Biblica* series.

29 June 1990   Scaria Kuthirakkattel, SVD

Feast of Sts. Peter and Paul

TABLE OF CONTENTS

CHAPTER TWO
THE PLAN OF THE GOSPEL ACCORDING TO MARK

CHAPTER THREE

INTERNAL COHESION AND LITERARY DIVISON OF MK 1,14-3,6

PART TWO

LITERARY ANALYSIS AND INTERPRETATION
OF MK 1,14-3,6

CHAPTER FOUR

THE PROCLAMATION OF THE KINGDOM (1,14-15)
AND THE CALL OF THE FIRST FOUR DISCIPLES (1,16-20)

CHAPTER FIVE

MANIFESTATION OF JESUS' MESSIANIC AUTHORITY
AND POPULAR ACCEPTANCE (1,21-45)

CHAPTER SIX

MANIFESTATION OF JESUS' MESSIANIC AUTHORITY AND
SCRIBAL AND PHARISAIC OPPOSITION (2,1-3,6)

PART THREE

FUNCTION OF MK 1,14-3,6
IN THE WHOLE OF THE GOSPEL

CHAPTER SEVEN

MK 1,14-3,6 IN THE FRAME OF THE GOSPEL

CHAPTER EIGHT

THE PROGRAMMATIC CHARACTER OF MK 1,14-3,6

CONCLUSION

ABBREVIATIONS

We have used the abbreviations as given in the "Instructions for Contributors", *Biblica* 1982, 1-19, except for the books of the Bible for which the abbreviations of *The Holy Bible,* Revised Standard Version, London 1966, xi-xii, are being followed. For abbreviations not found in the "Instructions for Contributors", we have used S. SCHWERTNER, *Internationales Abkürzungsverzeichnis für Theologie und Grenzgebiete,* Berlin - New York 1974, 3-88.

We have also used the abbreviations Mt, Mk, Lk and Jn for each of the four Gospels or the respective evangelists. The context will make the difference evident.

INTRODUCTION

I. Statement of the Problem

A. Organization of the Text

Departing from the traditional view, a growing number of exegetes affirm that the introduction to Mk consists of 1,1-15. The first section begins at 1,16 and concludes with the summary in 3,7-12 [1]. Is this contention valid? Within 1,14-3,6 authors recognize mainly two units, namely, 1,21-45 and 2,1-3,6 [2]. How are these two units structured?

Secondly, there are problems in the organization of specific pericopes in 1,14-3,6. Are 2,13-14 and 2,15-17 two literary units? [3] Is there a literary or logical necessity to divide 1,21-28 into two paragraphs: 1,21-22 and 1,23-28? [4] Similarly, is it meaningful to divide 2,1-12 into two paragraphs? [5]

B. Importance of 1,14-3,6

An accurate, perceptive and critical reading of Mk reveals that the evangelist gives great importance to the beginning of Jesus' public ministry.

---

[1] Cf. p. 3, nn. 2-3.

[2] Cf. p. 65-66, 71-72.

[3] So in NESTLE-ALAND, BJ, NEB, RSV; LANE, 99-107; TAYLOR, 191, 201-208.

N.B. Every commentary on Mk will be referred to (even the first time) only by the surname of the commentator, the volume number (if more than one), and the page number (e.g., GNILKA, I, 35). Similarly, other books and articles too will be abbreviated (e.g., JEREMIAS, *Theology*, 72; KOCH, "Aufriss", 154). For full details about every work referred to, see the bibliography.

Those authors who have the same surname are differentiated by their initials. Full details about every author referred to are given in the bibliography as well as in the index of authors.

[4] See for instance, NESTLE-ALAND; ALAND, *Synopsis*; BJ.

[5] Cf. NEB, Vg (nova).

First, significant and distinctive Marcan themes commence in this section: kingdom of God (1,15), discipleship (1,16-20)[6], Jesus' teaching (1,21-22.27; 2,2.13) and preaching (1,14-15.38-39), and the Messianic secret (1,34.43-44). Another characteristic Marcan theme, εὐαγγέλιον, already initiated in the title of the book (1,1), is further specified in 1,14-15.

Secondly, Jesus' ministry in this section is characterized by an authority that is extraordinary and unique and a sense of his mission that is conscious and deliberate. Jesus in his very first utterance summons man to radical conversion and authentic faith (1,15). He calls apparently strange men to be the nucleus of his disciples (1,17.20a; 2,14b) and their response to his summons is quick and unconditional (1,18.20b; 2,14c). People sense exceptional authority in his word and deed (1,22.27); and he himself claims unique authority in forgiving sins (2,10) and in exercising lordship over the sabbath (2,28). In 1,38 and especially in 2,17 he unequivocally spells out the purpose of his mission.

Thirdly, there seems to be a contrast between 1,21-45 and 2,1-3,6: in the former people's response to Jesus is very positive and their enthusiasm towards him steadily grows[7] whereas in the latter Jesus faces consistent and mounting opposition from Jewish leaders[8] which reaches its culmination in their decision to kill him (3,6).

Finally, as Albertz[9] long ago noted, the counsel to destroy Jesus (3,6) — which could logically be followed by the Passion narrative — occurs too early in the Gospel.

In light of these observations it is reasonable to ask: Why did Mk compose this section in this particular way? What is the theological significance of 1,14-3,6? What is the place and function of 1,14-3,6 in Mk?

C. Tradition and Redaction

Several authors consider 1,21-34(39) a pre-Marcan unit which Mk integrated into his Gospel while compiling it[10]. A greater number of exegetes

---

[6] See also Mk 1,29.37; 2,14-16.18.23.

[7] Cf. 1,22.27-28.31c.32-33.37.40.45.

[8] Cf. 2,6-7.16.18.24; 3,2.

[9] ALBERTZ, *Streitgespräche*, 5.

[10] Cf. BAARLINK, *Anfängliches Evangelium*, 84; ERNST, 11; GRUNDMANN, 57; JEREMIAS, *Theology*, 38; id., *Eucharistic Words*, 92; PESCH, I, 64; id., "Ein Tag", 114-115; RADERMAKERS, 21; SCHMIDT, *Rahmen*, 67, 76-77; TAYLOR, 91,171; TROCMÉ, *Formation*, 22.

hold that 2,1-3,6 is a pre-Marcan tradition [11]. Even those who admit redactional elements in 2,1-3,6 differ among themselves as to the limit of redaction [12].

An accurate redaction-critical study of 1,14-3,6 may hopefully enable us to come to a more precise and balanced conclusion.

II. Methodological Clarifications

Our investigation of Mk 1,14-3,6 has two principal steps: literary analysis and interpretation or exegesis. Literary analysis is mainly comprised of textual criticism, synoptic comparison, distinction between tradition and redaction, and literary structure. A thorough textual criticism will be undertaken only in those cases where important MSS evidence offers almost equally compelling evidence for two or more variant readings that a choice has to be made. Again, synoptic comparison will be done not in all its details but only insofar as it sheds light on Marcan perspectives. The exegesis will not be extensive but brief and to the point.

What do we mean by 'programmatic character' in Mk 1,14-3,6? Here the nature of the programmatic character is a bit different from what authors generally mean by it in Lk 4,16-30. The programmatic character of Lk 4,16-30 may be summarized as follows.

After a brief introduction (4,16-17) which narrates Jesus' coming to the synagogue at Capernaum and his opening of the book of Isaiah, Lk highlights the scope of Jesus' mission in 4,18-19. His mission has not only a theological and spiritual orientation but also an existential, personal and societal thrust and exigency. Verses 20-22 narrate Jesus' closing of the book, his comment – "Today this scripture has been fulfilled in your hearing" (4,21b) – and the

---

[11] ALBERTZ, *Streitgespräche*, 5-16; BAARLINK, *Anfängliches Evangelium* 84; DUNN, "Bridge", 397; ERNST, 11, 83; GRUNDMANN, 71-72; HULTGREN, *Jesus and His Adversaries*, 21, 152-162; JEREMIAS, *Theology*, 38; id., *Eucharistic Words*, 92; H.C. KEE, *Community*, 32; LANE, 91; MARXSEN, *Introduction*, 130; NINEHAM, 89; PESCH, I, 149; RADERMAKERS, 21; SCHMID, 7, 55-56; SCHMIDT, *Rahmen*, 104; TAYLOR, 91-92, 191; id., *Formation*, 177-179; TROCMÉ, *Formation*, 22.

[12] For instance, KUHN, *Sammlungen*, 52-98, holds that Mk 2,1-28 is pre-Marcan. Substantiating his evidence from Paul and Acts, he points out that the collection had its origin in the conflicts between the Church and Judaism. On the other hand, MAISCH, *Heilung*, 105, 112-118, is of the view that 2,15-3,6 is a pre-Marcan collection but 2,1-14 should be attributed to Mk.

appreciation of the audience. These verses form a miniature of the first part of Jesus' ministry characterized by his success and acceptance by people. In verses 23-27, however, Jesus confronts his audience and citing OT examples he insists on the need for faith. This corresponds to the second part of the Gospel where a growing opposition begins to mount between Jesus and the Jewish leaders. The audience's plan to take him to the brow of the hill and throw him down headlong (4,28-29) gives us an inkling of the events of the Passion. Finally, Jesus' passing through the midst of them and his escape from them (4,30) allude to the Resurrection.

In Mk, as will be established in Ch. II, there are two parts: 1,14-8,30 and 8,27-16,8. The main thrust of the first part is the progressive revelation of the mystery of Jesus' Messiahship whereas the predominant theme of the second part is the mystery of the suffering Son of Man. But in contrast to the second and third sections (3,7-6,6a; 6,6b-8,30) of the first part, the first section (1,14-3,6) contains allusions to Jesus' suffering Messiahship [13], the main theme of the second part. Thus, 1,14-3,6 is the first step of the revelation of Jesus' Messiahship and it is also the first step of the mystery of the suffering Messiahship. This feature of Mk 1,14-3,6 we call the programmatic character.

III. Plan of Procedure

Our investigation is divided into three parts: I. The Place of 1,14-3,6 in Mk; II. Analysis and Interpretation of 1,14-3,6; III. The Function of 1,14-3,6. Each of the above will be explained at some length in the introduction to the respective parts.

---

[13] Cf. p. 260-263.

PART ONE

MK 1,14-3,6 IN THE PLAN OF MARK

The main purpose of the first part of our investigation is to situate Mk
1,14-3,6, the area of our research, in the context of the whole Gospel. In the
first chapter, critically evaluating the views among modern scholars regarding
the extent of the introduction to Mk, we hold that it consists of 1,1-13. The
first section of the Gospel, therefore, begins at 1,14 and it ends at 3,6. The
second chapter attempts to place 1,14-3,6 in the frame of the second Gospel.
After a classification and brief exposition of various proposals on the structure
of Mk based on different criteria, the second chapter proceeds to establish
this according to literary and theological indices. In chapter three, attention
is focused on the internal cohesion of 1,14-3,6 where the literary and thematic
indices contributing to the internal coherence of this section as a whole are
pointed out and where the literary structures of its two main units are
proposed: 1,21-45 (A B A') and 2,1-3,6 (A A' C B B').

CHAPTER ONE

DELIMITATION OF THE SECTION (1,14-3,6)

I. The Problem

With regard to the delimitation of the first section of Mk's Gospel, there are in the main two opinions [1] among modern exegetes: (1) Primarily inspired by the two articles of Keck [2] on Mk 1,1-15 and 3,7-12 respectively, many exegetes hold that Mk 1,14-15 is an integral part of the introduction to the second Gospel [3]. So the introduction or prologue consists of Mk 1,1-15. The first section therefore begins at 1,16 and, according to some, it concludes with the summary in 3,7-12. (2) The introduction comprises Mk 1,1-13; 1,14-15 is, in fact, the beginning of the first section that ends at 3,6. Mk 3,7-12, therefore, constitutes the introduction to the second section which concludes at 6,6a.

---

[1] There are other isolated opinions. FENEBERG (*Markusprolog*, passim) holds that the prologue consists of Mk 1,1-11. A few others think that 1,1-13 is the introduction, 1,14-15 and 3,7-12 are transitional summaries, and the first section then consists of 1,16-3,6 (cf. DONAHUE, *Christ*, 206-208; H.C. KEE, *Community*, 56-62; KELBER, *Kingdom*, 2-7; PERRIN, "Interpretation", 5-6, 11-12; id., *Introduction*, 145-147). The view of PERRIN and his followers is critically evaluated by HEDRICK, "Composition", 289-297, 310-311.

[2] Cf. KECK, "Introduction", 352-370; id., "Mark 3,7-12", 341-358.

[3] Cf. ANDERSON, 58, 62, 83-86; Belo, 144-145; id., "Lecture", 19-25; BLATHERWICK, "Silhouette", 187; DAUTZENBERG, "Zeit", 219-234; ERNST, 17-18; GALIZZI, "Inizio", 4-18; GIBBS, "Prologue", 159, 174-175, 177-178; GNILKA, I, 30, 39-40; GRUNDMANN, 34 (compare with ³1965, v, 25); GUELICH, "Beginning", 5-15; VAN IERSEL, "Aanvang", 169-170; S.E. JOHNSON, 23-24 (compare with 1960, 24); KECK, "Introduction", 358-362; LÜHRMANN, *Markusevangelium*, VII, 31-34; MANGATT, *Way*, 23-25; PESCH, I, 32-33, 71-72; id., "Anfang", 109-113; SEITZ, "Praeparatio", 201-206; id., "Prologues", 262-268; SÖDING, *Glaube*, 134-136; TREVIJANO ETCHEVERRIA, *Comienzo*, 199 et passim.

II. The Beginning of the First Section

A. Mk 1,1-15: The Prologue

1. *Reasons for the Opinion*

The main arguments for considering Mk 1,1-15 as the prologue may be summarized as follows [4]. First, εὐαγγέλιον is the key word and the main theme in Mk's Gospel [5], and "Mark presents Jesus as the beginning (ἀρχή not γένεσις!) of the Christian gospel . . . the gospel 'begins' when Jesus begins preaching" [6], namely, at 1,14-15. Mk 1,14-15 therefore complements not only the title of the book (1,1) but also rounds out the whole introduction in such a way that the entire fifteen verses stand as a genuine prologue to the whole subsequent text [7]. In the second place, connecting words link 1,1-13 and 1,14-15: Ἰησοῦς at the beginning of a pericope (1,1.9.14, later only in 3,7), Ἰωάννης (1,4.6.9.14, next occurrence in 2,18), κηρύσσειν (1,4.7.14, next occurrence at 1,38-39), μετάνοια-μετανοεῖν (1,4.15, next occurrence only at 6,12), ἔρχομαι (1,7.9.14) and Γαλιλαία (1,9.14) [8]. Thirdly, the term εὐαγγέλιον in 1,1 and 1,14-15 forms an inclusion, thus framing 1,1-15 as a unit [9]. And finally some authors [10] point out that there is a parallelism between Mk 1,2-8 and 1,9-15.

2. *Critical Evaluation*

1) An adequate response to the contention that the gospel 'begins' when Jesus begins preaching, namely, at 1,14-15, requires a systematic and accurate

---

[4] See particularly KECK, "Introduction", 358-362; PESCH, I, 32-33, 71-72; DAUTZENBERG, "Zeit", 219-225; ERNST, 31-32; GNILKA, I, 39-40; LÜHRMANN, *Markusevangelium*, 32-34.

[5] Cf. KECK, "Introduction", 357-359, 365-366, 368; GRUNDMANN, 34; PESCH, I, 72.

[6] KECK, "Introduction", 359.

[7] KECK, "Introduction", 359-360. See also DAUTZENBERG, "Zeit", 231; EGGER, *Frohbotschaft*, 40; GNILKA, I, 39-40.

[8] Cf. PESCH, I, 72; id., "Anfang", 111. See also EGGER, *Frohbotschaft*, 39; MANGATT, *Way*, 24-26.

[9] Cf. DAUTZENBERG, "Zeit", 225, 227; GNILKA, I, 39; MANGATT, *Way*, 24.

[10] Cf. ERNST, 31; GNILKA, I, 39; PESCH, I, 71-72.

literary analysis of 1,1-8. Because this task is undertaken in the next section of this chapter, only the pertinent conclusions are mentioned here to show where ἀρχὴ τοῦ εὐαγγελίου takes place. The reading of the Vatican codex is certainly to be preferred in 1,4 (ἐγένετο Ἰωάννης ὁ βαπτίζων ἐν τῇ ἐήρμῳ κηρύσσων) where ὁ βαπτίζων is a title [11]. From syntactic considerations verse 1 has no verb at all but consists of six nouns only (the first in the nominative case and the rest in the genitive), and the conjunction καθώς in verse 2 begins a subordinate clause introducing a direct discourse (1,2bc) and an indirect discourse (1,3); and so the first main verb in 1,1-4 is ἐγένετο in verse 4 which grammatically depends on the present participle κηρύσσων and governs the subject Ἰωάννης ὁ βαπτίζων [12]. Therefore, ἀρχὴ τοῦ εὐαγγελίου is realized in ἐγένετο Ἰωάννης ὁ βαπτίζων . . . κηρύσσων. It must also be noted that ἀρχή in 1,1 means beginning in the sense of a historical event, and εὐαγγέλιον, unlike in Paul, includes Jesus' earthly ministry too and connotes the person of Jesus Christ [13]. Moreover, there is an intrinsic connection between εὐαγγέλιον in 1,1 and κηρύσσειν in 1,2-8 not merely because εὐαγγέλιον frequently has κηρύσσειν as its subject or object, but also because in 1,1 and in 1,7 they have the same content, namely, Jesus Christ [14]. Finally, the way Mk has portrayed John and his ministry in 1,2-8 (and in other pericopes on John the Baptist) clearly demonstrates that for him John and his mission function as a key to explain the identity of Jesus and the nature of his mission [15].

Therefore, based on these literary considerations and the particular theological perspective from which Mk views John and his mission, we hold that the historical event of the beginning of the Gospel concerning Jesus Christ takes place not in 1,14-15 but in 1,2-8 where John the Baptist as the Messianic forerunner proclaims through his person and mission Jesus Christ and his mission.

2) Regarding the connecting words that link Mk 1,1-13 and 1,14-15 the argument is not so strong or convincing. The proper name, Ἰησοῦς, is found 82 times in Mk. Of these, it occurs only 14 times at the beginning of a pericope: in the nominative case (1,9.14; 3,7; 8,27; 9,2; 10,23.32; 12,35; 14,27), in the genitive (1,1; 5,21), and in the accusative (6,30; 14,53;

---

[11] For details see p. 7-9.
[12] For details see p. 8-9.
[13] For details see p. 90-92, 100-102.
[14] For details see p. 90-91.
[15] Note the parallelism between John the Baptist and Jesus in Mk (1,2-8 in particular) and the evangelist's theological intention in drawing the parallelism between these two personages.

15,1) [16]. It is without the article only in 1,9; from 1,14 onwards it invariably has the article [17]. The pericopes with the proper name, ὁ Ἰησοῦς, at the beginning indicate in varying degrees more of a discontinuity than a continuity [18]. Therefore, the use of ὁ Ἰησοῦς in 1,14 argues in favour of a discontinuity from the preceding pericopes (1,1-13). The proper name Ἰωάννης occurs at 1,4.6 in a pericope that portrays his active ministry (1,2-8) and in 1,9 Jesus is baptized by John. Mk 1,14-15, however, does not pertain to John's ministry; therefore, the occurrence of Ἰωάννης at 1,14 does not necessarily indicate a literary continuity with the preceding pericopes.

Concerning the term Γαλιλαία, Mk 1,9 mentions the village of Nazareth in Galilee whereas 1,14 specifically speaks of Galilee as a region. Galilee occurs at 1,16 in reference to the lake of Galilee and at 1,28.39 in reference to the region of Galilee. Similarly, the verb ἔρχεσθαι and other verbs of movement in reference to Jesus are found not only in 1,7.9.14 but also in the pericopes that immediately follow (cf.1,16.19.21.24.29.31.35.38.39.45). And the frequent occurrence of verbs of movement in reference to Jesus is characteristic of Mk's Gospel [19]. The verb κηρύσσειν is predicated both of John (1,4.7) and of Jesus (1,14). Likewise both John (1,4) and Jesus (1,15) summon people to repentance. This similarity in vocabulary must be seen in the wider context of Mk's theological intention to draw a parallelism between John the Baptist and Jesus and to show the superiority of the latter [20].

3) Although only a few authors have held to an inclusion between 1,1 and 1,14-15 by virtue of the term εὐαγγέλιον, still none of them has established how it constitutes an inclusion. An inclusion necessarily requires literary connections among various literary units that it encloses, and it essentially implies a qualitative difference from those literary units that it excludes (by virtue of the inclusion). But in Mk 1,1-15, there are no literary links at all between 1,14-15 and the immediately preceding pericope (1,12-13); therefore, the first requirement is lacking. In the second place, the term, εὐαγγέλιον, in 1,1 is the key term of the title of Mk's work; consequently, all that follows

---

[16] The fourteen occurrences are dispersed in eleven chapters (except chapters 2, 4, 7, 11, 13). So statistically the presence or the absence of the name Jesus at the beginning of a pericope hardly proves anything.

[17] In three cases the article is omitted: (a) vocative (1,24; 5,7; 10,47); (b) where an anarthrous appositional phrase is added (10,47; 16,6); and (c) in the title of the work (1,1).

[18] This is most conspicuous in 5,21; 6,30; 8,27; 9,2; 10,32; 12,35; 14,53; 15,1.

[19] Cf. MANICARDI, Il cammino, 14-16.

[20] Cf. BUETUBELA, Jean-Baptiste, passim ; DE LA POTTERIE, "Mors Johannis Baptistae", 142-151.

– from the beginning (1,2) till the end (16,8) – pertains to εὐαγγέλιον. Hence, it is not clear how the term, εὐαγγέλιον, qualitatively distinguishes 1,1-15 from the rest of the evangelist's work (1,16-16,8). Mere occurrence of the term, εὐαγγέλιον, in 1,1 and 1,14-15 (bis) does not constitute an inclusion. What the evangelist has, in fact, done is to repeat the term in 1,14-15 to mark a new beginning, the beginning of Jesus' ministry [21].

4) We do not find enough literary indices for a parallelism between 1,2-8 and 1,9-15; on the contrary, 1,1-13 consists of a distinctive concentric structure (A B C B' A') [22].

3. Conclusion

An accurate reading of Mk 1,1-4 sufficiently demonstrates that the beginning, ἀρχή, of the Gospel takes place in John the Baptist's ministry. A critical assessment of the argument that connecting words link Mk 1,1-13 and 1,14-15 reveals its incongruity on many counts. No satisfactory literary evidence is found for an inclusion between v. 1 and vv. 14-15; nor is there a parallelism between 1,2-8 and 1,9-15.

B. Mk 1,1-13: Introduction to the Gospel

In the preceding pages it was clearly established that the reasons adduced by Keck, Pesch and others for the opinion that the introduction to Mk consists of 1,1-15 are not well founded. Now in the following pages we proceed to show that the introduction to the second Gospel does consist of 1,1-13. This is done in four steps: (1) textual and syntactic clarifications; (2) literary coherence of 1,1-13; (3) literary structure of 1,1-13; and (4) function of 1,1-13.

1. Textual and Syntactic Clarifications

a. *Textual Problem in Mk 1,4*

Mk 1,4 has four variant readings:

1) βαπτίζων ἐν τῇ ἐρήμῳ καὶ κηρύσσων (A W f [1.13] al.) [22a]

---

[21] Cf. p. 21-22.
[22] Cf. p. 15-18.
[22a] HUCK-GREEVEN and MERK opt for this reading.

2) ἐν τῇ ἐρήμῳ βαπτίζων καὶ κηρύσσων (D Θ *al.*)

3) ὁ βαπτίζων ἐν τῇ ἐρήμῳ καὶ κηρύσσων (ℵ L Δ *al.*) [22b]

4) ὁ βαπτίζων ἐν τῇ ἐρήμῳ κηρύσσων (B 33 *al.*) [22c]

The definite article ὁ before βαπτίζων is omitted in the first and the second variants because the scribes, used to the exclusive usage of Ἰωάννης ὁ βαπτιστής to refer to John the Baptist in Mt (7 times) and in Lk (thrice), interpreted βαπτίζων as a verbal form and connected it to κηρύσσων with καί without realizing that Mk uses ὁ βαπτίζων in the nominal form as a title (6,14.24) just as he uses ὁ βαπτιστής (6,25; 8,28). Therefore Metzger's view that "it is easier to account for the addition than for the deletion of the definite article before βαπτίζων" [23] is untenable.

According to the third variant, if καί is read before κηρύσσων both the participles (βαπτίζων and κηρύσσων) should be interpreted in the same way: either in the nominal form [24] or in the verbal form. But this is impossible because βαπτίζων is preceded by the definite article ὁ – so it has to be in the nominal form – and κηρύσσων is followed by the direct object βάπτισμα – so it must be in the verbal form. Therefore to avoid an anomaly and a lack of logic καί must be deleted. This is actually the fourth variant, the text of B.

According to the text of B, ὁ βαπτίζων is a title for John, the subject of ἐγένετο and κηρύσσων is the predicate; it is a construction typical of Mk (cf. 9,3.7). And verse 4 (together with 1,2a) should be translated: As it stands written in Isaiah the prophet (1,2a) . . . (so) it occurred that John the Baptist was preaching a baptism of repentance for the forgiveness of sins in the wilderness (1,4) [25]. This option also avoids the anomaly of baptizing in the desert (that is, how could there be water in the desert!); in fact, John was baptizing in the river Jordan (cf. 1,5.9).

[22b] GNT/NESTLE-ALAND and VOGELS prefer this variant.

[22c] This is the choice of WESTCOTT-HORT, ALAND (*Synopsis*, 21) and the translations of BJ, RSV and TOB.

[23] METZGER, *Commentary*, 73. Equally unacceptable is the translation of several commentators such as LANE, 41; RADERMAKERS, 39; etc.

[24] So the rendering of SCHWEIZER, 10; and SWETE, 3.

[25] Among different translations of recent years, the rendering of PESCH, I, 74; and SCHMITHALS, I, 73 is to be preferred.

b. *Syntactic Clarifications in Mk 1,1-4*

Mk 1,1 does not have a verb but consists of a cluster of six nouns, the first in the nominative case and the rest in the genitive; of these six nouns only the second (εὐαγγελίου) has a definite article (τοῦ). And 'Ιησοῦ Χριστοῦ is objective genitive [26] and υἱοῦ θεοῦ is an apposition to 'Ιησοῦ Χριστοῦ. There must be a period after the last noun (θεοῦ) [27]. The conjunction καθώς in verse 2 begins a subordinate clause introducing a direct discourse (1,2bc) and an indirect discourse (1,3). Although verse 2 is connected to verse 1, the conjunction καθώς in 1,2a has a value of comparison and it orients the whole clause (1,2a) towards the subsequent verses (1,2b-4). The relative pronoun ὅς in 1,2c refers to τὸν ἄγγελον in 1,2b; and φωνὴ βοῶντος (the subject in 1,3) is in apposition to ὅς and it is a circumstantial complement to ἐν τῇ ἐρήμῳ. The aorist ἐγένετο in verse 4 grammatically depends on the present participle κηρύσσων and governs the subject 'Ιωάννης ὁ βαπτίζων ἐν τῇ ἐρήμῳ. The main verb or the first independent verb in 1,2-4 is thus ἐγένετο in verse 4. Therefore to indicate the syntactic relation accurately, it is preferable to place a comma (a dash is also possible) after αὐτοῦ in 1,3b but not a period [28].

2. *Literary Coherence of Mk 1,1-13*

a. *Literary Unity of Mk 1,1-8*

As mentioned above, although verse 2 is connected to verse 1, it is also distinct from it because the subordinate clause (1,2a) introduced by καθώς is oriented to the subsequent verses (1,2b-4). And verses 2-4 are closely connected by linking nouns and pronouns on the one hand, and parallelisms, on the other. There are three series of linking nouns and pronouns in 1,2-4:

τὸν ἄγγελον — ὅς — φωνὴ βοῶντος — 'Ιωάννης ὁ βαπτίζων

τὴν ὁδόν — τὴν ὁδόν — τὰς τρίβους

σου — σου — Κυρίου — αὐττοῦ

---

[26] Against DAUTZENBERG "Zeit", 221-225; GNILKA, I, 43; SCHNACKENBURG, "Evangelium", 322.

[27] With most of the critical editions and translations, but against LOHMEYER, 9; and SCHWEIZER, 10, 12.

[28] With most of the critical editions and several translations, but against NEB; ERNST, 32; GNILKA, I, 40; S.E. JOHNSON, 33-34; LANE, 41; and SCHWEIZER, 10.

However, what gives solid unity to 1,2-4 is the following parallelism:

καθὼς γέγραπται . . . φωνὴ βοῶντος ἐν τῇ ἐρήμῳ
ἐγένετο ᾽Ιωάννης ὁ βαπτίζων ἐν τῇ ἐρήμῳ κηρύσσων [29]

The immediate link between 1,2-4 and 1,5-6 is evident from the perfect correspondence in narration between John the Baptist's proclamation (1,4) and the people's response (1,5) to it.

1,4	*1,5*
ἐγένετο ᾽Ιωάννης ὁ βαπτίζων	καὶ ἐξεπορεύετο πρὸς αὐτὸν . . . πάντες
ἐν τῇ ἐρήμῳ	ἐν τῷ ᾽Ιορδάνῃ ποταμῷ
κηρύσσων βάπτισμα	καὶ ἐβαπτίζοντο ὑπ᾽ αὐτοῦ
εἰς ἄφεσιν ἁμαρτιῶν	ἐξομολεγούμενοι τὰς ἁμαρτίας αὐτῶν

In contrast to 1,2-4, the verbs in verses 5 and 6 are in the imperfect tense which marks the continuity in narration between these two verses. Regarding vv. 7-8 although the verb βαπτίζειν occurs in verse 5 as well as in verse 8 (bis), the primary literary link is between 1,2-4 and 1,7-8, for the latter complements and perfects the former.

1,2-4	*1,7-8*
κηρύσσων	ἐκήρυσσεν
ἀποστέλλω τὸν ἄγγελόν μου	ἔρχεται ὁ ἰσχυρότερός μου
πρὸ προσώπου σου	ὀπίσω μου
βάπτισμα μετανοίας	βαπτίσει ὑμας ἐν πνεύματι ἁγίῳ

Again, differing from the narrative style in 1,4-6, verse 7a, just as verse 2, introduces a direct discourse (1,7b-8) in which John proclaims the coming of the mightier one and the latter's incomparable superiority. John's proclamation comes to a climactic conclusion in v. 8 where, by means of the anti-

---

[29] Mk 1,2c and 1,3b are synonymously parallel; so also 1,3b and 1,3c.

thetic parallelism, the evangelist emphatically highlights the contrast between John and the stronger one who comes after him.

ἐγὼ ἐβάπτισα ὑμᾶς ὕδατι

αὐτὸς δὲ βαπτίσει ὑμᾶς ἐν πνεύματι ἁγίῳ

Thus the precursor's ministry of proclamation [30] comes to a decisive conclusion in 1,7-8 [31].

To establish clearly the relation between Mk 1,1 and 1,2-8, it is necessary to clarify the meaning of the terms ἀρχή and εὐαγγέλιον in verse 1. Lexicons give at least four meanings to ἀρχή: beginning, first cause, authority, domain, etc. The specific meaning of ἀρχή in our verse must be determined from the context, taking into due consideration the Marcan usage. The four occurrences of ἀρχή in Mk are found in two ways: (1) without an article followed by a genitive (1,1; 13,8); (2) with the preposition ἀπό (10,6; 13,19). Because of the preposition ἀπό the meaning is clear in 10,6 and 13,19, namely, a temporal nuance is implied. In 13,8 the syntactic relation of ἀρχὴ ὠδίνων ταῦτα is as follows: subject = ταῦτα, verb = ἐστίν (understood), attribute = ἀρχὴ ὠδίνων. Here ἀρχή means beginning (the beginning of the sufferings). In Mk 1,1 too, ἀρχή has the same meaning, viz., beginning (the beginning of the Gospel) understood in the sense of a historical event.

Regarding the term, εὐαγγέλιον, a brief exposition is sufficient [32]. Borrowing the term εὐαγγέλιον from the missionary vocabulary of the early Church, Mk employs it in two ways: in the absolute sense (τὸ εὐαγγέλιον: six times) and determined by a genitive of person (1,1.14); both ways are typical of Paul. For Paul, the content of the gospel consists of Jesus' saving Death and Resurrection whereas for Mk, Jesus' earthly ministry is also εὐαγγέλιον. Furthermore, in Mk εὐαγγέλιον has also a Christological accentuation: more precisely, for him the gospel is Jesus Christ (cf. 8,35; 10,29).

Having ascertained the meaning of ἀρχή and εὐαγγέλιον in verse 1, we are better equipped to clarify the relation between Mk 1,1 and 1,2-8. In

---

[30] The key event predicated of John is κηρύσσειν, occurring in cardinal verses (1,4.7).

[31] John's ministry as the herald of the Messiah concludes with verse 8. The main theme in vv. 9-11 is not John's ministry as such but Jesus' baptism. Moreover, καὶ ἐγένετο at the beginning of v. 9 marks a certain discontinuity from the preceding verses as it does in 2,23 and 4,10.

[32] For details see p. 92.

Mk 1,1, generally recognized as the title of the work [33], the author announces the main theme: the gospel concerning Jesus Christ, the Son of God [34]. In 1,2-8, as previously noted, the evangelist's primary thrust is to portray the precursor's proclamation about the imminent coming of the mightier one and the key action predicated of the precursor is κηρύσσειν (1,4.7). But κηρύσσειν is a typical NT verb for the presentation of the Christian message which Mk uses in combination with the noun εὐαγγέλιον: in the active voice with εὐαγγέλιον as its direct object (1,14; 16,15) and in the passive with εὐαγγέλιον as its subject (13,10; 14,9). Therefore, since for Mk εὐαγγέλιον includes also Jesus' earthly ministry (not merely Jesus' Death and Resurrection as in Paul) and it has a Christological accentuation too (that the Gospel is identified with the person of Jesus Christ) and since John the Baptist's mission primarily consists in proclaiming (κηρύσσειν: a typical NT verb for announcing the Christian message, the Gospel, especially in Mk) the imminent advent of the stronger one, the Messiah, it follows that, according to Mk, there is an intrinsic connection between τὸ εὐαγγέλιον in 1,1 and κηρύσσειν in 1,2-8. In other words, τὸ εὐαγγέλιον connotes Jesus Christ and the object of κηρύσσειν in 1,7 is the imminent advent of the mightier one, the Messiah. Thus both εὐαγγέλιον and κηρύσσειν have the same content, Jesus Christ.

Furthermore, the way Mk has depicted John's ministry in 1,2-8, particularly the parallelism between John and Jesus, also shows the literary connection between 1,1 and 1,2-8.

John	*Jesus*
John was preaching in *the desert* (1,4).	Jesus sojourns in *the desert* (1,13ab).
John *preaches a baptism of repentance and the imminent advent of the mightier one* (1,4.7a).	Jesus *preaches the gospel of God* (1,14c).
John is *mighty* (as implied in 1,7b).	Jesus is *mightier* (1,7b).
John as the herald *precedes* Jesus (cf. 1,2b.7b).	Jesus *comes after* John (1,7b.14a).
John *baptizes with water* (1,5.8a).	Jesus *will baptize with the Holy Spirit* (1,8b).

---

[33] It was customary among some biblical authors to place the titles (consisting of a cluster of nouns but without a verb) at the beginning of their works (cf. Eccles 1,1; Prov 1,1a; Hos 1,2a (LXX); Mt 1,1; etc.).

[34] WIRKGREN, "APXH", 11-20, exposes six main interpretations of Mk 1,1.

The parallelism between John and Jesus in this pericope and in other pericopes on John the Baptist [35] is not a mere juxtaposition of the activities of these two persons, but it has a profound theological significance. It emphasizes the similarity between these two personages and the incomparable superiority of Jesus. By virtue of the similarity, the evangelist deliberately insists on the unity of their actions and the unity of their purpose: both have come to fulfil one and same design of God (cf. 11,27-33). Yet there is a qualitative difference between them: on the one hand, Jesus' person and ministry surpass and excel those of John (cf. 1,8), and, on the other hand, John begins the mission but Jesus continues and perfects it. In other words, Mk has presented an original portrait of John the Baptist – his person, his message and his martyrdom – in such a way that it derives its meaning and relevance from its function as a key to explain Jesus' identity (the principal theme in the second Gospel) and to shed light on the beginning of the Gospel (an issue in which the early Christians were keenly interested). In 1,2-8 too, the evangelist does not narrate John's ministry for its own sake but almost exclusively to announce and to prefigure Jesus, the Messiah, and the beginning of his mission. Therefore, the evangelist conceives John's ministry in 1,2-8 as the beginning of the Gospel: ἀρχὴ τοῦ εὐαγγελίου Ἰησοῦ Χριστοῦ (1,1) is realized in the historical event of John's ministry(1,2-8).

The evidence for this particular theological perspective of Mk can be reinforced by comparing it with the other synoptic Gospels. In Mk, unlike in Mt (11,2-15) and in Lk (7,18-30), John does not send two of his disciples to ask Jesus whether he is the Christ, for, it would be contradictory to do so since, according to Mk, John himself is a key to explain Jesus' identity. Besides, in Mk 1,2-8 attention is primarily focused on Jesus and the beginning of his mission. Consequently our evangelist does not allude to the theme of judgment as in Mt 3,7-10.12 and Lk 3,7-14.17; nor does he provide biographical details about John as such.

Regarding the literary connection between Mk 1,1 and 1,2-8 we summarily state that, on the one hand, there is an intrinsic connection between εὐαγγέλιον in 1,1 and κηρύσσειν in 1,2-8 and John and his ministry in 1,2-8 foreshadow Jesus and his mission, and, on the other hand, ἀρχή in 1,1 means beginning understood in the sense of a historical event. Therefore ἀρχὴ τοῦ εὐαγγελίου (1,1) takes place in John's ministry (1,2-8) [36] and John, according to Mk, belongs to the Christian era.

---

[35] See Mk 1,14a; 6,14-29; 9,9-13; 11,30.
[36] Therefore ἀρχή applies only to Mk 1,2-8 but not to the whole Gospel.

b. *Mk 1,1-8 and 1,9-13*

Although Mk 1,9-13 is distinct from 1,1-8, there are also literary connections between them. Of the various literary links between 1,1-8 and 1,9-13, the parallelism between 1,2-4 and 1,7.9, particularly between verse 4 and verse 9, is most striking:

1,2-4

Καθὼς γέγραπται . . . φωνὴ βοῶντος ἐν τῇ ἐρήμῳ . . .
ἐγένετο Ἰωάννης ὁ βαπτίζων ἐν τῇ ἐρήμῳ κηρύσσων

1,7.9

καὶ ἐκήρυσσεν . . . ἔρχεται ὁ ἰσχυρότερός μου ὀπίσω μου (1,7)
καὶ . . . ἦλθεν Ἰησοῦς (1,9)

These verses show also a progression in narration: just as ἐκήρυσσεν in 1,7a takes up κηρύσσων from 1,4a so also ἦλθεν in 1,9a takes up ἔρχεται announced in 1,7b.

Further, the phrase ἐν ἐκείναις ταῖς ἡμέραις in verse 9 connects Jesus' appearing for baptism with the Baptist's ministry in 1,4-8. Moreover, just as καὶ εὐθύς links 1,10 to 1,9 so also καὶ εὐθύς connects 1,12 to 1,11. The first two stiches in verse 13 have the construction καί + verb (καὶ ἦν . . . καὶ ἦν) whereas in the third stich the pattern is changed (καί + subject + verb). By this deliberate change the evangelist wants the readers to understand that 1,13c is the conclusion of the pericope [37].

Mk 1,1-13 is connected also by connecting words. The most frequent word is βαπτίζειν: verbal form five times (1,4.5.8(bis).9) and the noun βάπτισμα once (1,4). The term πνεῦμα binds the three pericopes together: one who comes after John will baptize ἐν πνεύματι ἁγίῳ (1,8), τὸ πνεῦμα descends upon Jesus at his baptism (1,10), and τὸ πνεῦμα drives him into the wilderness (1,12). And ἡ ἔρημος (the absolute usage) is exclusively reserved to the introduction (1,3.4.12.13); otherwise Mk uses ἔρημος τόπος (1,35.45; 6,31.32.35).

There is an inclusion between 1,2 and 1,13; more precisely between τὸν ἄγγελόν μου πρὸ προσώπου σου (1,2b) and οἱ ἄγγελοι διηκόνουν αὐτῷ (1,13c). God's messenger (τὸν ἄγγλον) identified as John the Baptist is the herald of the Messiah (1,2-8) and in 1,9-13 where the relation of various

---

[37] Cf. ZERWICK, *Markus-Stil*, 76-77.

celestial beings to Jesus is treated, the angels are servants to Jesus, the Messiah (1,13c).

There is further literary and theological correspondence between the first and the last literary units (1,1-4; 1,12-13): ἡ ἔρημος, the locus of the events in these two units, occurs twice in the first unit (1,3.4) as well as in the second (1,12.13). Based on the soteriological significance attached to ἔρημος in the OT, there arose the belief in Judaism that the last and decisive age of salvation would begin in the ἔρημος and that here the Messiah would appear [38]. Mk, differing from the first and the third evangelists [39], employs ἡ ἔρημος (the absolute usage, singular) exclusively in the introduction and attaches to it not a geographical but a theological significance. Thus, for our evangelist, ἔρημος is the locus theologicus for the beginning of the age of salvation and for the appearance of the Messiah.

3. Literary Structure of Mk 1,1-13 (A B C B' A')

While it is not necessary for the present study to enumerate and to critically evaluate the various structures proposed by different authors for the introduction to Mk, it would be helpful to give a brief assessment of the views in rather recent commentaries. We will then establish the literary structure of Mk1,1-13.

The commentaries of Ernst and Gnilka state that there is parallelism between 1,2-8 and 1,9-15, but they neither state clearly the nature of the parallelism nor offer satisfactory literary evidence for it [40]. Pesch clarifies the parallelism as follows [41]:

1,2-4	//	1,9-11
1,5-6	//	1,12-13
1,7-8	//	1,14-15

However, he does not sufficiently demonstrate the literary evidence for the parallelism; in the first and third pairs parallel elements are meagre and in the second none.

---

[38] Cf. KITTEL, *TDNT* II, 658-659.

[39] In the singular (Mt 11,7; 24,26; Lk 7,24; 15,4) and in the plural (Lk 1,80; 5,16; 8,29).

[40] Cf. ERNST, 31; GNILKA, I, 39-40.

[41] PESCH, I, 72-73.

The heterogeneous views regarding the structure of the introduction to Mk result primarily from inadequate attention to the literary data in verses 2-8 [42]. Therefore, in proposing a structure, we shall pay utmost attention to the literary data in these verses, most of which have been previously mentioned.

The usage of tenses in 1,1-8 is quite revealing:

1,2-4	γέγραπται	=	perfect
	ἀποστέλλω	=	present
	κατασκευάσει	=	future
	ἑτοιμάσατε	=	aorist
	ποιεῖτε	=	present
	ἐγένετο	=	aorist
1,5-6	ἐξεπορεύετο	=	imperfect
	ἐβαπτίζοντο	=	imperfect
	ἦν	=	imperfect
1,7-8	ἐκήρυσσεν	=	imperfect
	ἔρχεται	=	present
	εἰμί	=	present
	ἐβάπτισα	=	aorist
	βαπτίσει	=	future

Thus there is a great variation in the usage of tenses in 1,2-4 and 1,7-8 whereas in 1,5-6 all the verbs are in the imperfect tense. This is an important literary index in the division of 1,1-8.

Furthermore, as was already pointed out, verses 2-4 constitute a literary unit, for, among other elements which contribute to the literary unity of these verses, the parallelism between 1,3a and 1,4 is very striking:

φωνὴ βοῶντος ἐν τῇ ἐρήμῳ

᾽Ιωάννης ὁ βαπτίζων ἐν τῇ ἐρήμῳ κηρύσσων

---

[42] BENOIT-BOISMARD (*Synopse* II, 69-70) proposes the structure A B B' A' (respectively vv. 2-3, 4, 5, 6). But verses 2-3 (A) are not parallel to verse 6 (A') for, the former does not deal with the activity of John the Baptist as such. FENEBERG (*Markusprolog*, 49) advocates another division: 1,2-3: OT; 1,4-8: John the Baptist; 1,9-11: NT. This structure reflects the theological preoccupation to consider John the Baptist as the bridge between the OT and the NT. Moreover, the separation between verses 3 and 4 is not justified. RADERMAKERS, 39, also separates v. 4 from vv. 2-3.

This parallelism indicates a progression of thought by identifying God's messenger as John the Baptist: τὸν ἄγγελόν μου of 1,2b corresponds to φωνὴ βοῶντος in 1,3a and the latter in turn corresponds to 'Ιωάννης ὁ βαπτίζων . .. κηρύσσων in 1,4. Verses 5-6 form a separate unit, for in contrast to vv. 2-4, all the verbs in vv. 5-6 are in the imperfect tense, and, from another point of view, the subject of the verb in v. 4 is John the Baptist but in v. 5 the subject of the verbs is people. Again, differing from the narrative style in vv. 5-6, there is a direct discourse in vv. 7-8 whose literary unity is indubitable [43].

In summary, vv. 1-13 consists of five literary units (1-4, 5-6, 7-8, 9-11, 12-13). Our next task then is to find the interrelationship among these five literary units.

Mk 1,1-4 and 1,12-13 are characterized by parallel elements:

1,1-4 (A)	*1,12-13 (A')*
τὸν ἄγγελον	οἱ ἄγγελοι
φωνὴ βοῶντος ἐν τῇ ἐρήμῳ	ἐκβάλλει εἰς τὴν ἔρημον
'Ιωάννης ... ἐν τῇ ἐρήμῳ	ἦν ἐν τῇ ἐρήμῳ

Just as 1,3a and 1,4 are synonymously parallel so also are 1,12 and 1,13a; the former verses treat the activity of the precursor in the desert whereas the latter verses deal with the sojourn of the Messiah in the desert.

Likewise, 1,5-6 and 1,9-11 are also parallel, for, the people's baptism corresponds to that of Jesus in respect to the movement towards the Baptist, the event, the agent, and the place:

1,5-6 (B)	*1,9-11 (B')*
ἐξεπορεύετο ... ἡ 'Ιουδαία	ἦλθεν 'Ιησοῦς
ἐβαπτίζοντο	ἐβαπτίσθη
ὑπ' αὐτοῦ	ὑπὸ 'Ιωάννου
ἐν τῷ 'Ιορδάνῃ ποταμῷ	εἰς τὸν 'Ιορδάνην

And, finally, 1,7-8 (C) constitutes the centre of 1,1-13. Mk 1,2-6 leads to 1,7-8. As was noted earlier, vv. 7-8 complement and perfect vv. 2-4 and John's activity of baptizing with water (1,5) is recalled in 1,8a ("I have

---

[43] Cf. p. 9-11 above.

baptized you with water") and contrasted in 1,8b ("but he will baptize you with the Holy Spirit"). And 1,9-13 flows from 1,7-8: ἔρχεται ὁ ἰσχυρότερός μου ὀπίσω μου (1,7b) is taken up in ἦλθεν ᾿Ιησοῦς (1,9a) and he who will baptize with the Holy Spirit (1,8b) receives the Spirit (1,10b), and the same Spirit drives him out into the wilderness (1,12). John's ministry comes to a climax in 1,7-8 where he announces the imminent coming of the mightier one and 1,9-13 deals with Jesus' two preparatory acts before he begins his ministry in 1,14-15.

In conclusion, Mk 1,1-13 consists of a concentric structure as follows:

> A (1,1-4)
>> B (1,5-6)
>>> C (1,7-8)
>> B' (1,9-11)
> A' (1,12-13)

4. The Function of Mk 1,1-13

From the literary considerations in the preceding pages there are two points to be noted: (1) Within 1,1-13 the first eight verses have a special literary unity, (2) and at the same time verses 1-13 are concentrically structured. Now we ask: What is the function of 1,1-13 in Mk? Here too we proceed in two stages: the function of 1,1-8 and the function of 1,1-13 as a whole.

The early Christians, just as Christians of all times, were convinced that the newness of the Christian message is founded on Jesus: his person and ministry, his Death and Resurrection. But the early Christians were particularly interested in and intensely sensitive to the question: When is the ἀρχή of the Christian message? The response of the NT to a great extent depends on the theological perspective of the particular author [44]. Our evangelist has

---

[44] Lk conceives the beginning of Christian message in a double sense: (1) the beginning of Jesus' ministry (cf. Lk 3,23), and (2) the beginning of the mission of the Church. These two beginnings are typologically and theologically related: the Church's mission is patterned and based on Jesus' mission.

Jn also distinguishes two aspects of the beginning: one in the life of Jesus, the other in the Christian community. For Jn the beginning does not consist in the commencement of Jesus' preaching as in Lk but the beginning of a personal relationship between Jesus and his disciples (cf. Jn 2,11; 6,64; 15,27; 16,4).

given an original and ingenious answer to this question: the newness of Christianity commences (ἀρχὴ τοῦ εὐαγγελίου) in John the Baptist's ministry (1,2-8) for, as previously mentioned, John through his person, ministry, and martyrdom announces and prefigures Jesus, the Messiah, and his mission. In other words, unlike Lk who considers John the Baptist a figure still belonging to the OT ("The law and the prophets were until John; since then the good news of the kingdom of God is preached" Lk 16,16), Mk holds that John pertains to the NT and his function is unique as the herald of the Messiah.

After a brief digression on the function of Mk 1,2-8 in relation to ἀρχὴ τοῦ εὐαγγελίου in 1,1, we focus attention on the function of 1,1-13 as such. It was amply noted before that in 1,2-8 John proclaims Jesus, the Messiah, but a few salient points are still to be mentioned. By placing John's proclamation (1,4) just after the scriptural citations (1,2-3) Mk shows that John's mission as herald corresponds to the announcement of Scripture and his role precisely consists in preparing the way of the Messiah. The description of John's clothing [45] (possibly also his food) [46] alludes to Elijah who, according to the common belief of the time, was to return to prepare the way of the Messiah [47]. John's ministry concludes with the climactic proclamation stating the incomparable superiority of the one who comes after him in respect to his strength [48], his dignity [49], and the mode of his activity [50]. Thus through his person and mission John proclaims Jesus, the Messiah.

The same theme, the revelation of Jesus' identity, is further developed in 1,9-13. By receiving John's baptism Jesus identifies himself with sinful

---

[45] The description of John's garment in 1,6 corresponds to the identification of Elijah in 2 Kings 1,8. Referring to the story of 2 Kings 1,1-8 JOSEPHUS FLAVIUS states that Elijah was identified by his garment (cf. Antiquities, IX,22).

[46] John's diet possibly implies that in him the Messianic feast has not begun (cf. Mk 2,18-19; Lk 7,33-34; Jn 3,28-29) though he is closely associated with the Messiah.

[47] Cf. GRELOT, L'espérance juive, 252-255; SCHÜRER, History II, 515-516; VOLZ, Eschatologie, 195-197.

[48] The adjective ἰσχυρός is used in the synoptics in two contexts: description of the relation between John and the one who comes after (Mk 1,7 par.) and the discussion on the nature of Jesus' exorcisms (Mk 3,27 par.) Out of the four occurrences of the verb ἰσχύειν in Mk twice it is used in the context of the expulsion of demons (5,4; 9,18). Therefore by ἰσχυρότερος Mk probably refers to Jesus' power over demons.

[49] Only a servant was obliged to untie and carry the sandals of his master. A certain rabbi was of the opinion that this obligation bound not a Hebrew slave but only a pagan slave (cf. STR.-B., Kommentar I, 121). John is not worthy even to be a slave of the Messiah.

[50] Just as Mk describes John's ministry in terms of baptism with water, so also he summarizes Jesus' ministry in terms of baptism with the Holy Spirit.

mankind though he himself was sinless [51]. The heavens, the barrier between man and God, are rent asunder; God once again begins to communicate with man; thus the long-awaited and fervently-prayed-for eschatological time is inaugurated [52]. Jesus is endowed with the Spirit for the Messianic task whereby the new Israel too is constituted [53]. The voice from heaven declares that Jesus is God's Son and confirms him in his Messianic mission as the suffering Servant according to Is 42,1. Like Israel Jesus is tempted in the wilderness (by Satan, the archenemy of God), but unlike Israel Jesus overcomes the temptation.

Thus in 1,9-11 Jesus is presented in essential relationships: Jesus is the Son of God endowed with the Spirit to undertake the Messianic task as the suffering Servant. And Mk1,9-13 as a whole gives an inkling of the nature of Jesus' ministry: Jesus remains fully loyal to God as the suffering Messiah in establishing the kingdom of God and he constantly endeavours to overthrow the reign of Satan and his allies [54].

5. Conclusion

By showing the literary coherence of 1,1-13, we delimit the extent of the introduction to Mk. As regards the intent, 1,1-13 introduces Jesus to the readers and gives them an inkling of the nature of his mission. Mk does it in a masterful way: Jesus does not introduce himself but is introduced by others. Thus 1,1-13 functions as a curtain-raiser introducing Jesus, the main character, before he himself begins his key role by announcing his proclamation in 1,14-15 [55].

---

[51] One should note that the parallel to "confessing their sins" (1,5) is absent in 1,9.

[52] After the era of the prophets God's Spirit was no more active in Israel and God's voice was no longer heard. Even the holiest rabbis were allowed to hear only the echo of God's voice, 'daughter of the voice' (בַּת קוֹל) as it was called (cf. STR.-B., *Kommentar* I, 125-134). Heavens constituted a fixed barrier in the communication between God and Israel. So Israel prayed to God and hoped for his definitive intervention — to rend the heavens and come down — (cf. Is 63,7-64,11; Test. Levi 18; Test. Judah 24,2-3). Mk 1,9-11 is the fulfilment of this cherished hope.

[53] The descent of the Spirit upon Jesus has both a personal and a communitarian character. Jesus is personally equipped to be the Messiah but his Messiahship is for the sake of the community. The communitarian aspect is emphasized by the symbolism of dove as in Judaism dove signified Israel (cf. STR.-B., *Kommentar* I, 123-125; GOODENOUGH, *Symbols* VIII, 42-44.

[54] Cf. BURKILL, *Mysterious Revelation*, 16-23; ROBINSON, *History*, 33-34.

[55] Critically evaluating the views that 1,1-13 constitutes the introduction, KECK ("Introduction", 353-356) poses the question: What/whom does Mk introduce in 1,1-13? In light of our study on 1,1-13 the answer is obvious: it introduces Jesus, the Messiah whose identity is the primary concern of Mk.

C. Mk 1,14-15: The Beginning of the First Section

1. Literary Indices

Mk does not begin 1,14-15, a new pericope, with his preferential conjunction καί but with the less frequent conjunction δέ [56]. He employs δέ at the beginning of a pericope in two contexts: (1) to indicate a new beginning or a totally new dimension in Jesus' ministry (7,24; 10,32; 14,1) [57]; (2) to mark a contrast or a turning point within the same story or trend of thought (5,11; 13,14.28.32; 15,6.16). In 1,14 δέ is used to mark a new beginning, the commencement of Jesus' ministry.

None of the connecting words (βαπτίζειν, πνεῦμα, ἡ ἔρημος) that unite 1,1-13 as a unit are found in 1,14-15. As mentioned before, there is no literary connection between 1,14-15 and the pericope that immediately precedes (1,12-13). The episodes presented in 1,1-13 pertain to the space and time of John but not to that of Jesus. Moreover, the key nouns ὁ καιρός and ἡ βασιλεία τοῦ θεοῦ and the important verbs παραδιδόναι, πληροῦν, ἐγγίζειν, μετανοεῖν and πιστεύειν of vv. 14-15 do not occur in vv. 1-13 at all. Lastly, 1,14 (ἦλθεν ... εἰς Γαλιλαίαν) and 1,16 (καί παράγων παρά τήν θάλασσαν τῆς Γαλιλαίας) are connected; and 1,21a (καί εἰσπορεύονται plural) takes up the connection from 1,16-20.

2. Thematic Indices, Dramatis Personae, and Scene

The main theme in 1,1-13 is baptism whereas the central theme in 1,14-15 is Jesus' proclamation of the kingdom of God. As mentioned previously, in 1,2-8 John proclaims Jesus the Messiah; the spiritual beings in 1,9-13 (Father, Spirit, angels and Satan) also have Jesus as the focal point of their action. In 1,14-15, in contrast, one meets a very concrete historical person, Jesus. Unlike the ethereal actions and cosmic events (rending asunder of the heavens, the voice from heaven) of 1,9-13, the events in 1,14-15 are more concrete and extremely personal. Finally, the events in 1,1-13 take place in the wilderness or at the Jordan whereas the events of 1,14-15 occur in Galilee.

---

[56] Following GNT ³1975 there are 95 pericopes in Mk 1,1-16,8. Of these 79 pericopes begin with the conjunction καί ten with δέ and other constructions in six instances.

[57] At 7,24 Jesus enters into the territory of Tyre and Sidon for the first time. The first mention of Jerusalem as the destination of Jesus' journey is in 10,32. And 14,1 marks the beginning of the Passion narrative.

3. *Orientation of Mk 1,14-15*

It is a rather widespread view (one that will be explained in the second chapter) that Mk has composed the first part of the Gospel (1,14-8,30) in such a way that the mystery of Jesus' Messiahship is gradually unveiled. It consists of three sections, each begins with a summary on Jesus' ministry. Mk 1,14-15 is, then, the summary that commences the first section.

4. *Conclusion*

The literary evidence, therefore, favours the view that Mk 1,14-15 is more connected with what follows than with what precedes.

III. The End of the First Section

A. Mk 3,7-12: The Conclusion of the First Section

1. *Reasons for the Opinion*

Keck challenged the commonly accepted opinion that 3,7-12 is the introduction to the second section of Mk. He contended that "instead of beginning a new section, 3,7-12 is the conclusion of the section begun at 1,16" [58]. His argument is based on two correlated reasons: on the one hand, 3,7-12 does not introduce anything and, on the other hand, it stands as a good summary of what has been said so far. Similarly, Mangatt argues that 3,6 cannot be considered the conclusion of the first section which unfolds the rare success and the positive response of the people but that 3,7-12 wonderfully fulfils this function [59].

2. *Critical Evaluation*

Keck has adduced three reasons [60] to prove that 3,7-12 is the conclusion of the first section. But none of them is sufficiently supported by literary

---

[58] KECK, "Mark 3,7-12", 343.

[59] Cf. MANGATT, *Way*, 28-32.

[60] Cf. KECK, "Mark 3,7-12", 344.

evidence ⁶¹. Regarding Mangatt's arguments, one should note that he does not take due consideration of the consistent and steadily growing opposition to Jesus in 2,1-3,6. His claim that the confession of the unclean spirits (3,11) and Jesus' prohibition to make him known (3,12) bring to a climax the theme in 1,23-27.34.39 is not fully correct because 3,11 is rightly a confession ⁶² whereas there is no confession in 1,23-27.34.39 ⁶³.

B. Mk 3,7-12: Introduction to the Second Section (3,7-6,6a)

Mk 3,7-12 has no literary or thematic connections with the preceding pericopes (2,18-3,6). On the contrary, there are literary and thematic features that show that 3,7-12 is a new beginning and that it connects the pericopes that follow it. The use of ὁ 'Iησοῦς at the beginning of a pericope, as observed before, implies a certain discontinuity from the preceding pericopes. The verb ἀναχωρεῖν and the mention of a new scene, θάλασσα, also indicate a break from the preceding pericope (3,1-6).

The order in which the names of places are given implies an orientation to the Gentiles: it begins with the people of Israel (Galilee, Judea and Jerusalem – the latter two places are also religiously important) continues with marginal groups that are also religiously suspect (Idumea and beyond the Jordan) and concludes with the pagan territory (Tyre and Sidon). In 1,14-3,6 Jesus' ministry had been exclusively devoted to Galilee whereas in the subsequent chapters he extends his ministry to pagan territory as well (5,1-20; 7,24-30). The boat is a means of separation from the crowd (3,9; 6,32; 8,10) and from the Pharisees (8,13). It functions as a conveyance where the question of Jesus' identity is posed (4,35-41; 6,45-52; 8,14-21). And it is also a "platform" for his teaching (4,1) and encounter with people (5,2.18.21). Likewise, θάλασσα is used as a "springboard" for various activities: the locale to which Jesus retreats (3,7), where he manifests himself to his disciples (4,35-41; 6,47-51) and where the people gather to him (3,7; 4,1;

---

⁶¹ KECK'S arguments are consistently challenged and systematically refuted (cf. BURKILL, "Dualism", 409-417; EGGER, "Verborgenheit", 476-478; id., Frohbotschaft, 100, 108-109, 111; SNOY, "Miracles", 75-82).

⁶² The use of the verbs θεωρεῖν (cf. 15,40.47; 16,4) and προσπίπτειν (cf. 5,33; 7,25) and the revelatory formula σὺ εἶ (cf. 1,11; 8,29) indicate the confessional character of 3,11.

⁶³ Mk 1,23-27.34.39 narrate exorcisms (note the Marcan expression τὰ δαιμόνια ἐκβάλλειν). But in 3,11-12 there is no exorcism at all.

5,21). Finally, there is literary affinity between 3,7-10 and 5,24-34 and between 3,11 and 5,6-7 [64].

Jesus retreated μετὰ τῶν μαθητῶν (3,7) from the scenes of confrontation with the Jewish leaders (2,1-3,6) and from the crowd. And Mk 3,7-12 marks the beginning of a turning point in Jesus' ministry: on the one hand, he engages himself in intensifying his relationship with his disciples and in the formation of those who accept him and, on the other hand, he separates himself from the crowd [65]. The question of Jesus' identity confessed by the unclean spirits (3,11) becomes more important in the chapters that follow.

Therefore there are ample literary and thematic indications to support the view that 3,7-12 is not the conclusion of what precedes but is an introduction to what follows. And according to the structural pattern of the first part of Mk, 3,7-12 constitutes the introduction to the second section (3,7-6,6a).

C. Mk 3,5-6: The End of the First Section (1,14-3,6)

1. Preliminary Remarks

In determining the delimitation of a section the following interrelated methodological principles have to be kept in mind: (1) the delimitation of a section is conditioned not only by the internal organization and coherence of a section but also by the internal organization and coherence of the work as a whole; (2) consequently the literary and thematic indices that give structural

---

[64] *3,7-10*
καὶ πολύ πλῆθος...
ἠκολούθησεν (3,7)

θλίβειν (3,9) hapax in Mk

ἅπτεσθαι αὐτοῦ (the sick touch Jesus) 3,10

μάστιξ (3,10)

5,24-34
καὶ ἠκολούθει ὄχλος πολύς
(5,24)

συνθλίβειν (Mk 5,24.31).

5,27.28.30.31; 6,56 (otherwise nowhere else in Mk)

5,29.34 (this term occurs nowhere else in Mk).

3,11
ὅταν αὐτὸν ἐθεώρουν
προσέπιπτον αὐτῷ
καὶ ἔκραζον λέγοντες
οὐ εἶ ὁ υἱὸς τοῦ θεοῦ

5,6-7
καὶ ἰδὼν τὸν Ἰησοῦν
προσεκύνησεν αὐτῷ
καὶ κράξας φωνῇ μεγάλῃ λέγει
Ἰησοῦ υἱὲ τοῦ θεοῦ τοῦ ὑψίστου

[65] Cf. p. 48-52.

unity to the work as a whole have to be respected and given priority in determining the delimitation of a section. For it is in and through the totality of the work that an author conveys his message and a section has a role and relevance only in relation to the whole.

2. Mk 3,5-6: The End of the First Section

The principal question in the first part of Mk is the progressive revelation of the mystery of Jesus' Messiahship. The literary indices in the first part are therefore primarily oriented to achieve this basic aim.

Each section of the first part ends on a note of hardness of heart or incomprehension from the part of men: the Pharisees' hardness of heart (3,5-6), the incomprehension of his own countrymen (6,1-6a), and the incomprehension of his own disciples (8,17-21). However, the above climax on a very positive note. The healing of the blind man at Bethsaida (8,22-26) which has a symbolic and prefigurative value functions as a transitional pericope leading to Peter's confession of Jesus' Messiahship (8,27-30) which is the terminus ad quem of the first part.

Thus, according to the structural pattern in the first part of Mk 3,5-6 marks the end of the first section.

D. Conclusion

Based on literary and thematic grounds we have established that Mk 3,7-12 is not the conclusion of the first section; on the contrary, it is the introduction to the second section (3,7-6,6a). Mk 3,5-6 marks the end of the first section. Its place and function should be understood in the context of the structure of the first part of Mk.

CHAPTER TWO

THE PLAN OF THE GOSPEL ACCORDING TO MARK

I. The Problem

Our redaction-critical investigation of Mk 1,14-3,6 endeavours to study the significance and function of this section in Mk. The primary step for such an investigation is to determine the overall structure of the Gospel as a whole. For only within the context and according to the theological orientation and purpose of the whole Gospel can one determine the significance and function of a particular section [1]. However, the question of the structure of the second Gospel has elicited extremely variant and even contrary responses from scholars, ranging from utter silence, systematic and cynical scepticism [2] to constructive proposals for the structure. Furthermore, the structures propounded by various authors based on different criteria are extremely varied. Therefore, a critical appraisal is absolutely necessary in order to know which structure is consonant with the texture of Mk.

---

[1] PESCH, *Naherwartungen*, 48: "Eine redaktionsgeschichtliche Untersuchung muß sich ganz besonders um den Aufbau des Evangeliums kümmern. Denn im Aufriß, in der literarischen Struktur des Evangeliums—und gerade auch des ersten Evangeliums—müssen Tendenzen des Evangelisten greifbar sein". See also BAARLINK, *Anfängliches Evangelium*, 73; BLATHERWICK, "Silhouette", 186; GNILKA, "Martyrium", 78; KOCH, "Aufriss", 145; K. STOCK, "Gesù è il Cristo", 242-243, 253.

[2] BULTMANN, *Geschichte*, 375: "Mk ist eben noch nicht in dem Maße Herr über den Stoff geworden, daß er eine Gliederung wagen könnte". JEREMIAS, *Theology*, 38: "The whole of the Gospel of Mark consists of complexes of tradition . . . the search for a systematic structure of the gospel is a lost labour of love".

Similar opinions in HAENCHEN, 34; KUHN, *Sammlungen*, 217; LOISY, 9; NINEHAM, 27; S. SCHULZ, *Stunde*, 25; TAGAWA, *Miracles*, 2.

II. A Critical Appraisal of Various Approaches

A. Geographical Structure

Most scholars whether of the German, French or British/American school propose a structure that is primarily and fundamentally based on geographical criteria. This approach presupposes that Mk's outline basically corresponds to the actual progression of Jesus' ministry beginning in Galilee and culminating in Jerusalem [3]. And Mk 10,52 is generally considered as the demarcation line between these two geographical areas. In spite of using the same criteria, viz., fundamentally geographical, the structures proposed by various authors are considerably heterogeneous.

1. *Classification*

(a) Introduction (1,1-13)
     Jesus' ministry in Galilee (1,14-9,50)
     Jesus' journey from Galilee to Jerusalem (10,1-52)
     Jesus' ministry and death in Jerusalem (11,1-16,8) [4]

(b) Introduction (1,1-13)
     Jesus' ministry in Galilee (1,14-8,26)
     The way of the Passion (8,27-10,52)
     Ministry in Jerusalem (11,1-13,37)
     Passion and Resurrection (14,1-16,8) [5]

(c) Introduction (1,1-13)
     Ministry in Galilee (1,14-7,23)
     Journeys outside Galilee (7,24-10,52)
     Ministry in Jerusalem (11,1-13,37)
     Passion and Resurrection (14,1-16,8) [6]

---

[3] Cf. BAARLINK, *Anfängliches Evangelium*, 79; LANE, 9-12; MARXSEN, *Einleitung*, 120; S. SCHULZ, *Stunde*, 25-26; SOUBIGOU, "Plano", 84-96, etc.

[4] Cf. CONZELMANN, *Grundriβ*, 161-163; CONZELMANN-LINDEMANN, *Arbeitsbuch*, 242-245; GRANT, 645-646; LIGHTFOOT, *Gospel Message*, 9.

[5] Cf. BOUMAN, "Reflections", 326-331; BRANSCOMB, ix-xii; KOCH, "Aufriss", 145-166; RIGAUX, *Témoignage*, 32-51; SCHILLE, *Offen*, 64-65; URICCHIO-STANO, 43-45; VIELHAUER, *Geschichte*, 331-332, etc.

[6] Cf. *La Bible de Jérusalem*; CERFAUX, *La voix vivente*, 58-59; HUBY, 91-95.

(d)   Introduction (1,1-13)
      Jesus' ministry in Galilee (1,14-6,6a)
      Jesus' itinerant wandering (6,6b-10,52)
      The last days in Jerusalem (11,1-16,8) [7]

(e)   Introduction (1,1-13)
      Jesus in Galilee (1,14-5,43)
      Jesus as itinerant within and outside Galilee(6,1-9,50)
      Jesus on the way to Jerusalem (10,1-52)
      Jesus in Jerusalem (11,1-13,37)
      Passion and Resurrection (14,1-16,8) [8]

(f)   Prologue (1,1-13)
      The initial phase of the Galilean ministry (1,14-3,6)
      Later phases of the ministry in Galilee (3,7-6,13)
      Withdrawal beyond Galilee (6,14-8,30)
      The journey to Jerusalem (8,31-10,52)
      Ministry in Jerusalem (11,1-13,37)
      The Passion Narrative (14,1-15,47)
      The Resurrection of Jesus (16,1-8) [9]

2. *Critical Remarks*

A perusal of the opinions classified above offers relevant insights into the lack of cogency and aptness of the structure based on geographical criteria. In the first place, there is a common consensus regarding Jesus' ministry in Jerusalem (11,1-13,37) and his Passion and Resurrection (14,1-16,8). However, there are drastically divergent opinions concerning the demarcation of Jesus' ministry in Galilee: 1,14-5,43; 1,14-6,6a; 1,14-6,13; 1,14-7,23; 1,14-8,26; 1,14-9,50; 1,14-10,52. It means, in spite of using the same criteria, there is disagreement about the specific designation of more than one third of Mk (i.e., 6,1-10,52 = 233 verses out of the total 666/678 verses).

Secondly, to avoid this pandemonium authors have recourse to various remedies. Some give an ambiguous geographical designation to Mk 1,14-

---

[7] Cf. DEHN, 9-14; HERMANN, I, 18-20; SCHMID, 7-10; WIKENHAUSER, *Einleitung*, 114-116, etc.

[8] Cf. KLOSTERMANN, 1; KÜMMEL, *Introduction*, 82-84.

[9] Cf. CRANFIELD, 14; LANE, 29-34; TAYLOR, 107-111.

10,52 [10]. A few others introduce further divisions in 1,14-10,52; yet the basic lack of clarity remains [11]. A third group also integrates other criteria (topological, topical and theological) within the geographical frame; such an approach too has not met with success [12]. Thirdly, various models of the geographical structure so far proposed consist of two (e.g., Marxen, Soubigou) to six main parts (e.g., Lane, Taylor). Such a differentiation indicates the incoherence of the structure founded on geographical indices. Fourthly, even an extensive geographical structure (e.g., of Lane or of Taylor) presents only a general and exterior structure of the Gospel. These authors do not take into account the diversity and complexity of themes and narratives.

Fifthly, geographical and topographical notices are not precise enough (cf. Mk 5,1; 7,31; 10,1) to be the primary bases of the structure. Finally (and most important too), the geographical structure does not take into account the secrecy motif and the incomprehension of the disciples, both key themes in the first part of the Gospel.

Therefore, in conclusion, we hold that geographical and topographical criteria are not the primary basis for the structure of Mk.

B. Outline Based on Topic

1. *Exposition*

Radically rooted in the conviction that there is no cohesive factor which logically or theologically binds Mk as a whole, some scholars propose outlines based on topics [13]. A less rigid application of this principle is seen in the New English Bible:

---

[10] For instance, Mk 1,14-10,52 is given the title "die Wirksamkeit Jesu vor dem Jerusalemer Aufenthalt" by MARXSEN (*Einleitung*, 120); likewise, SOUBIGOU ("Plano") gives the heading "the ministry outside Jerusalem" for 1,14-10,52.

[11] ERNST gives the heading "Jesus auf dem Wege außerhalb von Galiläa" for 7,1-8,26. LANE gives the title "withdrawal beyond Galilee" to 6,14-8,30; similarly, TAYLOR has the title "the ministry beyond Galilee" for 6,14-8,26.

[12] For instance, LANG ("Kompositionsanalyse"), in addition to geographical and theological criteria, makes use of other elements such as stichometry, scenic difference of place, time and persons, etc. However, his title "Erweiterter Aktionsradius" for 6,6b-8,21 is vague and enigmatic. KOCH ("Aufriss") integrates the criteria of content into the geographical structure. Yet he finds no unity based on content for 6,6b-8,26 (cf. p. 156-157).

[13] Cf. FAW, "Outline", 19-23, etc.

The coming of Christ (1,1-13)
In Galilee: Success and opposition (1,14-4,34)
Miracles of Christ (4,35-6,56)
Growing tension (7,1-10,31)
Challenge to Jerusalem (10,32-13,37)
The final conflict (14,1-16,8)

2. *Critical Remarks*

The section entitled "Miracles of Christ" (4,35-6,56) contains six miracles and one summary whereas there are five miracles and three summaries
before it and six miracles after it. Secondly, compared to 2,1-3,6, there is no
growth of tension in 7,1-10,31 so as to give it the title "Growing tension".
Mk 8,27-10,52 is generally recognized as a coherent unit [14]; yet NEB breaks
this coherence. Finally, it lacks a single overarching principle for division.

C. Structuralist Approach

1. *Exposition*

Applying the categories and models of structuralism, some recent studies [15] envision the coherence of Mk in a new way. The common parameter
in most of them is the distinction between surface and deep structure and the
conviction that the deep structure discloses the true meaning of Mk.

Among the structuralist contributions van Iersel's study is stimulating.
The topographic structure of Mk is analysed as a means of finding sense in
this Gospel. There are five constitutive parts in Mk, forming a concentric
structure around the lexemes:

A:'desert' (1,1-13)
   B: 'Galilee'(1,16-8,21)
      C: 'the way' (8,27-10,45)
   B': 'Jerusalem' (11,1-15,39)
A': 'the tomb' (15,42-16,8)

---

[14] See for instance, PERRIN, "Interpretation", 7-30; QUESNELL, *Mind*, 134-138; K. WEIB,
"Ekklesiologie", 414-438, etc.

[15] Cf. CALLOUD, "Structural Analysis", 92-132; VAN IERSEL, "Locality", 45-54; MALBON,
"Elements", 155-170; id., "Mythic Structure", 97-132; id., "Galilee and Jerusalem", 242-255;
VIA, *Kerygma*, 71-169.

Therefore, the semantically most important part of the book is situated in the centre (8,27-10,45). All sorts of relations are constructed on the model of the square of oppositions transformed into a semiotic square [16]. Via, however, applies a number of categories and models to Mk in order to demonstrate its unity and progression from different points of view [17].

2. *Critical Remarks*

In the first place, deep structure must be based on the literary evidence of the surface structure. And in the second place, although under different nomenclature, Malbon and van Iersel clearly presuppose the validity of the structure based on geographical criteria.

D. Outline Based on the Structure of Drama

1. *Exposition*

There is a tendency, especially in recent years, to posit the hypothesis that in composing the Gospel Mk has followed the literary paradigm of drama, prevalent in Graeco-Roman antiquity. Applying the Aristotelian canons of drama some claim that the plan of Mk conforms to the three-part structure of Greek tragedy: complication, crisis and denouement [18].

prologue (1,1-13)

narration (1,14-6,13)

argumentation (6,14-10,52)

dramatic denouement (11,1-15,47)

epilogue (16,1-8) [19]

---

[16] Cf. VAN IERSEL, "Locality", 45-47, 51-54.

[17] On the basis of Barthes' categories Mk is a sequence composed of three cardinal functions which open, maintain and close the narrative (cf. VIA, *Kerygma*, 115-118). According to Bremond's categories the three sequential functions are virtuality, amelioration and goal (*ibid.*, 119-120). Again, Gerimas' analysis offers a third model: sender — object — receiver, helper — subject — opposer (*ibid.*, 132-133).

[18] Cf. BILEZIKIAN, *Liberated Gospel*; STANDAERT, *Composition*; A. STOCK, "Mystery Play", 1909-1915; id., *Discipleship*.

[19] Cf. STANDAERT, 24; id., *Composition*, 263-372.

2. Critical Observations

Advocates of this view assert that Mk has the structure of Greek tragedy. However, scholars of distinction in ancient literature do not subscribe to the view that Mk is modelled on ancient tragedy. On the contrary, they assert that the Gospels cannot be placed in any literary genre of antiquity; the Gospels, in fact, gave birth to a new literary genre [20]. Literary antecedents of particular themes or individual pericopes are traceable from the OT and Judaism. The claims that the author of the second Gospel must have been trained in rhetoric (Standaert) and that he must have been conversant with tragedy (A. Stock) remain in the realm of conjecture. The Gospels are founded on the Jesus' event and are controlled by oral tradition and living faith. In this sense they are not free compositions; they lack the freedom which ancient literature enjoyed [21].

E. Structure Based on Patternism, Stichometry, and Theological Content

Anchored on the redaction critical principle that Mk is an author in his own right with a specific theological intention in his writing, and founded on certain literary indices, a number of attempts at establishing the structure of Mk have been made during the last three decades. Despite this basically sound approach, the literary indices employed are considerably heterogeneous with the result that there is a noticeable variation in the resultant structures.

1. Patternism

A regular three-part pattern detectable in the whole of Mk, some claim, forms the basis of the Marcan structure.

---

[20] NORDEN, *Kunstprosa*, II, 480: "Die Evangelien stehen abseits von der kunstmäßigen Literatur. Auch rein äußerlich als literarische Denkmäler betrachtet tragen sie den Stempel des absolut Neuen zur Schau". In the same vein AUERBACH, *Mimesis*, 47-49, asserts that the Gospels portray something which neither the poets nor historians of antiquity ever set out to portray.

[21] Cf. NORDEN, *Kunstprosa*, II, 451-480.

a. *Exposition*

(i) Ellis [22] finds triads and triadic arrangements the constitutive feature of the Marcan structure both at the macro- and micro-levels. He divides the second Gospel into three parts:

 1,1-13: Introduction
I. 1,14-8,30: the arrival of the kingdom
II. 8,31-10,52: the suffering Son of Man and discipleship
III 11,1-16,8: the last seven days and the Resurrection

Each part contains three sections (ABC) and each section consists of three parts: introductory summary, apostleship, and narrative complex. This three-part pattern extends to the whole Gospel except the Passion narrative where the second part, 'apostleship', is lacking.

(ii) According to Robbins [23] the three-step progression evident in the context of the three passion predictions (Mk 8,27-9,1; 9,30-50; 10,32-45) is also present in scenes throughout the Gospel in which Jesus calls disciples (1,14-20; 3,7-19; 6,1-13; 8,27-9,1; 10,46-11,11; 13,1-37). These passages function as interludes establishing the basic outline of Mk. The outline thus comprises an introduction (1,1-13), six sections (1,14-3,6; 3,7-5,43; 6,1-8,26; 8,27-10,45; 10,46-12,44; 13,1-15,47), and a conclusion (16,1-8).

b. *Critical Observations*

First, an attentive reading of Mk reveals that patternism is to a great extent a projection of one's own ideas into the Gospel rather than a discovery of what is given in it.

Secondly, formal and stereotyped patterns are inadequate to bring out the internal texture and the organic unity of the Gospel. Nor do they enable the reader to comprehend fully the diversity and growth of themes and the complexity and progression of narrations.

Thirdly, among a number of critical observations of Ellis' structure I will mention a few more conspicuous ones. The first part (1,14-8,30) is given the title "The Arrival of the Kingdom". However, the expression, 'kingdom of God', occurs only six times in 1,14-8,30 whereas it is found ten times in 8,31-16,8. He considers 11,1; 16,1, etc. introductory summaries, but these

---

[22] ELLIS, "Patterns", 88-103.
[23] ROBBINS, "Summons", 97-114.

are, in fact, no summaries at all. Again, it is only to suit his pattern that he names 11,1c-6 a pericope on apostleship. Likewise, to be consistent with his pattern he includes 9,2-29 and 10,1-9 in Jesus' instruction on discipleship though these pericopes have hardly anything to do with discipleship.

Finally, the structure proposed by Robbins is less convincing and more problematic. It is solely to fit his three-step progression that he breaks single pericopes (e.g., 1,16-20; 3,7-12; 6,1-6; 10,46-52, etc.) into two literary units. Again, it is hard to see how some pericopes (e.g., 11,1-11; 13,3-37, etc.) deal with discipleship. Moreover, his structure does not clearly establish how the bulk of the material (1,21-3,6; 3,20-5,43; 6,14-8,26; 9,2-10,45; 11,12-12,44; 14,1-15,47) is related to and integrated within the overall plan of Mk.

In conclusion, the structure based exclusively on patterns, like an outer garment that does not touch the person, remains attractive on the exterior level only. It does not touch the Gospel in its deeper and interior level. Therefore such a structure is inadequate.

2. Stichometry

a. Exposition

Basing himself primarily on stichometry, Pesch [24] divides the second Gospel (exclusive of ch. 13) into six major sections (1,2-3,6; 3,7-6,29; 6,30-8,26; 8,27-10,52; 11,1-12,44; 14,1-16,8). Each major section comprises three units; the first and third units are of almost equal length whereas the second (middle) unit is invariably the shortest. Thus Pesch claims, each major division is concentrically structured. In his commentary, however, he divides the first two major sections not into three but four units [24a].

b. Critical Remarks

Pesch's use of the formal criteria does not take into account the inter-relationship and progression between various pericopes. His elimination of chapter 13 seems to be unwarranted because eschatological elements are also found elsewhere in Mk (cf. 8,38; 14,62, etc.) [25].

---

[24] Cf. PESCH, Naherwartungen, 54-68.

[24a] Cf. PESCH, I, 32-36.

[25] See the critical remarks on PESCH's view in BAARLINK, Anfängliches Evangelium, 101-102; KOCH, "Aufriss", 147, 160; id., "Christologie", 399-400; LANG, "Kompositions-analyse", 3.

3. *Structure Based on Theological Content*

a. *Exposition*

Primarily based on theological indices, a few rather recent studies divide the second Gospel into five or six major sections [26]. It is claimed that an overarching principle of design for the Marcan construction is extremely difficult though within a section there are ample unifying factors.

Gnilka and Schweizer affirm a progressive development of the theme of discipleship in 1,16-20; 3,13-19; 6,7-13. Gnilka argues that the progressive development of the theme of discipleship in Mk should be understood in the context of the rejection of Jesus by the Jews on the one hand, and the role of the Twelve in constituting the new people of God on the other [27].

Gnilka's outline [28]:

The beginning (1,1-15)
Jesus' mighty work before the people (1,16-3,12)
The teaching and the miracles of Jesus (3,13-6,6a)
Jesus' itinerant wandering (6,6b-8,26)
Invitation to cross-bearing (8,27-10,45)
Jesus' ministry in Jerusalem (10,46-13,37)
Suffering and victory (14,1-16,8)

The outline of Schweizer [29]:

The beginning (1,1-13)
The authority of Jesus and the blindness of the Pharisees (1,14-3,6)
Jesus' ministry in parables and signs and the blindness of the world (3,7-6,6a)
Jesus' ministry to the Gentiles and the blindness of the disciples (6,6b-8,26)
Jesus' open revelation and the meaning of discipleship (8,27-10,52)
The Passion and Resurrection of the Son of Man (11,1-16,8)

---

[26] Cf. BLATHERWICK, "Silhouette", 184-192; GNILKA, I, 30-32; SCHWEIZER, "Theologische Leistung", 337-355; id., "Portrayal", 387-399.

[27] Cf. GNILKA, I, 26-29.

[28] *Ibid.*, 32.

[29] SCHWEIZER, 223.

b. *Critical Observations*

These studies do not present adequate literary indices which would form the basis for their theological division. Further, as will be established in the next section, Mk does have an overarching principle of design for his Gospel. Gnilka's outline is not satisfactory: for the miracles of Jesus are not confined to 1,16-6,6a. Besides, nothing specific is conveyed by 'Jesus' itinerant wandering'. In fact, Jesus begins his journey even earlier: "he went throughout all Galilee" (1,39) and he journeyed to the country of the Gerasenes in a boat (5,1-2), etc.

As Fusco [30] has pointed out, Schweizer underscores the insuperable and radical blindness of man in recognizing Jesus. Each of the first sections, says Schweizer, concludes with the obduracy or blindness of Jesus' adversaries (3,1-6), of his countrymen (6,1-6a) and of his own disciples (8,14-21). There is no more room for any teaching or miracles except to follow the way to the cross. Such an interpretation undoubtedly emphasizes the centrality of theologia crucis. But the centrality of theologia crucis does not mean that the prepaschal ministry of Jesus has no positive value at all, especially regarding the relationship between Jesus and his disciples. Thus the key role of 8,27-30 which is also structurally central is not properly understood and interpreted. We will establish in the next section that the first three sections are progressively structured so that the veil of the disciples' blindness is lifted in 8,27-30.

F. Conclusion

In the preceding pages we have tried to present a brief and synthetic classification of the various prevalent opinions on the structure of Mk. It is evident that before redaction criticism became an accepted exegetical method, geographical outline was predominant. But after that there is a growing tendency either to integrate other criteria within the geographical division or to abandon the geographical structure altogether and then search for other criteria for structuring Mk. At first sight some of these attempts appeared strikingly ingenious and meticulously systematic. Yet our critical scrutiny has, at least to some extent, unveiled their flaws and incongruities. Now we proceed to present the structure that according to us is theologically in tune with Mk's plan.

---

[30] Cf. FUSCO, *Parola e regno*, 122-123.

III. The Structure Based on Literary and Theological Indices

The primary objective is to discover the basic question about which the evangelist is concerned. And the basic question becomes manifest by a frank and attentive dialogue with the text [31]. In this process the criteria employed by the evangelist to structure his Gospel also become transparent.

First of all, one perceives the key vocabulary whether noun or verb, their interrelation and place in the narrative, the mode and frequency of their occurrence. The redactional vocabulary should undoubtedly receive particular attention. Other literary indices such as inclusion, chiasm, parallelism between pericopes and between sections, correspondence between pericopes, etc. also become perceptible. Secondly, the key vocabulary indicates the main theological thrust of the Gospel. Consistent development of particular themes and their place and organization within the narrative, and the way secondary themes are subordinated to the main theme, etc. are elements that help to find the plan of the evangelist. Thirdly, various pericopes are linked by geographical notices which, though in a subordinate way, are also means by which the structure is decided. Finally, other criteria such as the change of audience, a difference in the way Jesus or others act or react may also serve in determining the structure.

A. Peter's Confession (8,27-30): The Watershed of Mark's Gospel

That Peter's confession (8,27-30) is the watershed of Mk is upheld by a number of exegetes [32] for, as de la Potterie aptly points out, it is the terminus ad quem of all that precedes and the terminus a quo of all that follows [33]. It is at 8,29 that for the first time a human being — Peter, the leader and spokesman of the disciples — declares Jesus' true identity: Σὺ εἶ ὁ Χριστός. The first part of Mk is composed so as to attain this dramatic climax and the second part elucidates what Jesus' Messiahship implies.

---

[31] Cf. PALMER, *Hermeneutics*, 7, 42, 81, 86, 114, 149, 183, 185, 197-200, 212, 233-237.

[32] Among others see FUSCO, *Parola e regno*, 127-132; GROB, *Einführung*, 6, 119-120; HEIL, *Jesus Walking*, 119; H.C. KEE, *Community*, 57, 62; LÉON-DUFOUR, *Introduzione* II, 45-47, 51-52; LIGHTFOOT, *Gospel Message*, 34-35; QUESNELL, *Mind*, 126-138; TILLESSE, *Le secret messianique*, 303-326; WREDE, *Messiasgeheimnis*, 115-124.

[33] DE LA POTTERIE, "De compositione", 137; id., "Confessione", 59; id., "Multiplication", 317.

1. *Progressive Revelation of the Mystery of Jesus' Messiahship: The Main Thrust of the First Part*

The selection and arrangement of materials in the first part of Mk are geared to a particular aim, viz., the progressive revelation of Jesus' Messiahship. All the protagonists are in one way or another involved in the question: Who is Jesus? The demons knew him but he prohibited them from making him known (1,34; 3,11-12). Those who were beneficiaries of Jesus' interventions, which had Messianic overtones, were commanded not to speak about those events (1,44; 5,43; 7,36; 8,26) though the command was unheeded in certain instances (cf. 1,45; 7,36).

People marvelled at his authority and perceived something unique in him (1,22.27). The scribes questioned in their hearts concerning him (2,7); they also affirmed that he was possessed by Beelzebul (3,22). His relatives held that he was insane (3,21). His own townsmen had a view about him that was too human (6,2-3). Herod and many others did not manage to have an exact view about his identity (6,14-16).

While all other protagonists had already taken a stand concerning Jesus' identity, the disciples remain open. They for the first time pose the question at the end of the calming of a storm: "And they were filled with awe, and said to one another, 'Who then is this, that even wind and sea obey him?'" (4,41; diff. par. Mt 8,27). And according to Mk it was imperative for the disciples to recognize Jesus' true identity. For they were his close followers right from the beginning [34] and his intimate companions (3,14); they had the unique privilege of sharing in his own mission (3,14-15; 6,7-13.30). Among various categories of Jesus' audiences, only they were given [35] the mystery of the kingdom of God (4,11). They alone experienced the epiphanies (4,35-41; 6,45-52) and participated in the Messianic banquet (6,34-44). In spite of all this they did not understand him. The question posed in 4,41 — who then is this? — remained unanswered. So Jesus repeatedly urges them to understand.

As the narrative progresses, Jesus' identity becomes glaringly transparent (4,35-41; 6,45-52), his Messiahship is revealed with almost compelling

---

[34] It is specific to Mk that from the beginning of his ministry, Jesus is accompanied by his followers (cf. 1,16-20; 2,14-15; 3,7; 6,1; 8,10.27). By the use of the third person plural of the verb, the evangelist stresses that Jesus is not alone but accompanied by his disciples (cf. 1,21.29; 5,1.38; 6,53; 8,22).

[35] In Mk 4,11 δέδοται is theological passive (cf. GNILKA, I, 163; id., *Verstockung*, 28-29; NOLLI, *Marco*, 80).

evidence (6,34-44), the miracles become more and more symbolic (7,31-37; 8,22-26) and he urges his disciples with utmost insistence to understand his identity (6,52; 8,17-21). The pericope of the healing of a blind man at Bethsaida (8,22-26) symbolizes the gradual spiritual enlightenment of the disciples concerning Jesus' identity. Thus the question of Jesus' identity progressively revealed and yet intentionally concealed in the first eight chapters finds a definitive answer in Peter's acknowledgement and confession of Jesus' Messiahship: "You are the Christ" (8,29).

As at the middle of each of the three sections stands the question of Jesus' identity, so also the first part comes to a climax in Peter's acknowledgement and confession of Jesus' true identity:

2,7:   Who can forgive sins but God alone?

4,41:   Who then is this, that even wind and sea obey him?

6,49-51:   But when they saw him walking on the sea they thought it was a ghost and they cried out; for they all saw him, and were terrified. But immediately he spoke to them and said, "Take heart, it is I; have no fear". . . . And they were utterly astounded.

8,29:   "But who do you say that I am?" Peter answered him, "You are the Christ".

2. The Mystery of the Suffering Son of Man: The Main Thrust of the Second Part

a. The Mystery of the Suffering Son of Man

The principal theme that dominates the second part of Mk is the mystery of the suffering Son of Man. All the occurrences of the title, Son of Man, employed by Jesus to describe his Passion, Death and Resurrection, are found in the second part [36]. From the outset Mk in unequivocal terms stresses that Jesus undergoes his Passion and Death because they are willed by God. And all the affirmations regarding the divine necessity of Jesus' Passion and Death are invariably placed on the lips of Jesus. These affirmations occur in manifold ways in different contexts in the second part of Mk. The very first prediction of Jesus' Passion (8,31) commences on a note of divine necessity

---

[36] Mk 8,31; 9,9.12.31; 10,33.45; 14,21.41.

(δεῖ). He emphasizes it also by showing that it is scripturally necessary: πῶς γέγραπται (9,12), καθὼς γέγραπται (9,13; 14,21), ὅτι γέγραπται (14,27) and πληροῦν αἱ γραφαί (14,49). It is underscored also by the use of the theological passive in 9,31and 10,33. Further, Mk underlines it by pointing out the contrast between the divine will and the human will (8,33). Finally, and most importantly, at Gethsemane Jesus as a human being with the fullness of feeling and emotion prays authentically and spontaneously to Abba, Father, that if possible he would remove the cup from him; however, the final and most significant element is obedience to God's will (14,36).

God wills the death of his Son as a total and selfless service for the sake of mankind, "as a ransom for many" (10,45). And through Jesus' Death the new and definitive covenant is established which implies God's absolute covenantal faithfulness to mankind through the blood of his own Son "poured out for many" (14,24).

Jesus' Passion and Death, willed by God, are historically realized through human agents. The Sanhedrin, the supreme religious authority, composed of chief priests, scribes, and elders who had the lion's share in putting Jesus to death, figures solely in the second part [37]. Likewise, the chief priests and scribes appear together as a body only in the second part (10,33; 11,18; 14,1). Of the 22 occurrences of the term ἀρχιερεύς in Mk, 21 are in the second part, and 17 in the Passion narrative. And in the trial before the Sanhedrin it is the high priest, ὁ ἀρχιερεύς, who is primarily responsible in condemning Jesus to death (cf. 14,61-64). The verbs that one or the other way pertain to the description of Jesus' Passion, Death and Resurrection also occur almost exclusively in the second part (cf. 8,31; 9,31; 10,33-34; 12,12; 14,1-16,8).

Thus in the second part Mk portrays the mystery of Jesus' Passion and Death willed by God for the salvation of mankind; Jesus in full freedom adheres to God's will; and this mystery is concretely realized through the complicity of the Jewish and Roman authorities.

b. *Progression in the Narration of the Son of Man's Suffering*

In the first three chapters of the second part there are three predictions about the fate of the Son of Man (8,31; 9,31; 10,32-34) composed in such a way as to reach their peak in 10,32-34 [38]. The events predicted are fulfilled in the Passion narrative:

[37] Mk 8,31; 11,27; 14,43.53; 15,1.
[38] Mk 8,31 and 9,31 foretell the Passion in three stages, but 10,33-34 consists of six stages.

Predictions	Fulfilment in the Passion Narrative
The Son of Man will be delivered (παραδιδόναι) into the hands of the Sanhedrin (9,31; 10,33).	Jesus is betrayed and delivered into the hands of the Sanhedrin (14,43-50; παραδιδόναι in 14,44).
They will condemn him (κατακρίνειν) to death (10,33).	They condemned him to death (14,53-65; κατακρίνειν in 14,64; diff. par. Mt. 26,66).
They will deliver him (παραδιδόναι) to the Gentiles (10,33).	Sanhedrin delivered him to Pilate (15,1-5; παραδιδόναι in 15,1.10; 15,1 diff. par. Lk 23,1).
They will mock him (ἐμπαίζειν), spit upon him (ἐμπτύειν) and scourge him (μαστιγοῦν) (10,34).	They maltreated him by mocking, spitting and striking (14,65; 15,16-20.29-32; ἐμπαίζειν in 15,20.31; ἐμπτύειν in 14,65; 15,19).
They will kill him (ἀποκτείνειν in 8,31; 9,31;10,34).	They plotted to kill him (ἀποκτείνειν: 14,1), they crucified him (15,21-32; σταυροῦν in 15,24.25) and he died on the cross (15,37).
And after three days he will rise (8,31; 9,31; 10,34).	And after three days he rose (15,42-16,6).

Each of these three predictions is immediately followed by a statement on the failure of the disciples to assimilate the mystery of the suffering Messiah. After this Jesus instructs his disciples on the absolute necessity to follow the path of suffering and service. The incomprehension of the disciples in chs. 8-10 works up to a tragic climax in the Passion narrative: Judas' betrayal (14,44-46), Peter's denial (14,66-72) and the flight of the rest (14,50-52).

Unlike chapters 8-10, there are no predictions about the Passion and Death of the Son of Man, nor any statement regarding the divine necessity of Jesus' Death in chapters 11-13. The predominant thrust in chapters 11-12 is the plot of the Jewish authorities to destroy Jesus and their specific attempts to entrap him — the former temporarily obliterated by the fear of the multitude and the latter by the apt and bold answers of Jesus to their questions. Both, however, reach full realization in the Passion narrative. This increasingly hostile attitude of the Jewish authorities towards Jesus and their calculatingly destructive ways are schematically demonstrated on the following folder.

Jewish authority's plot to destroy Jesus (chapters 11-12

Jesus' action	Drives out the dealers from the temple (11,15-16) and teaches there... "My house shall be called a house of prayer for all the nations. But *yo have* made it a den of robbers"(11,17)		Jesus is God's beloved son, the last and definitive envoy of God to Israel. Jewish *leaders' rejection of God's son* leads to *God's rejection of the leaders* (12,6-11)	
Opponents' reaction	*Opponents' plot*	The chief priests and the scribes sought [39] a way to *destroy Jesus* (11,18a)	*Opponents' plot*	The chief pries and the scribes and the elders tried to *arrest him* (12,12a)
	Obstacles	They feared him be-cause the multitude was astonished at his teaching (11,18b)	*Obstacles*	They feared th multitude (12,12b)
Their attempt	The chief priests, the scribes and the elders *question* Jesus' authority (11,27-28)		They send Pharisses and Herod-ians to *entrap Jesus* in talk (12,13) who ask an *intriguing question*: "Is it lawful to pay taxes to Caesar or not?"(12,14)	
Jesus' counter-action	Jesus' *counter-question*: "Was the baptism of John from heaven or from men?" (11,30)		*Jesus' response*: "Render to Caesar the things that are Caesar's and to God the things that are God's" (12,17a)	
Final outcome	They pretend ignorance. In turn, Jesus too refuses to answer them (11,33)		Amazement (12,17b). (A series of questions in which Jesus emerges victorious. "And after that no one dared to ask him any question" (12,34)	

---

[39] Note the imperfect ἐζήτουν in all the three summaries of the plot against Jesus (11,18; 12,12; 14,1).

Realization of the Plot in the Passion Narrative

Opponents' plots	The chief priests and the scribes tried to *arrest him by stealth and kill him* (14,1bc)	*Obstacle overcome*	Judas volunteered to betray Jesus to the chief priests and they promised to give him money (14,10-11). Crowds won over by the chief priests (14,43; 15,11-15)
		FINAL ACT	*CRUCIFIXION* (15,21-37)
Obstacle	Not during the feast lest there be un uprising of the people (14,2)	*Plot executed*	Betrayal (14,44-45) Arrest (14,46-48) Trial (14,55-65; 15,1-15)

This scheme shows a vertical as well as a horizontal progression. The vertical progression consists of two parallel chain-reactions clearly perceptible in the scheme:

Jesus' action (accusation: 11,17; 12,6-11) —->

opponents' plot (11,18a; 12,12a) —->

obstacle (11,18b; 12,12b) —->

their attempt (11,27-28; 12,13-15) —->

Jesus' counteraction (11,30; 12,16-17a) —->

Jesus' victory (11,33; 12,17b.34).

The horizontal progression is most obvious in the linear development and gradual specification of the plot: in 11,18 it is very general (destroy Jesus), in 12,12 it is specific (arrest him), and in 14,1 it is more specific and articulated clearly (arrest him by stealth and kill him). This horizontal progression is transparent also from other perspectives. The crowds, who are Jesus' admirers during his ministry in Jerusalem (11,9-10.18b; 12,12b; 14,2) and, as a result, an obstacle to the Jewish authorities in executing their plot, are won over in the Passion narrative (14,43; 15,11-15). Thus the obstacle to the plot is gradually eliminated. Furthermore, in chapters 11-12 the Jewish authorities could not succeed in finding a legitimate cause for accusation against Jesus through just and honest means, whether by themselves (11,27-28: questioning Jesus' authority) or by their agents (12,14: the intriguing question whether to pay taxes to Caesar or not). Therefore, in the Passion narrative they employ occult and deceptive ways to achieve their aim: reward of money to the betrayer (14,11), instigating the crowd (15,11), and false accusations brought against Jesus (14,56-59; 15,10).

The progression is shown also by means of the contrasts between Jesus' ministry in Jerusalem and his Passion. The key contrasts are the following:

Jerusalem Ministry	*Contrast in the Passion Narrative*
A prophetic, symbolic act foreshadowing the destruction of the temple (11,12-17.20-21) and the prediction of its destruction (13,2).	Construction of another temple in three days not made with hands (14,58b; 15,29c).
Jesus the teacher confronts the true robbers (11,17).	Jesus the teacher is seized as if he were a robber (14,49).
Jesus warns about the scribes (12,38-40).	The scribes (together with others) condemn Jesus as deserving death (14,64) and they mock him (15,31).

| The crowds' ovation and crying out, "Hosanna!" (11,7-10). | The crowds' derision and crying out, "Crucify him" (15,12-14). |

Thus various literary elements and thematic aspects of Jesus' ministry in Jerusalem come to a climax in the Passion narrative.

The main contacts of Mk 13 with the Passion narrative are the conjunction of the sufferings of Christians with that of Jesus (compare 13,9-13 with 14,32-42), the exhortation to watch and pray (13,33; 14,38), the verb γρηγορεῖν exclusively in 13,34.35.37 and 14,34.37.38, the absolute use of 'the hour' (13,11; 14,41), the coming of the Son of Man in clouds with great power and glory (13,26; 14,62) and the use of the verb σώζειν in the soteriological sense (13,13.20; 15,30.31).

In 14,1-42 Mk highlights the role of Jesus' own disciples in his Passion. Their role prophesied in 14,1-42 is fulfilled in 14,43-72:

Prophecy	*Fulfilment*
Betrayal by one of the Twelve (14,18-21)	Actual betrayal by one of the Twelve (14,44-46)
Defection by the disciples (14,27)	Actual defection of the disciples (14,50-52)
Denial by Peter (14,30-31)	Actual denial by Peter (14,66-72)

In brief, our evangelist has structured the second part of the Gospel in a way that emphasizes the three key facets of the mystery of Jesus' Passion and Death: the three predictions (chs. 8-10), the plot of the Jewish authorities (chs. 11-12), and the role of the disciples (14,1-42). These are gradually unveiled and dramatically fulfilled in the arrest, trial, condemnation and crucifixion of Jesus (14,43-15,39). These three aspects are depicted below:

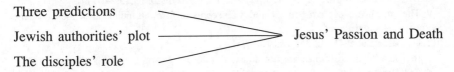

Three predictions

Jewish authorities' plot ————————————> Jesus' Passion and Death

The disciples' role

3. *Confirmation*

In Mk Χριστός, after its use in the heading of the book, never again occurs before Peter's confession (8,29)[40]. Thus up to 8,29 Jesus' true identity remains concealed[41]. However, in the second part the title Χριστός is rather frequent[42]. Further, οὐ νοεῖν, οὐ/οὔπω συνιέναι, ἀσύνετος, πεπωρωμένη (καρδία) and πώρωσις (τῆς καρδίας) are characteristic of the first part but not of the second. As pointed out previously, all the occurrences of the title, the Son of Man, employed by Jesus to describe his Passion, Death and Resurrection and the verbs that narrate these events, are found exclusively in the second part.

Secondly, after Peter's confession the disciples do not express surprise or amazement when encountering Jesus. Nor are the verbs ἐκθαμβεῖσθαι, ἐκθαυμάζειν, θαμβεῖν, θαυμάζειν and ἐκπλήσσειν predicated of the disciples in the second part but of the crowd, Pilate, the women, the Pharisees and Herodians etc[43]. The disciples have only fear in face of the mystery of suffering (cf. 9,32; 10,32).

Finally, in the second part the events that have Messianic overtones are not accompanied by the command to silence as in the first part. For instance, the blind Bartimaeus twice addressed Jesus, Son of David (10,47.48), a Messianic title[44]; but he is not silenced. Unlike the blind man at Bethsaida (8,26) there is no imposition of secrecy on Bartimaeus when he is healed (cf. 10,52). Furthermore, Jesus' entry into Jerusalem (11,1-11), especially the manner and the public ovation, has Messianic overtones[45]; yet Jesus does not object to these revelations, on the contrary, he tacitly seems to approve them.

[40] Differ Mt (cf. 1,16.17.18; 2,4; 11,2) and Lk (cf. 2,11.26; 3,15; 4,41).

[41] The presence of Χριστός in 1,1 and 8,29 seems to form an inclusion of the first part, indicating its principal theme.

[42] Cf. Mk 8,29; 9,41; 12,35; 13,21; 14,61; 15,32.

[43] In 10,24.26 the disciples are not amazed at Jesus' person but at his words.

[44] Cf. BURKILL, "Strain", 33; LOHSE, TDNT VIII, 480-482, 484-486; LOHMEYER, *Davidssohn*, 66-67, 71-72, 76-84; MICHAELIS, "Davidssohnschaft", 320-324.

[45] Zech 9,9 narrates the Messiah's coming "humble and riding on an ass, on a colt the foal of an ass". Zech 14,4 associated the Mount of Olives with the coming of the Messiah. Furthermore, ὁ ἐρχόμενος is probably a Messianic title (cf. SCHNEIDER, TDNT II, 670). Finally, Mk 11,10, a comment on Ps 118,25-26, is based on the Messianic title, Son of David (cf. AMBROZIC, *Hidden Kingdom*, 39).

4. *Conclusion*

Therefore, there are ample literary indications and thematic bases for the assertion that 8,27-30 is the watershed of Mk and that the main thrust of the first part is the progressive revelation of the mystery of Jesus' Messiahship while the chief thrust of the second is the mystery of the suffering Son of Man. In other words, the main question in the first part is: Who is Jesus? The answer: Σὺ εἶ ὁ Χριστός (8,29). The principal question in the second part is: What sort of Messiah is he? Mk answers: He is the suffering Son of Man. The identity of Jesus as the Messiah (part I) and his specific characteristic as the suffering Messiah (part II) merge into one basic theme: the mystery of the person of Jesus.

The mystery of Jesus' Messiahship is progressively revealed in the first part and ultimately acknowledged and confessed by Peter in 8,29. Similarly the mystery of Jesus' suffering is gradually unveiled in the second part and finally realized in 15,37 by Jesus' Death crowned by his Resurrection (16,1-8).

B. The Structure of Mark's Gospel

Introduction (1,1-13)

Part I: Progressive Revelation of the Mystery of Jesus' Messiahship (1,14-8,30)

a. Manifestation of Jesus' Authority: Popular Acceptance and Scribal and Pharisaic Opposition (1,14-3,6)

b. Manifestation in Parabolic Teaching and Stupendous Miracles: Jesus and 'His Own' (3,7-6,6a)

c. Jesus Reveals Himself to His Disciples (6,6b-8,30)

Part II: Revelation of the Mystery of the Suffering Son of Man (8,27-16,8)

a. The Way of the Son of Man and Discipleship (8,27-10,52)

b. Revelation in Jerusalem and the Definitive Break with the Jews (11,1-13,37)

c. Fulfilment and Culmination of the Mystery: Passion, Death and Resurrection of the Son of Man (14,1-16,8)

Mk has provided sufficient literary indications for further divisions within the Gospel, particularly for the first part. There are three summary statements regarding Jesus' ministry (1,14-15; 3,7-12; 6,6b) which, as noted in Ch. I, are not primarily conclusions of the preceding pericopes nor are they mere transitional summaries. Rather they mark the beginning of a section. These summaries, though linked to what precedes, have mainly a prospective function within the respective sections that indicate the progression of Jesus' ministry in the first part of Mk. Each of these summaries is immediately followed by a pericope on discipleship (call: 1,16-20; appointment: 3,13-19; mission: 6,7-13). These three pericopes on discipleship show the increasing role of the disciples in terms of their personal relation to Jesus and their participation in his mission. Thus a summary statement together with a pericope on discipleship constitutes an introduction to each of the three sections in the first part (1,14-15 + 1,16-20; 3,7-12 + 3,13-19; 6,6b + 6,7-13).

The end of each of the three sections is indicated by a statement on the hardness of heart or incomprehension concerning the mystery of Jesus' person: of the Pharisees and Herodians in 3,5-6, of Jesus' own townspeople in 6,1-6a and of his own chosen disciples in 8,17-21. In contrast to the first two sections, Mk does not conclude the third section on a totally negative note. The healing of the blind man at Bethsaida (8,22-26) is a most fitting transition to Peter's confession of Jesus' Messiahship (8,29). Thus there are three sections in the first part of Mk: (a) 1,14-3,6; (b) 3,7-6,6a; and (c) 6,6b-8,30. So Mk 1,1-13 constitutes but the introduction to the Gospel.

1. Introduction (1,1-13)

It was established in Ch. I that Mk 1,1-13 is a coherent literary unit and that the primary function of 1,1-13 was to introduce Jesus, the main character of the Gospel.

2. Part I: Progressive Revelation of the Mystery of Jesus' Messiahship (1,14-8,30)

a. Manifestation of Jesus' Authority: Popular Acceptance and Scribal and Pharisaic Opposition (1,14-3,6)

Mk 1,14-3,6 is characterized by the manifestation of Jesus' unique authority in his exorcisms and healings, teaching and controversies. The proclamation of the kingdom and the call of the first four disciples constitute the introduction to this section(1,14-20) . For the rest, Jesus receives two contrasting responses: popular acceptance (1,21-45) and opposition from scribes and Pharisees (2,1-3,6). As there is a steady growth in appreciation and acceptance of Jesus by the common people (cf. 1,22.28.32-34.37.45), so also there is a mounting opposition to him by the scribes and Pharisees (cf. 2,6-7.16.18.24; 3,2.4). The plot of the Pharisees and Herodians to destroy Jesus (3,5-6) marks the end of the section.

b. *Manifestation in Parabolic Teaching and Stupendous Miracles: Jesus and 'His Own' (3,7-6,6a)*

After the introduction (3,7-12 and 3,13-19), Mk narrates the reactions of Jesus' relatives and the scribes. His relatives are convinced that he is insane while the scribes accuse him of being possessed by Beelzebul. He disproves the latter and explains to the former the nature of his true family (3,20-35). He then continues his ministry of teaching about the kingdom of God in parables (4,1-34) [46]. He performs greater miracles than those recorded in the preceding section (4,35-5,43) [47]. This section concludes with the rejection of Jesus by his own townspeople (6,1-6a), "a text shaped under strong redactional influence" [48].

However, what specifically characterizes 3,7-6,6a is the formation of 'his own' or of his new 'family'. The tone is already set right at the beginning in Jesus' withdrawal with his disciples (3,7) and the foundation is laid in the institution of the Twelve (3,13-19), a decisively new and unique act. The Twelve are to be with him (3,14: ἵνα ὦσιν μετ' αὐτοῦ) and they constitute the nucleus of the true 'family' of believers who are seated around him (περὶ αὐτόν: 3,32.34) in contrast to the unbelieving relatives who stand outside (ἔξω: 3,31.32). It is the Twelve encircled by οἱ περὶ αὐτόν to whom are given the mystery of the kingdom of God whereas for οἱ ἔξω everything in parables (4,10-12). Again, only the disciples (and not the crowd) are privileged to experience the manifestation of Jesus' power over natural forces (4,35-41). Finally, only Peter, James and John (the innermost circle of his disciples) are

---

[46] Of the 13 occurrences of παραβολή the first nine are in this section (3,23; 4,2.10.11.13(bis).30.33.34). The next is in 7,17.

[47] The stilling of the storm (4,35-41) with its profound OT symbolism recalls Yahweh's victory over evil forces; and this goes beyond his ministry of healing and exorcism (cf. ACHTMEIER, "Storm-Tossed Sea", 169- 176; HEIL, *Jesus Walking*, 118-127).

The vivid and detailed narration of the expulsion of an entire 'legion' of demons (5,1-20) certainly surpasses any previous exorcism (cf. ANNEN, *Heil für die Heiden*, 103-110; DERRETT, "Gerasene Demoniac", 2-17; LAMARCHE, "Le possédé de Gérasa", 582-589).

The healing of the woman with hemorrhage (5,24-34) reveals that not only Jesus' words and touch have healing power but also his garment (5,27). Thus it supercedes all previous healings. Finally, to crown it all, the resuscitation of Jairus' daughter shows Jesus' victory over death itself.

[48] GRÄSSER, "Jesus in Nazareth", 18; see also MAYER, "Mk 6,1-6a", 187-198.

permitted to witness the crowning miracle of the section, the resuscitation of
Jairus' daughter (5,37-43).

Thus the specific theme that unites various pericopes in 3,7-6,6a is the
formation of those who hear the word and enter into a personal relationship
with or nearness to Jesus. In this way the true 'family' of Jesus is constituted,
forming, so to say, a concentric circle: Jesus, the Three, the Twelve, the
disciples, and οἱ περὶ αὐτόν.

c. Jesus Reveals Himself to His Disciples (6,6b-8,30)

After the introduction (6,6b and 6,7-13) [49] Mk narrates two apparently
contrary themes: on the one hand, Jesus' ministry opens itself to ever wider
horizons (universalism), and on the other hand, his whole effort is geared to
revealing himself to his disciples even though they continue to remain blind.

The key word that unites various pericopes in 6,6b-8,30 is ἄρτος. Of
the 21 occurrences of this term in Mk, eighteen are in this section. And by
placing the popular opinion concerning Jesus' identity at the beginning (6,14-
15) and at the end (8,27-28) of this section, the evangelist has not only
redactionally framed the 'bread' section by this inclusion, but he has also
indicated the main theme of the section, viz., Jesus' identity as the Messiah [50].

6,14-15	*8,28*
Some said, "John the baptizer has been raised from the dead"	and they told him, "John the Baptist;
But others said, "It is Elijah"	and others say, Elijah;
And others said, "It is a prophet, like one of the prophets of old".	and others one of the prophets".

The theme of Jesus' identity is verified in various pericopes of 6,6a-
8,30. The martyrdom of John the Baptist (6,17-29) is narrated in such a way
as to foreshadow Jesus' own Passion [51]. The pericope on the multiplication

---

[49] LANG ("Kompositionsanalyse", 7) finds 6,6b "viel zu kurz und nichtssagend, um eine
neue Sektion einleitend zu kennzeichnen". It should be born in mind that it is not the summary
(6,6b) alone but 6,6b plus the pericope that immediately follows (the mission of the Twelve,
6,7-13) constitute the introduction to the third section. Moreover, 6,6b shows terminological
affinity to what follows (cf. 6,36.56; 8,23.26.27).

[50] KOCH ("Aufriss", 156) states concerning this section: "Ein inhaltlich neues Thema,
das für den gesamten Abschnitt leitend wäre, ist hier nicht zu erkennen". His reliance on
geographical criteria, failure to note the key word and Mk's strong emphasis on the Messianic
revelation and on the disciples' incomprehension account for his statement.

[51] Cf. BUETUBELA, *Jean-Baptiste*, 220-233.

of the loaves (6,31-44), the key event of this section [52], contains many redactional elements intended to bring out specific theological motifs.

Jesus' invitation to the apostles to rest (6,31; cf. Mt11,28-29; Ps 23,2) and the mention of "sheep without a shepherd" (6,34b) and of "green grass" (6,39; cf. Ps 23,2) allude to the theme of Jesus the Shepherd [53]. The expression κατ' ἰδίαν (6,31.32), a typical formula of the Messianic secret in Mk, is generally used in the context of imparting special instruction to the disciples. Among the synoptic Gospels only Mk narrates the ironical response of the disciples, "Shall we go and buy two hundred denarii worth of bread, and give it to them to eat?" (6,37). This remark underlines the incomprehension of the disciples [54], a theme much emphasized in this section (cf. 6,52; 8,17-21). The crowd, mentioned only once (6,34), functions as the backdrop to the key actions and important dialogue which take place exclusively between Jesus and his disciples. The arrangement of the crowd into field-groups of hundreds and fifties is striking because the documents of Qumran use these subdivisions to describe the eschatological assembly and meal of the true Israel, the children of the Alliance [55]. The verbs ἀναπίπτειν and ἀνακλίνειν also suggest the context of a meal. The occurrence of ἔρημος (6,31.32.35) evokes the exodus experience. Thus both the setting and the event indicate that the multiplication of the loaves in Mk 6,31-44 is primarily a symbolic event, the symbol of the Messianic banquet: "Jésus est le vrai pasteur, qui nourrit son peuple par son enseignement et avec du pain véritable" [56]. The principal thrust of Mk 6,45-52 is Jesus' self-revelation [57] to his disciples who fail to understand the profound significance of these two miracles (cf. 6,52) [58].

---

[52] The importance the evangelist attaches to 6,31-44 is indicated not only by the length of the narrative (Mt 14,13-21: 157 words; Mk 6,31-44: 221 words; Lk 9,10b-17: 156 words) but also by its position in the parallelism between 6,31-7,37 and 8,1-26.

[53] The description of Israel as "sheep without a shepherd" is almost stereotypic in the OT (cf. Num 27,17; 1 Kings 22,17; 2 Chron 18,16; Jud 11,19; Ezek 34,2-24).

[54] FOWLER, *Loaves and Fishes*, 74: the disciples' "cold insensitivity to the crowd"; 81: they "think Jesus wants them to spend their own money to feed the crowd!"; 83: "the disciples fear that they will have to relinquish 200 denarii to feed the hungry crowd". These statements of Fowler clearly evince his failure to understand the true meaning of Mk 6,37b in its context.

[55] Cf. CD 13,1; 1 QS 2,21-22; 1 QM 13,1.

[56] DE LA POTTERIE, "Multiplication", 316.

[57] Cf. HEIL, *Jesus Walking*, 69-74, 83, 130-131.

[58] The verb συνιέναι is a quasi-technical term for the deeper understanding of mysteries, proverbs and parables. Mk uses it always in reference to understanding the mystery of the person of Jesus (cf. 4,12; 6,52; 8,17.21). Hardening of hearts, primarily an anti-Jewish phrase in NT, is applied to the apostles in Mk 6,52 (note the perfect πεπωρωμένη). Thus underlining the total incomprehension of the apostles, 6,52 well concludes both 6,31-44 and 6,45-52.

In the discussion on defilement (7,1-16) and in the ensuing private instruction to the disciples on true defilement (7,17-23) Jesus attacks Jewish ritualism. This serves as a fitting prelude to Jesus' ministry on Gentile soil (7,24-8,9). The healing of the Syrophoenician woman's daughter (7,24-30) not only illustrates the participation of Gentiles in the eschatological salvation but also prefigures the Church's mission to the Gentiles. The healing of the deaf and dumb man (7,31-37), with its twofold references to Is 35,5-6, symbolizes the dawn of the Messianic era. Thus it certainly has Messianic overtones. In the second feeding narrative (8,1-10) in which there is greater emphasis on universalism [59] Jesus reveals himself once again. Yet the disciples fail to understand the significance of the miracle (cf. 8,20). In the dialogue with his disciples (8,14-21) Jesus most emphatically urges them to understand. He cautions them saying, "Beware of the leaven of the Pharisees and the leaven of Herod" (8,15) which in the context means false messianic conceptions (cf. 6,16; 8,11-13). Nowhere else does Mk emphasize the urgency to understand as in 8,17-21. The whole of 8,17-21 consists of a chain of seven questions in which Jesus reprimands his disciples for their blindness and strongly urges them to understand:

> Do you not yet perceive or understand? Are your hearts hardened? Having eyes do you not see, and having ears do you not hear? . . . Do you not yet understand? (8,17-18.21)

Jesus' strong reprimands regarding the blindness of his disciples are immediately followed by the healing of a blind man at Bethsaida (8,22-26), an event narrated only by Mk and parallel to Peter's confession of Jesus' Messiahship (8,27-30):

Mk 8,22-26	*Mk 8,27-30*
Jesus and his disciples arrived in Bethsaida (8,22a).	Jesus and his disciples came to Caesarea Philippi (8,27a).
Imposition of hands: Jesus questions the blind man whether he sees anything (8,23).	Jesus questions the disciples as to whom people think him to be (8,27bc).

---

[59] The expression "some have come a long way" (8,3) suggests Gentile participation. For "those come a long way" or "those far away" generally refer to Gentiles (cf. Josh 9,6; 2 Chron 6,32; Is 5,26; Jer 4,16; 6,20; Ezek 23,40; Acts 2,39; 22,21; Eph 2,11-13). The term σπυρίς (8,8) is Hellenistic, but κόφινος (6,43) is Jewish. Secondly, elements that are religiously evocative for Jews are missing. Finally, the event probably took place in a predominantly pagan territory (cf. 7,31; 8,10).

The blind man's answer: imperfect sight (8,24)	The disciples' answer: incorrect view (8,28)
Again, imposition of hands and intent look (8,25ab)	Jesus again questions the disciples as to whom they think him to be (8,29a).
Perfect sight (8,25cd)	Peter's confession:correct view (8,29b)
Command to secrecy (8,26)	Command to secrecy (8,30)

This parallelism in the composition and theme is too precise to be fortuitous. It shows that for the evangelist the miracle at Bethsaida is a pericope of transition, which has a profound symbolical and prefigurative character, towards the following pericope, the confession of Peter. The progressive healing of the blind man symbolizes the spiritual enlightenment of the disciples, their transition from blindness (cf. 8,17-18) to faith in Jesus, the Messiah [60].

Mk narrates the authentic faith of the disciples in Jesus, the Messiah, acknowledged and confessed by Peter, their leader and spokesman, in sharp contrast to the popular opinion concerning Jesus:

Mk 8,27-28	*Mk 8,29*
Jesus' question: "Who do men (οἱ ἄνθρωποι) say that I am?"	Jesus' question [61]: "But (δέ) who do you (ὑμεῖς) say that I am?"
They told him: "John the Baptist . . . Elijah . . . one of the prophets"	Peter answered him: "You are the Christ".

Thus in Peter's confession (8,29) the tension that was being built up in the first eight chapters is released, blindness has given way to sight. For the evangelist the confession of Peter revealed Jesus' true identity which corresponded to the faith of the apostolic Church. Therefore the opinion that Peter confessed Jesus to be a nationalistic kingly Messiah [62] and then Jesus

---

[60] DE LA POTTERIE, "Confessione", 64 (translation mine).

[61] Note the emphatic use of personal pronouns thrice in 8,29 (αὐτός, ὑμεῖς, σύ).

[62] Cf. G. FRIEDRICH, "Beobachtungen", 292; GRUNDMANN, 218; S.E. JOHNSON, 148; KLOSTERMANN, 80; SCHMID, 155; VÖGTLE, "Messiasbekenntnis", 255; WEEDEN, *Tradition*, 64-65, 154, etc.

corrected the false messianic conception of his disciples by revealing himself to be the suffering Messiah lacks evidence in the text. Again, the conception that Jesus considered Peter's confession "nothing less than . . . a satanic temptation" [63] is totally ill-founded.

3. Part II: Revelation of the Mystery of the Suffering Son of Man (8,27-16,8)

Just as the first part, so the second is also divided into three sections: (a) way of the Son of Man and discipleship (8,27-10,52), (b) revelation in Jerusalem and the final break with the Jews (11,1-13,37), and (c) fulfilment of the Mystery: the Passion, Death and Resurrection of the Son of Man (14,1-16,8).

a. *Way of the Son of Man and Discipleship (8,27-10,52)*

The pillars on which the structure of 8,27-10,52 is founded are the three predictions of the Passion, Death and Resurrection of the Son of Man. Each of these predictions is immediately followed by the incomprehension of the disciples and Jesus' instruction to them on the inevitable demands of discipleship. Thus the basic structure of this section is developed in three parallel steps:

	Predictions of the Passion Death and Resurrection of the Son of Man	Incomprehension of the Disciples	Instruction on Discipleship
A	8,31	8,32-33	8,34-9,1
A'	9,30-31	9,32-34	9,35-37
A"	10,32-34	10,35-37	10,38-45

The key terms that hold this section together as a coherent literary unit, some of which undoubtedly were intentionally placed in strategically

---

[63] CULLMANN, *Christology*, 122. DINKLER, "Petrusbekenntnis", 142: "Jesus hat das Ansinnen des Petrus, der verheiβene Messias zu sein, explicite abgewiesen, als satanisch verurteilt, als menschliches, d. h. widergöttliches Denken". OSBORNE ("Stumbling-Block", 187-190) and ROBINSON (*History*, 52) concur with CULLMANN.
"But this is untenable, because the first Christian community, which confessed Jesus as the Messiah, would never have transmitted unaltered an account in which Jesus rejected this confession as satanic" (KÜMMEL, *Theology*, 69-70).

important passages, are the sayings on the suffering Son of Man [64], the phrase ἐν τῇ ὁδῷ [65] and the verb ἀκολουθεῖν [66]. The principal theme of this section, the way of the Son of Man, the way of his Passion and Death, is not comprehended by the disciples. Therefore, Jesus instructs them on the absolute necessity of living a life of suffering and service, typical of the Son of Man himself (10,45).

This section is demarcated by a double inclusion. The first is the occurrence of the phrase ἐν τῇ ὁδῷ both at the beginning (8,27) and at the end (10,52) of this section. It is also found in the context of the predictions of the Passion (9,33.34;10,32). It is indeed a theological theme: Jesus' way towards Jerusalem (10,32.52; 11,1) is the way of suffering, culminating on the cross. The disciples too must follow this path. The second inclusion is indicated by the correspondence between the healing of the blind man at Bethsaida (8,22-26) and the healing of the blind Bartimaeus at Jericho (10,46-52). The first healing, as mentioned before, symbolizes the spiritual enlightenment of the disciples while the second depicts Bartimaeus as a true follower of Jesus (10,52) [67]. The faith of the blind Bartimaeus demonstrates what kind of faith the disciples must have to follow Jesus on the way to the cross.

Thus both from the literary and thematic point of view 8,27-10,52 is a coherent section whose unity is generally recognized by exegetes [68].

b. *Revelation in Jerusalem and the Definitive Break with the Jews (11,1-13,37)*

This section is structured on the basis of spatio-temporal categories. The spatial demarcations are indicated in three successive steps: Jesus' journey towards Jerusalem and his entry into the city and temple (A), his activity in

---

[64] Of the nine sayings on the *suffering* Son of Man, six are found in this section (8,31; 9,9.12.31; 10,33.45).

[65] Of the six occurrences of ἐν τῇ ὁδῷ in Mk, five are in this section (8,27; 9,33.34; 10,32.52).

[66] Of the 18 occurrences of ἀκολουθεῖν in Mk, seven are in this section (8,34(bis); 9,38; 10,21.28.32.52).

[67] Despite a few literary connections between 10,46-52 and 11,1-11, it is more fitting to link 10,46-52 to what precedes rather than to what follows because of the abundant literary links and thematic affinities (cf. DUPONT, "Il cieco di Gerico", 106-113; E.S. JOHNSON, "Blind Bartimaeus", 198-204).

[68] This coherence is broken in the outlines of NAB, NEB, etc., commentaries of RADERMAKERS, URICCHIO-STANO, etc., and the articles of BLATHERWICK ("Silhouette", 188-190, 192) RAMAROSON ("Plan", 226, 233), etc.

the temple (B), and his exit from the city or temple (A'). Between A and A'
a twofold contrast is implied: the contrast between the departure towards
Jerusalem and the departure from Jerusalem (to Bethany); and the contrast
between the entry into the city and temple and the exit from the city or
temple. And Jesus' activity in the temple (B) is intercalated between A and
A'. This literary device (A B A') known as 'sandwich' composition or
intercalation is frequently found in Mk [69]. The temporal designations are
shown on three successive days. It is noteworthy that the spatial demarcations
coincide with the temporal designations [70]. The literary structure of Mk 11,1-
13,37, therefore, may be demonstrated according to the following scheme:

	1st day	2nd day	3rd day
A. Journey towards Jerusalem and entry into city and temple.	11,1-11a	11,12-15a	11,20-27a
B. Activity in the temple	11,11b	11,15b-18	11,27b-12,44
A' Exit from the temple and departure from Jerusalem (to Bethany)	11,11c	11,19	13,1.2-37

The geographical designations, Ἱεροσόλυμα and ἱερόν, characteristic of this
section [71], occur in units allotted to each of the three days. The temporal
designations also render compositional unity insofar as the events on each of
the three days presuppose and prepare for the next.

---

[69] Cf. 1,21-28; 3,20-35; 5,21-43; 6,7-30; 11,13-26; 14,54-72.

[70] 11,11c: As it was *already late*, he *went out to Bethany*.
11,12: On the *following day* when they *came from Bethany*.
11,19: When *evening* came they *went out of the* city.
11,20: As they *passed by* in the *morning* (v. 27: *came again to Jerusalem*).
14,1: It was *two days before the Passover* (v. 3: he *was at Bethany*).
The argument of Manicardi (*Il cammino*, 34) and Biguzzi (*Il tempio*, 98-101) who
reject the temporal designations in Mk 11,1-13,37 is not convincing.
It is instructive to note that S.H. Smith ("Structure", 120-121) employs only temporal
designations in structuring chs. 11-12.

[71] 'Jerusalem' occurs in 11,1.11.15.27. In other instances it is not the place of Jesus'
ministry but whence the crowd (3,8) and the scribes (3,22; 7,1) come to Jesus, or the destination
of Jesus' journey (10,32.33) or of the women who accompanied him (15,41).
The term ἱερόν occurs as follows: 11,11.15(bis).16.27; 12,35; 13,1-3. Otherwise it
occurs only once (14,49), that too in reference to his ministry of teaching in chs. 11-12.

The main theme of Mk 11,1-13,37 is Jesus' self-revelation. On the first day Jesus enters Jerusalem riding on a colt — which in the light of Zech 9,9 (cf. n. 45) is a symbolic action revealing his identity as God's promised Messiah. People acclaimed him with jubilation and connected his arrival with their own expectation of the Davidic Messiah (11,8-10), a notion which Jesus on his own initiative will radically modify by pointing out that the Messiah is not only David's son but also David's Lord (cf. 12,35-37). The self-revelation through his words and deeds in the temple and his sayings about the temple mark a sharp progression:

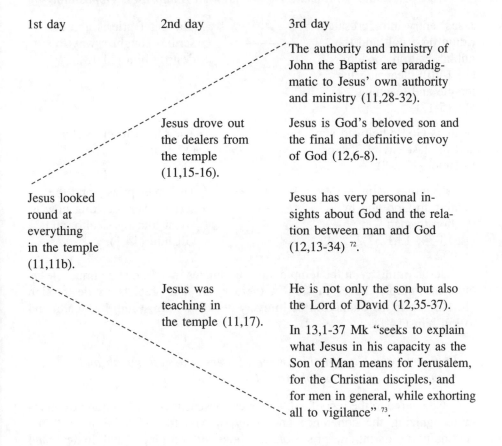

1st day

2nd day

3rd day

The authority and ministry of John the Baptist are paradigmatic to Jesus' own authority and ministry (11,28-32).

Jesus drove out the dealers from the temple (11,15-16).

Jesus is God's beloved son and the final and definitive envoy of God (12,6-8).

Jesus looked round at everything in the temple (11,11b).

Jesus has very personal insights about God and the relation between man and God (12,13-34) [72].

Jesus was teaching in the temple (11,17).

He is not only the son but also the Lord of David (12,35-37).

In 13,1-37 Mk "seeks to explain what Jesus in his capacity as the Son of Man means for Jerusalem, for the Christian disciples, and for men in general, while exhorting all to vigilance" [73].

---

[72] In no other section is θεός as frequent as in 12,13-34 (twelve occurrences out of a total of 48).

[73] MALLY, 50.

Thus, on the first day, Jesus only looks around at everything with no word or deed. On the second day, his authoritative deed is followed by his teaching. On the third day, he is engaged exclusively in dialogue, often controversial, in which the nature of his person and mission is glaringly revealed.

As Jesus progressively reveals himself through his ministry, so also the Jewish authorities' opposition to him mounts steadily. This contrast between the progression of revelation and of opposition is graphically illustrated below:

Jesus' Revelatory Ministry		*Jewish Authorities' Opposition*
Jesus' entry into Jerusalem riding on a colt and the public ovation for him (11,1-10); cleansing the temple and teaching (11,15-17).	<———>	The chief priests and the scribes sought a way to destroy him (11,18).
Jesus is God's beloved son and the last envoy of God to Israel (12,6-8).	<———>	They tried to arrest him (12,12).
Jesus' unique status in relation to God and in relation to man (12,13-34; 13,1-37).	<———>	The chief priests and the scribes were seeking how to arrest him by stealth, and kill him (14,1).

Jesus' ministry in the temple thus culminates in a dramatic climax: Jesus quits the temple, never to step in there again and predicts its destruction (13,1-2) while the Sanhedrin definitively decides to arrest him by stealth and to kill him (14,1).

c. *Fulfilment and Culmination of the Mystery: Passion, Death and Resurrection of the Son of Man (14,1-16,8)*

Compared to the rest of Mk a greater consensus prevails among exegetes in recognizing the coherence and unity of Mk 14,1-16,8 because of the continuity in narration, precision of time and of place, and logical and dramatic progression of the story. A critical and perceptive investigation of 14,1-16,8 furnishes additional literary and thematic indices that form the bases of a concentric structure consisting of seven scenes as demonstrated below.

The scene in 14,1-11 contains elements parallel to the scene in 15,40-16,8:

Mk 14,1-11 (A)	*Mk 15,40-16,8 (A')*
The scene consists of *three pericopes*. The *first* (14,1-2: Jewish authorities plan to arrest Jesus and kill him) and the *last* pericope (14,10-11: Judas agreed with them to betray Jesus) strikingly similar, *frame the central pericope* (14,3-9: a woman anoints Jesus).	This scene also consists of *three pericopes*. The *first* (15,40-41: pious women witness Jesus' death) and the *last* pericope (16,1-8: they plan to anoint Jesus' body), similar to some extent, *frame the central pericope* (15,42-47: Joseph of Arimathea buries Jesus).
A time factor: "two days before the Passover and the feast of the Unleavened Bread" (14,1).	*A time factor*: "the day of Preparation, that is, the day before the sabbath" (15,42).
A woman, despite other's indignation and reproaches, does *homage* to Jesus by *anointing him in the house of Simon the leper* (14,3-6).	*Joseph of Arimathea* daringly asked Pilate for Jesus' body and *honourably buried it in the tomb* (15,42-46).
Jesus' body in the physical sense (14,8)	*Jesus' body* in the physical sense (15,43.45) [74]
To *anoint* (14,8)	To *anoint* (16,1) [75]
Ointment of pure nard (14,3-5)	*Spices* for anointing (16,1)
Anointment without burial (14,8)	*Burial without anointment* (15,46-16,1)
Jesus' comment about the *woman's action*: "What she has done will be told" (14,9).	*A young man tells* the *women*: "Go, tell his disciples" (16,7).

These two scenes (A A'), then, frame the Passion narrative in the second Gospel.

---

[74] The noun σῶμα in reference to Jesus' body in the physical sense occurs nowhere else in Mk.

[75] Elsewhere it occurs only once more (6,13).

There is correspondence also between the scene of Jesus' last Passover in the upper room (14,12-25) [76] and the scene of his last night on the Mount of Olives (14,26-52):

Mk 14,12-25 (B)	*Mk 14,26-52 (B')*
The *main dramatis personae, Jesus and his disciples*, are engaged in frequent *dialogue* concerning the Passover, betrayal, etc. (14,12-15.18-25).	The main dramatis *personae, Jesus and his disciples*, are engaged in frequent *dialogue* concerning the disciples' flight, Peter's denial, etc. (cf. 14,27-45).
Jesus came with the Twelve to the *upper room* (14,17)	*They went out* to *the Mount of Olives* (14,26)
Jesus' prayer of blessing over the bread and the cup (14,22.24)	*Jesus' prayer* at Gethsemane (14,36.39)
παραδιδόναι (14,21)	παραδιδόναι (14,41.42.44)
ποτήριον (14,23)	ποτήριον (14,36) [77]
J*esus predicts the betrayal of the Son of Man by one of the Twelve* (14,18-21).	*Jesus predicts the betrayal of the Son of Man by one of the Twelve* and its realization (14,41.44-46).
Defection by the disciples is foretold (14,27).	Actual *defection by the disciples* takes place (14,50-52).

Thus these two scenes contain parallel elements. Besides, a comparison of B and B' shows progression in the latter: Jesus predicts the betrayal of the Son of Man by one of the Twelve(14,21) and Judas betrays him (14,44-46); Jesus foretells the defection of the disciples (14,27) and they flee (14,50-52).

As in B and B', so also in C (15,1-20c: the scene of Jesus' trial in the Praetorium) and C' (15,20d-39: the scene of Jesus' Crucifixion and Death on Golgotha) there are parallel features:

---

[76] Of the five occurrences of πάσχα in Mk, four are found in 14,12-25 (14,12(bis).14.16).

[77] In 14,1-16,8 ποτήριον occurs only in 14,23 and 14,36.

Mk 15, 1-20 (C)	*Mk 15,20d-39 (C')*
The *main dramatis personae* are Jesus, the Sanhedrin, Pilate, soldiers, and the crowds.	The *main dramatis personae* are Jesus, chief priests with the scribes, soldiers, and those who passed by.
A *time factor*: in the morning the Sanhedrin held a consultation (15,1).	A *time factor*: at the third hour they crucified Jesus (15,25).
σταυροῦν (15,13.14.15)	σταυροῦν (15,20b.24.25.27)
Jesus is *silent except* for his brief answer to Pilate: "You have said so" (15,2).	*Jesus* is *silent except* for the cry of dereliction: "My God, my God, why hast thou forsaken me?" (15,29-32).
The soldiers *mocked Jesus* (15,17-19).	Various groups *mocked Jesus* (15,29-32).
They stripped him of the purple cloak and put his *own clothes* on him (15,20bc).	They divided *his garment* among them casting lots (15,24b).
"King of the Jews" (15,2.9.12.18)	*"King of the Jews"* (15,26); "King of Israel" (15,32)
Barabbas, *a murderer*, is *released* (15,7.11.15).	Jesus, the *innocent one*, is *crucified* in between two robbers (15,32).

Some of these parallel features show also the progression of the narrative: the cry of the crowd for Jesus' crucifixion (15,13.14) and Pilate's consent to it and the actual crucifixion of Jesus (15,24.25); mockery of Jesus by one group (15,17-19) and the mockery by groups (15,29-32); the contrast between the release of the criminal Barabbas (15,7.11.15) and the crucifixion of the innocent Jesus (15,27).

Mk 14,53-72 (D)

The events in the first three scenes (A: 14,1-11; B: 14,12-25; B': 14,26-52) are preparatory to and work up to a climax in the fourth and central scene, the process before the Sanhedrin (14,55-65). Likewise, the event in the last three scenes (C: 15,1-20c; C': 15,20d-39; A': 15,40-16,8) flow from and are consequences of the key event in the central scene: the Sanhedrin "condemned Jesus as deserving death"(14,64).

Intercalated between two statements concerning Peter, Peter followed Jesus from a distance (14,54) and he denied Jesus thrice (14,66-72), the central scene focuses attention on the process before the Sanhedrin (14,55-65). In it the high priest plays the key role [78]. The core of this scene consists of three supremely important and intrinsically interrelated verses:

A   The high priest's question: "Are you the Christ, the Son of the Blessed?" (14,61)

 B   Jesus' asseveration: "I am; and you will see the Son of Man sitting at the right hand of Power, and coming with the clouds of heaven" (14,62).

A'   The Sanhedrin's final decision: "And they all condemned him as deserving death" (14,64).

These verses (14,61-64) constitute the Christological climax of the Passion narrative. And the Sanhedrin's condemnation of Jesus to death (14,64) is the arithmetical centre of the Passion narrative: it is preceded by 63 verses (14,1-63) and followed by 63 verses (14,65-16,8) [79].

In brief, the Passion narrative in Mk, composed of seven scenes, has a concentric structure as follows:

> A: Anointing at Bethany (14,3-9 + 14,1-2.10-11)
>> B: Passover meal in the upper room (14,12-25)
>> B' Last night on the Mount of Olives (14,26-52)
>>> D: Process before the Sanhedrin (14,53-72)
>> C: Trial in the Praetorium (15,1-20)
>> C' Crucifixion and Death on Golgotha (15,21-39)
> A' Burial and the empty tomb (15,40-16,8)

Just as at the centre of his Gospel where Mk has placed Peter's acknowledgement and confession of Jesus' Messiahship (8,29), so also at the centre of the Passion narrative stand Jesus' self-revelation (14,62: Ἐγώ εἰμι and the Sanhedrin's condemnation of him to death (14,64).

---

[78] Of the eight occurrences of the title "high priest" ὁ ἀρχιερεύς (singular) six are found in this scene (14,53.54.60.61.63.66). Moreover, the decisive charge against Jesus is alleged by the high priest himself (cf. 14,61-64).

[79] FELDMEIER, *Gethsemaneerzählung*, argues that the Gethsemane scene is the key to Jesus' Passion in Mk. But for this he does not adduce any literary evidence.

CHAPTER THREE

INTERNAL COHESION AND LITERARY DIVISION
OF MK 1,14-3,6

It was established in the previous chapters that 1,14-3,6 constitutes the first section of the first part of Mk. In the present chapter an attempt is made to point out the internal coherence of various pericopes in this section and to establish the literary structure of its two main subunits.

I. Elements of Internal Coherence in 1,14-3,6

A. Key Words and Basic Themes

What impresses the reader most in 1,14-3,6 is Jesus' unique authority. The central point in the healing of the paralytic is the ἐξουσία of Jesus to forgive sins (2,10) and his mission is characterized by the exercise of this authority in calling men to authentic conversion (2,17). Though the term ἐξουσία is not used, the same idea is conveyed in 2,28 where his lordship over the sabbath is asserted and he exercises it in genuine need (3,2-5). By the redactional insertion of 1,22 (ἦν γὰρ διδάσκων αὐτοὺς ὡς ἐξουσίαν ἔχων καὶ οὐχ ὡς γραμματεῖς) and 1,27 (διδαχὴ καινὴ κατ᾽ ἐξουσίαν) into the exorcism of 1,23-26, our evangelist not only interprets the tradition in 1,21-28 but also introduces a key theme of this section. The next occurrence of ἐξουσία in reference to Jesus is after eight chapters (11,27-33) where the Sanhedrin questions Jesus' authority.

Jesus' ministry, especially his teaching, is characterized by a certain newness (cf. 1,22.27). Jesus' authority to forgive sins, his association with sinners, the failure of the disciples to observe the laws of fasting and the breaking of sabbatical laws are something new (καινός: 2,21.22) [1] — signs

---

[1] The next and the last occurrence of καινός is in 14,25.

of the inbreaking of the kingdom — in contrast to the practice of Judaism (παλαιός: thrice in 2,21-22) [2].

Another important Marcan emphasis in this section is his insistence that the beginning of Jesus' ministry was oriented to the Jews. In no other section does the evangelist stress so much as in 1,14-3,6 that Jesus' ministry primarily takes place in the synagogue. This is shown not merely by the frequency of συναγωγή in this section [3], but also by the programmatic development of his ministry in the synagogue. Jesus begins his paradigmatic 'one day' ministry (1,21-34) in the synagogue at Capernaum (1,21-28) and by means of a summary statement in 1,39, Mk shows that his ministry at the synagogue extends to the whole of Galilee. The concluding episode of this section also takes place in the synagogue (3,1-6). So the synagogue scene primarily unifies this section. Moreover, the five controversies in 2,1-3,6 are typically Jewish both in origin and in content.

The frequent occurrence of σάββατον is characteristic of our section [4]. In fact, all the references to τοῖς σάββασιν are found in this section (1,21; 2,23.24; 3,2.4). Jesus' 'one day' ministry is on the sabbath (1,21-34) and the last two controversies also take place on the sabbath (2,23-3,6).

Finally, by means of the theme of Jesus' preaching in Galilee our evangelist connects 1,14 with 1,39:

Mk 1,14	*Mk 1,39*
ἦλθεν κηρύσσων	ἦλθεν κηρύσσων
εἰς τὴν Γαλιλαίαν	εἰς ὅλην τὴν Γαλιλαίαν

Likewise, by virtue of the theme of calling men to discipleship he links 1,16-20 with 2,13-14 [5].

B. Geographical and Scenic Connections

One of the impressive literary features in the initial stage of Jesus' ministry is the frequency of the verbs of movement, especially ἔρχεσθαι and

---

[2] The adjective παλαιός occurs in Mk only in 2,21-22.

[3] The term συναγωγή occurs 8 times in Mk. Of these five are in our section (cf. 1,21.23.29.39; 3,1); the next is in 6,2.

[4] The noun σάββατον occurs 12 times in Mk. Of these 8 are in our section (1,21; 2,23.24.27(bis). 28; 3,2.4), and the next is in 6,2.

[5] There are five features of structural similarity between 1,16-18 and 2,14 (cf. p. 202).

its compound forms, predicated of Jesus [6] and the oft-repeated occurrence of the adverb εὐθύς [7]. Other protagonists in their responses and reactions to Jesus also move quickly. By means of this literary device the evangelist shows the rapid progression of Jesus' ministry and the swiftness of the inbreaking of God's kingdom.

The geographical background for Jesus' swift activity in these pericopes is the region of Galilee. It is in Galilee that he commences the proclamation of the kingdom (1,14-15). Again, he calls his first disciples from Galilee (1,16-20). Because of his unique, authoritative teaching and exorcism, his fame spreads to all the surrounding region of Galilee (1,28). Then he extends his ministry to the whole of Galilee (1,39). The cure of the leper may be considered an isolated event that occurred during his Galilean ministry [8].

By means of πάλιν Mk links 2,1-3,6 to the preceding pericopes whereby scenic connections are made between 1,14-45 and 2,1-3,6:

Jesus' entry into Capernaum in 2,1 is thus linked to 1,21a:

1,21: καὶ εἰσπορεύονται εἰς Καφαρναούμ

2,1: καὶ εἰσελθὼν πάλιν εἰς Καφαρναούμ

Again, the scene in 2,13 is connected to 1,16:

1,16: καὶ παράγων παρὰ τὴν θάλασσαν

2,13: καὶ ἐξῆλθεν πάλιν παρὰ τὴν θάλασσαν

Finally, the scene in 3,1 is linked to 1,21b:

1,21: καὶ εὐθὺς τοῖς σάββασιν εἰσελθὼν εἰς τὴν συναγωγήν

3,1: καὶ εἰσῆλθεν πάλιν εἰς τὴν συναγωγήν ... τοῖς σάββασιν

Thus the geographical background of 1,14-3,6 is the region of Galilee which functions as one of the unifying elements of this section [9]. Galilee is important for Mk not only because Jesus began his ministry there but also

---

[6] Cf. 1,14.16.19.21(bis).24.28.29(bis).31.35(thrice).38.39.45. Of these 16 occurrences of the verbs of movement predicated of Jesus in 1,14-45, thirteen instances originate from ἔρχεσθαι and its compound forms.

[7] Cf. 1,18.20.21.23.28.29.30.42.43 (= 9 times).

[8] Cf. MANICARDI, Il cammino, 58.

[9] One should note that after 3,6 Mk does not mention about Jesus' ministry in Galilee. In 3,7-8 Galilee is one among other regions whence the multitudes flocked to Jesus. In 7,31 and 9,30 Jesus merely passes through Galilee.

because he himself preached the Gospel there [10]. According to our evangelist, then, the period of the Galilean ministry is, indeed, the time par excellence in Jesus' ministry.

C. Conclusion

Therefore, by means of key words, thematic indices, and geographical and scenic connections, our evangelist links various pericopes of 1,14-3,6 together, thereby giving literary and thematic unity to this section.

II. Literary Division of 1,14-3,6

As stated in the second chapter of our study, 1,14-20 is the introduction to the first section of Mk. Regarding the literary unity of 1,21-3,6 we have already mentioned a number of literary indices in the preceding pages. Here we show the parallelism between Mk 1,21-28 and 3,1-6 by virtue of which 1,21-3,6 is framed as a literary unit:

Mk 1,21-28	*Mk 3,1-6*
εἰσελθὼν εἰς τὴν συναγωγήν	εἰσῆλθεν πάλιν εἰς τὴν συναγωγήν
τοῖς σάββασιν (1,21)	τοῖς σάββασιν (3,2.4)
Mention of Jesus' enemies: the scribes (1,22)	Mention of Jesus' enemies: Pharisees and Herodians (3,2.6)
Jesus encounters a man with an unclean spirit (1,23-24).	Jesus encounters a man with a withered hand (3,1b.3a).

---

[10] The locus of κηρύσσειν in Mk is as follows:

κηρύσσειν	*person*	*place*
1,4.7.	John the Baptist	the wilderness
1,14.38.39	Jesus	Galilee
1,45	the leper	'Galilee' from the context
5,20	Gerasene demoniac	Decapolis
7,36	the deaf-mute	Decapolis
3,14; 6,12	the Twelve	no precise place (possibly the places of Jesus' activity)
13.10; 14,9	verb in the passive with no agent	all nations (13,10) the whole world (14,9).

Jesus expels the unclean spirit by word (1,25).	Jesus heals the man by word (3,3b.5b).
The man is liberated from the unclean spirit (1,26).	The man is healed (3,5c).
Reaction of the audience: amazement (1,27).	Reaction of the enemies: held counsel how to destroy him (3,6).

Within 1,21-3,6, however, there are two literary units: 1,21-45 and 2,1-3,6. Each of these units consists of a distinctive concentric structure. So now we focus our attention on the literary structure of these two units.

III. Literary Structure of Mk 1,21-45 and 2,1-3,6

A. Literary Structure of Mk 1,21-45

1. *Structures Proposed* [11]

a. *Exposition*

The article of Dideberg and Mourlon Beernaert and the commentary of Radermakers proposed a chiastic structure (A B C D C' B' A') for Mk 1,21-45 [12]:

First stage: In Capernaum on the sabbath (1,21-31):

A (1,21-27): In the synagogue Jesus teaches and casts out an impure spirit from a man (silence imposed); inclusion between 1,22 and 1,27.

B (1,28): Jesus' fame spreads to the whole of Galilee.

C (1,29-31): In the house of Simon, his mother-in-law is cured on the intervention of the four companions.

---

[11] MARCHESELLI ("La ricerca di Dio", 289-313) proposes an asymmetrical structure for 1,21-45: 1,21-28 (a); 1,29-31 (b); 1,32-34 (b'); 1,35-39 (c) and 1,40-45 (a'). From literary considerations MARCHESELLI'S structure is defective. There is no literary evidence for a parallelism between 1,29-31 (b) and 1,32-34 (b'). Verses 32-34 deal not only with healings but also with exorcisms. The literary evidences mentioned by him for the parallelism between 1,21-28 and 1,40-45 are very meagre. Finally, he does not offer any literary basis for his contention that 1,35-39 is the centre of the asymmetrical structure. Instead he theologically presupposes it.

[12] Cf. DIDEBERG and MOURLON BEERNAERT, "Jésus vint en Galilée", 306-323; RADERMAKERS, 41-43.

Hinge of the narration: in front of the door, on the sabbath.
D (1,32-34): All gather (the sick and the possessed) to Jesus
(silence imposed).

Second stage: In Galilee, the day after the sabbath (1,35-45):

C' (1,35-38): Jesus' departure to a lonely place and the intervention of
the four companions.

B' (1,39): Jesus goes to the whole of Galilee.

A' (1,40-45): Jesus cleanses a leper (silence imposed); inclusion between
1,40 and 1,45.

b. *Critical Remarks*

Perhaps the weakest point of this structure is the failure to establish the
literary evidence for the parallelism between C (1,29-31) and C' (1,35-38).
The intervention of the first four disciples in 1,29-31 and of Simon and those
with him in 1,35-38 hardly suffices for a well-grounded literary basis. The
occurrence of ἔρχεσθαι and its compound forms [13] (three times each) both
in 1,29-31 and in 1,35-38 is not a distinctive literary feature of these two
pericopes. For ἔρχεσθαι and its compound forms are found 16 times in 1,21-
45, spread out from the beginning to the end.

Again, Mk 1,21-28 is a well-structured literary unit [14]. Therefore, its
division into two units (1,21-27 and 1,28) is unwarranted. Moreover, the
distinction between the first stage at Capernaum (1,21-31) and the second
stage in Galilee (1,35-45) is not adequate. In fact, as already stated, Mk
considers the whole of 1,14-3,6 Jesus' Galilean ministry. He schematically
depicts the events narrated in 1,21-34 as a sample of Jesus' one-day-activity
centered around Capernaum which is a village in the region of Galilee.
Finally, there is no one-day-scheme in 1,35-45 at all. Mk 1,35 only indicates
the beginning of another day but does not state the terminus ad quem of the
day in the subsequent verses.

---

[13] *Ibid.*, 316, 323.
[14] Cf. p. 125-126.

2. *Literary Structure of Mk 1,21-45*

A
- a (1,21-28): Jesus' teaching and exorcism in the synagogue and the amazement of his audience; the spreading of his fame to the surrounding region of Galilee
- b (1,29-31): The cure of Simon's mother-in-law

B
- (1,32-34): Many healings and exorcisms

A'
- a' (1,35-39): Jesus' withdrawal to a lonely place; people's search for him; Jesus' ministry to the whole of Galilee: preaching and exorcisms
- b' (1,40-45): The cure of the leper

a. *Internal Cohesion of 1,21-45*

Mk 1,21-45 is a well-demarcated unit on Jesus' ministry to the public. It is preceded by a pericope on the call of the first four disciples (1,16-20) and followed by a cluster of controversies in which there is a steadily mounting opposition to Jesus that culminates in the plot of the Pharisees with the Herodians to kill him. As previously mentioned, 1,21-45 is characterized by the frequent occurrence of verbs of movement predicated of Jesus and by the oft-repeated occurrence of the adverb εὐθύς. There is also an enthusiastic response to Jesus and a whole-hearted acceptance of him (cf. 1,22.27-28.32-34.37.45) that 1,21-45 may rightly be considered the heyday of his public ministry. A comparison between the beginning (1,21-22) and the end (1,45) of this literary unit demonstrates the steady growth of Jesus' popularity:

1,21-22	*1,45*
They went into Capernaum, entered (εἰσέρχεσθαι) the synagogue and taught.	Jesus could no longer openly enter (εἰσέρχεσθαι) a town [15], but was out in the country.
People were astonished at his teaching.	People came to him from every quarter.

The end of this literary unit marks the rising popularity of Jesus that to escape the crowd he had to go out into the country (1,45bc); nevertheless,

---

[15] The first occurrence of εἰσέρχεσθαι in Mk is at 1,21 and the second at 1,45.

they came to him from every quarter (1,45d). Within 1,21-45, however, there are contrasts and differentiations between 1,21-31 and 1,35-45:

1,21-31	*1,35-45*
Closed scene: synagogue and house	Open scene: ἔρημος τόπος (1,35.45) and Galilee (1,39)
Jesus goes to the synagogue (1,21); there he encounters a man with an unclean spirit.	Jesus withdraws (1,35); yet people come to him (1,37).
Again, he goes to Simon's house (1,29) where he cures Simon's mother-in-law.	A leper on his own initiative begs Jesus to cure him (1,40) and Jesus cures him.
By means of the temporal designations (cf. 1,21.32) Mk demarcates 1,21-34 as a specimen activity of Jesus on a sabbath.	In contrast to 1,21-34, the events in 1,35-45 take place in the open scenes and by means of ἔρημος τόπος our evangelist frames these two pericopes [16].

b. *Parallelism between 1,21-28 and 1,35-39*

1,21-28 (a)	*1,35-39 (a')*
a temporal designation	
καὶ εὐθύς τοῖς σάββασιν (1,21)	καὶ πρωῒ ἔννυχα λίαν (1,35)
verbs of movement and local designation	
καὶ εἰσπορεύονται εἰς Καφαρναούμ ... εἰσελθὼν εἰς τὴν συναγωγήν (1,21)	καὶ ... ἀναστὰς ἐξῆλθεν καὶ ἀπῆλθεν εἰς ἔρημον τόπον (1,35)
Jesus' initial activity	
ἐδίδασκεν (1,21; imperfect)	προσηύχετο (1,35; imperfect)
action of the protagonist	
A man with an unclean spirit confronts Jesus (1,23-24).	Simon and those with him search for Jesus (1,36-37).

---

[16] The first occurrence of ἔρημος τόπος is at 1,35 and the second at 1,45. The next is at 6,31.

Jesus' response

Jesus' counteraction: exorcism (1,25-26)

Jesus' response: explanation of the nature of his mission (1,38)

scope of Jesus' mission

ἦλθες ἀπολέσαι ὑμᾶς; (1,24)

Ἄγωμεν ... ἵνα καὶ ἐκεῖ κηρύξω
εἰς γὰρ τοῦτο ἐξῆλθον (1,38)

Jesus' main activities

teaching and exorcism

preaching and casting out demons

Jesus' impact on Galilee

καὶ ἐξῆλθεν ἡ ἀκοὴ αὐτοῦ ...
εἰς ὅλην τὴν περίχωρον τῆς
Γαλιλαίας (1,28)

καὶ ἦλθεν ... εἰς ὅλην
τὴν Γαλιλαίαν (1,39)

This schematic presentation indicates the literary and thematic bases for the parallelism between 1,21-28 and 1,35-39.

c. *Parallelism between 1,29-31 and 1,40-45*

1,29-31 (b)   1,40-45 (b')

setting

Jesus goes to Simon's house (1,29).

A leper comes to Jesus (1,40).

request

καὶ λέγουσιν αὐτῷ
περὶ αὐτῆς (1,30)

ἐὰν θέλῃς δύνασαί
με καθαρίσαι (1,40)

Jesus' action

καὶ προσελθὼν ἤγειρεν αὐτὴν
κρατήσας τῆς χειρός (1,31)

καὶ σπλαγχνισθεὶς ἐκτείνας
τὴν χεῖρα αὐτοῦ ἥψατο (1,41)

cure

καὶ ἀφῆκεν αὐτὴν ὁ πυρετός (1,31)

καὶ εὐθὺς ἀπῆλθεν ἀπ' αὐτοῦ ἡ
λέπρα (1,42)

demonstration of the cure

καὶ διηκόνει αὐτοῖς (1,31).

ὁ δὲ ἐξελθὼν ἤρξατο κηρύσσειν
πολλὰ καὶ διαφημίζειν τὸν λόγον (1,45).

Thus these literary, formal and thematic features show the parallelism between 1,29-31 (b) and 1,40-45 (b').

d. *The Centrality of 1,32-34 (B)*

We have shown that 1,21-31 and 1,35-45 constitute two blocks within 1,21-45. We have also indicated the parallelism between 1,21-28 (a) and 1,35-39 (a'), on the one hand, and the parallelism between 1,29-31 (b) and 1,40-45 (b'), on the other hand. Thus by implication 1,32-34 (B), generally considered a summary of Jesus' ministry, is the central pericope.

The relation between B (1,32-34) and A (a b: 1,21-31) is twofold. First, the whole of 1,21-34 presents Jesus' one-day-activity. Secondly, in 1,21-28 the evangelist narrates a single exorcism and in 1,29-31 a single healing, whereas 1,32-34 is a summary of many exorcisms and multiple healings. Thus the main theme of 1,21-31 is carried on in 1,32-34.

Similarly, the relation between B (1,32-34) and A' (a' b': 1,35-45) is also twofold. First, there is an injunction to secrecy in 1,34 and in 1,44. Secondly, in 1,35-45 people search for Jesus which was already initiated in 1,32-34 in a very spectacular manner. Thus there is a thematic unity in 1,32-45.

Therefore, 1,32-34 (B) is rightly the central pericope of 1,21-45. This summary has a concentric structure (A B A') [17] of which v. 33 is the core. This verse is also the core of 1,21-45.

e. *Significance of the Structure*

If one excludes the mention of Jesus' teaching, preaching and prayer, Mk 1,21-45 as a whole deals with Jesus' ministry of healing and exorcism. The structure we have proposed adequately explains this literary and thematic feature of 1,21-45. The fact that the central pericope, 1,32-34 (B), is a summary exclusively of Jesus' healing and exorcism reinforces the validity and relevance of the structure.

The core of 1,21-45, as explained above, is verse 33: "the whole city was gathered together about the door". A linear development of the theme of the people's gathering to Jesus is gradually developed in 1,21-45. The audience at the synagogue is amazed at his unique authority in teaching and exorcism (1,22.27). His fame spreads to the whole of Galilee. The people gather to Jesus bringing the sick and the possessed. He withdraws to a lonely place. People search for him. After the cure of the leper, people come to

---

[17] Cf. p. 152.

Jesus from every quarter (1,45). Thus the theme of the people gathering to Jesus highlighted in 1,33 (the core of the structure) reaches its apex in 1,45.

B. Literary Structure of 2,1-3,6

The unity of Mk 2,1-3,6 is generally recognized because of certain common literary features perceptible in each pericope of this unit [18]. Our concern in the following pages is to examine whether there is any literary structure that adds further unity and throws light on the theology of 2,1-3,6.

1. *Structures of Mourlon Beernaert and Dewey*

a. *Structure of Mourlon Beernaert*

Mourlon Beernaert's starting point in proposing the structure for 2,1-3,6 is the theologically significant Son of Man sayings in 2,10 and 2,28 [19]. Based on this presupposition he constructs the following structure which is found in other studies as well [20]:

A (2,1-9): Cure by Jesus, silence of the adversaries, questioning in their hearts

    B (2,10-12): Declaration of the Son of Man

        C (2,13-17): Action of Jesus, reaction of opponents

            D (2,18-22): Sayings of Jesus on bridegroom and newness

        C' (2,23-26): Action of the disciples, reaction of opponents

    B' (2,27-28): Declaration of the Son of Man

A' (3,1-6): Cure by Jesus, silence of the adversaries, hardness of their hearts

b. *Critical Remarks*

In Mk 2,1-3,6 there are five self-contained pericopes. For the sake of his chiastic structure Mourlon Beernaert divides 2,1-12, a very well-structured

---

[18] Already ALBERTZ, *Streitgespräche*, 5-16; among rather recent studies see KUHN, *Sammlungen*, 53-98, 214-234; THISSEN, *Erzählung*, 114-151; DEWEY, *Markan Public Debate*, 65-130; DOUGHTY, "Son of Man", 161-181.

[19] MOURLON BEERNAERT, "Jésus controversé", 138-141.

[20] Cf. HARRINGTON, 24-25; MANGATT, *Way*, 31; RADERMAKERS, 43-45.

pericope [21], into two units: 2,1-9 and 2,10-12. In doing so the semantic unity of 2,1-12 is impaired. Again, the full significance of 2,23-28 can be comprehended only in the light of the sayings in 2,27-28. For vv. 23-26 work up to a climax in vv. 27-28 [22], especially the Christological saying in 2,28. So 2,23-28 constitutes a single literary unit. Furthermore, the elements of parallelism between 2,1-9 and 3,1-6 most probably do not pertain to the essential constitutive factors of these two pericopes [23]. Likewise, most of the elements that form the parallelism between 2,13-17 and 2,23-26 seem necessary to these pericopes only at the peripheral level [24].

c. *Structure of Dewey*

Dewey first in an article and later in her doctoral dissertation argued for the recognition of "a single literary unit with a tight and well worked out concentric or chiastic structure: A B C B' A'" [25]:

A (2,1-12): The healing of the paralytic

   B (2,13-17): The call of Levi and the dining with sinners

      C (2,18-22): The sayings on fasting and on the old and the new

   B' (2,23-28): Plucking grain on the sabbath

A' (3,1-6): The healing on the sabbath [26]

d. *Critical Remarks*

1. Dewey calls her rhetorical criticism method "one particular branch of literary criticism" [27]. She asserts that her study does not enter into the field of structuralism but focuses "on the surface structure or patterns in all their particularity and concreteness" [28]. Yet a few of the literary indices she adduces

---

[21] Cf. p. 181-182.

[22] Cf. p. 220-221, 223-225.

[23] The common elements are: 'and he entered again' (2,1; 3,1), 'there' (2,6; 3,1), 'paralysis' of the legs and 'paralysis' of the hand, etc. For details see MOURLON BEERNAERT, "Jésus controversé", 139.

[24] The elements are: 'his disciples' (2,15; 2,23), 'to eat' (2,16 (bis); 2,26 (bis); 'to have need' (2,17; 2,25). See MOURLON BEERNAERT, *ibid.*, 140.

[25] DEWEY, "Controversy Stories", 394.

[26] DEWEY, *Marcan Public Debate*, 109-116.

[27] *Ibid.*, 10.

[28] *Ibid.*, 6.

for parallelism are certainly the result of abstraction. For instance, the formal element for the parallelism between the healing of the paralytic (2,1-12) and the healing of the man with a withered hand (3,1-6) is that they are a resurrection-type of healing [29]. Undoubtedly, this results from abstraction.

2. Dewey admits: "Rhetorically, the double use of the Son of Man title stands outside of the symmetrical pattern of 2,1-3,6" [30]. Why do these two key sayings, so crucial for the understanding of 2,1-3,6, stand outside of the symmetrical pattern? She attributes the absence of the symmetry "to the redactor's unmodified incorporation of tradition" [31]. The reason why they stand outside the symmetrical pattern is probably due to Dewey's faulty structure.

3. "Literary structure is an avenue toward understanding theological meaning" [32]. Her theological contribution on 2,1-3,6 is minimal and superficial [33]. Finally, she has not succeeded in showing how the central pericope, 2,18-22, is a guide to understanding the whole of 2,1-3,6.

2. Literary Structure of 2,1-3,6

Mk 2,1-3,6 may schematically be structured as follows:

A (2,1-12): Jesus, the Son of Man, has authority to forgive sins.

A' (2,13-17): Jesus has come to call sinners.

C (2,18-22): Jesus, the Bridegroom, ushers in a total innovation.

B (2,23-28): Jesus, the Son of Man, has authority over the sabbath.

B' (3,1-6): Jesus exercises authority over the sabbath.

a. Preliminary Observations

Mk 2,1-3,6 constitutes a coherent literary unit which is dominated by the theme of the opposition of the scribes and the Pharisees to the acts of Jesus or of his disciples. It is sharply set off from its surrounding context

---

[29] *Ibid.*, 111-112, 115, 138.

[30] *Ibid.*, 123.

[31] *Ibid.*, 123.

[32] *Ibid.*, 137. Similar statements also on p. 5-7.

[33] The subtitle of her doctoral dissertation reads, "Literary technique, concentric structure, and theology in Mark 2,1-3,6". She has devoted over 80 pages to literary technique and concentric structure while not even seven full pages on the theology of 2,1-3,6. Her superficial theological content is an answer to ALBERTZ' objections and themes such as the role of healing and eating, the theme of life versus death, etc.

which displays Jesus' popularity (cf. 1,45; 3,7-12). Within 2,1-3,6, however, there are three units, each characterized by key terms that occur exclusively in that particular unit. In this way these key words bind one particular unit together and at the same time separate it from the other two units.

Mk 2,1-12 and 2,13-17 are linked by the key words ἁμαρτίαι (2,5.7.9.10 = four times) and ἁμαρτωλοί (2,15.16 (bis).17 = four times). These key terms do not occur in 2,18-3,6 at all. Furthermore, the key issue that pervades both pericopes is sin: Jesus' authority to forgive sins and his association with sinners. This issue is specifically articulated in 2,7.10.16-17.

Likewise Mk 2,23-28 and 3,1-6 are connected by the key words σάββατον (2,23.24.27(bis).28; 3,2.4 = seven times) and ἔξεστιν (2,24.26; 3,4 = three times). These key terms are totally absent in 2,1-22. Moreover, the key issue that pervades both pericopes is the observance of sabbatical laws. It is most conspicuous in 2,24.26; 3,2.4.

Finally, the key terms that unite 2,18-22 are νηστεύειν (2,18(thrice). 19(bis).20 = six times), νυμφίος (2,19 (bis).20 = thrice), καινός (2,21.22 = twice), νέος (2,22 = twice) and παλαιός (2,21 (bis).22 = thrice). These key terms occur neither in 2,1-17 nor in 2,23-3,6 [34]. Besides, the key issue in 2,18-22 is the question of fasting and Jesus' answer to it.

b. *Parallelism between 2,1-12 and 2,13-17*

2,1-12 (A)	2,13-17 (A')
	adversaries
scribes (2,6.8.10)	scribes (2,16-17)
	place
house (cf. 2,1-4)	house (cf. 2,15-16)
	introduction
καὶ εἰσελθὼν πάλιν εἰς Καφαρναοὺμ (2,1)	καὶ ἐξῆλθεν πάλιν παρὰ τὴν θάλασσαν (2,13a)
καὶ συνήχθησαν πολλοὶ ὥστε μηκέτι χωρεῖν (2,2a)	καὶ πᾶς ὁ ὄχλος ἤρχετο πρὸς αὐτόν (2,13b)
καὶ ἐλάλει αὐτοῖς τὸν λόγον (2,2b).	καὶ ἐδίδασκεν αὐτούς (2,13c).

---

[34] Except for καινός the other key terms, namely, νηστεύειν, νυμφίος, νέος and παλαιός occur exclusively in 2,18-22 in the whole of Mk.

setting of the controversy

Four men brought a paralytic to Jesus. Seeing their faith, Jesus said, "My son, your sins are forgiven" (2,5).	Many tax collectors and sinners were sitting and eating with Jesus and his disciples (2,16).

adversaries' question

Scribes were questioning in their hearts, "Who can forgive sins but God alone?" (2,7)	They asked his disciples, "Why does he eat with tax collectors and sinners?" (2,16)

Jesus' answer in two steps

καὶ εὐθὺς ἐπιγνοὺς λέγει αὐτοῖς (2,8):	καὶ ἀκούσας ὁ Ἰησοῦς λέγει αὐτοῖς (2,17):
(1) "But that you may know that the Son of Man has authority on earth to forgive sins" (2,10).	(1)"I came not to call the righteous but sinners" (2,17).
(2) "Rise, take up your pallet and go home" (2,11).	(2) "Those who are well have no need of a physician" (2,17).

This scheme clearly indicates the literary and thematic indices for the parallelism between 2,1-12 (A) and 2,13-17 (A').

c. *Parallelism between 2,23-28 and 3,1-6*

2,23-28 (B)	3,1-6 (B')

adversaries

Pharisees (cf. 2,24.25.27)	Pharisees (cf.3,2.4.5.6.)

setting

disciples plucked ears of grain	event	a man with a withered hand
sabbath	time	sabbath
grainfields	place	synagogue

problem posed

| Pharisees questioned him: "Why are they doing what is not lawful on the sabbath?" (2,24) | Pharisees watched him whether he would heal on the sabbath so that they might accuse him (3,2). |

Jesus' answer in two steps

καὶ λέγει αὐτοῖς:	καὶ λέγει αὐτοῖς:
(1) direct question (2,25)	(1) direct question (3,4)
(2) explicatory narration (2,26)	(2) explicatory narration of Jesus' emotional reaction (3,5a)

Final vindication

| in words: superiority of man over sabbath and Jesus' lordship over sabbath" (2,27-28) | in action: healing the man with a withered hand (3,5) |

Thus there are ample literary and thematic indications for for the parallelism between 2,23-28 (B) and 3,1-6 (B').

d. *Centrality of 2,18-22 (C)*

Mk 2,1-17 and 2,23-3,6 then constitute two units within 2,1-3,6. But 2,1-12 and 2,13-17 are parallel (A A'); likewise, 2,23-28 and 3,1-6 are also parallel (B B'). Hence, by implication 2,18-22 is the central pericope.

As mentioned earlier, by virtue of the key words and the specific issue, Mk 2,18-22 is differentiated both from 2,1-17 and from 2,23-3,6. There are also other elements by means of which 2,18-22 is clearly set off from the other four controversies. First, in the other four controversies the opponents are specifically named whereas in 2,18-22 the adversaries are unspecified (cf. 2,18). Secondly, in the other four controversies there is a setting (house, grainfield, synagogue) but in 2,18-22 a setting is totally lacking. Lastly, in 2,18-22 Jesus' answer consists of two parables (2,19-20; 2,21-22), a feature totally absent in the other four pericopes. Therefore, 2,18-22 is clearly differentiated from both 2,1-17 and 2,23-3,6 and it rightly constitutes the central pericope in the structural frame.

e. *Significance of the Structure*

This structure preserves the literary unity of each of the five pericopes. Thus it avoids the main shortcoming of the structure proposed by Mourlon

Beernaert. In the second place, the key words and the main theme of each pericope are duly taken into consideration. Therefore, the theological insufficiency that flows from Dewey's structure may hopefully be overcome. The structure that we have proposed will serve as the foundation for an accurate exegetical study of 2,1-3,6 which is undertaken in Ch. VI.

Finally, the central pericope 2,18-22 (C) is the pivotal point of the structure which is also the hinge of the theology in 2,1-3,6, namely, Jesus' person and mission created a unique newness that is absolutely incompatible with the old. On a par with the authority of God in the OT, Jesus enjoys the authority to forgive sins and his mission is oriented towards bringing sinners to genuine conversion. Similarly, Jesus has absolute authority over the sabbath which he exercises for the betterment and wholeness of man.

PART TWO

LITERARY ANALYSIS AND INTERPRETATION OF MK 1,14-3,6

It was established in the third chapter that Mk 1,14-3,6 consists of three literary units: 1,14-20; 1,21-45; 2,1-3,6. Now in the second part of our study (and the most important part too) the literary analysis and interpretation of these three units are undertaken. In the fourth chapter entitled, "The Proclamation of the Kingdom and the Call of the First Four Disciples" the first unit (1,14-20) is analysed and interpreted. In chapter five, attention will be focused on 1,21-45 where people appreciate and accept Jesus. The title of this chapter is derived primarily from the leading and the longest pericope (1,21-28) where Jesus' authority is manifested in word and deed. The area of our analysis and exegesis in chapter six will be 2,1-3,6 where the scribes and the Pharisees oppose Jesus. The title of this chapter is based on the main thrust of the first and longest pericope (2,1-12).

CHAPTER FOUR

THE PROCLAMATION OF THE KINGDOM (1,14-15)
AND THE CALL OF THE FIRST FOUR DISCIPLES (1,16-20)

I. The Proclamation of the Kingdom (1,14-15)

A. *Literary Analysis*

1. *Textual Criticism*

In this pericope there are two textual problems: one in v. 14 and the other in v. 15. The first has two variant readings:

1) καὶ μετά (B D *al.*) [1]

2) μετὰ δέ (א A L W Θ *al.*) [2]

Although in respect to the date and qualities of the MSS evidence both variants have almost equal claims, the second reading (μετὰ δέ) is attested to by an appreciable number of MSS pertaining to all text types. Moreover, even though Mk shows a clear preference for καί to δέ [3] he does use δέ to indicate a significant break in the narration (cf. 7,24; 10,32; 14,1). In 1,14 too he employs δέ to show a new turning point, namely, the end of John's ministry and the beginning of Jesus' ministry. Therefore both external evidence and internal evidence favour the second variant (μετὰ δέ). The first

---

[1] TASKER; WESTCOTT-HORT; EGGER, *Frohbotschaft*, 44; MARXSEN, *Evangelist*, 32; CRANFIELD, 61; LAGRANGE, 14; and SWETE, 12 opt for this reading.

[2] GNT/NESTLE-ALAND, HUCK-GREEVEN, MERK, VON SODEN, TISCHENDORF and VOGELS choose this reading. Among authors AMBROZIC, *Hidden Kingdom*, 3; MUßNER, "Gottesherrschaft", 82; SCHMIDT, *Rahmen*, 32-33; TAYLOR, 165; TURNER, "Commentary", 152, etc. opt for this variant.

[3] Cf. n. 25 below.

reading most probably originated from a copyist's attempt to replace the Marcan preferential καί.

The second textual problem concerns the first two words of 1,15: καὶ λέγων. There are three variant readings:

1) καὶ λέγων omitted (ℵ* c sy⁵ al.) [4]

2) λέγων (ℵ¹ A D al.) [5]

3) καὶ λέγων (B K L W Δ Θ f¹·¹³ al.) [6]

Among these three readings, the third variant alone is supported by a variety of witnesses from all text-types and has wide geographical distribution. The quality of the manuscripts (B W Θ) that support this reading is also good. Furthermore, Mk nowhere else introduces a direct discourse by the verbal forms of κηρύσσειν followed by the conjunction ὅτι. So the first reading does not seem to suit Marcan style. The second variant can appeal to ὅτι recitativum, a characteristic style which is invariably preceded by a verb like λέγειν [7]. However, it should be noted that although ὅτι recitativum occurs frequently in Mk [8] and it is often preceded by the verbal forms of λέγειν [9], still it is generally not preceded by a double participial construction as in 1,14-15 (κηρύσσων ... λέγων ὅτι) [10]. Therefore appeal to ὅτι recitativum to justify the second variant is not convincing.

---

[4] TISCHENDORF and TASKER opt for the first variant.

[5] HUCK-GREEVEN and TURNER prefer the second variant; VON SODEN doubts the authenticity of καί.

[6] Cf. GNT/NESTLE-ALAND, MERK, VOGELS, and the commentaries of LAGRANGE, SWETE and TAYLOR accept the third variant.

[7] Cf. BLASS-DEBRUNNER, *Grammar*, § 470; ZERWICK, *Markus-Stil*, 39-48.

[8] According to ALAND (*Konkordanz* I/2, 1017-1021, II 202-203) the frequency of ὅτι and ὅτι recitativum is as follows:

	Mt	Mk	Lk
ὅτι	141	101	174
ὅτι recitativum	15	29	17

[9] Except in seven instances, in all others the verbal forms of λέγειν are used.

[10] The verbal forms preceding ὅτι recitativum in Mk are as follows:

indicative +				ὅτι recitativum	18
indicative +	pr. ptc. +			"	7
ἤρξατο +	inf. +			"	2
infinitive +	pr. ptc. +			"	1
pr. ptc. +	pr. ptc. +			"	1

Following the third variant the syntactic structure of our text is as follows: main verb + subject + participle + καί + participle + ὅτι (ἦλθεν ὁ Ἰησοῦς ... κηρύσσων ... καὶ λέγων ὅτι). In this syntactic structure double participial construction and ὅτι recitativum are combined. Double participial construction, a typical literary style of Mk [11], features mainly in two syntactic relations and word-order: (1) verb + subject + participle + καί + participle [12]; (2) participle + participle + verb [13]. In the former both participles are joined by the conjunction καί whereas in the latter the participles are not joined by καί or any other conjunction. In our text the first syntactic pattern of double participial construction is followed. Thus an accurate and critical study of the syntax of our text reveals that here double participial construction and ὅτι recitativum, both typical of Mk, are combined. And it is this syntactic consideration that sheds light on and justifies the third variant.

2. Synoptic Comparison

Mk 1,14-15	*Mt 4,12.17*	*Lk 4,14-15*
---------------	---------------	In the power of the Spirit
John's arrest	John's arrest	---------------
coming into Galilee	withdrawal into Galilee	return into Galilee
---------------	---------------	teaching in their synagogues
preaching the gospel of God	began to preach	---------------
The time is fulfilled,	---------------	---------------
and the kingdom of God is at hand;	repent,	---------------
repent,	for the kingdom of heaven is at hand	---------------
and believe in the gospel	---------------	---------------
---------------	---------------	being glorified by all.

---

[11] Cf. NEIRYNCK, *Duality*, 82-84.
[12] Cf. 1,4.6.15.32.39.40; 2,6; 4,8; 5,5.15; 6,31; 14,54.62; 15,29(bis).
[13] Cf. 1,41; 3,5; 6,41; 7,7-8.25; 8,6.13.23; 10,50; 14,3(bis).22.23.45.67; 15,1.7.43.46.

a. *Mk 1,14-15 and Mt 4,12-17*

Although the immediate context of the beginning of Jesus' Galilean ministry is similar both in Mk and in Mt, namely, preceded by Jesus' baptism and temptation and followed by the call of the first four disciples, there is a conspicuous difference in content and in emphasis. While Mk emphasizes a temporal sequence between John's arrest and Jesus' arrival in Galilee (μετὰ ... ἦλθεν), Mt probably stresses a withdrawal from a hostile situation (ἀκούσας ... ἀνεχώρησεν) [14]. Again, the second evangelist speaks about Jesus' coming into Galilee without referring to any specific localization as such but the first evangelist adds further geographical specifications by affirming that Jesus, leaving Nazareth, went and dwelt in Capernaum which later is given the appellation, "his own city" (9,1). And by adding the geographical details "in the territory of Zebulun and Naphtali" to Capernaum in 4,13, an immediate connection is prepared for the quotation (Is 9,1-2) in Mt 4,15-16. Thereby a literary coherence is created in 4,12-16 as a whole [15] and two theologically relevant and thematically interrelated results are achieved.

First, the Jewish criticism and objection to Jesus' Messianic manifestation in Galilee are clarified as well as answered: there is no anomaly in Jesus' Galilean provenance because it is founded on the prophecy of Is 9,1-2. And secondly, by means of this quotation from Isaiah Mt provides the starting point for a missionary vision that embraces also the Gentiles [16] right from the beginning of Jesus' ministry. He highlights this universal missionary vision by bringing in the motif of the dawn of a great light for those "who sat in darkness . . . and shadow of death" (4,16 = Is 9,2), a typically Messianic theme [17]. And Isaiah whom the first evangelist frequently quotes to demonstrate that in Jesus' person and work the scriptures are being fulfilled characterizes the universal mission of the servant to be a light to the nations (Is 42,6; 49,6). Therefore by quoting Is 9,1-2 in 4,15-16 Mt interprets Jesus' manifestation in Galilee with a missionary perspective that includes the Gentiles too. To sum up, Jesus' Messianic manifestation at Capernaum in Galilee corresponds to God's plan of salvation as promised in Is 9,1-2.

---

[14] Mt primarily employs his favourite verb ἀναχωρεῖν (Mt 10, Mk 1, Lk 0) to denote withdrawal from a hostile situation (2,12.13.14.22; 4,12; 12,15; 14,13).

[15] The geographical data in 4,12-16 form a chiastic structure (A B C C' B' A'; cf. FABRIS, *Matteo*, 94).

[16] See Mt 12,18-21; 15,21-28; 21,43; 24,14 and, most importantly, the final missionary command in 28,19-20.

[17] Cf. STR.-B., *Kommentar* I, 161-162; Jn 1,8-9; 8,12; 12,36.46.

To this quotation from Isaiah is appended Jesus' proclamation, "Repent, for the kingdom of heaven is at hand" (4,17), which, however, adds nothing new but only repeats John the Baptist's preaching in 3,2. In other words, according to the first evangelist, the content of the preaching of John and Jesus is the same [18]. As a consequence what primarily counts in Mt 4,12-17 is not Jesus' preaching as such (4,17) but his settling down at Capernaum in Galilee and the Isaian quotation to justify it (4,12-16). On the other hand, for Mk the introduction (1,14) has only a secondary and subordinate role; what is of paramount significance for him is Jesus' proclamation in 1,15 which he alone characterizes as τὸ εὐαγγέλιον τοῦ θεοῦ. Compared to the Matthean parallel Mk 1,15 has two additional elements: "The time is fulfilled" (1,15a) and "believe in the gospel" (1,15d). Furthermore, for our evangelist Jesus' proclamation in 1,15 is kerygmatic whereas for the first evangelist it is primarily exhortative.

Finally, Mk 1,14-15 is certainly the key pericope of 1,14-3,6, but Mt 4,12-17 does not appear to have such a role. Mt 4,12-17, in fact, forms part of the narrative section (3,1-4,25) leading to the key event, the Sermon on the Mount (5,1-7,29), a magisterial discourse in which Jesus spells out the spirit that should animate and guide Christians in contrast to the norms and practices of the OT and Judaism.

b. *Mk 1,14-15 and Lk 4,14-15*

The only similarity between these two pericopes is that Jesus, after being tempted, returns (ὑποστρέφειν, a favourite verb of Lk) [19] to Galilee. In all other respects they differ. For instance, Lk does not envisage an immediate connection between Jesus' return to Galilee and John's arrest, for, the latter was already shut up in prison (3,20) prior to Jesus' baptism. Likewise, no element of Jesus' proclamation as in Mk 1,15 appears in Lk 4,14-15. The Lucan emphasis in 4,14-15 (a summary) is to mark the beginning of Jesus' ministry as an act commenced under the impulse of the Spirit [20]. But the rest of the pericope does not have great theological significance. Lk has composed this brief summary and placed it here as the introduction to the first part of

---

[18] That John preached the dawn of the kingdom of God is probably a Matthean redactional perspective. In respect to time, attitude and main thrust, John belongs to Jesus and his disciples (Mt 3,2; 4,17; 10,7) in contrast to the unbelieving Israel. Therefore, John is in the forefront proclaiming the same message as Jesus himself.

[19] Mt 0, Mk 0, Lk 21, Jn 0, Acts 11, Paul 1, Rest 2.

[20] "And Jesus returned in the power of the Spirit into Galilee" (Lk 4,14a) recalls the role of the Spirit in Jesus' life from the beginning (cf. 1,35; 3,22; 4,1.18; 10,21).

his Gospel (4,14-9,50) but without a key role as in the Marcan parallel (1,14-15). It is precisely so because Lk's main interest lies not in 4,14-15 but in what follows, viz., 4,16-30, the programmatic proclamation of Jesus in the synagogue at Nazareth.

3. Tradition and Redaction

In Mk, μετά with the accusative is comparatively more frequent [21]. The verb παραδιδόναι which acquired a deep Christological significance in the early Church [22] is a key word in the Passion tradition of the Gospels. Taking over this term from tradition, Mk uses it in the absolute sense exclusively for Jesus [23] and for John (1,14); its use in the passive is also reserved for Jesus (9,31; 10,33; 14,21.41) and for John (1,14). Jesus' movement to Galilee is expressed in Mk 1,14 by ἦλθεν, a verb, as previously noted, frequently predicated of Jesus in the second Gospel. 'Galilee' is a Marcan preferential term [24]. Among the Synoptics κηρύσσειν, πιστεύειν and εὐαγγέλιον are more frequent in Mk [25]. In the NT εὐαγγέλιον is used absolutely only in Mk and in Paul [26]. Although πληροῦν and καιρός are not Marcan preferential terms, their use in the second Gospel is revealing [27].

As stated before, ὅτι recitativum is characteristic of Mk. Double participles (κηρύσσων ... λέγων) [28], direct discourse preceded by a qualifying

---

[21] Mt 10, Lk 12, Mk 9+2: 1,14; 8,31; 9,2.31; 10,34; 13,24; 14,1.28.70; (16,12.19).

[22] Cf. Acts 3,13; Rom 4,25; 8,32; I Cor 11,23; Eph 5,2.25.

[23] Cf. Mk 3,19; 14,11.18.21.42.44.

[24] Cf. GASTON, Horae Synopticae., 58, 70.

[25]

	Mt	Mk	Lk	Jn	Acts	Paul	Rest		Total
δέ	491	160	548	196	558	633	185	=	2771
εὐαγγέλιον	4	8	0	0	2	60	2	=	76
καί	1169	1078	1455	818	1108	1529	190	=	8947
κηρύσσειν	9	14	9	0	8	19	2	=	61
πιστεύειν	11	14	9	98	37	54	18	=	241
πληροῦν	16	2	9	15	16	23	5	=	86
fulfilment of Ss	12	1	5	8	1	0	1	=	28
πληροῦν + καιρός	0	1	1	1	0	0	0	=	3

[26] Mk 1,15; 8,35; 10,29; 13,10; 14,9; (16,15). There are 30 occurrences of the absolute use of εὐαγγέλιον in Paul.

[27] Cf. p. 93-94. Absolute usage of καιρός is Marcan (Mt 0, Mk 3; Lk 1).

[28] NEIRYNCK (Duality, 82-84) mentions 56 occurrences of the double participial construction in Mk. Same as in Mk: Mt 17 instances and Lk 8; no parallel: Mt 10, Lk 18; modified: Mt 29, Lk 30.

verb (κηρύσσων τὸ εὐαγγέλιον τοῦ θεοῦ καὶ λέγων ὅτι πεπλήρωται ὁ καιρός) [29] and synonymous expression (πεπλήρωται ὁ καιρὸς καὶ ἤγγικεν ἡ βασιλεία) [30] are typical of Mk.

In 1,15d πιστεύειν and εὐαγγέλιον are Marcan preferential terms [31] and, as mentioned above, the absolute use of εὐαγγέλιον and synonymous expressions are characteristic features of the second evangelist. Besides, the double imperative is typical of Mk [32]. It must also be noted that 1,15d is in tune with Mk's theological thinking [33].

Based on vocabulary, style and themes, we conclude that vv. 14.15ad are redactional, but 1,15bc is from tradition [34]. Compared to Mt 4,17 (= 3,2), Mk 1,15bc is secondary. However, it is not easy to decide whether the Marcan text depends exclusively on the Matthean source (4,17) [35] or possibly on oral tradition.

4. *Structure of the Text*

Mk 1,14-15 consists of an introduction (v. 14) and the proclamation (v. 15). The introduction (A), consisting of three stiches, narrates the time, place and circumstance of the proclamation. The proclamation consists of a pair of synonymously parallel indicatives linked by καί and a pair of synonymously parallel imperatives (also linked by καί). In the indicatives the verb (perfect,

---

[29] NEIRYNCK (*Duality*, 122-124) points out 36 occurrences of direct discourse preceded by a qualifying verb. Same as in Mk: Mt 17 occurrences and Lk 10; no parallel: Mt 3 and Lk 11; modified: Mt 16 and Lk 15.

[30] NEIRYNCK (*Duality*, 101-106) notes 104 instances of synonymous expression in Mk. Same as in Mk: Mt 28, Lk 20; no parallel: Mt 15, Lk 27; modified: Mt 61, Lk 57.

[31] Cf. n. 25 above.

[32] NEIRYNCK (*Duality*, 84-85) lists 31 occurrences of double imperative. As in Mk: Mt 16, Lk 9; no parallel: Mt 4, Lk 10; modified: Mt 11, Lk 12.

[33] On thematic congruency see p. 100-101.

[34] Our distinction between the redactional and traditional elements in Mk 1,14-15 calls into question the view of AMBROZIC, *Hidden Kingdom*, 4-5 and PRYKE, *Redactional Style*, 151-152 who ascribe the whole of these two verses to Marcan redaction. It also challenges CHILTON's opinion (*God in Strength*, 27) that assigns 1,14a.15 to tradition. PESCH's contention (I, 100, 104; id., "Anfang", 115) that 1,14-15 (with the exception of 1,15d) should be attributed to pre-Marcan redactor is unwarranted. STRECKER's view ("εὐαγγέλιον-Begriff", 93-94, 96) that 1,15b is redactional whereas 1,15d is pre-Marcan is not convincing. Finally, it challenges SCHLOSSER's opinion (*Le règne de Dieu* I, 93) that ascribes v. 14 to pre-Marcan tradition but v. 15 to redaction.

[35] Cf. BENOIT-BOISMARD, *Synopse* II, 88.

third person, singular) is placed in the first place followed by the subject.
Both the imperatives are present, plural.

The structure of the text is, therefore, as follows:

14 A   Μετὰ δὲ τὸ παραδοθῆναι τὸν Ἰωάννην
          ἦλθεν ὁ Ἰησοῦς εἰς τὴν Γαλιλαίαν
          κηρύσσων τὸ εὐαγγέλιον τοῦ θεοῦ καὶ λέγων ὅτι

15 B a Πεπλήρωται ὁ καιρὸς καὶ
    a'   ἤγγικεν ἡ βασιγεία τοῦ θεοῦ·
    b   μετανοεῖτε καὶ
    b'   πιστεύετε ἐν τῷ εὐαγγελίῳ.

B. Interpretation

1. Introduction (1,14)

a. Time

In the NT μετὰ τό followed by an infinitive has always a temporal
meaning, "after" [36]. The use of παραδιδόναι "as a technical term in police
and law-court jargon for 'deliver up as a prisoner' is attested in papyri and
inscriptions" [37]. In LXX παραδιδόναι (almost always used with a complement) acquires its meaning from the context: the most frequent complement
is εἰς (τὰς) χεῖρας (τῶν) ἐχθρῶν or the like. In Jewish literature, however,
it acquires a specific nuance: it describes the fate of the prophets [38]. The early
Christian community adopted this term from Judaism and applied it in the
absolute sense to the handing over of Jesus. Mk employed this specific
Christian terminology to describe the fate of John the Baptist although he
could have used other terms (cf. Mk 6,16.17.19.27). As mentioned before,
he uses it in the absolute sense and in the passive voice exclusively for Jesus
and for John.

Therefore Mk's choice of the term and its specific use clearly indicate
that his main concern is not so much to emphasize the historical fact of

---

[36] Cf. Mk 14,28; 16,19; Mt 26,32; Lk 12,5; 22,20; Acts 1,3; 7,4; 10,41; 15,13; 19,21;
20,1; 1 Cor 11,25; Heb 10,15.26.
[37] CRANFIELD, 61-62.
[38] Cf. HAHN, Hoheitstitel, 49, 62-66; POPKES, Christus traditus, 13-83.

John's imprisonment (and beheading) as to stress a theological motif: John is handed over as Jesus will be handed over; thus, according to the divine plan [39], the forerunner anticipates the destiny of the Messiah.

b. *Place*

The coming of the mightier one as announced by John (1,7) is realized in the coming of Jesus into Galilee (1,14). In contrast to John who appeared in the wilderness preaching only βάπτισμα μετανοίας Jesus came into Galilee proclaiming τὸ εὐαγγέλιον τοῦ θεοῦ. Furthermore, differing from the synoptic parallels, in Mk Jesus' coming into Galilee is closely linked with his proclamation of the Gospel there. In fact, he comes to Galilee proclaiming the Gospel of God (ἦλθεν ... κηρύσσων τὸ εὐαγγέλιον τοῦ θεοῦ) [40]. Thus the coming of Jesus into Galilee is significant precisely because he proclaims the Gospel of God there. So the main event is the proclamation of the Gospel.

For Mk Galilee is not a pure geographical designation [41]; rather it has primarily a theological value, even if the exact theological meaning is still in dispute [42]. As far as 1,14 is concerned, Galilee is the privileged place (locus

---

[39] In 1,14 παραδοθῆναι is a theological passive (cf. GNILKA, I, 65). Mk 9,13: "But I tell you that Elijah has come, and they did to him whatever they pleased, as it is written of him".

[40] MUBNER, "Gottesherrschaft", 82: "Gegenüber dem prosaisch wirkenden 'zurück-kehren' des Matthäus und des Lukas hat das des Markus eher epiphanischen Klang: Jesus 'kommt' mit einer wichtigen Botschaft nach Galiläa".

Note the period after 'Galilee' in Mt 4,12 and Lk 4,14. In Mt Jesus' coming into Galilee (4,12) is separated by five verses from his preaching there (4,17); he does not mention that Jesus preached the Gospel of God. In Lk 4,15 there is no notice about Jesus' preaching the Gospel at all.

[41] Against KATO (*Völkermission*, 23-24: "Galilaa ist also kein theologischer Begriff . . . sondern es bleibt ein geographischer Begriff im historischen Sinn").

[42] The views on the theological significance of Galilee may summarily be classified as follows: (1) According to LOHMEYER (*Galiläa*, 26-36) Jesus founds his eschatological community in Galilee, supports it with his salvific activity and there his followers must await the Parousia. In contrast, Jerusalem is the city of deadly enmity towards Jesus, the city of sin and death. While LOHMEYER presupposes two distinct Christian groups (one of Galilee and the other of Jerusalem), MARXSEN (*Evangelist*, 93-94) speaks about a single Christian community, namely, that of Galilee. (2) Based on the OT background and the ethnic situation of Galilee in the first century AD, BOOBYER ("Galilee and Galileans", 334-348) claims that for Mk Galilee means Galilee of the pagans. For KARNETZKI ("Die galiläische Redaktion", 238-272) Galilee is significant because it is the starting point of the Gentile mission. SCHREIBER (*Theologie*, 170-184) goes a step further: Galilee is not only the starting point of the Gentile mission, but it is there that Jesus himself began his mission to the Gentiles. (3) A third group of authors attempt to combine the two views mentioned above but at times with slight modifi-

theologicus) where Jesus himself first proclaimed the Gospel. In the Matthean parallel, in contrast, the geographical connotation is stressed: it is the place of Jesus' domicile (cf. Mt 4,12-13).

c. Circumstance

The primary meaning of κηρύσσειν is to proclaim publicly a message that one is commissioned to announce, not in one's own name but by the authority of the sender. In classical Greek, unlike the noun κῆρυξ, the verb κηρύσσειν is neither frequent nor significant [43]. In passages of religious significance it is used for a sacral proclaiming of contests and divine festivals [44]. It is not very frequent in the LXX (only 29 times) and has a direct object only in six instances [45]; of these six texts only Is 61,1 appears to have a noun of soteriological significance. "Against all expectation κηρύσσειν is seldom used of the proclamation of the prophets" [46]. Its use in rabbinic writings breaks no fresh ground [47].

In the NT, however, κηρύσσειν is considerably frequent (61 times). The most frequent use is with τὸ εὐαγγέλιον either as the direct object or as the

---

cations (cf. VAN CAGH, "Galilee", 74-76; KELBER, *Kingdom*, passim; MALBON, *Mythic Meaning*, 40-46). (4) DE LA CALLE (*Situación*, 75-149) argues that for Mk Galilee is significant because in Galilee Jesus began his ministry, founded the first Christian community, and the post-Easter appearances also took place there. MANICARDI (*Il cammino*, 51-72, 171-182) adds: for Mk there is no real contrast between Galilee and Jerusalem and it is in Galilee that the disciples came to know who Jesus really was.

The views of LOHMEYER and BOOBYER on Galilee constitute the basis or, at least, the starting point for the theories of others. First of all, an accurate reading of Mk reveals that there is no radical opposition between Galilee and Jerusalem from the redactional point of view. Although Jesus' initial ministry in Galilee found a very favourable response (1,14-45), a steady and consistent opposition to him also developed there (2,1-3,5), culminating in the decision of the Pharisees and Herodians to destroy him (3,6). In Jerusalem too people are enthusiastic about and appreciative of Jesus (cf. 11,8-10.18; 12,12.37; 14,2). And in the second place, Mk does not portray a link between Galilee and the Gentile mission. The Isaian text (8,23-9,1) is not cited in Mk but in Mt (4,15-16). The basis of the Gentile mission, in fact, emerges from Mk 7,24-30; 11,17; 13,10; and 14,9.

For Mk Galilee is the privileged place where Jesus himself preached the gospel and received a very positive response from people (der galiläische Frühling). It is in Galilee that the disciples, after their failure at Jesus' Passion, were reconstituted.

[43] Cf. H. FRIEDRICH, *TDNT* III, 683-685, 697-698.

[44] *Ibid.*, 691, 698.

[45] 2 Chron 20,3; Prov 8,1; Is 61,1; Jon 3,5; Joel 1,14; 2,15.

[46] H. FRIEDRICH, *ibid.*, 701.

[47] *Ibid.*, 702.

subject [48]. In both Acts and in Paul Jesus or Christ is the object of this verb [49]. In the synoptic Gospels κηρύσσειν is used mainly in four contexts: (a) in the active, for the preaching of John (Mt 3,1; Mk 1,4.7; Lk 3,3); (b) for the preaching of Jesus [50]; (c) for the preaching of the Twelve [51]; and (d) in the passive, for the preaching of the post-Easter Church [52].

These philological considerations lead us to three conclusions. First, κηρύσσειν acquired a profound theological significance in the NT: it is a typical NT word for the presentation of the Christian message, the Gospel. Second, by means of κηρύσσειν John, Jesus, the Twelve and the post-Easter Church are all linked in the synoptic Gospels [53]. Third, the use of the active voice for the preaching of John, Jesus and the Twelve seems to indicate that their role of preaching pertains to the constitutive level of the kerygma whereas the use of the passive for the preaching of the post-Easter Church probably shows that her role consists in preaching the kerygma which is already constituted (cf. Mk 13,10 par. Mt 24,14; Lk 24,47).

In Mk κηρύσσειν is used with the direct object τὸ εὐαγγέλιον exclusively in reference to Jesus' first proclamation in 1,14-15. It is significant to note the progression: in 1,1 Mk proposes to narrate the gospel whose content is Jesus Christ. The beginning of this gospel is in John's proclamation (1,4). John, having proclaimed the coming of the mightier one (1,7-8), disappears from the scene (1,14a) and then Jesus enters the scene κηρύσσων τὸ εὐαγγέλιον. Thus Mk takes up the theme, τὸ εὐαγγέλιον, from v. 1 and commences a new beginning in 1,14-15. In v. 14 Jesus is both the herald and the content of the gospel he proclaims. It is also instructive to note that τὸ εὐαγγέλιον is qualified by τοῦ θεοῦ. Therefore, according to Mk, Jesus is the herald par excellence who is authenticated to proclaim τὸ εὐαγγέλιον τοῦ θεοῦ [54].

---

[48] Direct object: Mt 4,23; 9,35; Mk 1,14; Gal 2,2; Col 1,23; I Thess 2,9. The passive of κηρύσσειν with τὸ εὐαγγέλιον as subject: Mt 24,14; 26,13; Mk 13,10; 14,9.

[48] Direct object Jesus: Acts 9,20; 19,13; 2 Cor 4,5; 11,4. Direct object Christ: Acts 8,5; 1 Cor 1,23; Phil 1,15.

[50] Mt 4,17.23.35; 11,1; Mk 1,14.38.39; Lk 4,18.19.44; 8,1.

[51] Mt 10,7.27; Mk 3,14; 6,12; Lk 9,2.

[52] Mt 24,14; 26,13; Mk 13,10; 14,9; Lk 24,47.

[53] John preaches before Jesus commences his ministry. Jesus' kerygmatic activity is concentrated at the initial stages of his ministry. But once the Twelve are constituted and empowered to preach, the verb 'preach' is not predicated of Jesus in Mk (in contrast Mt 11,1; Lk 8,1). The Church's preaching is to take place after Jesus' Death and Resurrection.

[54] In the Gospels τὸ εὐαγγέλιον τοῦ θεοῦ is the object of κηρύσσειν only in Mk 1,14.

Among the Greeks εὐαγγέλιον is a technical term for the news of victory, often used for the victory in battle [55]. The term (בְּשׂרָה) occurs six times in OT: good news (2 Sam 18,19.20.25.27) or reward for good news (2 Sam 4,10; 18,22); but it has no religious significance in any of these texts. In Roman times εὐαγγέλιον was used for the good news of the birth of an heir of Caesar or the accession of a Caesar to the throne [56]. The NT probably took over the term from this Roman imperial background and gave it a new content by applying it to the Christ-event [57]. In the NT εὐαγγέλιον occurs 76 times, predominantly in Paul for whom the main content of the Gospel is Jesus' saving Death and Resurrection.

As mentioned before, Mk uses εὐαγγέλιον in two ways: in the absolute sense (τὸ εὐαγγέλιον) and determined by a genitive of person (1,1.14). Both ways are typical of Paul. In 1,14 it is determined by τοῦ θεοῦ which again is characteristic of Paul [58]. The genitive τοῦ θεοῦ in 1,14 is not objective but subjective (from God). And καὶ λέγων is epexegetic. Therefore grammatically and syntactically the proclamation that follows spells out τὸ εὐαγγέλιον. In other words, Mk adopting the term εὐαγγέλιον and even the expression τὸ εὐαγγέλιον τοῦ θεοῦ from the missionary vocabulary of the early Church (particularly from Paul) gave it a new content, namely, not only Jesus' Death and Resurrection but also his earthly ministry is εὐαγγέλιον. He also links τὸ εὐαγγέλιον τοῦ θεοῦ and ἡ βασιλεία τοῦ θεοῦ, the main content of Jesus' proclamation in 1,15.

To sum up v. 14, at the divinely preordained moment Jesus came into Galilee as the unique herald κηρύσσων τὸ εὐαγγέλιον τοῦ θεοῦ. This is the setting for the proclamation in v. 15 which elucidates the meaning of τὸ εὐαγγέλιον τοῦ θεοῦ. The double participle (κηρύσσων ... λέγων) literally and logically connects the introduction (1,14) and the proclamation (1,15).

---

[55] Cf. H. FRIEDRICH, *TDNT* II, 722.

[56] *Ibid.*, 724-725.

[57] With KÄSEMANN (*Romans*, 7-8) against GNILKA (I, 66) who bases its origin on Deutero-Isaiah. One should note that Dt-Is does not use the noun εὐαγγέλιον at all but the verb εὐαγγελίζειν (cf. Is 40,9; 41,27; 52,7; 60,6; 61,1). In fact, Mk does not use this verb at all.

[58] Rom 15,16; 2 Cor 11,7; 1 Thess 2,2.8.9; in Rom 1,1 (without the article). Otherwise in NT only once (1 Pt 4,17).

2. *Proclamation (1,15)*

a. *Fulfilment of the Time*

In the non-biblical literature the verb πληροῦν (predominantly constructed with genitive) is generally used in the physical sense [59]. In the LXX the physical (particularly spatial) sense is most prevalent though the metaphorical sense is also rather frequent [60], and a few times the theological sense is also used (e.g., 2 Chron 36,22: to fulfil a word of Yahweh).

The lexicons give at least five meanings for πληροῦν in the NT but in the Gospels it is frequently used to mean the fulfilment of the Scriptures (word of God), particularly in Mt [61]. Thrice it is used with καιρός as the subject (Mk 1,15; Lk 21,24; Jn 7,8).

A comparison of the Marcan usage of πληροῦν (only twice: 1,15; 14,49) with the rest of the NT shows that the second evangelist uses it exclusively in a theological sense: fulfilment of the Scriptures (14,49) and fulfilment of the time determined by God (1,15).

In the secular use καιρός primarily means "the decisive moment" [62] or "the moment in time which is especially favourable for an undertaking" [63]. The use of καιρός is rather frequent in the LXX where in many instances the emphasis falls on its divine appointment (καιρός is divinely ordained) [64]. In this sense καιρός is an established term in salvation history.

In the NT the most frequent use of καιρός is with a preposition. It is also used with demonstrative adjectives such as ἐκεῖνος, οὗτος, etc. and in the absolute sense. Of the five instances of καιρός in Mk (invariably in the singular) thrice he uses it in the absolute sense (1,15; 12,2; 13,33), once with a demonstrative adjective coupled with a preposition (10,30: ἐν τῷ καιρῷ τούτῳ) and once with a genitive (11,13: καιρὸς ... σύκων). In 12,2 by τῷ καιρῷ is meant "when the season came" (NEB) or "at the proper season" [65]. And ὁ καιρός in 13,33 means the eschatological time of Parousia.

Mk's choice of the term in 1,15 is greatly influenced by the LXX use of καιρός to mean God's time, particularly in its prophetic-apocalyptic

---

[59] Cf. DELLING, *TDNT* VI, 286-287.
[60] *Ibid.*, 287-288.
[61] See n. 25 above.
[62] DELLING, *TDNT* III, 455.
[63] CULLMANN, *Christ and Time*, 39.
[64] See the texts in DELLING, *TDNT* III, 458.
[65] TAYLOR, 474.

colouring (cf. Ezek 7,12; Dan 2,21; 7,22). According to the context, therefore, ὁ καιρός in 1,15 means the particular time [66] determined by God for the commencement of the eschatological salvation in and through the ministry of the Messiah [67]. More precisely, by virtue of the parallelism between 1,15a and 1,15b it is evident that the fulfilment of the time takes place in Jesus' proclamation of the kingdom of God.

To sum up, the time of preparations and promises have come to an end; the long-awaited eschatological time is definitively fulfilled in the commencement of Jesus' ministry inaugurating the inbreaking of the kingdom of God. The eschatological NEW, active here and now [68], is brought about by God himself [69]. Yet it is Jesus who announces the definitive fulfilment of the Messianic time determined by God. Concerning the beginning of the Messianic time Rabbi Jose (c. 150) said: "Wer das Ende (= Tage des Messias) angibt (berechnet), hat keinen Teil an der zukünftigen Welt" [70].

Wenn Jesus also jetzt die Vollendung verkündet, dann ist entweder für jüdische Ohren sein Wort Blasphemie oder es ist für urchristliche Ohren Gottes eigene Stimme und Gottes eigenes Wort. Dann ist auch der Träger dieser Verkündung so eng mit Gott zusammengeschlossen, daß Sein Wort und Gottes Wort eines und dasselbe ist [71].

Thus Jesus' proclamation of the definitive fulfilment of the time (= Messianic time) demonstrates also his unique status in relation to God [72].

---

[66] Die festgesetzte Zeit, der Zeitpunkt, differs from χρόνος (Zeitraum, Zeitdauer).

[67] The theme of the fulfilment of the time (the day of the Messiah) was frequent in Jewish eschatology. The Syriac Apocalypse of Baruch 30,1: "When the time of the advent of the Messiah is fulfilled"; 30,3: "For they know that the time has come of which it is said, that it is the consummation of the times". According to Pesher on Habakkuk, although the teacher of righteousness did not know the fulfilment of the time, still he held that the community at Qumran was the community of the last times (cf. 1 QpHab VII, 1-5).

[68] LOHMEYER, 30: "Jetzt eingetretene, hier wirklich gewordene Vollendung". TRILLING, "Botschaft", 46: "Markus . . . will den Tag hervorheben, an dem die Ausrufung der Gottesherrschaft im Wort Jesu geschah. An diesem 'Tag' fängt das Neue an, indem es ausgerufen wird. Sein 'Erfülltsein' hat den Klang des 'Jetzt und heute und hier'".

[69] Not only that ὁ καιρός is predetermined by God Himself, but also πεπλήρωται is theological passive (cf. GRUNDMANN, 50; MUBNER, "Gottesherrschaft", 88).

[70] Quoted by STR.-B., *Kommentar* I, 671. For analogous opinions see *ibid.*

[71] LOHMEYER, 30.

[72] Jewish eschatology refers to God as the bringer of the Messianic time, but it also states that the Messiah himself is the bringer of the Messianic time. Compare STR-B., *Kommentar* IV, 558-572 with 572-580.

b. *Drawing Near of the Kingdom of God*

In the non-biblical literature and in the LXX ἐγγίζειν is primarily used either in the spatial or in the temporal sense [73]. In the LXX, depending on the context, it also attains various theological overtones. Deutero-Isaiah employs it to denote the approach of the time of salvation [74].

In the NT ἐγγίζειν followed by dative has a spatial sense in the Lucan writings [75] whereas in Heb 7,19 and Jas 4,8 it denotes nearness to God. When followed by the preposition εἰς it always has spatial significance [76]. When used absolutely, depending on the context, it has either spatial [77] or temporal [78] meaning. The perfect active (ἤγγικεν) with the subject ἡ βασιλεία τοῦ θεοῦ/τῶν οὐρανῶν occurs six times in the NT: the content of the preaching of John (Mt 3,2), of Jesus (Mt 4,17; Mk 1,15) and of the Twelve (Mt 10,7; Lk 10,9.11). The expression, ἤγγικεν ἡ βασιλεία τοῦ θεοῦ was probably quasi-technical, current in the primitive Christian community, to proclaim the effective presence of the new way of life inaugurated by Jesus [79]. As far as Mk is concerned, it is the exclusive prerogative of Jesus to proclaim ἤγγικεν ἡ βασιλεία τοῦ θεοῦ. Unlike Mt and Lk, in Mk neither John nor the Twelve preach ἤγγικεν ἡ βασιλεία τοῦ θεοῦ.

The exact translation of ἤγγικεν is difficult: some give a 'realized' interpretation (has come) whereas a few others favour a 'futuristic' option (come near) [80]. In Mk ἐγγίζειν occurs thrice. In 11,1 and in 14,42 it has spatial meaning whereas in 1,15 (absolute use) it has a temporal nuance. In

---

[73] Cf. PREISKER, *TDNT* II, 330.

[74] Cf. Is 46,13; 50,8; 51,5; 56,1.

[75] Cf. Lk 7,12; 15,1.25; 22,47; Acts 9,3; 10,9; 22,6.

[76] Cf. Mt 21,1; Mk 11,1; Lk 18,35; 19,29; 24,28.

[77] Cf. Mt 26,46; Mk 14,42; Lk 12,33; 18,40; 19,41; 24,15; Acts 21,33; 23,15.

[78] Cf. Mt 21,34; 26,45; Lk 21,8.20.28; 22,1; Acts 7,17; Rom 13,12; Heb 10,25; Jas 5,8.

[79] Cf. BUETUBELA, *Jean-Baptiste*, 285; EGGER, *Frohbotschaft*, 59; SCHLOSSER, *Le règne de Dieu* I, 101.

[80] DODD (*Parables*, 36-37) holds that ἤγγικεν translates the Aramaic original (*m'ta*) and that in Mk 1,15 ἤγγικεν should be rendered 'has come'. CAMPBELL ("Kingdom", 91-94) challenged DODD's opinion asserting that it renders *qrb* which meant 'come near'. BLACK ("Kingdom", 289-290) and HUTTON ("Kingdom", 89-91) also defend DODD's translation (ἤγγικεν = 'has come'). On the other hand, CLARK ("Eschatology", 367-383) and KÜMMEL (*Promise*, 19-25) hold the second opinion (ἤγγικεν = 'come near'). MARXSEN (*Evangelist*, 133), quoting KÜMMEL, opts for a futuristic interpretation. FULLER (*Mission and Achievement*, 125) found it necessary to explain "the impending event, while emphatically future, is nevertheless operative in advance". BERKEY ("Realized Eschatology", 177-187) attempts to reconcile the 'realized' and 'futuristic' interpretations.

1,15 ἤγγικεν is indicative perfect whose full meaning must be duly recognized, namely, "it denotes the continuance of completed action" [81]. This shows that the action has taken place, the kingdom of God is already inaugurated [82]. Furthermore, 1,15a and 1,15b are synthetically parallel in which the second member explicates the first. Therefore the time is fulfilled inasmuch as the kingdom of God is inaugurated. Consequently, the translation 'come near' which presupposes a distance is inadequate [83]. On the other hand, the translation 'has come' also appears inadequate because it does not sufficiently emphasize the aspect of continuance. In order to emphasize both aspects (continuance of a completed action) some authors offer a descriptive or a metaphorical rendering [84].

In brief, the eschatological kingdom of God is already inaugurated as Jesus begins his Messianic ministry.

The term βασιλεία (= מַלְכוּת) in relation to God is rarely found in the early OT books and not so frequently in later books of the OT and intertestamental writings [85]. Based on a detailed analytical study of the occurrences of 'kingdom of God' in the OT and intertestamental literature Camponovo concludes:

> Gottes Königtum über Israel, die Schöpfung und die Welt waren am Anfang des AT anerkannt. Die Herrschaft Gottes als des Königs ist eine bekannte Glaubensaussage. Der Verweis darauf ist zu einem Kennwort für die eschatologische Heilserwartung geworden [86].

---

[81] BLASS-DEBRUNNER, *Grammar*, § 340. MOULTON-TURNER, *Grammar* III, 182: "a combining of the Aktionsarten of aorist and present".

[82] MUßNER, "Gottesherrschaft", 89: "in Mk 1,15 durch das Perfekt ἤγγικεν *die unmittelbare Nähe der Gottesherrschaft* angekündigt. Wenn der Anbruch der eschatologischen Gottesherrschaft noch eine Weile auf sich warten ließe, dann ist die Zeit eben noch nicht erfüllt. Sie ist nur dann wirklich erfüllt, wenn sich nun auch sofort die Gottesherrschaft zu verwirklichen beginnt".

[83] MUßNER, "Gottesherrschaft", 91: "es duldet auch kein Zwischen dem Ende der Wartezeit und der Ankunft des Gottesreiches".

[84] EGGER, *Frohbotschaft*, 58: "Erfüllt ist die Zeit: machtvoll ist die Gottesherrschaft nahegekommen". KLOSTERMANN, 12: "Das Maß der in Aussicht genommenen Wartezeit ist voll, der entscheidende Zeitpunkt ist erreicht, das Heil, die βασιλεία τοῦ θεοῦ steht vor der Tür". BERKEY ("Realized Eschatology", 184) compares it to a knock on the door by which the arrival of an expected guest is recognized.

[85] Regarding the frequency of 'kingdom/reign of God' in Jewish literature and sources thereof cf. JEREMIAS, *Theology*, 32, with the observation that its occurrences in Qumran are more frequent (cf. CAMPONOVO, *Reich Gottes*, 259-307).

[86] CAMPONOVO, *ibid.*, 127.

Das Thema der Königsherrschaft Gottes ist kein Hauptthema der früh-jüdischen Literatur . . . . Es ist nur im Buch Daniel so zentral, dass es das Werk als Ganzes bestimmt [87].

In contrast, in the synoptic Gospels βασιλεία τοῦ θεοῦ/τῶν οὐρανῶν is not only very frequent [88] but also occurs almost exclusively on the lips of Jesus. Many of these expressions in which βασιλεία τοῦ θεοῦ occurs have no parallels (not even secular ones) in the language of Jesus' contempo-raries [89]. And kingdom of God certainly constitutes the key message of Jesus. Kingdom of God is a global expression for the sum total of eschatological salvation. It is a relational and experiential reality; consequently it is beyond definition. Jesus never attempts to define it. Instead he explains it in metaphors, parables and short sayings, offers personal and experiential insights into this polyvalent symbol and enables people to experience it personally [90].

Mk has given pointers about his understanding of the kingdom of God. By commencing his ministry in words and deeds, Jesus ushers in the kingdom of God. By his exorcisms and healings he wages the eschatological battle against the reign of Satan (who according to the opinion of Jesus' contempo-raries was the archenemy of God's kingdom) [91], a key theme in the second Gospel (cf. 3,22-30). Mk's description of a typical day spent by Jesus at Capernaum (1,21-34) is a concrete illustration of the inbreaking of the kingdom of God. This way Mk spells out how the kingdom of God breaks into salvation history.

Furthermore, the expression, kingdom of God, is typical of Jesus' earthly ministry [92]. Mk in 1,15 (diff. par. Mt 4,17 and Lk 4,15) links this basic message of Jesus' earthly ministry with εὐαγγέλιον, a term typical of the early missionary Church, insofar as the main content of τὸ εὐαγγέλιον τοῦ

---

[87] *Ibid.*, 437.

[88] For a statistical survey on 'kingdom/reign of God' and related terms in various books of NT see SANTRAM, "Kingdom of God", 83.

[89] Cf. JEREMIAS, *Theology*, 32-34, 96-97.

[90] PERRIN views 'Kingdom of God' as a polyvalent symbol (cf. *Kingdom*, 1-2, 22, 32-33, 202-203; id., "Biblical Symbol", 367-369). This basic insight of PERRIN is generally accepted by others (SCHLOSSER, CAMPONOVO, etc.).

[91] Cf. BECKER, *Heil Gottes*, 205-209; FOERSTER, *TDNT* VII, 158-160; KRUSE, "Das Reich Satans", 29-61; STR.-B., *Kommentar* IV, 801-804, 814-815.

[92] Cf. JEREMIAS, *Theology*, 96-102.

θεοῦ is ἡ βασιλεία τοῦ θεοῦ. Thereby he points out the continuity between Jesus' preaching and the Gospel proclaimed by the early Church.

Finally, Mk closely connects the kingdom of God and the person of Jesus. This is evident in Mk 4,11:

ὑμῖν δέδοται γνῶναι τὰ μυστήρια τῆς βασιλείας (Mt 13,11 par.)

ὑμῖν τὸ μυστήριον δέδοται τῆς βασιλείας (Mk 4,11)

Compared with the parallels (Mt 13,11 par. Lk 8,10) Mk 4,11 is secondary, for he has intentionally omitted γνῶναι [93] and changed τὰ μυστήρια into τὸ μυστήριον. By these redactional changes Mk has interpreted the meaning of τὸ μυστήριον τῆς βασιλείας (which is given to those who were about him with the Twelve), namely, it is the mystery of Jesus' Messianic identity [94]. From this close connection between the kingdom of God and the person of Jesus, Origen develops the expression αὐτοβασιλεία [95].

In summation, Jesus ushers in the kingdom of God in his ministry, particularly in his eschatological battle against the reign of Satan. The main content of the Gospel that is proclaimed by Jesus is the kingdom of God; thus Mk shows the continuity between Jesus' preaching and the preaching of the early Church. Though the kingdom of God is theocentric, in Mk it is also Christocentric, for it is equated with the Messianic identity of Jesus. Jesus is thus not only the herald of the kingdom but also its content.

c. *Repentance*

Compared with the Matthean parallel, our evangelist has inverted the order of the indicative and the imperative whereby he has changed the moralizing tone of the first evangelist into a kerygmatic one. The irruption of God's kingdom (God's definitive revelation) demands final and unconditional decision on man's part. These demands are stated by means of a pair of synthetically parallel imperatives: (1) μετανοεῖτε (2) πιστεύετε ἐν τῷ εὐαγγελίῳ. Repentance and faith were already connected in the missionary

---

[93] The knowledge of Jesus' identity is a secret till Peter's confession (8,29). Consequently Mk cannot use the verb to know in 4,11.

[94] SCHMID, 95: "Das Geheimnis des Gottesreiches ist demnach gleichbedeutend mit dem Messiasgeheimnis Jesu".

[95] Cf. LAMPE, *Lexicon*, 268.

preaching of the early Church as the foundation of Christian life [96]. However, it is Mk who links them as direct consequences flowing from the irruption of God's kingdom.

The verb μετανοεῖν (to change one's mind) and the noun μετάνοια are neither frequent in classical Greek nor related to any specific concept in pre-biblical and extra-biblical usage [97]. In the LXX μετάνοια occurs only five times and μετανοεῖν 22 times, of which in 14 instances it translates the niphal נָחַם (be sorry, suffer grief, regret something). But sometimes its meaning is similar to ἐπιστρέφειν [98] which is the normal rendering of שׁוּב (turn back, return), the technical term in the OT for the profound and personal conversion to Yahweh.

By μετάνοια/μετανοεῖν the NT on the whole means the profound and personal conversion to God as accentuated by the prophets and expressed by the verb שׁוּב rather than the feeling of remorse for wrongdoing (i.e., נָחַם = μετανοεῖν); however, the exact meaning of μετάνοια/μετανοεῖν in a particular NT text must be decided from the context.

In Mk μετάνοια occurs once (1,4) and μετανοεῖν twice (1,15; 6,13). In 1,4 μετάνοια pertains to the content of John's preaching; in 1,15 μετανοεῖτε is part of Jesus' preaching; and in 6,13 it is the object of the preaching of the Twelve. Two conclusions may be drawn from Mk's use of μετάνοια/μετανοεῖν. First, in Mk the appeal to repentance is preceded by κηρύσσειν. Second, repentance is the object of the preaching of John (who through his ministry proclaims the Messiah), of Jesus himself and of the Twelve (Jesus' official emissaries who carry on his own mission). Thus through the ministry of preaching repentance, a link is established between John, Jesus and the Twelve.

In 1,15 the imperative μετανοεῖτε is dependent on the indicative ἤγγικεν ἡ βασιλεία τοῦ θεοῦ and it is a necessary consequence flowing from the dawn of the kingdom of God. Because it is present imperative plural, it has a universal and personal appeal. Unlike the appeal to repentance in the

---

[96] Excluding Mk 1,15 there are two explicit texts in the NT (Acts 20,21; Heb 6,1) in which repentance (μετάνοια) is immediately followed by faith (πίστις). Acts 20,21 is the quintessence of Paul's missionary appeal both to Jews and to Greeks. Repentance and faith are closely connected in Heb 6,1: repentance from dead works (negative element) and faith toward God (positive element). Heb 6,1 is an important text for the connection between repentance and faith because it is an instruction for catechumens. See also Acts 3.19; 26.20; 1 Thess 1,7-8.

[97] Cf. BEHM, *TDNT* IV, 976-979.

[98] In Ex 32,12; Is 46,8; Jer 4,28 the two verbs (שׁוּב and נָחַם) are parallel and have almost the same meaning.

OT it is not a return to the old covenant [99]. Distinct from the summons to repentance of the OT prophets, it does not necessarily presuppose faith [100]. It is a total change of the heart and a complete transformation of one's attitudes that affect every sphere of one's life [101]. It is a conversion even from the OT pattern of life in which Israel so far had found security and salvation [102].

d. Faith in the Gospel

In the NT πιστεύειν when followed by a preposition, mainly εἰς (frequent in Johannine writings) or ἐπί, governs a personal object (generally Jesus or Lord). In Mk 1,15d, however, the object is τῷ εὐαγγελίῳ. Furthermore, here πιστεύειν is followed by the preposition ἐν. According to Doudna, the Marcan expression πιστεύειν ἐν has no parallel in the classical Greek or in the papyri [103]. But there are instances of πιστεύειν ἐν in the LXX where it is a literal rendering of the Hebrew אמן ב (Jer 12,6; Dan 6,24; Ps 77,22; 105,12). Although in the NT πιστεύειν followed by the preposition ἐν is very rare, it probably corresponds to the Pauline ἐν ᾧ [104]. This view is reinforced by the fact that in the composition of 1,14-15 our evangelist is dependent upon the missionary vocabulary (especially Pauline) of the early Church.

The meaning of πιστεύειν ἐν τῷ εὐαγγελίῳ must be decided in the context of 1,14-15. It was already noted that in the composition of 1,14-15 Mk has adopted and integrated vocabulary (κηρύσσειν, εὐαγγέλιον) and phraseology (μετανοεῖτε . . . πιστεύετε) from the missionary theology of the early Church. Paul operates with a rich vocabulary to denote the proclamation of the

---

[99] WOLFF, "Kerygma", 184: "Die Umkehr als Rückkehr in den Väterbund, den Jahwe noch nicht vergessen hat, ist das einzige, was Israel zu tun übergeblieben ist".

[100] The prophetic summons to repentance necessarily presupposed faith. Cf. RAITT, "Repentance", 30-49; WOLFF, "Umkehr", 129-148; WÜRTHWEIN, TDNT IV, 984-988.

[101] Cf. GNILKA, I, 67-68; SOARES PRABHU, Formula Quotations, 113; TRILLING, "Botschaft", 48, 51-52.

[102] MERKLEIN, "Umkehrpredigt", 35: "Umkehr erfordert daher nicht nur Bekenntnis der individuellen Sünden, sondern Eingeständnis dieser Verlorenheit und damit radikal Abkehr von allem Bisherigen, auch von dem, woraus Israel bisher Heil und Heilssicherheit bezogen hat".

[103] Cf. DOUDNA, Greek, 23.

[104] In Eph 1,13 πιστεύειν is preceded by ἐν (ἐν ᾧ καὶ πιστεύσαντες). Here ἐν ᾧ may mean "in him" (RSV) referring to ἐν τῷ Χριστῷ in v. 12 or "in it" (NEB) referring to 'gospel' in 1,13. Here ἐν ᾧ καὶ ὑμεῖς ἀκούσαντες... ἐν ᾧ καὶ πιστεύσαντες are parallel and so the second ἐν ᾧ should refer to Christ.

Gospel and its corresponding acceptance [105]. Among various pairing terms to express this correlation, the most frequent is κηρύσσειν and πιστεύειν (Rom 10,8.14-17; 1 Cor 15,11; 2 Cor 1,19-20). It is also clear that the specific purpose and the ultimate goal of preaching the Gospel is to instil faith: preach the gospel . . . hear . . . believe (Col 1,23), preach the gospel . . . hear . . . receive . . . believe (1 Thess 2,9.13), preach the gospel . . . receive . . . believe (1 Cor 15,1-2). In these texts *to believe* is synonymous with *to become a Christian*. Adopting this correlation between κηρύσσειν τὸ εὐαγγέλιον and πιστεύειν current in Paul, Mk integrates it in the composition of 1,14-15.

Furthermore, in Paul one discovers a tendency to personify τὸ εὐαγγέλιον and to make it an object of faith, the faith of the Gospel (Phil 1,27). Rom 10,16, synonymously parallel, is particularly instructive:

'Αλλ' οὐ πάντες ὑπήκουσιν τῷ εὐαγγελίῳ . . .

Κύριε, τίς ἐπίστευσεν τῇ ἀκοῇ ἡμῶν;

By virtue of the synonymous parallelism ὑπακούειν τῷ εὐαγγελίῳ has the same content as πιστεύειν τῷ εὐαγγελίῳ. Therefore, τὸ εὐαγγέλιον as the object of πιστεύειν, at least in a latent and incipient form, is part of Pauline thinking and preaching. As far as Mk is concerned the clause πιστεύετε ἐν τῷ εὐαγγελίῳ is not strange at all because for him faith is usually in a person (either implicit in the context or explicitly stated) and because he identifies Jesus and τὸ εὐαγγέλιον (8,35; 10,29). Therefore 1,15d corresponds to Mk's thinking and the expression means to believe in Jesus Christ, the content of the gospel (cf. 1,1).

In brief, πιστεύετε ἐν τῷ εὐαγγελίῳ primarily implies personal relationship: faith in Jesus Christ who is not only the herald of the Gospel but also its content. Further, as 1,15b explicated 1,15a, so also πιστεύετε ἐν τῷ εὐαγγελίῳ is the complement of μετανοῖετε: repentance consists in adhering to Jesus Christ in faith. In other words, as the prophetic summons to repentance in the OT was a call to return to Yahweh (personal adherence to Yahweh and obedience of his will) so also the demand to conversion in Mk 1,15c is a call to adhere to Jesus Christ in faith. Finally, the summons πιστεύετε ἐν τῷ εὐαγγελίῳ is equally unconditional, universal, personal and radical just as the summons to repentance.

---

[105] For the proclamation of the gospel is employed καταγγέλειν (1 Cor 9,14), ἱερουργεῖν (Rom 15,16), λαλεῖν (1 Thess 2,2), etc. Likewise there are typical verbs for the acceptance of the gospel: ἀκούειν (Eph 1,13; Col 1,23), δέχεσθαι (2 Cor 11,4), ὑπακούειν (Rom 10,16; 2 Thess 1,8), etc.

C. Concluding Remarks

1. In the composition of 1,14-15 Mk has combined Jesus' tradition and select words and expressions from the missionary vocabulary of the early Church (some of them with new nuances and original insights). The net result is a well-compact and carefully constructed redactional unit which Mk places at the beginning of Jesus' ministry. This proclamation constitutes the very first utterance of Jesus in the Gospel of Mk [106].

2. In the proclamation the indicative (the time is fulfilled, and the kingdom of God is at hand) may be considered God's gift and the imperative (repent, and believe in the Gospel) man's response. So the proclamation consists of a gift and a task. In the indicative by placing the verbs in the first position Mk draws attention to the fact that the emphasis is not on 'time' and 'kingdom of God' but rather on the verbs πεπλήρωται and ἤγγικεν [107].

3. The two elements that constitute the core of the proclamation (ἤγγικεν ἡ βασιλεία τοῦ θεοῦ. μετανοεῖτε) were already linked together in the pre-Marcan tradition (cf. Mt 3,2; 4,17) although in Mk 1,15 the order is reversed. Among these two elements, the proclamation of the kingdom is more characteristic of Jesus than the summons to repentance. For, on the one hand, the expression 'the kingdom of God' is not a key theme in the OT and in the intertestamental writings, except in Daniel, and, on the other hand, it is the key message of Jesus found almost exclusively in Jesus' own sayings and discourses. In contrast, the call to repentance is frequent in the OT, especially in the prophets. In the NT the preaching of repentance is more characteristic of John (cf. Mk 1,4; Lk 3,3.8; Acts 13,24; 19,4) than of Jesus; moreover, the early Church does not present Jesus as the preacher of repentance, on the contrary, repentance is preached in his name (cf. Lk 24,47; Acts 2,38; 5,31; etc.).

4. The kingdom of God, the innermost core of the proclamation, is original to Jesus. The originality may be viewed from two angles: the originality is probably derived from his filial experience of the Father, the abba-experience [108], but Jesus' own sovereignty and lordship are founded not so much on his filial experience as on his Resurrection (cf. Rom 1,4; Phil 2,10-11, etc.).

---

[106] Differ Mt (cf. 3,15; 4,4.7.10) and Lk (2,49; 4,4.8.12).

[107] A valid observation by ZERWICK (*Markus-Stil*, 102) and later repeated by others (MUBNER, "Gottesherrschaft", 90; REPLOH, *Markus-Lehrer*, 20; AMBROZIC, *Hidden Kingdom*, 7).

[108] CAMPONOVO, *Reich Gottes*, 445: "Seine Originalität liegt meines Erachtens darin, dass er das Symbol von seiner Erfahrung Gottes her angeht. Gott ist für Jesus abba, Vater—und das prägt Gottes Herrschaft".

II. The Call of the First Four Disciples (1,16-20)

A. Literary Analysis

1. *Synoptic Comparison*

a. *Mk 1,16-20 and Mt 4,18-22*

Compared to the Marcan parallel, Mt 4,18-22 is secondary as the vocabulary, style and the attempt to improve upon the Marcan text indicate. The Marcan παράγων is replaced with περιπατῶν in Mt 4,18a. The replacement of καί with δέ (4.18.20.22), ὀλίγον with ἐκεῖθεν (4,21), εὐθύς with εὐθέως and ἀμφιβάλλοντας with βάλλοντας ἀμφίβληστρον (4,18) and the insertion of δύο ἀδελφούς (4,18), ἄλλους δύο ἀδελφούς (4,21) and τὸν λεγόμενον Πέτρον (4,18) are to be attributed to the Matthean hand [109]. The use of the personal pronoun αὐτοῦ (4,18) instead of repeating the proper name Σίμωνος (Mk 1,16), improvement upon the Marcan Greek by the omission of αὐτούς in 4,21 and the attempt to make the narrative more coherent and logical [110] are indications of Mt's endeavour to improve upon the Marcan text.

---

[109]

	Mt	Mk	Lk	Jn	Acts	Paul	Rest		Total
ἀκολουθεῖν	25	18	17	19	4	1	6	=	90
ἀφιέναι	47	34	31	14	3	5	8	=	142
Γαλιλαία	16	12	13	17	3	0	0	=	61
δύο	40	19	28	13	14	10	12	=	136
ἐκεῖθεν	12	5	3	2	4	0	1	=	27
εὐθέως	11	0	6	3	9	1	3	=	33
εὐθύς adj.	1	1	2	0	3	1	0	=	8
εὐθύς adv.	7	42	1	3	1	0	0	=	54
θάλασσα	16	19	3	9	10	4	30	=	91
καλεῖν	26	4	43	2	18	33	22	=	148
ποιεῖν	84	47	88	110	68	82	86	=	565

[110] Without giving any notice in 1,19 that the father of James and John was also in the boat, Mk states in 1,20: "They left their father Zebedee in the boat . . . and followed him". Mt overcomes this incoherence by anticipating the presence of Zebedee, their father, with them in 4,21. By the transposition of εὐθέως from 4,21 to 4,22 and by changing the Marcan ἀπῆλθον ὀπίσω into ἠκολούθησαν the prompt response in 4,22 is made identical with that in 4,20.

b. *Mk 1,16-20 and Lk 5,10-11*

Unlike Mk, Lk's narration of Jesus' encounter with the first three disciples is preceded by a rather long ministry (4,14-44). The encounter takes place in the setting of a miraculous event in which Peter experiences the divine in Jesus (5,8-9) as in a theophanic scene (cf. Ex 33,20; Is 6,5). Jesus dispels Peter's fear and offers a totally new orientation to him: "Henceforth you will be catching men" (5,10b). Peter and his companions, James and John who also had experienced the event, left everything and followed Jesus.

The core of the narrative (5,10b: μὴ φοβοῦ· ἀπὸ τοῦ νῦν ἀνθρώπους ἔσῃ ζωγρῶν), to a great extent redactional [111], is a call to mission. This call is founded not only on Jesus' authoritative word as in Mk 1,17 but on his word and deed. The call is effective not only in the missionary task of Peter in the post-Easter Church but also in the pre-Easter ministry [112]. In fact, it commences from the very moment of the call (ἀπὸ τοῦ νῦν).

2. *Tradition and Redaction*

In 1,16 παρὰ τὴν θάλασσαν τῆς Γαλιλαίας is redactional because compound verbs followed by the same preposition are typical of Mk [113] and θάλασσα and Γαλιλαία are characteristically Marcan terms [114]. Possibly εὐθύς in 1,18.20 is from the Marcan hand to emphasize the promptness in following Jesus in the former and the suddenness of the call in the latter. The rest is in all probability from tradition.

The main reason why the rest is considered to be from tradition is the occurrence of hapax legomena spread out in 1,16b-20: ἀμφίβαλλειν, καταρτί-ζειν, προβαίνειν, δεῦτε ὀπίσω and μισθωτός [115]. A corroborative factor is that the nouns ἁλιεύς (1,16.17) and δίκτυον (1,18.19) occur nowhere else in Mk. The adverb ὀλίγον is found only twice in the second Gospel. It should

---

[111] μὴ φοβοῦ ..... Mt 0, Mk 1, Lk 5
ἀπὸ τοῦ νῦν .. Mt 0, Mk 0, Lk 5

[112] SCHÜRMANN, *Lukas* I, 264: "Das Hauptinteresse gilt dem Bemühen, die Primatialgewalt und apostolische Sendung im vorösterlichen Willen Jesu zu begründen".

[113] NEIRYNCK, (*Duality*, 75) notes 63 instances of compound verbs followed by the same preposition in Mk. Same as in Mk: Mt 17 instances and Lk 15; no parallel: Mt 24 and Lk 35; modified : Mt 22 and Lk 13.

[114] Cf. n. 109 above.

[115] The first (ἀμφιβάλλειν) hapax in the NT and the rest hapax in Mk.

be noted that semitic features are perceptible in 1,16-20 [116]. A negative support for our opinion is that no typical Marcan term except εὐθύς as noted above occurs in 1,16b-20.

3. *Literary Structure*

Mk 1,16-20 consists of a doublet: the call of Simon and of his brother Andrew (1,16-18) and the call of James and of his brother John (1,19-20). Both units have an identical structure.

The narrative begins with a movement of Jesus, expressed by a participle (1,16a: παράγων, 1,19a: προβάς), along the Sea of Galilee. Jesus sees (aorist indicative: εἶδεν) Simon and his brother Andrew (1,16a) and James and his brother John (1,19a). They were engaged in activities pertaining to their daily occupation, indicated by present participle (1,16b: ἀμφιβάλλοντας, 1,19b: καταρτίζοντας). He calls them with the verb in the aorist indicative (1,17: εἶπεν, 1,20a: ἐκάλεσεν). On hearing the call they promptly responded: leaving their day-to-day task (and father), expressed by the aorist participle ἀφέντες (1,18.20b), they followed Jesus — verb in aorist indicative: ἠκολούθησαν (1,18), ἀπῆλθον ὀπίσω (1,20b).

Based on these literary indications the literary structure of 1,16-18 and 1,19-20 may be delineated as follows:

16 A   Καὶ παράγων παρὰ τὴν θάλασσαν τῆς Γαλιλαίας εἶδεν Σίμωνα καὶ Ἀνδρέαν τὸν ἀδελφὸν Σίμωνος

    B   ἀμφιβάλλοντας ἐν τῇ θαλάσσῃ· ἦσαν γάρ ἁλιεῖς.

17   C καὶ εἶπεν αὐτοῖς ὁ Ἰησοῦς, Δεῦτε ὀπίω μου, καὶ ποιήσω ὑμᾶς γενέσθαι ἁλιεῖς ἀνθρώπων.

18   B' καὶ εὐθὺς ἀφέντες τὰ δίκτυα

    A' ἠκολούθησαν αὐτῷ.

---

[116] Semitism is more frequent in traditional material than in redactional. Imperative + καί + future in 1,17 is due to semitic influence (cf. K. BEYER, *Semitische Syntax*, 252). The use of θάλασσα in the sense of λίμνη is possibly semitic (cf. CRANFIELD, 69; LAGRANGE, 18). Possibly δεῦτε ὀπίσω μου is also semitic in origin (cf. AERTS, *À la suite de Jésus*, 38).

19 A   Καὶ προβὰς ὀλίγον εἶδεν Ἰάκωβον τὸν τοῦ Ζεβεδαίου καὶ
        Ἰωάννην τὸν ἀδελφὸν αὐτοῦ,

   B   καὶ αὐτοὺς ἐν τῷ πλοίῳ καταρτίζοντας τὰ δίκτυα,

20   C καὶ εὐθὺς ἐκάλεσεν αὐτούς.

   B'   καὶ ἀφέντες τὸν πατέρα αὐτῶν Ζεβεδαῖον ἐν τῷ πλοίῳ μετὰ
        τῶν μισθωτῶν

   A'   ἀπῆλθον ὀπίσω αὐτοῦ.

Thus there is a movement of Jesus towards the would-be disciples whom
he sees (A) to which corresponds their movement towards him by following
him (A'). They are engaged in their daily occupation (B) which they abandon
(B'). At the core of this concentric structure stands Jesus' call of his disciples
(C) [117].

B. Interpretation

1. *Jesus' Initiative (1,16a.19a)*

Generally at the beginning of the call narratives there is a movement
of the one who calls towards the one being called [118]. This initial movement
is conveyed by παράγων in 1,16a and προβάς in 1,19a. The verb παράγειν
(Mt 3, Mk 3 Lk 0) is used by Mk only intransitively and in the participial
form: twice in reference to Jesus (1,16; 2,14) and once in reference to Simon
of Cyrene (15,21). In 1,16 and 2,14 Jesus passes by in view of calling men
to discipleship. In 15,21 Simon of Cyrene, a passerby, figuratively fulfils the
function of a disciple (cf. 8,34). Hence there is a link between παράγειν and
discipleship in Mk. Likewise the verb προβαίνειν is used by Mk only in the
context of discipleship (1,19).

---

[117] Our structure drastically differs from that proposed by FABRIS (*Matteo*, 94), PESCH
("Berufung", 9) and A. SCHULZ (*Nachfolgen*, 98-99) consisting of three parts: encounter, call
and response.

[118] In the case of Moses and Gideon an angel of the Lord appeared (Ex 3,2; Judg 6,11).
The Lord came to Jeremiah (1,4) and Elijah passed by Elisha (1 Kings 19,19), etc.

In general θάλασσα has two (almost contrary) symbolic meanings: a hostile element and a primal element or mother symbol [119]. In Mk the term, θάλασσα, has various nuances. In 2,13; 3,7-10; 4,1-2 it is a place of veiled revelation. In 4,35-41 and 6,45-52 Jesus subdues the hostile sea in his disciples' presence whereby he manifests himself to them [120]. In 5,1.21; 7,31 where Jesus is in transit, θάλασσα seems to function as a bridge between Jewish and Gentile territory. In the light of the disciples' function as fishers of men in 1,17 the Sea of Galilee in our verse seems to have two interrelated symbolic nuances: (1) discipleship is born at the Lake of Galilee (mother symbol), (2) to fish for men from the whole world (hence it stands for the world or nations) [121].

The key event in 1,16a is Jesus' seeing (εἶδεν). In Mk the verb ὁράω is predicated of Jesus 13 times. Of these, in four instances (1,10.16.19; 2,14) he employs the construction: aorist indicative + accusative with the present participle and once (6,48) aorist participle + accusative with the present participle. Except in the first instance (1,10), the object of Jesus' seeing is either the would-be disciples (1,16.19; 2,14) or those already constituted as disciples (6,48). It is not two brothers in their blood relationship as in Mt 4,18.21 that Jesus perceives but the two as persons, Simon and Andrew, James and John. Hence the Marcan narration is more personal. Again, it is not stated that they saw Jesus, or that they and Jesus saw each other; instead, he (and only he) saw them. Therefore the whole initiative is on the part of Jesus. Furthermore, Jesus' seeing is accompanied by his effective word by virtue of which the disciples cease to be in the same situation in which Jesus found them.

2. Context of Daily Task (1,16b.19b)

Jesus encounters his would-be disciples while they were engaged in activities connected with their occupation, fishing. The first two were casting their nets whereas the other two were mending their nets. This setting corresponds to the OT call narratives where those who were being called were usually encountered while they were performing their daily tasks [122].

---

[119] Cf. GOODENOUGH, Symbols VIII, 105; HILGERT, Symbols, 43-47.

[120] Cf. HEIL, Jesus Walking, 127-129.

[121] Cf. HILGERT, Symbols, 73; PESCH, "Berufung", 27; SCHREIBER, Theologie, 171-174. On p. 47-49 HILGERT observes that in the apocalyptic literature there are instances where 'sea' means nations.

[122] Moses was keeping watch over the flock of his father-in-law (Ex 3,1). Gideon was beating out wheat in the wine press (Judg 6,11) and Elisha was ploughing (1 Kings 19,19), etc.

The twin activities, casting nets and mending them, possibly have a veiled symbolic meaning in Mk. There are four pericopes in the NT where the disciples' activity of fishing is mentioned: Mk 1,16-20; Mt 4,18-22; Lk 5,1-11; Jn 21,1-14. They contain common literary features. First, those engaged in fishing are the disciples. Second, in the NT the nouns δίκτυον and ἁλιεύς and the verb ἁλιεύειν occur only in these four pericopes. Third, the expression, casting nets, also occurs in all the four (Mk 1,16; Mt 4,18; Lk 5,4.5; Jn 21,6). Fourth, the new task entrusted to these fishermen as fishers of men is found in Mk 1,17; Mt 4,19; Lk 5,10. But in Lk 5,1-11 and Jn 21,1-14 the metaphor, fishing, signifies the missionary activities of the apostles [123]. If in Lk and Jn the disciples' fishing means their missionary endeavour, the same meaning can be implied in a latent form in Mk and Mt too because in Mk 1,17 and in Mt 4,19 they are called to be fishers of men.

3. *The Call (1,17.20a)*

The call in 1,17 is composed of an introductory formula (καὶ εἶπεν αὐτοῖς ὁ 'Ιησοῦς) and the call proper (Δεῦτε ὀπίσω μου, καὶ ποιήσω ὑμᾶς γενέσθαι ἁλιεῖς ἀνθρώπων). The importance of the call is evident from the fact that 1,17 and 1,20a occupy the central position in the concentric structure respectively of 1,16-18 and 1,19-20. The emphatic use of ὁ 'Ιησοῦς in 1,17 shows the importance of the saying in this verse. Mk often employs καὶ εἶπεν αὐτοῖς ὁ 'Ιησοῦς or similar phrases to introduce a saying of Jesus [124]. The content consists of a present imperative (δεῦτε ὀπίσω μου) and a future indicative (καὶ ποιήσω ὑμᾶς γενέσθαι ἁλιεῖς ἀνθρώπων).

In the OT call-narratives the person who calls is ultimately God [125]. Generally the call is preceded by a brief dialogue between the one who calls and the one being called so that a familiarity is created between them (cf. Ex 3,4-5; Judg 6,12-13, etc.). However, in Mk 1,17 Jesus on his own authority, without a word of introduction, summons totally strange fishermen to be his disciples with a command: Δεῦτε ὀπίσω μου.

In Mk δεῦτε (δεῦρο + ἴτε) is rarely used: of the three occurrences once it is followed by an imperative (6,31), once by a subjunctive (12,7) and once by ὀπίσω μου (1,17). The adverb ὀπίσω occurs once as adverb of place

---

[123] Cf. BARRETT, *John*, 581; MARSHALL, *Luke*, 200; PANIMOLLE, *Giovanni* III, 483-484; SCHÜRMANN, *Lukas* I, 265.

[124] Cf. 1,25.38.44; 2,5.8.10.17.19.25.27; 3,4.23.33; 4,2.11.13.21.26.30, etc.

[125] Cf. HENGEL, *Charismatic Leader*, 17, 73; LÉON-DUFOUR, *Résurrection*, 114.

(13,16) and five times as an improper preposition (with the genitive): once of time (1,7) and four times of place (1,17.20; 8,33.34). All these four instances, expressing spatial nearness to (1,17.20; 8,34) or distance from (8,33) Jesus, signify their personal relation to Jesus [126]. The first two appear in the context of the call to discipleship: the call to follow Jesus (1,17) and the response to the call by following him (1,20). The last two (8,33.34) are found in a context where the absolute necessity of suffering, whether for the Messiah or for his disciples, is stressed most emphatically. Hence there is a relation between the two contexts: following Jesus (1,17.20) inevitably leads to suffering (8,34).

It is instructive to note that the call to follow Jesus is placed at the beginning of the first part of Mk and the emphatic statement on the necessity of suffering for the disciples at the beginning of the second part. As the disciples continue to follow Jesus uninterruptedly from the moment of their call so they also constantly fail to assimilate the necessity of suffering right through the second part. Thus the theme of 'following after' Jesus and the theme of the necessity of suffering for a disciple, initiated respectively in 1,16-20 and 8,34, are progressively developed in the second Gospel [127].

Summing up, δεῦτε ὀπίσω μου (used only at 1,17 in Mk) is at the surface level a spatial category; but at the deeper level, it signifies a personal relation to Jesus, a call to be his disciples. The call is founded exclusively on Jesus' authority, the Messianic authority, and the efficacy of his call is manifested in the promptness with which they follow him.

The conjunction καί, the link between 1,17b and 1,17c, is most probably to be understood as consecutive or final. The consecutive καί "is especially frequent after imperatives" [128]. Hence the indicative (1,17c) explicates the purpose of the call in 1,17b. The construction in 1,17c, ποιεῖν followed by the accusative with infinitive, means 'to cause someone to do something'.

---

[126] As observed in Ch II, Mk employs spatial categories to denote personal relationships to Jesus. The flight of the disciples (14,50), Peter's following Jesus at a distance (14,54) leading to the denial (14,66-72) are also spatial categories implying a rupture of discipleship.

[127] Note the parallelism between 1,16-20 and 8,34:

1,16-20	8,34
καλεῖν	προσκαλεῖσθαι
εἶπεν αὐτοῖς	εἶπεν αὐτοῖς
δεῦτε ὀπίσω μου	εἴ τις θέλει ὀπίσω μου ἀκολουθεῖν
ἠκολούθησαν αὐτῷ	ἀκολουθείτω μοι
names of four disciples	τοῖς μαθηταῖς αὐτοῦ

[128] BLASS-DEBRUNNER, *Grammar*, § 442 (2); ZERWICK, *Biblical Greek*, § 455.

Thus Mk 1,17c strongly emphasizes that becoming fishers of men is not an achievement of the disciples but wholly a task of Jesus.

Compared with the rest of the NT, the verb ποιεῖν is not so frequent in Mk [129]. It is predicated of Jesus in the following contexts: (a) Jesus' miracles (3,8; 5,20; 6,5; 7,37; 10,51); (b) the request of James and John (10,35.36); (c) the questioning of Jesus' authority (11,28.29. 33); (d) the question of Pilate to the crowd (15,14); (e) the institution of the apostles (1,17; 3,14.16). In each context ποιεῖν explicitly or implicitly refers to Jesus' authority.

The clause, καὶ ποιήσω ὑμᾶς γενέσθαι ἁλιεῖς ἀνθρώπων, may be considered a promise which is being fulfilled in 3,13-16 and 6,7-13.30. The future ποιήσω is realized in the aorist ἐποίησεν in 3,14.16 and the metaphor, 'become fishers of men' in the mission of the Twelve (cf. 3,14c-15; 6,7-13.30). The metaphor, fishermen, in the OT (Jer 16,16; Ezek 47,10; cf. Amos 4,2; Hab 1,14-15) and in Qumran (1 QH 3,26; CD 4,15-16, etc.) had a negative colouring, viz., it referred to God's punitive eschatological judgment. In the Greek diatribe too this metaphor had a predominantly negative ring [130]. In Mk 1,17, however, it acquires a positive significance in a soteriological perspective. Here the object of fishing is men [131] (ἁλιεῖς ἀνθρώπων which has a universalistic nuance) and, as noted before, 'sea' stands for the world. In other words, this metaphor symbolizes the missionary activity of the apostles who after being with Jesus are sent out in his name and with his authority to carry on his own mission (3,13-16; 6,7-13.30) [132].

To conclude, the indicative (1,17c: "I will make you become fishers of men") spells out the scope of the call in 1,17b. The disciples' becoming fishers of men is not their own achievement but a task of

---

[129] Cf. n. 109 above.

[130] Cf. HAENCHEN, 81, n. 9; HENGEL, *Charismatic Leader*, 77-78, n. 151; KLOSTERMANN, 10-11.

[131] As in Judaism 'fish' symbolized the Messiah and 'little fishes' the faithful, so also in early Christian tradition 'fish' meant Christ and 'fishes' Christians.

[132] The metaphor 'fishers of men' is interpreted in two ways. (1) Eschatological perspective: C.W.F. SMITH ("Fishers of Men", 187-203) with the background of Jer 16,16; Amos 4,2; Hab 1,14-15 and Qumran argues that by this metaphor Jesus commands the apostles to bring the people to judgment. AGNEW ("Vocatio", 141-143) concurs with C.W.F. SMITH and adduces Mt 13,47-50 for further support. (2) Majority of the authors opt for an interpretation in soteriological perspective as we have done. Cf. HENGEL, *Charismatic Leader*, 76-80; MÁNEK, "Fishers of Men", 138-141; PESCH, "Berufung", 13, 15-16, 21-22; WUELLNER, *Fishers of Men*, 121-123, 135, 146-173, 211-212, 223-231.

Jesus himself. And this task is realized in the appointment and the mission of the Twelve [133].

In 1,20a the call of James and John is narrated in indirect discourse. The key word in verse 20a is ἐκάλεσεν. Although καλεῖν is infrequent in Mk [134], another picture emerges when the agent of calling is considered. In the Gospels Jesus is the subject of καλεῖν as follows: Mt 2 (4,21; 9,13) Mk 2 (1,20; 2,17), Lk 1 (5,32), Jn 0. Mk and Mt use καλεῖν in the absolute sense only in these references. The absolute use is most probably a technical term (frequent in Paul) to signify God's offer of salvation [135]. Mk's absolute use of καλεῖν is intentional to underscore the fundamental call of Jesus to discipleship.

4. Leaving Daily Task and Father (1,18a.20b)

The verb ἀφιέναι occurs predominantly in the Gospels and it is comparatively more frequent in Mk [136]. It has a wide spectrum of usage in the second Gospel, various ways and different shades of meanings: (1) In the sense of let go, send away, with a personal object (4,36; 8,13) and an impersonal object (15,37). (2) In certain instances it means to remit, forgive with an impersonal object, sins (2,5.7.9.10). (3) It also means to leave with a personal object in 1,20.31; 12,12; 14,50 and with an impersonal object in 10,28.29; 13,34. (4) To let, let go, tolerate (with an accusative object) in 5,19; 11,6; 14,6 and allow, permit (with accusative and infinitive) in 1,34; 7,12.27; 10,14.

As regards to discipleship ἀφιέναι is used with personal objects (1,20) and impersonal objects, viz., material possessions (1,18; 10,28.29). The syntax of 1,18a (καὶ εὐθὺς ἀφέντες ... ἠκολούθησαν αὐτῷ) and 1,20b (καὶ ἀφέντες τὸν πατέρα ... ἀπῆλθον ὀπίσω αὐτοῦ) implies that leaving property and father is logically (possibly also chronologically) prior to following Jesus. This is evident also from the narrative about the rich young man (cf. 10,21-

---

[133] KLEIN ("Berufung", 12-13) states that in Mk it is not clear when the disciples were made fishers of men. We have shown that the promise 'I will make you become fishers of men' is realized in the making and the mission of the Twelve (3,13-16; 6,7-13.30). Note also the literary affinity between 1,16-20; 3,13-16; and 6,7-13.30.

[134] Cf. n. 109 above.

[135] Cf. Rom 8,30; 1 Cor 1,9; Gal 1,6.15; 1 Thess 2,12; 5,24; 2 Thess 2,14.

SCHMIDT (*TDNT* III, 489-490) traces the origin of the absolute use of καλεῖν in NT to Dt-Is where the verb is employed for the relation between God and Israel.

[136] Cf. n. 109 above.

22) and from Peter's comment: "Lo, we have left everything and followed you" (10,28).

Compared with 1,18a there is a progression in 1,20b, for James and John leave not only their property but also their father: the root of one's existence for a Jew in his socio-cultural milieu [137]. Leaving father implies forsaking also other family ties (cf. 10,29). By leaving property and forsaking family ties those called are enabled to make a more radical and intimately personal commitment to Jesus.

In brief, abandoning material possessions and relinquishing family ties constitute a step towards the key event, the following after Jesus. This renunciation derives its meaning and purpose from a totally free and radical commitment to Jesus (cf. 10,29-30).

5. *Following Jesus (1,18b.20c)*

Jesus' call to follow him receives an immediate response from his would-be disciples [138]. Contrary to one's spontaneous expectation, the characteristic feature by which the relation between Jesus and his μαθηταί is distinguished, is neither the cognate verb μανθάνειν nor the abstract substantives derived from the same root [139] but the phrase 'to follow after' Jesus. Again, the emphasis is not on the abstract idea but on the concrete action of following after Jesus [140].

In the OT 'follow after' הָלַךְ אַחֲרֵי and its synonyms are used in three contexts [141]. (1) A human being follows after another human being: warriors-general (1 Sam 17,13-14; 25,13), partisans-leader (Ex 23,2), wife-husband (Gen 24,5.8.61; Ruth 3,10; Jer 2,2), disciple-master (1 Kings 19,20-21), etc. (2) It is a technical term for apostasy into heathenism (Deut 4,3; 6,14; Judg 4,12; Jer 11,10, etc.). (3) Follow Yahweh (Deut 1,36; 13,4, etc.) or walk the

---

[137] Cf. HENGEL, *Charismatic Leader*, 13-15, 33.

[138] Not only that there is no dialogue between Jesus and his would-be disciples but also there is no objection (cf. Ex 3,11; 1 Kings 19,20; Jer 1,6; Judg 6,15-16, etc.) or an assuring sign (cf. Ex 3,12; Jer 1,7-10; Judg 6,17-21, etc.).

[139] Both μαθητής and μανθάνειν are derived from the same root μάθ. The abstract nouns derived from the same root do not occur in NT at all: μάθη, μάθημα, μάθησις, μαθημοσύνη, μαθητεία, κτλ.

[140] The abstract nouns ἀκολούθησις, ἀκολουθυία, and παρακολούθησις do not occur in NT at all.

[141] For a detailed study of הָלַךְ אַחֲרֵי and synonyms and their significance, cf. HELFMEYER, *Die Nachfolge Gottes*, 6-63, 152-222.

way of the Lord (Deut 13,5; Ps 86,11, etc.) is employed to connote observance of the law and faithfulness to the covenant. Its use in Qumran also
does not break new ground except that there is a stress on following the
community and an accent on imitation [142].

In the NT ἀκολουθεῖν (a verb that occurs predominantly in the Gospels) [143] is used in the sense: (1) to go after or follow those who go before
(Mk 11,9; 14,13); (2) to accompany, go along with (Mt 8,1.10; 12,15; 14,13;
19,2, etc.) and (3) the figurative use to mean discipleship. The latter occurs
primarily in the call-narratives (Mk 1,16-20 par.; 2,14 par.) and in the sayings
on discipleship (Mk 8,34 par.; 10,28 par.; Lk 9,59.61 par.).

The most frequently used phrase to denote discipleship is ἀκολουθεῖν
with the dative [144]. Other expressions signifying discipleship are: ἀπέρχεσθαι
ὀπίσω (Mk 1,20), ἀκολουθεῖν ὀπίσω μου (Mk 8,34; Mt 10,38), δεῦτε ὀπίσω
μου (Mk 1,17 par.), ὕπαγε ὀπίσω μου (Mk 8,33 par.), συνακολουθεῖν (Mk
5,37; 14,51; Lk 23,49), and ἔρχεσθαι ὀπίσω (Lk 9,23; 14,27).

The disciples' following of Jesus is more strongly emphasized in Mk
than in the first and the third Gospels. The mention of their following Jesus
is more frequent in Mk (Mt 17, Mk 18, Lk 15) whereas the crowds' following
him is less frequent (Mt 8, Mk 3, Lk 5). According to Mk only the disciples
and those positively disposed to him (at least not opposed to him) follow
him. Others express no inclination to follow him (in contrast cf. Mt 8,19).
Unlike the first evangelist Mk never mentions that Jesus follows anybody [145].

Mk 1,18b (ἠκολούθησαν αὐτῷ) is the prompt response to Jesus'
summons in 1,17b (δεῦτε ὀπίσω μου) and ἀπῆλθον ὀπίσω αὐτοῦ in 1,20c is
the answer to Jesus' call in 1,20a (ἐκάλεσεν). Following Jesus implies a free
self-commitment, a personal attachment to Jesus which shapes the whole life
of his μαθηταί. This personal attachment to Jesus extends not only to the
exterior aspects of the disciples' life but also to the inner core of their life:
it is indeed a participation even in his destiny (8,34).

To sum up, the figurative use of the expression to 'follow after' meaning
discipleship is without parallel both in OT and in Qumran. The expression
ἠκολούθησαν αὐτῷ in 1,18b and the synonym, ἀπῆλθον ὀπίσω αὐτοῦ (the
sole occurrence in the NT), in 1,20c are on the surface level spatial categories.
But at the deeper level they denote free self-commitment of the four men to

---

[142] Cf. HELFMEYER, "'Gott Nachfolgen' in den Qumrantexten", 81-104.
[143] Cf. n. 109 above.
[144] Cf. AERTS, À la suite de Jésus, 16.
[145] Compare Mt 9,19 with the par. in Mk 5,24

Jesus as his disciples [146]. As the call is founded on Jesus' Messianic authority, so also the free response is oriented to the person of Jesus, the Messiah, and by implication in his mission and destiny too.

C. Concluding Remarks

1. Compared to the synoptic parallels the Marcan narration of the call of the first four disciples is primary, to a great extent pre-Marcan. It is stereotypic and woodcut in form and patterned on the call of Elisha by Elijah (1 Kings 19,19-21). According to Mk, Jesus calls totally strange men to discipleship. By placing the call to discipleship in the context of a miraculous catch of fish, Lk, however, tones down the radicality so conspicuous in Mk.

2. As our analysis has shown, the whole initiative in calling the four fishermen to discipleship is from Jesus. Jesus' words are so powerful and efficacious that man has no way but to obey. Their response to Jesus' call is radical and personal. Leaving their boats and nets implies a total renunciation of all material possessions; and leaving their father, the root of one's familial and personal existence, accents the free commitment of themselves to Jesus [147]. This sudden and radical commitment may by interpreted as genuine faith: "Vera fides non habet intervallum: statim audit, statim credit, statim sequitur, statim piscator efficitur" [148].

3. Jesus calls men to discipleship on his own authority just as in the OT Yahweh summons men to specific tasks in salvation-history [149]. The basis of this authoritative call is rooted in the awareness of his Messianic mission. Likewise, the meaning and purpose of total renunciation and unconditional commitment to Jesus become transparent only in the light of Jesus' Messianic

---

[146] NEUHÄUSLER, *Anspruch*, 186: "Der Jünger erfährt nur in der Bindung an Jesus den Heilsplan Gottes. Diese Verbindung drückt das Evangelium mit dem Wort 'Nachfolge' aus".

[147] The invitation from Jesus in contrast to the disciples choosing their master, and their self-commitment to Jesus in contrast to dedication to the study of Thorah or philosophy are two fundamental differences distinguishing Jesus' disciples from those in rabbinate and Hellenism.

[148] HIERONYMUS, 462.

[149] M. SMITH, *Tannaitic Parallels*, 152-157, notes that Jesus uses expressions typical of Yahweh in OT.

authority. It is this Messianic authority and mission that distinguish his disciples from the followers of the Zealot movement [150].

4. Unlike the OT call-narratives and differing from Mk 2,14 and 10,17-22, in 1,16-20 not individuals but Simon and his brother Andrew, James and his brother John are called to discipleship. Hence 1,16-20 is a narration not of vocation but of con-vocation to discipleship. A natural brotherhood gave birth to a Christian brotherhood.

5. In 1,16-20 one can distinguish a call to follow after Jesus and a call to be fishers of men. The former is realized from the moment of the call and the latter from the constitution and mission of the apostles. The second point is aptly expressed by Jerome: "Felix piscationis mutatio: piscatur eos Iesus, ut ipsi piscentur alios piscatores. Ipsi primum pisces efficiuntur, ut piscentur a Xpisto [= Christo], postea ipsi alios piscaturi" [151].

---

[150] In the Zealot movement also 'follow after' demanded an unconditional ultimacy: renunciation of possessions and family, and even the risk of one's own life. But unlike Zealot leaders, (1) Jesus never placed himself at the head of a crowd, (2) his eschatological struggle was against demonic powers and sickness, (3) he excluded any form of violence, (4) and he associated himself with pariahs (tax gatherers, prostitutes, sinners, etc.) whom Zealots hated.

It is no accident that ζῆλος and ζηλοῦν do not occur in the Synoptic Gospels.

[151] HIERONYMUS, 462.

CHAPTER FIVE

MANIFESTATION OF JESUS' MESSIANIC AUTHORITY AND POPULAR ACCEPTANCE (1,21-45)

I. Jesus' Authority in Teaching and Exorcism (1,21-28)

A. Literary Analysis

1. *Text-Critical Problems*

In this pericope there is only one textual problem [1] that has to be clarified: Was the participle εἰσελθών in 1,21 accidentally omitted? Or was it inserted to ameliorate a seemingly awkward construction?

Mk 1,21 has the following variant readings:

1) εἰσελθὼν εἰς τὴν συναγωγὴν ἐδίδασκεν (A B W *al.*)
2) εἰσελθὼν εἰς τὴν συναγωγὴν ἐδίδασκεν αὐτούς (D Θ *al.*)
3) εἰσελθὼν ἐδίδασκεν εἰς τὴν συναγωγήν (33)
4) ἐδίδασκεν εἰς τὴν συναγωγήν (ℵ L *al.*)
5) ἐδίδασκεν εἰς τὴν συναγωγὴν αὐτῶν (892 (syrᵖ) *al.*)

---

[1] Another minor textual problem concerns verse 27. Among the welter of variant readings in 1,27 which variant should be preferred? The reading preserved in ℵ B L 33 accounts best "for the rise of others. Its abruptness invited modifications, and more than one copyist accommodated the phraseology in one way or another to the parallel in Lk 4,36" (METZGER, *Commentary*, 75) and made the three clauses into one. In fact, Mk is fond of such triple co-ordinate clauses (cf. 1,24; 2,7; 14,64; 16,6). Some critical editions (TREGELLES, WESTCOTT-HORT, etc.) and commentaries (SWETE, TAYLOR, etc.) punctuate the text as follows: τί ἐστιν τοῦτο; διδαχὴ καινή· κατ' ἐξουσίαν. But in view of 1,22 it is preferable to take κατ' ἐξουσίαν with διδαχὴ καινή.

Among these five variants, attempts at improvement on the original text are obvious in three: the addition of αὐτούς in the second variant and αὐτῶν in the fifth and the transposition of ἐδίδασκεν in the third are obviously geared to clarity. However, a choice between the remaining two readings, the first and the fourth, is not easy; critical editions and authors are almost equally divided [2]. Yet, one should note that the use of compound verbs followed by the same preposition is a typical stylistic feature of Mk [3] and there is a predominant weight of external evidence (A B D W Θ *al.*) for εἰσελθών. Therefore, it is highly probable that εἰσελθών was accidentally omitted in copying because of the following εἰς and ἐδίδασκεν was transposed before εἰς τὴν συναγωγήν.

2. Synoptic Comparison

a. Mk 1,22 and Mt 7,28b-29

Although Mt 7,28b-29 is a word for word reproduction of Mk 1,22 (except for the addition of οἱ ὄχλοι as subject of the impersonal verb ἐξεπλήσσοντο and the personal pronoun αὐτῶν after οἱ γραμματεῖς), both differ in context, purpose and content [4]. Mt 7,28b-29 is the conclusion of Jesus' instruction to his disciples in which he authoritatively interprets God's will, not by appealing to the authority of the tradition as was the practice among the scribes, but founded on his personal conviction and consciousness that he has come to reveal God's final and definitive will (cf. 5,17) [5]. Thus, according to Mt, Jesus teaches a new law, but unlike the scribes he teaches it with authority both personal and original. Moreover, the first evangelist, writing to a Jewish-Christian community, has a polemic aim in contrasting Jesus' teaching to that of the scribes [6].

---

[2] GNT/NESTLE-ALAND, MERK, TASKER, VOGELS and WESTCOTT-HORT and commentators such as LAGRANGE and SWETE opt for the first reading. In contrast, HUCK-GREEVEN, TISCHENDORF and VON SODEN and authors such as CRANFIELD, TAYLOR, TURNER ("Commentary", 153) choose the fourth variant.

[3] Cf. p. 104, n. 113.

[4] See our interpretation of Mk 1, 22 on p. 128-132.

[5] The antithesis, "You have heard that it was said . . . But I say to you . . . " occurs six times in Ch. 5 alone.

[6] Cf. FABRIS, *Matteo*, 187.

b. Mk 1,21-28 and Lk 4,31-37

Lk 4,31-37, a well-thought out literary unit, develops two themes: Jesus' teaching and his exorcism. Both are narrated in three successive stages, as demonstrated below, and the pericope concludes with a statement regarding the consequence of Jesus' teaching and his exorcism, namely, reports of him spread to the surrounding region:

Jesus' activity	Teaching (4,31)	Exorcism (4,33-35)
Reaction of the public	Astonishment at his teaching (4,32a)	Amazement at his word (4,36ab)
Reason for the reaction expressed by a ὅτι clause	His word was with authority (4,32b).	With authority and power he commands the unclean spirit (4,36cd).

Thus Jesus' teaching and exorcism are treated almost independently in Lk 4,31-37 whereas in Mk 1,21-28 these two activities of Jesus are more integrated as emphasized in 1,27 where the people are deeply amazed at his teaching as well as his exorcism.

Mk and, in particular, Lk link Jesus' teaching and his exorcism in the synagogue at Capernaum with the two preceding pericopes [7]. Lk deletes the Marcan favourite εὐθύς (Mk 1,21.23.28), as he does elsewhere [8], and the personal pronoun αὐτῶν after ἐν τῇ συναγωγῇ (Mk 1,23). He does not compare Jesus' teaching with that of the scribes as Mk does (1,22b). He has also considerably modified the Marcan text for clarity, difference of style, and distinctive emphasis on content. Because he uses ἐν πνεύματι for the possession of the Spirit of God [9] he substitutes ἔχων in 4,33 [10]; and φωνῇ μεγάλῃ has been brought forward from Mk 1,26 to associate it with the actual words of the man and to make the necessary modifications to Mk 1,26. Lk

---

[7] The subject of the verb εἰσπορεύονται in Mk 1,21 is obviously Jesus and the four disciples whom he had called (1,16-20). 'Galilee' in 1,28 evokes 'Galilee' in 1,14 where Jesus had commenced his ministry.

The verb κατῆλθεν in Lk 4,31 is an appropriate verb to be used for a descent from Nazareth (cf. 4,16-30) in the hills (over 1200 ft. high) to Capernaum situated at the shore (c. 686 ft. below sea level). There are literary links too between 4,31-37 and 4,14-30, in particular with the summary statement in 4,14-15.

[8] Cf. Mk 1,12 par. Lk 4,1; 1,29 par. 4,38; 1,30 par. 4,38; 2,8 par. 5,22; 2,12 par. 5,25; 3,6 par. 6,11, etc.

[9] Cf. Lk 2,27; 3,16; 4,1.14; 10,21; Acts 1,5, etc.

[10] See also 8,27; 13,11; Acts 8,7; 16,16, etc.

replaces ἐθαμβήθησαν ἅπαντες (Mk 1,27) with a characteristic periphrasis. Because συζητεῖν of Mk might suggest dissension among the audience, Lk substitutes it with συνελάλουν. To be more precise and true to the logic of the narrative he replaces ὑπακούσιν with ἐξέρχονται in 4,36. The Lucan addition, "when the demon had thrown him down in the midst . . . having done him no harm" (4,35b), indicates the immediate effect of Jesus' command ("Be silent, and come out of him" 4,35a) and it also intensifies the emotive basis for the amazement of the audience (namely, although the demon had thrown him down, he was not injured). Lk unequivocally emphasizes that both Jesus' teaching and his exorcism are effected by his word (ὁ λόγος), qualified by ἐν ἐξουσίᾳ in reference to the former and ἐν ἐξουσίᾳ καὶ δυνάμει in reference to the latter. Such a qualification of ὁ λόγος Ἰησοῦ is exclusive to this NT pericope. Again, the combination of ἐξουσία and δύναμις occurs only thrice in the Gospels: Lk 4,36; 9,1; 10,19. In 9,1 Jesus gives authority and power to the Twelve to perform exorcism and to cure diseases and in 10,19 too Jesus bestows on the seventy (seventy two) disciples authority and power to fight against evil forces. According to Lk, then, Jesus possesses authority and power which he shares with his apostles and disciples to fight against evil forces, but in 4,35-36 he himself employs the same authority and power in exorcising a man possessed by an unclean spirit.

In summation, in Lk 4,31-37 Jesus' teaching and exorcism are less integrated than in Mk 1,21-28 and the efficacy of these twin activities is attributed to Jesus' word whereas in Mk it is primarily attributed to Jesus in his capacity as the Messiah. Of these twin activities, teaching and exorcism, Mk emphasizes the former but Lk stresses the latter. In his narration of Jesus' teaching Mk deepens its intensity:

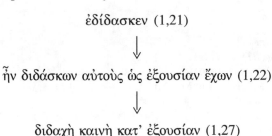

$$ἐδίδασκεν\ (1,21)$$

$$\downarrow$$

$$ἦν\ διδάσκων\ αὐτοὺς\ ὡς\ ἐξουσίαν\ ἔχων\ (1,22)$$

$$\downarrow$$

$$διδαχὴ\ καινὴ\ κατ'\ ἐξουσίαν\ (1,27)$$

On the contrary, Lk characterizes Jesus' teaching as ὁ λόγος ἐν ἐξουσίᾳ but his exorcism has an important additional element: ὁ λόγος ἐν ἐξουσίᾳ καὶ δυνάμει. Moreover, Lk does not compare Jesus' teaching with that of the scribes.

3. *Tradition and Redaction*

In 1,21 Marcan redaction is conspicuously perceptible. Compound verbs followed by the same preposition (εἰσπορεύονται εἰς . . . εἰσελθών εἰς) are characteristic of Mk [11]. Because the impersonal plural followed by the singular is a typical Marcan usage [12], there is another reason why εἰσπορεύονται . . . εἰσελθών should be reckoned redactional. Double statements, general and special (εἰσπορεύονται εἰς Καφαρναούμ . . . εἰσελθών εἰς τὴν συναγωγήν), are characteristic of the second Gospel [13]. Again, historic present (εἰσπορεύονται) is a feature frequently used by Mk [14]. Furthermore, the verbs διδάσκειν and εἰσπορεύεσθαι and the adverb εὐθύς are predominantly Marcan [15]. Although συναγωγή is not a preferential term in the second Gospel, its use is striking. A typical sabbath's ministry commences in the synagogue (1,21-23) where Jesus overcomes the representative of evil forces [16]. It is possible that he encountered evil forces in other synagogues too (cf. 1,39). According to 3,1-6, Jesus' ministry of healing at the synagogue climaxes in the plan of the Pharisees and Herodians to destroy him. And in the synagogue at his own town (6,1-2) he faces incredulity (6,3-6a). In the sayings in 12,39 and 13,9 too the opposition persists: in the former Jesus criticizes the scribes for taking the best seats in the synagogues and in the latter he foretells that his followers would be beaten up in the synagogues. From this overall picture of the use of συναγωγή what emerges is Mk's emphasis on the steadily growing opposition that Jesus faces in the synagogue [17].

Regarding Mk 1,22 the evidence for the Marcan redaction is more compelling. In Mk γάρ explanatory and periphrastic imperfect (ἦν διδά-

---

[11] Cf. p. 104, n. 113.

[12] Cf. Turner, *JTS* 26 (1925), 228-231.

[13] Neirynck (*Duality*, 96-97) mentions 28 occurrences of double statements, general and special, in Mk. Retained as in Mk: Mt 11 instances and Lk 4; no parallel: Mt 7 and Lk 14; modified: Mt 10 and Lk 10.

[14] Cf. Hawkins, *Horae Synopticae*, 143-149; Moulton-Turner, *Grammar* IV, 20; Zerwick, *Markus-Stil*, 49-57.

[15] Cf. n. 36 below.

[16] Cf. p. 132-134 below.

[17] Such an opposition to Jesus at the synagogue is lacking in Mt (4,23; 9,35) and Lk (4,15.44; 7,5; 8,41; 13,10).

[18] Cf. Pryke, *Redactional Style*, 126-135. Moulton-Turner, *Grammar* IV, 20; Turner, *JTS* 28 (1927), 349-351.

There are 26 instances of γάρ with imperfect tense in Mk. Of these Mt follows Mk in 7 instances and Lk 1; no parallel: Mt 7 and Lk 11; modifies: Mt 12 and Lk 14.

σκων) are frequently redactional [18]. Similarly, the causal use of ἐπί (ἐπί with dative) [19] and ἔχειν auxiliary [20] are characteristically Marcan. Multiplication of cognate verbs (1,21.22: ἐδίδασκεν ... ἦν διδάσκων) [21] and the repetition of the antecedent (ἐπὶ τῇ διδαχῇ αὐτοῦ cf. v. 21: ἐδίδασκεν) [22] are also typical literary devices of the second evangelist. Moreover, the verbs διδάσκειν and ἐκπλήσσειν and the nouns γραμματεύς, διδαχή and ἐξουσία are overwhelmingly Marcan [23]. The theme of Jesus' teaching has special Christological interest for Mk [24]. Finally, the connection of ἐκπλήσσειν with διδάσκειν/διδαχή is recognizable in 6,2 and there is a word for word parallel to 1,22 in 11,18 (πᾶς ὁ ὄχλος ἐξεπλήσσοντο ἐπὶ τῇ διδαχῇ αὐτοῦ).

In v. 23 by means of καὶ εὐθύς Mk connects the narrative of the man with an unclean spirit (1,23-26) with the astonishment of people at Jesus' teaching (1,22), a device the second evangelist employs also elsewhere (cf. 1,12.21b.29, etc.). To detect the redactional activity of the evangelist in v. 24 a comparison of this verse with 1 Kings 17,18 (since the former is presumably modelled on the latter) [25] and Mk 5,7 (the only close parallel in the second Gospel to 1,24) is very fruitful:

1 Kings 17,18-19	*Mk 1,24-25*	*Mk 5,7-8*
καὶ εἶπεν	καὶ ἀνέκραξεν λέγων	καὶ κράξας ... λέγει
τί ἐμοὶ καὶ σοί	τί ἡμῖν καὶ σοί	τί ἐμοὶ καὶ σοί
ἄνθρωπε τοῦ θεοῦ;	᾽Ιησοῦ Ναζαρηνέ;	᾽Ιησοῦ υἱὲ τοῦ θεοῦ τοῦ ὑψίστου;
εἰσῆλθες πρός με τοῦ ἀναμνῆσαι τὰς ἀδικίας μου	ἦλθες ἀπολέσαι ἡμᾶς;	ὁρκίζω σε τὸν θεόν, μή με βασανίσῃς
----------------------	οἶδά σε τίς εἶ	----------------------

[19] Cf. Mk 1,22; 3,5; 10,22.24; 11,18.
[20] Cf. TURNER, *JTS* 28 (1927), 357-360.
[21] NEIRYNCK (*Duality*, 77-81) notes 167 occurrences of the multiplication of cognate verbs in Mk. Retained as in Mk: Mt 50 instances and Lk 20; no parallel: Mt 22 and Lk 55; modified: Mt 95 and Lk 92.
[22] NEIRYNCK (*Duality*, 85-87) mentions 94 occurrences of the repetition of the antecedent in Mk. Retained as in Mk: Mt 25 instances and Lk 18; no parallel: Mt 13 and Lk 30; modified: Mt 56 and Lk 46.
[23] Cf. n. 36 below.
[24] See our observations on p. 126-127.
[25] Among several others see ARENS, ΗΛΘΟΝ-*Sayings*, 211; BAUERNFEIND, *Die Worte der Dämonen*, 3-10; GUILLEMETTE, "Un enseignement nouveau", 229-230; MUßNER, "Wortspiel", 285-286; PESCH, "Eine neue Lehre", 252.

	ὁ ἅγιος τοῦ θεοῦ	
καὶ εἶπεν Ηλιου	καὶ ἐπετίμησεν αὐτῷ	ἔλεγεν γὰρ αὐτῷ
πρὸς τὴν γυναῖκα	ὁ Ἰησοῦς λέγων	
----------------------	φιμώθητι	----------------------
Δός μοι τὸν	καὶ ἔξελθε ἐξ	ἔξελθε . . . ἐκ
υἱόν σου	αὐτοῦ	τοῦ ἀνθρώπου

This synopsis brings to light the redactional elements in 1,24-25. Mk 1,24a reads τί ἡμῖν καὶ σοί but the parallels have τί ἐμοὶ καὶ σοί. The singular form is most probably the original (MT: מַה־לִּי וָלָךְ = LXX: τί ἐμοὶ καὶ σοί in Judg 11,12; 1 Kings 17,18 and Mk 5,7 par. Lk 8,28) and the context requires it since the confrontation is between a man with an unclean spirit and Jesus. By substituting the plural ἡμῖν for the singular ἐμοί Mk underlines a theological motif, namely, the beginning of the confrontation between Jesus the Messiah and the realm of evil forces as portrayed in the apocalyptic literature [26]. The clause οἶδά σε τίς εἶ ὁ ἅγιος τοῦ θεοῦ is possibly a Marcan creation: on the one hand, it is absent in the parallels (cf. 1 Kings 17,18; Judg 11,12; Mk 5,7 par. Lk 8,28) and, on the other hand, the demons' knowledge of Jesus' true identity occurs in other redactional verses (cf. 1,34; 3,11). When the demons recognize or confess Jesus' identity, he imposes silence (cf. 1,34; 3,12); so the imperative φιμώθητι (absent in Mk 5,8 par. Lk 8,29) could be redactional. The clause ἦλθες ἀπολέσαι ἡμᾶς is most probably redactional due to the following reasons: Mk has replaced the original με with ἡμᾶς; the verb ἀπόλλυμι occurs also in other redactional verses (3,6; 11,18); the verb ἔρχεσθαι is frequently predicated of Jesus in the second Gospel [27]; and ἦλθον/ἦλθεν/ἦλθες with infinitive is a soteriologically intended expression to describe Jesus' salvific mission (cf. 2,17; 10,45). The occurrence of the double question in 1,24ab is another reason why v. 24b could be reckoned redactional [28]. There is a remote possibility that Mk has added φωνῆσαν φωνῇ μεγάλη [29] (v. 26) to express the intensity of the confrontation between Jesus and the evil spirit.

---

[26] Cf. n. 84 below.

[27] Cf. p. 6, n. 19.

[28] NEIRYNCK (*Duality*, 125-126) mentions 25 occurrences of double questions in Mk. Retained as in Mk: Mt 10 instances and Lk 8; no parallel: Mt 4 and Lk 7; modified: Mt 11 and Lk 10.

[29] NEIRYNCK (*Duality*, 76-77) points out 28 occurrences of verbs with cognate accusative or dative in Mk. Retained as in Mk: Mt 9 instances and Lk 2; no parallel: Mt 11 and Lk 18; modified: Mt 8 and Lk 8.

The redactional activity in Mk 1,27 is conspicuous. The construction ὥστε with infinitive indicating result is characteristically Marcan[30]. Direct discourse preceded by a qualifying verb (συζητεῖν λέγοντας) is Marcan[31]. Among the Gospels, Mk's preference of πρὸς ἑαυτούς to πρὸς ἀλλήους is obvious[32]. The verbs θαμβεῖν and συζητεῖν and the nouns πνεῦμα ἀκάθαρτον and διδαχή are typically Marcan[33]; and the verb ἐπιτάσσειν and the adjective καινός are relatively more frequent in the second Gospel[34]. There is considerable evidence for the redactional nature of Mk 1,28 too. Double statements, temporal or local (πανταχοῦ εἰς ὅλην τὴν περίχωρον τῆς Γαλιλαίας) are typical of Mk[35]. The verb ἐξέρχεσθαι, the adverb εὐθύς, the adjective ὅλος and the noun Γαλιλαία are predominantly Marcan[36].

To sum up the results of our investigation, v. 21 is to a great extent redactional but v. 22 is entirely redactional. Verses 23-26 are from tradition which Mk incorporated into his Gospel with possibly slight retouches in vv.

---

[30] Cf. Mk 1,27.45; 2,2.12; 3,10.20; 4,1.32.37; 9,26; 15,5.

[31] Cf. p. 87, n. 29.

[32]

	Mt	Mk	Lk	Jn
πρὸς ἑαυτούς	0	7	2	2
πρὸς ἀλλήλους	0	4	8	4

[33] Cf. n. 36 below.

[34] Cf. n. 36 below.

[35] NEIRYNCK (*Duality*, 94-96) notes 68 occurrences of double statement, temporal or local, in Mk. Retained as in Mk: Mt 17 occurrences and Lk 8; no parallel: Mt 14 and Lk 24; modified: Mt 37 and Lk 36.

[36]

	Mt	Mk	Lk	Jn	Acts	Paul	Rest		Total
Γαλιλαία	16	12	13	17	3	0	0	=	61
γραμματεύς	22	21	14	0	4	1	0	=	62
διδάσκειν	14	17	17	9	16	15	7	=	95
διδαχή	3	5	1	3	4	6	8	=	30
εἰσπορεύεσθαι	1	8	5	0	4	0	0	=	18
ἐκπλήσσειν	4	5	3	0	1	0	0	=	13
ἐξέρχεσθαι	43	39	44	29	29	8	24	=	216
ἐξουσία	10	10	16	8	7	27	24	=	102
ἐπιτάσσειν	0	4	4	0	1	1	0	=	10
εὐθύς	7	42	1	3	1	0	0	=	54
θαμβεῖν	0	3	0	0	0	0	0	=	3
καινός	4	5	5	2	2	7	17	=	42
ὅλος	22	18	16	6	19	14	13	=	108
πνεῦμα ἀκάθαρτον	2	11	5	0	2	0	2	=	22
συζητεῖν	0	6	2	0	2	0	0	=	10

23 and 26. Verses 24 and 25 may possibly have slight modifications and additions in them. It is likely that in the process of incorporating the exorcism story, Mk has shortened it, and he has also given it a time setting (sabbath) and a place setting (Capernaum/synagogue) of his own. The term 'synagogue' was possibly derived from v. 23 and 'Capernaum' was probably derived either from the exorcism story itself or from early tradition [37]. In v. 27, the original story contained the surprise of the people at the successful exorcism but Mk converted it into a general reaction to exorcisms (plural) as such and added the theme of Jesus' new and authoritative teaching.

Regarding v. 28, the opinion is sharply divided: many hold that v. 28 except τῆς Γαλιλαίας is from tradition [38] whereas several others consider the whole of it the product of Marcan redaction [39]. The main reason in favour of the first opinion is the occurrence of the hapax legomena περίχωρος and πανταχοῦ in v. 28. However, no proponent of this view has clearly established how v. 28 had been related to 1,21-27 and what function it had in tradition. In fact, v. 27 provides an excellent conclusion to the account in 1,21-26 just as elsewhere (cf. 4,41; 2,12; 7,37) and so v. 28 is not necessary for the pericope as such. It can hardly be an originally isolated verse because by itself it has no independent significance or function. Therefore, it is reasonable to conclude that Mk composed v. 28 to mark the overall success of Jesus' ministry from the beginning as he does elsewhere (cf. 1,32-34.37.45; 3,7-12; 6,56); the occurrence of the hapax legomena is no serious argument against its redactional character [40]. In brief, our distinction between redaction and tradition in 1,21-28 based on the evangelist's language, style and theological motif provides a balanced view: it attributes to Marcan redaction neither too little nor too much [41].

---

[37] See n. 51 below.

[38] Cf. ERNST, 64-65; GNILKA, I, 82; KERTELGE, Wunder, 51; LOHMEYER, 34; PERELS, Wunderüberlieferung, 93, etc.

[39] Cf. KLOSTERMANN, 18; KOCH, Bedeutung, 44-45; LUZ, "Geheimnismotiv", 18; SCHENKE, Wundererzählungen, 98-99; STEIN, "Markan Seam", 77; SUNDWALL, Zusammensetzung, 9; TAGAWA, Miracles, 86-87, etc.

[40] Hapax legomena do occur in verses generally recognized as redactional. E.g., πλεῖστος in 4,1; ἀναχωρεῖν in 3,7; πλοιάριον in 3,9; ἀπόστολοι in 6,30, etc.

[41] For example, PESCH, I, 117-118; id., "Ein Tag", 119; id., "Eine neue Lehre", 255-256, attributes to Marcan redaction only Mk 1,21a.22; διδαχὴ καινὴ κατ' ἐξουσίαν in 1,27 and τῆς Γαλιλαίας in 1,28. In contrast, PRYKE (Redactional Style, 152) considers the whole of 1,21-22; 1,26-28 and part of 1,23 (καὶ εὐθὺς ἦν ἐν τῇ συναγωγῇ αὐτῶν) to Marcan redaction.

4. *The Literary Structure*

21 A Καὶ *εἰσπορεύονται* εἰς Καφαρναούμ. καὶ *εὐθὺς* τοῖς σάββασιν *εἰσελθὼν* εἰς τὴν συναγωγὴν ἐδίδασκεν.

22   B καὶ ἐξεπλήσσοντο ἐπὶ τῇ διδαχῇ αὐτοῦ, ἦν γὰρ διδάσκων αὐτοὺς ὡς *ἐξουσίαν* ἔχων καὶ οὐχ ὡς οἱ γραμματεῖς.

23   C καὶ εὐθὺς ἦν ἐν τῇ συναγωγῇ αὐτῶν ἄνθρωπος ἐν πνεύματι ἀκαθάρτῳ καὶ ἀνέκραξεν

24   D λέγων, Τί ἡμῖν καὶ σοί, ᾽Ιησοῦ Ναζαρηνέ; ἦλθες ἀπολέσαι ἡμᾶς; οἶδά σε τίς εἶ, ὁ ἅγιος τοῦ θεοῦ.

25   D' καὶ ἐπετίμησεν αὐτῷ ὁ ᾽Ιησοῦς λέγων, Φιμώθητι καὶ ἔξελθε ἐξ αὐτοῦ.

26   C καὶ σπαράξαν αὐτὸν τὸ πνεῦμα τὸ ἀκάθαρτον καὶ φωνῆσαν φωνῇ μεγάλῃ ἐξῆλθεν ἐξ αὐτοῦ.

27   B' καὶ *ἐθαμβήθησαν* ἅπαντες, ὥστε συζητεῖν πρὸς ἑαυτοὺς λέγοντας, Τί ἐστιν τοῦτο; διδαχὴ καινὴ κατ᾽ *ἐξουσίαν* καὶ τοῖς πνεύμασι τοῖς ἀκαθάρτοις ἐπιτάσσει, καὶ ὑπακούουσιν αὐτῷ.

28 A' καὶ *ἐξῆλθεν* ἡ ἀκοὴ αὐτοῦ *εὐθὺς* πανταχοῦ εἰς ὅλην τὴν περίχωρον τῆς Γαλιλαίας.

Mk 1,21-28, as shown above, consists of a chiastic structure. Jesus' entry into the synagogue at Capernaum and teaching there (1,21: A) are parallel to the diffusion of Jesus' fame everywhere (1,28: A'). The astonishment of the audience at Jesus' authoritative teaching (1,22: B) has its parallel in 1,27 (B') where the audience is amazed at his new and authoritative teaching and the evil spirits' obedience to him. The presence of a man possessed by an unclean spirit in the synagogue and his cry (1,23: C) are parallel to the expulsion of the unclean spirit after a paroxysm (1,26: C'). The unclean spirit's confrontation of Jesus, stating the purpose of Jesus' coming and the recognition of his identity (1,24: D) and the parallel, Jesus' crushing rebuke of the unclean spirit ordering him to be silent and to come out of the man (1,25: D'), constitute the centre of the chiastic structure.

The two halves of the concentric structure in Mk 1,21-28 are equally divided: verses 21-24 (A B C D) consist of 61 words and verses 25-28 (D' C' B' A') 62 words. The first half works up to a climax in 1,24 (D): Jesus entering the synagogue at Capernaum teaches there (A) and the people were wonderstruck at his authoritative teaching (B); among them, there was a man possessed by an unclean spirit (C), who crying out, declared the purpose of

Jesus' coming and recognized the identity of Jesus' person (D). The second half flows from 1,25 (D'): Jesus' imposition of silence and the command to the unclean spirit to come out of the man (D') are immediately obeyed (C'). People were filled with awe at his authoritative teaching and the obedience of the unclean spirits (B'). As a consequence, his fame spreads into the surrounding region of Galilee (A'). Therefore, the arithmetical centre and the thematic core of the narrative concern the identity of Jesus' person and the scope of his mission (D D').

This structure is reinforced by studying the text from the perspective of the dramatis personae (the subject of the main verb) and their actions:

A *Jesus*, entering the synagogue, *was teaching* (1,21).

  B *People were astonished* at his teaching (1,22).

    C *A man possessed by an unclean spirit cried out* (1,23).

      D *The unclean spirit confronts Jesus* (1,24).

      D' *Jesus confronts the unclean spirit* (1,25).

    C' *The unclean spirit came out* (1,26).

  B' *People were amazed* at his teaching and exorcism (1,27).

A' *Jesus' fame spreads* (1,28).

B. Exegesis

1. *Jesus' Entry into and Teaching at the Synagogue (1,21)*

After being called (1,16-20), the disciples are continuously in Jesus' company throughout his ministry. This theological perspective, favourite and typical of the second Gospel and expressed in different ways, is emphasized in 1,21a by the plural verb (εἰσπορεύονται) [42]. In 1,21 he also provides a time setting (sabbath) and a place setting (Capernaum/synagogue) for the events that follow in 1,22-27. According to the synoptic tradition, Capernaum

---

[42] TURNER, *JTS* 26 (1925) 225-231, lists 21 instances of plural verbs denoting the coming and going of Jesus and his disciples. On five occasions Mt substitutes singular for the plural and Lk on eight occasions; omissions: Mt 3 and Lk 5. Therefore, the retension of Mk's plural is rare in Mt, rarer still in Lk.

was the centre of Jesus' ministry at its initial phase [43] and the synagogue, the place of his teaching and preaching [44].

In 1,21 Mk presents Jesus' teaching on the sabbath (τοῖς σάββασιν) [45] as part of the service at the synagogue, consisting of prayer, followed by readings from the Law and the Prophets, and exposition or sermon [46]. Among these, the sermon, which was open to any competent member of the congregation [47], was probably the most important part of the proceedings [48]. Mk's interest in mentioning ἐδίδασκεν in 1,21, however, lies not so much in the sermon of Jesus for the service at the synagogue as to mark the beginning of a typical day's ministry at Capernaum with διδάσκειν, a characteristic activity of Jesus. Of the 17 instances of διδάσκειν, (with the exception of 6,30 where his ἀπόστολοι teach), 16 have Jesus as the subject (differ Mt and Lk). And Mk uses this verb with deliberate, systematic and progressive Christological motif: in the first part of the Gospel the content of Jesus' teaching is not described at all (1,21; 2,13; 6,2.6b.34); it is qualified but not made explicit (1,22.27); and finally, it is described as parabolic and mysterious (4,1-34, and especially 4,11.33-34). In the second part, however, immediately after the confession of Jesus' Messiahship by Peter (8,29), the content of Jesus' teaching becomes very transparent: its primary object is the mystery of Jesus' person and mission. In 8,31 and 9,31 the object of Jesus' teaching is the revelation of his Passion, Death and Resurrection. In 11,17 it deals with the eschatological fulfilment of God's promises to be realized through his Passion and Death, and in 12,35-37 it is inextricably linked with the mystery of his person who is not only the son of David but also David's Lord. Mk's view of the theme of Jesus' teaching is then in total conformity with the main thrust of his Gospel: in the first part of the Gospel, as noted in chapter 2, Jesus progressively reveals himself in word and deed, but this revelation is closely tied in with the secrecy motif, whereas in the second part, the veil of secrecy regarding Jesus' identity is lifted. This theological preoccupation of the evangelist to conceal the identity of Jesus in the first part of the Gospel appears to be the reason why the content of Jesus' teaching is not mentioned in 1,21.

---

[43] Cf. Mk 1,21: 2,1: Mt 4,13: 8,5: Lk 4,23.31.

[44] Cf. Mk 1,21.39: 3,1: 6,2: Mt 4,23: 9,35: Lk 4.15-44: 6.6. etc.

[45] The LXX renders the MT שַׁבָּת both in plural and in singular. although in the Pentateuch and the Prophets the singular is very rare. In the NT both plural and singular are used. Even though the form is plural. it has a singular meaning as in the case of feasts: τὰ γενέσια (6,21). τὰ ἄζυμα (14.1). etc.

[46] Cf. Schürer. History II. 448: Str.-B.. Kommentar IV/1. 153-154.

[47] Cf. Schürer. ibid.. 453.

[48] See the text from Philo quoted by Schürer. ibid.. 448. n. 102.

2. *Astonishment of the Audience at Jesus' Teaching (1,22)*

In 1,22 the evangelist narrates the impact of Jesus' teaching on the audience and offers reasons for such an impact: one positive (ἦν γὰρ διδάσκων αὐτοὺς ὡς ἐξουσίαν ἔχων) and the other, a contrast (καὶ οὐχ ὡς οἱ γραμματεῖς).

In the LXX, the verb ἐκπλήσσειν is very rare (occurring only five times) and unrelated to teaching. In contrast, in the NT, of the 13 occurrences, eight times it is used to express the astonishment of the people at Jesus' teaching (Mt 7,28; 13,54; 22,33; Mk 1,22; 6,2; 11,18; Lk 4,32; Acts 13,12) and in two instances to denote the reaction of the disciples at a saying of Jesus (Mt 19,25 par. Mk 10,26). It is well to note that although Mk uses other verbs to describe people's astonishment at Jesus' miracles [49], he employs only ἐκπλήσσειν (thrice) and θαμβεῖν (once: 1,27) to depict people's reaction to Jesus' teaching. Therefore, ἐκπλήσσειν is the typical reaction to his teaching; in fact, it is caused by Jesus' teaching [50]. The specific reason for the astonishment in 1,22 is Jesus' διδαχή (all the five occurrences of διδαχή in Mk are attributed to Jesus) which is authoritative and new (1,22b.27c), meaning revelatory and Messianic [51]. Therefore by ἐξεπλήσσοντο in 1,22 is meant man's reaction of astonishment at Jesus' revelatory teaching and it possibly connotes the first step towards faith [52].

The positive reason for the astonishment of the audience is ἦν γὰρ διδάσκων αὐτοὺς ὡς ἐξουσίαν ἔχων. Here ἔχων is an idiomatic usage, meaning 'with' (accompanying) [53]. The noun ἐξουσία, derived from ἔξεστιν, denotes the ability to perform an action to the extent that there are no hindrances in the way, as distinct from δύναμις in the sense of intrinsic ability. "In the LXX ἐξουσία first means right, authority, permission or freedom in the legal or political sense, and it is then used for the right or permission given by God" [54]. The NT usage is closest to that of the LXX. In Mk ἐξουσία occurs ten times: nine times in the sense of authority, a quality proper to Jesus alone, and once in the sense of being in charge (13,34). Jesus' authority is manifested in his words, teaching (1,22.27) and forgiving sins (2,10), and in his deeds

---

[49] θαυμάζειν (5,20), ἐξιστάναι (2,12; 5,42; 6,51).

[50] 'Επί is used causatively.

[51] Cf. p. 129-130, 138-140.

[52] One should note that ἐκπλήσσειν is predicated only of those who are at least to some extent disposed to Jesus.

[53] Cf. BLASS-DEBRUNNER, *Grammar*, § 419.

[54] FOERSTER, *TDNT* II, 564.

(11,28. 29.33) and he shares his authority to cast out demons with the Twelve (3,15; 6,7).

What does ὡς ἐξουσίαν ἔχων in 1,22 mean? Daube has argued that by ἐξουσία is meant licence to teach authoritative doctrine conferred upon rabbis as distinct from inferior or elementary teachers of Jewish law such as the scribes, and that the people of Galilee who had hardly listened to a rabbi were astonished at the teaching of Jesus, as if he were an ordained rabbi [55]. Not only is the meaning of ἐξουσία in Mk 1,22.27 entirely different but 'scribes' is also the correct term for the ordained theologians in the oldest strata of the rabbinic tradition and in the NT [56]. Again, several modern commentators hold to the view that scribes taught according to the tradition handed down by the elders whereas Jesus taught the original will of God [57]. This view is evidently applicable to the first Gospel where one finds the frequent "You have heard that it was said . . . . But I say to you" (5,21-22.27-28.33-34.38-39.43-44, etc.). Such a distinction may have some basis in the second Gospel in certain passages (cf. 7,8-23; 10,6-9; 12,24-27); however, this interpretation is not adequate and precise enough as far as Mk 1,22b is concerned since Mk does not consider these responses of Jesus as his teaching. Daube and other modern commentators "err in seeking to explain from out of the first *Sitz im Leben* a description of Jesus whose origin took place in the third *Sitz im Leben*" [58].

An adequate answer demands a thorough analysis of both of the terms with which it is connected and of the context in which it occurs. In Mk 3,15 and 6,7 the authority conferred upon the Twelve has exorcism in view; these texts show no connection between authority and teaching as such. In 11,27-33 the opponents' question and Jesus' counterquestion are focused on the source of Jesus' authority (cf. 11,28b.30). Here the context suggests at least an indirect connection between Jesus' authority and his teaching. In 2,10 Jesus' authority is closely related to forgiveness of sins, a right reserved to God alone (2,7). Here Jesus' word and his authority are intrinsically connected (cf. 2,5c.10-11). And finally, in 1,27, which is parallel to 1,22, the connection between Jesus' authority and his teaching is very clear (διδαχὴ καινὴ κατ᾽ ἐξουσίαν).

---

[55] DAUBE, "Mark 1,22 and 27", 45-59; id., "Rabbinic Authority", 205-233.

[56] Cf. JEREMIAS, *Jerusalem*, 235-243; id., *TDNT* I, 740-742.

See further critical observations in ARGYLE, "Mark 1,22.27", 343; LÉGASSE, "Scribes et disciples de Jésus", 497-502.

[57] Among others see ERNST, 63; GNILKA, I, 78-80; PESCH, I, 120-121.

[58] STEIN, "Markan Seam", 90.

What does Mk mean by ἐξουσία in 1,27; 2,10 and 11,27-33? In 11,27-33 Jesus' counterquestion, "Was the baptism of John from heaven or from men?" (11,30), gives an inkling of the nature of Jesus' authority. By this question our evangelist implies that he who authorized John to offer the eschatological baptism has also authorized Jesus to proclaim and inaugurate the kingdom of God in word and deed [59]. But, according to Mk, John the Baptist is Elijah (cf. 1,2-8; 9,12-13) and Jesus is the Messiah (cf. 1,1; 8,29). As a consequence, John's authority is that of Elijah, and Jesus' authority is that of the Messiah. In the second text (2,10) the evangelist's prime intent is Jesus' authority as the Son of Man [60]. And lastly, in 1,27, a Messianic connotation is also implied [61]. Therefore, in light of Mk 1,27; 2,10 and 11,27-33, we conclude that in 1,22b ἐξουσία refers to Jesus' Messianic function — an interpretation that seems to be in tune with the patristic understanding [62]. Our exegesis of καὶ οὐχ ὡς οἱ γραμματεῖς will further reinforce this interpretation.

The second reason for the audience's astonishment is contained in the expression καὶ οὐχ ὡς οἱ γραμματεῖς. What does this phrase mean? The syntax of the sentence (ἦν γὰρ διδάσκων αὐτοὺς ὡς ἐξουσίαν ἔχων καὶ οὐχ ὡς οἱ γραμματεῖς) necessarily implies a contrast, a qualitative difference, between Jesus' teaching and the teaching of the scribes [63]. Regarding the point of comparison between Jesus' teaching and the teaching of the scribes, we have ruled out the interpretation of Daube as unfounded and the opinion of several modern commentators as inadequate. It was also established that Jesus' teaching is characterized ὡς ἐξουσίαν ἔχων, meaning Messianic authority. However, Mk does not explicitly mention any characteristic note of the scribes' teaching here or elsewhere. In chapter seven, the evangelist speaks about the preoccupation of the scribes and the Pharisees with observing the tradition (παράδοσις cf.7,3.5.8.9.13) of the elders but he does not employ the term teaching in these contexts. Nowhere in Mk are the scribes addressed as teachers or rabbis. Yet there are three texts where the view of Mk's Jesus and that of the scribes drastically differ (9,11-13; 11,27-33; 12,35-37). According to 9,11-13 and 11,27-33, the scribes do not acknowledge John the

---

[59] Cf. BUETUBELA, *Jean-Baptiste*, 147-149; SHAE, "Authority of Jesus", 27-28.

[60] Cf. p. 191-195.

[61] Cf. p. 138-140.

[62] BEDA, 447: "Illi enim ea dicebant populos quae scripta sunt in Moyse et prophetis, Iesus vero quasi Deus et dominus ipsius Moysi". HIERONYMUS, 465: "aliud est dicere, haec dicit dominius; et aliud est dicere, amen dico vobis".

[63] See JEREMIAS, *Jerusalem*, 233-245.

Baptist as Elijah and a fortiori Jesus as the Messiah. Furthermore, according to 12,35-37, the scribes affirm that Christ is from the Davidic lineage but they fail to realize that he is also David's Lord. In these three texts, then, our evangelist highlights the contrasting Christological opinions of the scribes and of Jesus. In other words, the scribes do not acknowledge Jesus as the Messiah and his authority as Messianic which, as stated before, is the prime thrust of Jesus' teaching. Therefore, the contrast between Jesus' teaching and the teaching of the scribes consists in the theological conviction of the evangelist that the scribes do not recognize Jesus' Messiahship and his Messianic mission. It is instructive to note that other Jewish groups such as the Pharisees and Herodians (12,14) and Sadducees (12,19) address Jesus as Teacher but never the scribes [64]. Therefore, according to Mk, the scribes do not recognize Jesus as a teacher.

Our interpretation is strengthened by the theological portrait of the scribes as depicted in the second Gospel. It is commonly agreed that among various hostile groups in Mk, the scribes are portrayed as deadly enemies of Jesus [65]. There are various literary indications to support this view [66] and the scribes do play a decisive role in putting Jesus to death. However, what interests us most in this context is their accusations against Jesus: they interpret Jesus' authority to forgive sins as blasphemy (2,6-7); they also charge that he "is possessed by Beelzebul, and by the prince of demons he casts out the demons" (3,22) — a charge the evangelist censures as blasphemous (3,28-30). Finally, among various groups who ridiculed Jesus, the scribes' mockery betrays their theological intent and personal conviction (15,31-32b):

Persons who mock Jesus	*Content of their mockery*
Those who passed by	"You who would destroy the temple and build it in three days, save yourself, and come down from the cross" (15,30).
The chief priests and the *scribes*	"He saved others; he cannot save himself. Let the *Christ* ... come down now from the cross, that *we may see and believe* (15,31-32b).
Those who were crucified with him	"reviled him" (15,32c).

---

[64] Mk 12,32 does not speak of scribes as a class but of an individual scribe.

[65] Among several others cf. AMBROZIC, "New Teaching", 116-121; COOK, *Jewish Leaders*, passim; PESCH, "Eine neue Lehre", 250, n. 34; SCHENKE, *Wundererzählungen*, 97; id., *Studien*, 39-41.

[66] Cf. p. 261, n. 1.

From these three texts (2,6-7; 3,22; 15,31-32b), the scribes' basic viewpoint about Jesus and their accusations against him become clear: they acknowledge neither Jesus' Messiahship nor his Messianic mission. Thus, here too, the content of the scribes' accusations against Jesus is diametrically opposed to Jesus' own teaching about his person and his mission. It is also worth noting that the first (1,22) and the last (15,31-32b) occurrence of 'the scribes' have the same content: they refuse to acknowledge the Messiahship of Jesus. This is implied in 1,22 and is made explicit in 15,31-32b.

3. A Man with an Unclean Spirit (1,23)

From v. 23 onwards the evangelist focuses attention on the confrontation between the demoniac described as ἄνθρωπος ἐν πνεύματι ἀκαθάρτῳ and Jesus. Here the preposition ἐν should be understood in a sociative sense, at least in part under the influence of Semitic בְּ [67] meaning 'with'. Also the adjective ἀκάθαρτος does not mean ceremoniously impure as in Leviticus [68] but in the sense of being estranged from God [69].

Sensing Jesus' presence, the man's immediate and spontaneous reaction is to cry aloud, ἀνέκραξεν. The verb ἀνακράζειν occurs in the NT (a total of five times) in three contexts: on sensing Jesus' presence the demoniacs cry out (Mk 1,23 par. Lk 4,33; 8,28); the cry of the crowd for Jesus' crucifixion (Lk 23,18); and the disciples' cry on seeing Jesus walking on the sea whom they mistook for a ghost (Mk 6,49). Although in all of these contexts ἀνακράζειν expresses a sudden emotional excitement and outburst [70], there seems to be a deeper meaning in the first three texts where the content of the demoniacs' outcry reveals their horror that Jesus has come to destroy them. This is particularly demonstrated in the concentric structure of 1,24.

4. He Confronts Jesus (1,24)

The unclean spirit's verbal confrontation of Jesus (1,24), consisting of a clearly distinctive concentric structure (A B A'), strongly emphasizes the

---

[67] Cf. ZERWICK, Biblical Greek, § 116-117.

[68] More than half of the occurrences of ἀκάθαρτος in the LXX are found in Leviticus: in the 11th chapter alone 29 instances and in the 15th chapter 24.

[69] Cf. GRUNDMANN, 59; SCHWEIZER, 24; SWETE, 19.

[70] CRANFIELD, 75; NINIHAM, 79.

fundamental reason why the evil spirits find Jesus a threat, viz., Jesus has come to destroy them:

A   Τί ἡμῖν καὶ σοί, Ἰησοῦ Ναζαρηνέ;

  B   ἦλθες ἀπολέσαι ἡμᾶς;

A' οἶδά σε τίς εἶ, ὁ ἅγιος τοῦ θεοῦ.

Previously it was pointed out that Mk probably changed the original ἐμοί into ἡμῖν thereby stressing the opposition between the realm of the evil spirits [71] and Jesus. This perspective of Mk becomes clear when one compares 1,24 with the close parallel in 5,7.9. In 5,9 a plurality of demons is evident: λεγιὼν ὄνομά μοι, ὅτι πολλοί ἐσμεν. Nevertheless, Mk uses the singular in 5,7: τί ἐμοὶ καὶ σοί. However, in the Matthean parallel the plural is used (Mt 8,29: τί ἡμῖν καὶ σοί, υἱὲ τοῦ θεοῦ; ἦλθες ὧδε πρὸ καιροῦ βασανίσαι ἡμᾶς). The phrase τί ἐμοὶ (ἡμῖν) καὶ σοί occurs in classical Greek too [72] where it means "What have we and you in common?" [73] In the OT it has two meanings: one expresses hostility and the other indicates lack of proper understanding [74]. In our verse the context makes it clear that the evangelist underlines the contrast between Jesus and the evil spirits: they pertain to diametrically opposing poles, enemies in the arena of salvation history. "Quae enim communicatio Xpisto [= Christo] et Beliae? Non poterant Xpistus et Belias in uno concilio commorari" [75].

The appellative Ἰησοῦ Ναζαρηνέ has mainly two interpretations in the present exegetical discussions: (1) Ναζαρηνός/Ναζωραῖος [76] derives from the name of a town, Nazareth [77], where Jesus grew up (cf. Mt 2,23; 4,13; Mk 1,9; Lk 1,26; 2,4.39.51; Jn 1,45-46); (2) Mußner's contention that in Mk 1,24 there is a play on words (נְזִיר אֱלֹהִים is rendered ἅγιος θεοῦ in codex Vaticanus) and so ὁ ἅγιος τοῦ θεοῦ in 1,24b could be "eine sachliche

---

[71] BÖCHER, Die dämonischen Mächte, 30.

[72] Cf. SWETE, 19.

[73] CRANFIELD, 75.

[74] Cf. DE LA POTTERIE, De matre Iesu, 45-46.

[75] HIERONYMUS, 465.

[76] For a discussion on the original Hebrew name, the transmutation of vowels, and the derivation of Ναζαρηνός/Ναζωραῖος cf. DIEZ MACHO, "Jesus 'Ho Nazoraios'", 9-26; RÜGER, "ΝΑΖΑΡΕΘ", 257-263.

Regarding the double form Ναζαρηνός/Ναζωραῖος one should note that there are similar variants in other instances as well: Ἐσσηνοί/Ἐσσαῖοι, Ἀγαρηνοί/Ἀγαραῖοι, κτλ.

[77] Cf. NINIHAM, 79.

Interpretation" of Ναζαρηνέ in 1,24a [78], a view upheld by several modern commentators [79]. Although the second opinion appears appealing at first sight, it lacks an adequate literary basis. Let us compare the MT texts with their rendering in the LXX:

	MT	LXX (Codex A)	LXX (Codex B)
Judg 13,5	נְזִיר אֱלֹהִים	ναζιραῖον τῷ θεῷ	ναζὶρ θεοῦ
Judg 13,7	נְזִיר אֱלֹהִים	ναζιραῖον θεοῦ	ἅγιον θεοῦ
Judg 16,17	נְזִיר אֱלֹהִים	ναζιραῖος θεοῦ	ἅγιος θεοῦ

If the word originates from the Hebrew נזר (= dedicate, consecrate), the form Ναζαραῖος might be expected as in codex A; but Mk 1,24a has Ναζαρηνός. Secondly, codex B has ἅγιος θεοῦ (= a holy man of God) whereas Mk 1,24b has ὁ ἅγιος τοῦ θεοῦ (= the Holy One of God). It should be noted that Mußner, having added the definite article ὁ to ἅγιος and τοῦ to θεοῦ proposes ὁ ἅγιος τοῦ θεοῦ as the original rendering of Judg 13,7; 16,17 in codex B [80]. In paraphrasing Mußner's view Arens deletes the second article and wrongly vocalizes the text of codex A [81]. And lastly, in Mk 1,24b ὁ ἅγιος τοῦ θεοῦ is probably a Messianic title [82], whereas in the texts cited above there is no messianic nuance at all. Since Jesus was not an ascetic (cf. Mt 11,18-19 par.; Mk 2,15-16 par.), there is no need to address him as a Nazorite. Therefore, in conclusion, we hold that Ναζαρηνός derives from the name of the town, Nazareth. In the context of the Marcan redaction, however, Ναζαρηνός has a particular nuance. Of the four occurrences (1,24; 10,47; 14,67; 16,6), twice it occurs in the context of the Passion: a maid said to Peter, "You also were with the Nazarene, Jesus" (14,67 differ par. Mt 26,69 and Lk 22,56); the young man said to the women, "You seek Jesus, the Nazarene, who was crucified" (16,6 differ par. Mt 28,5 and Lk 24,56). In the light of the above texts it is reasonable to presume that in 1,24 too it has a veiled allusion to the cross.

---

[78] Cf. MUßNER, "Wortspiel", 285-286.

[79] Cf. ARENS, HΛΘON-Sayings, 211-212; ERNST, 64; GNILKA, I, 81; PESCH, I, 122; SCHWEIZER, 24; id., "Nazoräer", 90-93.

[80] MUßNER, "Wortspiel", 285: "nach Ri 13,7 (16,17) übersetzt: ὁ ἅγιος τοῦ θεοῦ".

[81] Cf. ARENS, HΛΘON-Sayings, 212: "and was translated by MS A of the LXX as ναζιραῖων θεοῦ, and MS B as ὁ ἅγιος θεοῦ".

[82] Cf. p. 136.

The clause ἦλθες ἀπολέσαι ἡμᾶς explicitly states the reason for Jesus' coming and the consequence his presence had for the demoniac world. Although the verb ἦλθες has a local sense (the concrete action of Jesus' coming to the synagogue) at the story-level [83], it also has an eschatological meaning. For ἦλθον/ ἦλθεν predicated of Jesus and followed by an infinitive underlines Jesus' soteriologically intended career on behalf of mankind (2,17; 10,45). In 1,24 ἦλθες (Jesus' coming) followed by the infinitive of purpose ἀπολέσαι with the object ἡμᾶς (i.e., evil spirits) certainly evokes the Jewish apocalyptic imagery according to which the Messiah establishes the kingdom of God by defeating and destroying the realm of Satan and of his hosts [84]. On the basis of this imagery, the question of the demon (ἦλθες ἀπολέσαι ἡμᾶς) is all the more poignant: the prime thrust of the question is not that the demon has met his match or even his destroyer (hence, not ἦλθες ἀπολέσαι με) but that the evil spirits, meaning all the forces hostile to God, recognize Jesus as the final and definitive envoy of God and sense his coming and presence as a menace to their security, ultimately leading to their definitive destruction. "Praesentia Salvatoris tormenta sunt daemonum" [85]. In a word, by placing ἦλθες ἀπολέσαι ἡμᾶς on the lips of the demoniac who speaks as the representative of the evil spirits [86], Mk asserts that the destruction of the evil powers is a goal of Jesus' coming into this world. And the central position this clause occupies in the literary structure (A B A') shows the importance that the evangelist gives to it.

Perceiving the purpose of Jesus' coming, the demoniac tries to disarm Jesus by saying that he knows Jesus' true identity (οἶδά σε τίς εἶ) and his

---

[83] Cf. ARENS, ΗΛΘΟΝ-Sayings, 219-221.

[84] Cf. STR.-B., Kommentar IV, 802-804, 808. See also FOERSTER, TDNT II, 79-81, VII, 151-163; KÜMMEL, Promise, 105-109.

[85] BEDA, 447. 1 Jn 3,8: "The reason the Son of God appeared was to destroy the works of the devil".

[86] Various attempts have been made to explain the abrupt change from the plural (ἡμῖν ... ἡμᾶς) to the singular (οἶδα). (1) GRUNDMANN, 60; SCHWEIZER, 24, etc. consider it schizophrenia (Persönlichkeitsspaltung).This explanation tries to make Mk a modern psychologist. Our evangelist, on the contrary, is concerned with faith in Jesus Christ (cf. 1,1.15, etc.). (2) LANE, 73; VAN DER LOOS, Miracles, 380; and so on think that the demoniac identifies himself with the congregation and speaks from their perspective. But the congregation's comment in 1,27 contradicts this opinion. (3) LOHMEYER, 36: "ein Dämon ist Individuum nur als Glied seiner Gattung". (4) We would go beyond LOHMEYER and state that the plural denotes demons as a class and the demoniac speaks as the representative of the demoniac world as such (cf. ARENS, ΗΛΘΟΝ-Sayings, 212; H.C. KEE, "Terminology", 243; KLOSTERMANN, 17, etc).

name which he utters (ὁ ἅγιος τοῦ θεοῦ) [87]. This verbal confrontation of the demoniac does not seem to be a formula of confession as in 3,11; 8,29; 15,39; or of declaration as in 1,11 but of recognition (cf. 1,34; 5,7). It is aimed at gaining control over Jesus and making his work ineffective. By οἶδα is meant not a knowledge derived from observation or experience (for which γινώσκω would be the apt verb) but a knowledge gained from insight or intuition [88]. The use of σε here is probably not pleonastic or redundant [89] but emphatic. With regard to ὁ ἅγιος τοῦ θεοῦ there is no evidence that this title was used by the Jews in a messianic sense [90]; nevertheless, in our verse it does express the true identity of Jesus, particularly his divine origin. This is evident from the striking difference between the forms of address by demoniacs and others in the first part of the Gospel: the demoniacs address Jesus 'the Holy One of God' (1,24), 'the Son of God' (3,11) and 'the Son of the Most High God' (5,7) while the latter address him as 'Teacher' (4,38), 'Lord' (7,28), etc. Jesus imposes silence only when his true identity is revealed (cf. 1,24-25.34; 3,11-12; 8,29-30). Furthermore, it is likely that, based on the association of Ps 16,10 with Jesus' Resurrection in Acts 2,27, this title could have acquired a Messianic nuance in the early Church which the evangelist attributed to the demon in 1,24b [91]. One should note that, with the exclusion of the parallel in Lk 4,34, this title occurs only once more in the NT where a Messianic connotation cannot be denied: "You have the words of eternal life; and we have believed, and have come to know, that you are the Holy One of God" (Jn 6,68b-69) [92].

5. *Jesus' Reaction (1,25)*

Jesus' stern reaction to the verbal confrontation of the demoniac is expressed by a divine word of rebuke, ἐπετίμησεν, which is explicated in the form of a double command, φιμώθητι καὶ ἔξελθε ἐξ αὐτοῦ. The impera-

---

[87] Cf. ARENS, *ΗΛΘΟΝ-Sayings*, 211; BAUERNFEIND, *Die Worte der Dämonen*, 3-10, 14-16, 28-31; KERTELGE, *Wunder*, 53; ROBINSON, *History*, 43-46; SCHENKE, *Wundererzählungen*, 100; TAGAWA, *Miracles*, 83-84, etc.

[88] Cf. DE LA POTTERIE, "Οἶδα et γινώσκω", 709-713; id., *La vérité* II, 539-540, 576-578.

[89] So SWETE, 20 and TAYLOR, 174.

[90] Cf. HAHN, *Hoheitstitel*, 235-238; RAWLISON, 16, n. 6.

[91] Cf. KLOSTERMANN, 17; NINIHAM, 79; SWETE, 20.

[92] Compare with Jn 20,31: "but these are written that you may believe that Jesus is the Christ, the Son of God, and that believing you may have eternal life in his name".

tive φιμώθητι thwarts the revelation of Jesus' true identity (1,24) and ἔξελθε
ἐξ αὐτοῦ is the counterpart to the invasion of the man's spirit by an alien
power (1,23).

The verb ἐπιτιμᾶν (= גָּעַר) [93] has a particular theological nuance in 1,25.
There is evidence from the Qumran documents that גָּעַר is a technical term
for the commanding word uttered by God or his spokesman by which evil
powers are brought into submission and thereby the way is prepared for
establishing God's righteous rule in the world (cf. 1 QapGen 20,28-29; 1 QM
14,9; 1 QH 9,11, etc.). This meaning of גָּעַר is confirmed in several texts of
the OT [94] and in a few instances of the Jewish apocalyptic literature [95].

We have shown that structurally Mk 1,24 and 1,25 are parallel (D D')
and we have interpreted 1,24 against the background of the apocalyptic
soteriological perspective. Therefore, on the basis of the background of the
verb ἐπιτιμᾶν (גָּעַר) and in the context of Mk 1,24 we affirm that in Mk
1,25 ἐπετίμησεν means that Jesus uttered "the commanding word by which
the demon, as the representative of the forces opposed to God and his
purposes, is overcome" [96].

In Mk the verb φιμοῦν occurs only twice, both in the imperative (1,25;
4,39). In our verse it means to "tie shut" [97], analogous to the injunction in
1,34 and 3,12 to the unclean spirits to keep silent. The verb ἐξέρχεσθαι with
the preposition ἐκ is employed two ways in Mk: of place (1,29; 5,2; 6,54;
7,31) and of person (1,25.26; 5,8.30; 7,29; 9,25). All occurrences in the latter
group, except 5,30, are either Jesus' command (in the imperative) to the
unclean spirits to come out of the person (1,25; 5,8; 9,25) or the narration
(in the indicative) of the actual coming out of the unclean spirits from the
person (1,26; 7,29). Therefore, ἔξελθε ἐξ αὐτοῦ is a typical formula by which
Jesus commands the evil spirits to quit the person.

---

[93] All the eleven occurrences of ἐπιτιμᾶν in the LXX invariably translate the Hebrew
verb גָּעַר.

[94] Cf. H.C. KEE, "Terminology", 234-237.

[95] Cf. ibid. 237-238.

[96] Ibid. 242.

[97] CRANFIELD, 77, and RAWLISON, 17, remark that φιμοῦν is a technical term for binding
a person with a spell. But they too agree that in Mk 1,25 it is a command to silence.

6. *Exit of the Unclean Spirit (1,26)*

Jesus' word of command (1,25) effects a prompt response from the unclean spirit (1,26): σπαράξαν αὐτὸν... φωνῆσαν φωνῇ μεγάλη ἐξῆλθεν ἐξ αὐτοῦ. The verb σπαράσσειν in classical Greek meant to tear, rend, pull to and fro. It very rarely occurs in the NT [98] and in our verse it means to convulse. The verb φωνεῖν has three different nuances in Mk: (1) with the accusative of person, in the sense to call someone (9,35; 10,49; 15,35); (2) cock crows (14,30.68.72); (3) followed by φωνῇ μεγάλη (1,26). It is only in our verse that the subject of φωνεῖν is the evil spirit, and by φωνῆσαν φωνῇ μεγάλη is meant a very loud shriek. Mk employs φωνὴ μεγάλη in two contexts: loud shriek when the demon comes out of the possessed person (1,26; 5,7), and Jesus' loud cry at his death (15,34.37). What our evangelist seems to be emphasizing by the details, σπαράξαν... φωνῆσαν φωνῇ μεγάλη, is that Jesus' word of command to the unclean spirit was accompanied by a struggle, not a momentary one, but "part of a wider conflict, of which this is but a single phase" [99].

7. *Reaction of the Audience (1,27)*

Verse 27 which narrates the audience's reactions, when compared with the parallel verse (1,22), swells to a crescendo. The verb in 1,22 is the impersonal ἐξεπλήσσοντο whereas in 1,27 there is a very strongly emotive verb, ἐθαμβήθησαν, with an emphatic and all-embracing subject ἅπαντες. Again, the distinctive note of Jesus' teaching in 1,22 is that it was with authority but in 1,27 there is a significant additional attribute καινή to qualify his authoritative teaching. Finally, in 1,27 there is a totally new element: even the evil spirits obey Jesus' commands. It is not an isolated reaction to the exorcism narrated in 1,23-26 but a general principle (note the plural: καὶ τοῖς πνεύμασι τοῖς ἀκαθάρτοις ἐπιτάσσει, καὶ ὑπακούουσιν αὐτῷ).

The main event narrated in v. 27 is ἐθαμβήθησαν. The verb θαμβεῖν/ ἐκθαμβεῖσθαι (root meaning: to be struck, to strike) in classical Greek denotes emotions between astonishment and fear. In the NT these two verbs occur exclusively in Mk and except in 1,27 they are never found in the context of the audience's reaction to the miracles performed by Jesus.

---

[98] Mk 2 and Lk 1 = a total of 3.
[99] H.C. KEE, "Terminology", 243.

Furthermore, in Mk there is a good blend of astonishment and fear (particularly the latter) in most of these texts: θαμβεῖν (cf. 10,32), ἐκθαμβεῖσθαι (14,33; 16,5.6) [100]. Why does Mk employ such a strongly emotive verb in 1,27? It is surely not commensurate with the reactions to a single exorcism since the Jews were not at all that unfamiliar with exorcisms (cf. Mk 9,38; Lk 11,19; Acts 19,13, etc.). What justifies the use of θαμβεῖν becomes clear from the question asked by the audience and the reasons given for asking the question. We now explain these points step by step.

In Mk συζητεῖν has various nuances: seek (8,11), discuss (9,16), argue (9,14; 12,28), and question (1,27; 9,10). So filled with awe they questioned among themselves: τί ἐστιν τοῦτο [101]; The first reason for the question is διδαχὴ καινὴ κατ' ἐξουσίαν. We have already explained the meaning of διδαχή and ἐξουσία. The adjective καινός has different shades of meanings: (1) new, fresh; (2) newly invented, novel; (3) something not previously present, unknown, strange; (4) what has become obsolete should be replaced by what is new — especially in the eschatological sense. Even in the OT there are texts where καινός means the quality of those realities which belong to the definitive fulfilment of God's saving action (cf. Is 42,9; 43,18-19; 65,17) [102]. In this sense καινός "is the epitome of the wholly different and miraculous thing which is brought by the time of salvation . . . καινός becomes a slogan of the reality of salvation which we know already in Christ" [103]. It is in this sense that the NT speaks of a new covenant (Lk 22,20; 1 Cor 11,25; 2 Cor 3,6; Hebr 8,8; 9,15); a new commandment (Jn 13,34; 1 Jn 2,7.8; 2 Jn 5); a new man (Eph 2,15; 4,24); a new teaching (Mk 1,27). In these texts, therefore, καινός, distinct from νέος, has an eschatological content [104]. In our verse then διδαχὴ καινή connotes a teaching that is revelatory and Messianic, final and definitive.

And the second reason for the question is καὶ τοῖς πνεύμασι τοῖς ἀκαθάρτοις ἐπιτάσσει, καὶ ὑπακούουσιν αὐτῷ. The verb ἐπιτάσσειν is

---

[100] In 9,15 and 10,24 the emphasis seems to be on astonishment rather than on fear.

[101] In light of our exegesis of 1,21-28, the question — who is this? — is also logical. However, according to Mk only the disciples are privileged to ask such a question (cf. 4,35) and, paradoxically, only they themselves elicit the right answer (cf. 8,29).

[102] Intertestamental literature also uses this term in a similar manner. See 1 Enoch 45,4; 72,1; TgMic 7,14, etc.

[103] BEHM, *TDNT* III, 449.

[104] Καινός is 'new' with respect to quality or substance, as distinct from νέος, 'new' as regards time.

used in the NT with dative of persons (Mk 1,27; 6,39; 9,25; Lk 4,36; 8,31; Acts 23,2; Philem 8), dative of personified realities (Lk 8,25), accusative of things (Lk 14,22), and followed by an infinitive (Mk 6,27). It is worth noting that in all the instances where the subject of ἐπιτάσσειν is Jesus, it governs a dative of persons (personified realities) who are opposed to God (cf. Mk 1,27; 9,25; Lk 4,36; 8,25.31). According to Mk 1,27, therefore, Jesus commands the forces hostile to God and his purposes, and his authority thus extends even (καί) to the uncontrollable wills of spirits who defy all genuine obligations [105]. The corresponding verb to ἐπιτάσσειν in Mk 1,27 is ὑπακούειν. In the Gospels where Jesus is the object (dative) of ὑπακούειν its subject is invariably those forces hostile to God (cf. Mk 1,27; 4,41 par.) According to Mk 1,27, then, evil spirits diametrically opposed to God and his plans heed Jesus' commands. Thus, in brief, the second reason for the audience's amazement is that Jesus commanded the unclean spirits and they obeyed him: Jesus, the Messiah, has subdued the evil forces [106].

8. *Diffusion of Jesus' Fame (1,28)*

Even though there is an excellent conclusion for 1,21-26 in 1,27 where the impact of Jesus' teaching and exorcism on the audience is vividly narrated, our evangelist nonetheless describes the effect by a further reference to the spread of the tidings. His intent in adding v. 28 appears to be twofold: first, as our exegesis has demonstrated, in 1,21-27 Mk has depicted a Messianic portrait of Jesus; consequently, it is logical that his fame spreads throughout the surrounding region of Galilee. And secondly, Jesus' ministry from the beginning (1,14) up to 3,6 is exclusively restricted to the region of Galilee. However, in 3,7-8 Mk narrates: "A great multitude from Galilee followed; also from Judea . . . Tyre and Sidon a great multitude, hearing all that he did, came to him". Thus our evangelist makes a clear distinction between the multitude from Galilee (where Jesus had personally ministered) who followed him and the multitudes from other countries (where he had not ministered personally) who came to him. The fame (ἀκοή) that spread throughout the surrounding region of Galilee (1,28) is then a preparation for people's coming to Jesus ἀκούοντες ὅσα ἐποίει in 3,7-8.

---

[105] The order of words, τοῖς πνεύμασι τοῖς ἀκαθάρτοις, emphasizes the adjective (cf. Eph 4,30; 1 Thess 4,8).

[106] Our opinion differs from the view of several authors. Cf. GNILKA, I, 82; LANE, 76; PESCH, I, 124-125; SWETE, 22; THEIBEN, *Wundergeschichten* 165; TAYLOR, 176.

C. Concluding Remarks

Modifying the original story of the exorcism and introducing the theme of Jesus' teaching, Mk has placed his personal stamp on 1,21-28. His theological perspective and doctrinal emphases in 1,21-28 may be summarized thus:

(1) Jesus' uniquely qualified teaching in 1,22.27 has a revelatory function, viz., it alludes to Jesus' person and mission.

(2) Mk wants his readers to understand that what he narrates in 1,23-26 is not a mere exorcism but the eschatological encounter between the Messiah and the evil spirits and the definitive victory of the former over the latter.

(3) Both Jesus' teaching and his exorcism are thus channels of revelation, revelation of Jesus' person and of his mission [107]. The concentric structure we have proposed for 1,21-28 underscores the relation between Jesus' person and his mission on the one hand and his activities of teaching and exorcism on the other.

(4) The placement of this pericope at the beginning of Jesus' ministry is not fortuitous but intentional: 1,21-28 has a specific function in Mk.

II. The Healing of Peter's Mother-in-Law (1,29-31)

A. Literary Analysis [108]

1. Comparison with Mt 8,14-15 and Lk 4,38-39

a. *Mk 1,29-31 and Mt 8,14-15*

The healing of Peter's mother-in-law occurs in the first two Gospels in very dissimilar contexts. In Mk it is part of Jesus' ministry at Capernaum on a specific sabbath (1,21-34). It is preceded by his teaching and exorcism (1,21-28) and followed by a summary on his healing and casting out demons

---

[107] Cf. p. 247-249.

[108] In verse 29 ἐξελθόντες ἦλθον is more probable than ἐξελθὼν ἦλθεν because "the copyists would tend to change the plural to the singular in order (a) to focus attention on Jesus, (b) to conform the reading to the parallels in Mt 8,14 and Lk 4,38 and (c) to provide a nearer antecedent for αὐτῷ of v. 30" (METZGER, *Commentary*, 75). Moreover, impersonal plural is typical of Mk.

(1,32-34). In Mt it remotely pertains to a cycle of ten miracles whereby the first evangelist brings home the message that Jesus is the Messianic deliverer [109]. It proximately belongs to a group of three healings (8,1-4: leper; 8,5-13: the centurion's servant; 8,14-15: Peter's mother-in-law). This is followed by a succinct summary (8,16) [110], culminating in a formula quotation from the suffering servant (8,17 = Is 53,4) which underlines the theological significance of Jesus' healings. In Mt the healing narrated most succinctly [111] is wholly on the initiative of Jesus without an interlocutor [112]. According to Mt the healing takes place by Jesus' touch (καὶ ἥψατο τῆς χειρός αὐτῆς) and ἠγέρθη is the sign that she is cured whereas, according to Mk, Jesus lifts her up by the hand (καὶ προσελθὼν ἤγειρεν αὐτὴν κρατήσας τῆς χειρός) just as he does with Jairus' daughter (5,41) and the epileptic boy (9,27). For Mt then the healing of Peter's mother-in-law is one of the signs which symbolizes the redemption. In other words, by means of the fulfilment quotation (8,17 = Is 53,4) the first evangelist stresses the symbolic value of the healing as an anticipation of the redemption accomplished through Jesus [113]; for Mk, however, it is a revelatory event [114].

b. Mk 1,29-31 and Lk 4,38-39

Lk adds descriptive details about the intensity of the sickness (4,38b) and the immediate effect of the cure (4,39c). He also retains the name of Simon (but does not mention the names of the other three disciples), thereby preparing for the call of Simon in 5,1-11. Again, unlike Mk, for Lk the cure is effected by rebuking the fever (ἐπετίμησεν τῷ πυρετῷ) just as Jesus rebukes the demons (4,35.41; 9,42), the wind and the raging waves (8,24) and by ἀναστᾶσα the efficacy of the cure is stressed. Thus Lk highlights the miraculous aspect of the event but interprets it as if it were an exorcism. The following scheme sheds light on this Lucan perspective:

---

[109] Ex 7,8-13,16 narrates ten mighty acts worked by Moses, the first liberator. The repetition of such mighty acts was expected at the Messianic time (cf. Targum Pseudo-jonathan Exodus 12,42; Targum Lamentation 2,22). By narrating ten miracles in chs. 8-9, Mt presents Jesus as the new Moses, the Messianic deliverer.

[110] Mt 8,16 is a summary of Jesus' exorcisms (8,16ab) and healings (8,16c) parallel to Mk 1,32-34. Therefore, it is not a logical conclusion of 8,1-15 where only healings are narrated.

[111] Mt 31 words, Mk 44 words and Lk 38 words.

[112] The only healing in the first Gospel without any interlocutor.

[113] Cf. LÉON-DUFOUR, "La belle-mère", 136-137; LAMARCHE, "La belle-mère", 523.

[114] Cf. p. 249-250.

Situation	Rebuke	Result
A man with the spirit of an unclean demon (4,33-34)	Jesus rebuked him (4,35a)	The man is liberated from the evil spirit (4,35b).
Peter's mother-in-law ill with high fever (4,38b)	Jesus rebuked the fever (4,39a)	Immediate cure (4,39bc).
Jesus and his disciples in a boat in the stormy sea (8,23b-24a)	Jesus rebuked the wind and the raging waves(8,24b)	There was calm (8,24c).
The epileptic demoniac (9,38-42a)	Jesus rebuked the unclean spirit (9,42b)	The boy was healed (9,42cd).

2. Tradition and Redaction

In v. 29 καὶ εὐθὺς ἐκ τῆς συναγωγῆς ἐξελθόντες is redactional, for by means of Jesus' entry and exit our evangelist links various pericopes [115]. Moreover, as noted before, the impersonal plural, multiplication of cognate verbs, compound verbs with the same preposition, and the adverbial use of εὐθύς are typical of the second evangelist. The mention of the names of James and John is probably redactional, since Mk uses μετά for the secondary insertion of persons (cf. 3,6.7; 15,1.31). It is likely that εὐθύς in v. 30 comes from the Marcan hand. There is a very remote possibility that κατακεῖσθαι in v. 30 and κρατεῖν and χείρ in v. 31 are redactional [116].

---

[115] Cf. Mk 1,21 and 1,29; 2,1 and 2,13; 3,1 and 3,7; 5,38 and 6,1; 7,24 and 7,31; 8,22 and 8,27; 9,14 and 9,30; 11,11a and 11,11c; 11,15 and 11,19; 12,27 and 13,1.

[116]	Mt	Mk	Lk	Jn	Acts	Paul	Rest		Total
κατακεῖσθαι	0	4	3	2	2	1	0	=	12
κρατεῖν	12	15	2	2	4	2	10	=	47
χείρ.........................	24	25	26	15	45	17	24	=	176

3. *Literary Structure*

29 A Καὶ εὐθὺς ἐκ τῆς συναγωγῆς ἐξελθόντες ἦλθον εἰς τὴν οἰκίαν
       Σίμωνος καὶ ᾿Ανδρέου μετὰ ᾿Ιακώβου καὶ ᾿Ιωάννου

30   B ἡ δὲ πενθερὰ Σίμωνος κατέκειτο πυρέσσουσα, καὶ εὐθὺς λέγουσιν
          αὐτῷ περὶ αὐτῆς.

31   C καὶ προσελθὼν ἤγειρεν αὐτὴν κρατήσας τῆς χειρός

       B' καὶ ἀφῆκεν αὐτὴν ὁ πυρετός,

   A' καὶ διηκόνει αὐτοῖς.

Mk 1,29-31 thus constitutes a concentric structure (A B C B' A'). The
arrival into the house of Simon and Andrew (A) parallels the service done
to them by Simon's mother-in-law (A'). Similarly Simon's mother-in-law
sick with fever (B) is parallel to her being cured of fever (B'). The centre
of the structure (C), differing from A B B' A', consists of verbs predicated
exclusively of Jesus. This constitutes the cardinal event of the narrative.

B. Exegesis

1. *Arrival at the House of Simon and Andrew (1,29)*

After Jesus' teaching and exorcism in the synagogue, he enters a house
together with the four disciples whom he had called. The close association
of the disciples with Jesus indicates not a social fellowship but an embryonic
Christian community under the leadership of Jesus [117]. The names of the four
disciples are mentioned in the same sequence and combination (Simon and
Andrew, James and John) as in 1,16.19.

The house which Jesus enters is that of Simon and Andrew. Having left
his home in Nazareth (Mk 1,9) [118], Jesus does not have a home of his own
nor does he live with his parents (3,21.31) but he leads an itinerant life.
Sometimes he is the guest of Simon (1,29) and Levi (2,15) at Capernaum,
of Simon the leper (14,3) and Lazarus (Jn 12,1-8) at Bethany, of Zacchaeus

---

[117] Cf. RIGAU, *Témoignage*, 157-165.
[118] See also Mt 4,13; Lk 1,26; 2,4.39.51; 4,16.

at Jericho, etc. [119]. The same itinerant ministry Jesus recommends also to his apostles (Mk 6,10-11).

What does Mk mean by οἰκία in 1,29? In the second Gospel there are eleven instances when Jesus enters a house or is at a house: in four cases the owner of the house is specified (1,29; 2,15; 5,38; 14,3) and in seven instances unspecified (2,1; 3,20; 7,17.24; 9,28.33; 10,10). The house in 2,1 is presumably that of Simon [120]; in 3,20 and 9,33 it is certainly at Capernaum and in 7,17 it is probably at Capernaum. These could possibly be referring to the house of Simon.

The noun οἰκία/οἶκος [121], depending on the context and the event that takes place in the pericope, has different nuances in Mk. It is a locus theologicus of Jesus' private instruction to his disciples in four instances: (7,17; 9,28.33; 10,10) [122]. In four other instances (2,1.15; 3,20; 14,3) it is the locus theologicus of his revelatory words, and in three other cases (1,29; 5,38; 7,24) of his revelatory deeds. The noun οἰκία in 1,29 has a theological significance inasmuch as the first healing whereby Jesus reveals himself takes place in Simon's house. Furthermore, in light of our interpretation of the close association of Jesus and his disciples as an embryonic Christian community, it is reasonable to view the house which accommodates the Christian community as symbolic of the church [123].

2. Simon's Mother-in-Law Sick (1,30)

Simon's mother-in-law's condition is described as κατέκειτο πυρέσσουσα. In Mk κατακεῖσθαι is used in two senses: to lie down/lie in bed (1,30; 2,4) and to recline at table (2,15; 14,3). The verb πυρέσσειν which

---

[119] Mt 8,20 par. Lk 9,58: "And Jesus said to him, 'Foxes have holes, and the birds of the air have nests, but the Son of man has nowhere to lay his head'".

[120] The phrase τὴν θύραν in Mk 2,2 certainly evokes the same phrase from 1,33 where it refers to the door of Simon's house (1,29).

[121] Both οἰκία and οἶκος have basically two meanings: (1) house in the sense of dwelling; (2) family. But in Mk οἰκία shows a preference for the second meaning, that is, family as a place of sharing and intimacy.

[122] The house is the place where the question is asked by the disciples (7,17; 9,28; 10,10) or by Jesus himself (9,33). This is immediately followed by Jesus' private instructions to his disciples (7,18-23; 9,29.35-37; 10,11-12).

[123] Two reasons strengthen this symbolic interpretation. First, Simon's house was Jesus' own dwelling during his ministry. And second, the early Christians assembled in private houses (cf. Acts, 1,13; 2,1.46, etc.).

occurs only twice in the NT means to be feverish/to have a fever. So, according to Mk, she was lying down, suffering from fever. And by καὶ εὐθὺς λέγουσιν αὐτῷ περὶ αὐτῆς a request to heal her is implied (cf. Mk 1,32; 2,3-4; 3,9b-10; 6,55-56; 9,17-18) [124].

3. *Jesus' Healing Gesture (1,31a)*

In the second Gospel Jesus heals [125] by action (gestures) accompanied by words (1,41; 7,33-34; 8,23.25) or by words alone (2,5; 3,5; 10,52). The sick are also healed when they touch him or his garment (3,10; 5,27; 6,56). It is solely in the first healing that the sick woman is healed by a gesture alone — a gesture that is otherwise used in Mk for raising someone to life:

1,31a: καὶ προσελθὼν ἤγειρεν αὐτὴν κρατήσας τῆς χειρός

5,41: καὶ κρατήσας τῆς χειρὸς τοῦ παιδίου λέγει αὐτῇ ... σοὶ λέγω, ἔγειρε

9,27: ὁ δὲ Ἰησοῦς κρατήσας τῆς χειρὸς αὐτοῦ ἤγειρεν αὐτόν [126]

It should be noted that only in Mk Jesus lifts her up whereas in the parallels (Mt 8,15; Lk 4,39) "she rose and served them" (i.e., her rising demonstrates that healing has taken place). And according to the concentric structure we have proposed 1,31a constitutes the core of the narrative where ἤγειρεν is the main verb. This verb is the hinge of Mk 1,29-31.

Furthermore, Mk's favourite expression for Jesus' healing gesture is χεῖρ (-ας) ἐπιτιθέναι: there are in the second Gospel six instances while in the rest of the NT only five [127]. Why does he use ἐγείρειν in 1,31? In the NT this verb is primarily used for Jesus' Resurrection whether in the active [128] or in the passive [129]. It is also used in the sense to raise someone from the

---

[124] In other instances there is an explicit request for Jesus' intervention (Mk 1,40; 4,38; 5,22-23.27-28; 7,25-28.32; 8,22; 10,47-48).

[125] Exorcism is performed by word alone (1,25; 5,8; 9,25), resuscitation by word and gesture (5,41), and nature miracles either by word alone (4,39; 11,4) or by action alone (6,51).

[126] Note 9,26: "it (= the unclean spirit) came out, and the boy was like a *corpse*; so that most of them said, 'He is *dead*.'"

[127] Mk 5,23; 6,5; 7,32; 8,23.25; 16,8; Mt 9,18; Lk 13,13; Acts 9,12.17; 28,8.

[128] For example, Acts 3,15; 4,10; 5,30; 10,40; 13,30.37; Rom 4,24; 8,11; 10,9; 1 Cor 6,14; 15,15; 2 Cor 4,14; Gal 1,1; Eph 1,20, etc.

[129] For instance, Mt 16,21; 17,23; 26,32; 28,6; Mk 14,28; 16,6; Rom 6,4.9; 8,34; 1 Cor 15,12.20, etc.

dead, both in the active [130] and in the passive [131]. By using ἐγείρειν in 1,31, a verb so frequently employed for Jesus' Resurrection in the early Church, Mk probably attaches a symbolic significance to Jesus' first healing gesture: it is an anticipatory participation in Jesus' own Resurrection [132]. As ὁ Θεὸς ἤγειρεν Ἰησοῦν ἐκ νεκρῶν (Acts 3,15) [133] so also Ἰησοῦς ἤγειρεν αὐτὴν κρατήσας τῆς χειρός (Mk 1,31a).

4. *She is Cured from Fever (1,31b)*

The efficacy of Jesus' healing gesture performed effortlessly without any magic or special technique is narrated in 1,31b: καὶ ἀφῆκεν αὐτὴν ὁ πυρετός. The aorist (ἀφῆκεν) underlines the immediate and total efficacy of Jesus' healing gesture [134]. "Natura hominum istiusmodi est, ut post febrem magis lassescant corpora: et incipiente sanitate aegrotationis mala sentiant. Verum sanitas quae confertur a Domino, totum simul reddit" [135].

5. *Her Service to Them (1,31c)*

Verse 31c narrates: καὶ διηκόνει αὐτοῖς. The statement of the cure is expressed by the aorist tense (ἀφῆκεν) but the demonstration of the cure is in the imperfect (διηκόνει) even though Mk generally employs the aorist in similar instances (cf. 1,27.45; 4,41; 5,20; 8,26, etc.). Mk 1,31 and 10,52 are two conspicuous exceptions to this general practice where respectively διηκόνει and ἠκολούθει occur. What does διηκόνει in 1,31 mean? Several commentators interpret this verb in the sense to serve at table [136]. I think that by this verb Mk means service of a general nature, perhaps with waiting at table as part of it, and this for the following reasons. First, if it means only

---

[130] Cf. Mt 10,8; Jn 5,21; Acts 26,8, etc.

[131] Cf. Mt 11,5; 14,2; 27,52; Mk 6,14.16; 12,26, etc.

[132] But LAMARCHE, "La belle-mère", 519-521, and LÉON-DUFOUR, "La belle-mère", 138 find a baptismal symbolism in 1,29-31.

[133] Same formula in Acts 4,10; 5,30; 10,40; 13,30; Rom 10,9; 1 Cor 6,14, etc.

[134] To stress the immediate efficacy Mk always employs the aorist (cf. 1,26.31.34.42; 2,12; 3,5; 4,39; 5,42; 6,5, etc.).

[135] HIERONYMUS, *Matthaeus*, 53-54.

[136] For instance, CRANFIELD, 82; GRUNDMANN, 63; KLOSTERMANN, 19; LANE, 78; TAYLOR, 180, etc.

waiting at table, Mk would more likely have used the aorist tense as in other similar instances as noted above. Secondly, it is doubtful whether in Jesus' time women were permitted to wait on someone at table [137]. And thirdly, Mk does state that women from Galilee followed him and ministered to him (15,41) which presumably had begun in 1,31 where Peter's mother-in-law begins to serve Jesus and his disciples in a sense wider than serving at table. Therefore, her response to Jesus' healing consists in her continuous service to him and his disciples, the embryonic Christian community.

C. Conclusion

The healing of Peter's mother-in-law, the shortest miracle story in the Gospels, has received a few redactional touches from Mk's hands. By placing it in the scheme of Jesus' activity on a specific sabbath, our evangelist considers it particularly significant. It is the only healing in the second Gospel where the cure is effected through Jesus' gesture alone and it is comparable to a resuscitation whereby Jesus reveals himself [138]. The grateful response of Peter's mother-in-law consists in dedicated service to Jesus (and his disciples) which is a paradigm of Christian ecclesial service.

---

[137] Cf. STR.-B., *Kommentar* I, 480; GRUNDMANN, 63.
[138] Cf. p. 249-250.

III. The Summary on Healing and Exorcism (1,32-34)

A. Literary Analysis [139]

1. Delimitation of the Pericope

There are several authors who consider 1,29-34 as a single literary unit [140]. Schweizer, however, connects 1,32-34 not with 1,29-31 but with 1,35-39. According to him the pervading theme in vv. 32-39 is "die Bedeutung der Vollmacht Jesu" [141]. Finally, Merk considers the whole of 1,29-39 as a single literary unit.

Although the events narrated in 1,29-31 and 1,32-34 take place on the same day and in the same place, as Grundmann rightly observes [142], one should note that the dramatis personae in the former are Jesus, Simon's mother-in-law and the four disciples, but in the latter Jesus and the crowds. Besides, 1,29-31 narrates a particular healing while 1,32-34 summarizes both healings and exorcisms. Consequently, 1,32-34 is thematically connected not only with 1,29-31 but also with 1,21-28. Furthermore, 1,29-31 has its own literary structure just as 1,32-34 has its own literary structure too. As regards the relation between 1,32-34 and 1,35-39, there is no literary link between v. 34 and v. 35. There is both spatial and temporal discontinuity between 1,32-34 and 1,35-39. Finally in 1,35-38 no mention is made of a healing or exorcism which were the main themes in 1,32-34.

2. Synoptic Comparison

a. Mk 1,32-34 and Mt 8,16

The biblical quotation in 8,17 (= Is 53,4) is Mt's theological reflection on the meaning of Jesus' healings narrated in 8,16, the redactional composi-

---

[139] In v. 32 B D *al.* have ἔδυσεν whereas א A W Θ *al.* have ἔδυ. However, there is no difference in meaning between them. And in v. 34 the addition Χριστὸν εἶναι is probably an assimilation to the Lucan parallel (4,41).

[140] Among others see GNT; BELO, 148; GRUNDMANN, 62; KLOSTERMANN, 18.

[141] SCHWEIZER, 25.

[142] GRUNDMANN, 62.

tion of the evangelist [143]. According to Mt, it is the prophecy that interprets Jesus' miracles as God's activity and it is Jesus, the Messianic Servant, who brings the divine design to fulfilment [144]. For Mk, however, miracles by themselves reveal Jesus' person whose true identity is known to the demons. In contrast to Mk's ambiguous statement ("they brought to him all who were sick or possessed . . . he healed many who were sick . . . and cast out many demons" (1,32-34)), Mt emphasizes the all-powerful healing and exorcising potency of Jesus by stating that "they brought to him many who were possessed with demons; and he cast out the spirits with a word, and healed all who were sick" (8,16). Jesus' exorcism by a word (λόγῳ) in 8,16 is resonant of the centurion's faith in Jesus' efficacious and liberating word in 8,8. The order of events in Mk (healing—exorcism) is determined by the evangelist's interest in narrating the demons' knowledge of Jesus' identity and his command to secrecy as a climactic statement (1,34c). On the contrary, the order in Mt (exorcism—healing) is necessary because of the citation (8,17) concerned with infirmities and diseases only and not with exorcism.

b. Mk 1,32-34 and Lk 4,40-41

Lk has linguistically improved the Marcan text and rendered it more precise [145]. The following considerations are relevant for its content. Lk specifies that Jesus healed the sick by laying his hands on them (4,40c) and clarifies the Marcan ambiguity by stating that all the sick brought to him were healed by him (4,40). As in Mt, Mk 1,33 is absent in Lk too. The description in Mk 3,11-12 (the demons' confession of Jesus as the Son of God and the injunction to silence) is brought forward to Lk 4,41. And his elucidation of the title, 'Son of God', by means of another title, 'Christ', "may be to indicate that 'Son of God' must not be understood in purely Hellenistic categories as a reference to a charismatic, semi-divine figure" [146] but as the promised Messiah [147].

---

[143] The vocabulary in 8,16 is to a great extent typical of Mt. Cf. BENOIT-BOISMARD, *Synopse* II, 97-98.

[144] Cf. FABRIS, *Matteo*, 202; SCHWEIZER, *Matthew*, 217.

[145] Cf. MARSHALL, *Luke*, 195-197; SCHÜRMANN, *Lukas* I, 252-254.

[146] MARSHALL, *Luke*, 197.

[147] Cf. GRUNDMANN, *Lukas*, 125; SCHÜRMANN, *Lukas* I, 254.

3. Redactional Character of 1,32-34

Several authors assert that when composing 1,32-34, Mk was indebted to pre-Marcan tradition. However, their distinction between tradition and redaction in 1,32-34 has produced divergent results [148]. Prescinding from these opinions, let us examine the text in depth so as to answer these authors adequately.

V. 32 is certainly redactional. In Mk most of the genitive absolutes occur in redactional verses [149] and, in particular, all occurrences of ὀψίας (δὲ) γενομένης serve as a connecting link in the narrative (cf. 4,35; 6,47; 14,17; 15,42). Double temporal statements, typical of Mk, are frequently found in redactional verses [150]. Verbs of movement + πρός + αὐτόν ('Ιησοῦν) generally occur in redactional verses [151]. 'Impersonals' like ἔφερον are a typical feature of Marcan redaction [152]. The expression κακῶς ἔχοντες is thrice redactional (1,32.34; 6,55) and only once traditional (2,17). Also generally considered redactional is καὶ τοὺς δαιμονιζομένους [153]. Double participial constructions (ἔχοντας ... δαιμονιζομένους) are another characteristic literary feature of our evangelist [154]. And φέρειν is a Marcan preferential verb [155].

Verse 33 is also redactional. Periphrastic constructions, a favourite stylistic feature of Mk, frequently occur in redactional verses [156]. The phrase 'gather together about the door' occurs also in 2,2, a verse commonly considered redactional [157]. And the adjective ὅλος is most frequent in the second Gospel [158]. There is sufficient evidence that 1,34 is redactional. The verb θεραπεύειν occurs also in other redactional verses (cf. 3,10; 6,5.13); πολλά

---

[148] For instance, see EGGER, *Frohbotschaft*, 72; KERTELGE, *Wunder*, 32; PESCH, I, 133; id., "Ein Tag", 190; SCHENKE, *Wundererzählungen*, 115; SNOY, "Miracles", 59-71.

[149] PRYKE, *Redactional Style*, 62-67, considers 24 out of a possible 29 occurrences of genitive absolute redactional.

[150] Cf. n. 35 above.

[151] Mk 1,40.45; 2,3.13; 3,8.13.31; 4,1; 5,15; 6,30; 9,19.20; 10,1.14.50.

[152] Of the 46 occurrences of 'impersonals' PRYKE (*Redactional Style*, 107-115) allots 29 to redaction and 17 to tradition.

[153] Cf. GNILKA, I, 85-86; KOCH, *Bedeutung*, 161-166; SCHENKE, *Wundererzählungen*, 113.

[154] Cf. p. 86, n. 28.

[155] Cf. n. 160 below.

[156] PRYKE (*Redactional Style*, 103-106) assigns 20 occurrences to redaction and 10 to tradition.

[157] Cf. p. 180.

[158] Cf. n. 160 below.

accusative is usually redactional in the second Gospel [159]; δαιμόνια ἐκβάλλειν is also found in other redactional verses (cf. 1,39; 3,15); the adjective πολύς is most frequent in Mk [160]. And finally, the twin phrases — the demons' knowledge of Jesus' identity and the injunction to silence — pertain to the central theme of Mk, the Messianic secret. These twin phrases in 3,11-12 are considered redactional too.

4. *Literary Structure*

32 ---- Ὀψίας δὲ γενομένης, ὅτε ἔδυ ὁ ἥλιος

A ἔφερον πρὸς αὐτὸν *πάντας τοὺς κακῶς ἔχοντας καὶ τοὺς δαιμονιζομένους*

33 B καὶ ἦν ὅλη ἡ πόλις ἐπισυνηγμένη πρὸς τὴν θύραν

34 A' καὶ ἐθεράπευσεν *πολλοὺς κακῶς ἔχοντας ποικίλαις νόσοις, καὶ δαιμόνια πολλὰ ἐξέβαλεν*

---- καὶ οὐκ ἤφιεν λαλεῖν τὰ δαιμόνια, ὅτι ᾔδεισαν αὐτόν

Thus 1,32-34 consists of a clearly demarcated concentric structure (A B A') where the people's gathering to Jesus (B) is emphasized.

B. Interpretation

1. *The Sick and the Possessed Brought to Jesus (1,32)*

The narration begins with a double statement of time: that evening, at sundown. Of these two descriptions of time, the second further defines the time more precisely, a literary feature found elsewhere in Mk (cf. 1,35; 4,35; 13,11; 14,1.12; 16,2). The second more precise description of time in 1,32 (i.e., at sundown) perhaps suggests that neither the transportation of the sick

---

[159] PRYKE (*Redactional Style*, 70-72) is of the view that of the 10 occurrences, one (15,3) or utmost two (12,41?) are from tradition while the rest are redactional.

[160]	Mt	Mk	Lk	Jn	Acts	Paul	Rest		Total
ὅλος	22	18	16	6	19	14	13	=	108
πολύς	50	57	51	36	46	82	31	=	353
φέρειν	6	15	4	17	10	2	14	=	68

and the possessed nor Jesus' healings and exorcisms violated the sabbatical laws [161]. The verb ἔφερον is impersonal, meaning 'people were bringing' and in the imperfect tense [162], implying that these were not isolated instances but continuously repetitive: "case after case arrived" [163]. The idiomatic phrase τοὺς κακῶς ἔχοντας (cf. 1,34; 2,17; 6,55) describes the sick people and τοὺς δαιμονιζομένους means the possessed. The verb δαιμονίζομαι is derived from Hellenistic Greek and corresponds to the classical δαιμονάω which means to be under the power of a δαίμων. Mk thus clearly distinguishes the sick from those possessed (cf. 1,34; 3,9-12; 6,13).

2. The Whole City Gathered to Jesus (1,33)

The phrase ὅλη ἡ πόλις is hyperbolic like πᾶσα ἡ 'Ιουδαία χώρα in 1,5. The verb ἐπισυνάγειν, an intensive form of συνάγεν, occurs only twice in Mk: gathering his elect from the four winds (13,27) and gathering of a crowd (1,33). The noun θύρα is used six times in three different contexts: (1) the gate of someone's house (11,4; 13,29); (2) the door of Jesus' tomb (15,46; 16,3); (3) the door of Simon's house (1,33; 2,2) where the crowds gather. The crowds flocked to the door of Simon's house because Jesus, the Messiah, who performed an exorcism and healed Simon's mother-in-law is there. The gathering of the crowd, therefore, has an eschatological nuance in 1,33.

3. Jesus' Response (1,34)

Jesus' response is twofold: (1) καὶ ἐθεράπευσεν πολλοὺς κακῶς ἔχοντας ποικίλαις νόσοις, (2) καὶ δαιμόνια πολλὰ ἐξέβαλεν. The verb θεραπεύειν, predicated exclusively of Jesus(1,34; 3,2.10; 6,5) and of the Apostles (6,13), means in classical Greek to treat medically [164] and in Mk, as is clear from the context, it means to cure miraculously. The expression πάντες (v. 32) . . . πολλοὺς (v. 34) is a semitism [165], where the latter is

[161] GOULD, 26; KNABENBAUER, 56-57; RAWLISON, 18.
[162] Cf. TAYLOR, 180.
[163] SWETE, 24.
[164] Cf. CRANFIELD, 87; TAYLOR, 181.
[165] Cf. LOHMEYER, 87; GRUNDMANN, 64.

coextensive with the former [166]. By mentioning that people "with various diseases" were cured, our evangelist makes progress in his narration in 1,34 (compare with 1,30-31). The phrase δαιμόνια ἐκβάλλειν is frequently used in the synoptic tradition, particularly in Mk, for exorcism [167]. The pericope concludes with a statement on the Messianic secret. Unlike the first exorcism story where the evil spirit's verbal recognition of Jesus' identity (1,24) is followed by his injunction to silence (1,25), the exorcisms in 1,34 reverses the order. Here Jesus would not permit (ἤφιεν) the demons to speak, because they knew (ᾔδεισαν) him.

C. Mk 1,32-34 in Context

In conclusion, 1,32-34 should be considered a redactional composition of our evangelist which he placed at this point of the narrative. His aim in doing this has been aptly summarized by Nineham:

> The specimen day ends with the performance of a large number of exorcisms and healings. These are not described individually but their very number (all v.32 and many v.34) and variety (various diseases v.34) serve to show that the two cases just described in detail were not freaks or fortunate coincidences, but the manifestations of a power which can deal with 'all those who are in a bad way' (the literal translation in v.32), no matter what the various ills from which they may be suffering. A power so great and universally effective as this can be no other than the eschatological power of God [168].

---

[166] Cf. CRANFIELD, 87; SWETE, 24.
[167] Mk 1,39; 3,15.22; 6,13; 7,26; 9,18.28.38.
[168] NINIHAM, 82.

IV. Jesus' Departure from Capernaum and His Ministry in Galilee (1,35-39)

A. Literary Analysis [169]

1. *Delimitation of the Pericope*

Some authors affirm that there are two literary units in 1,35-39: Jesus' departure from Capernaum (1,35-38) and his preaching and healing in Galilee (1,39) [170]. This opinion is based mainly on two reasons: (1) ἐξῆλθεν in v. 35 and ἐξῆλθον in v. 38 constitute an inclusion; (2) v. 39 does not seem to fit into the theme of vv. 35-38 (withdrawal — search — response). However, a more appealing approach would consider 1,35-39 as a single literary unit because of the literary and thematic connections between v. 38 and v. 39. The subject of the verbs is Jesus both in 1,38 and in 1,39. Besides, in v. 38 Jesus expresses the wish to minister in the neighbouring towns, a wish which is realized in v. 39. Moreover, the verb κηρύσσειν is predicated of Jesus only thrice in the second Gospel: the first is in 1,14 while the second and the third occur in 1,38 and 1,39.

The critical edition of Nestle-Aland joins v. 39 to the healing of the leper (1,40-45). One can object to this for the following reasons. First, there is no literary or thematic connection between v. 39 and v. 40. Secondly, Mk 1,40-45 has a well-balanced concentric structure and so the inclusion of v. 39 to vv. 40-45 would create structural imbalance. And lastly, the wish expressed in v. 38 is actually fulfilled in v. 39.

2. *Mk 1,35-39 and Lk 4,42-44*

The Lucan parallel differs considerably from Mk 1,35-39 both in language and in content. Lk omits the reference to Jesus' prayer here but transposes it to 5,17. According to Mk, Simon and οἱ μετ' αὐτοῦ (i.e.,

---

[169] Accidental omission of a line or a conscious intention to prune away the apparent redundancy will account for the reading of B in verse 35. The MSS support for ἦλθεν in v. 39 is good and ἦν was probably introduced from the Lucan parallel (4,44). Having substituted ἦν for ἦλθεν the copyists standardized the grammar by changing εἰς to ἐν.

[170] Cf. ALAND, *Synopsis*, § 39-40; BELO, 149; HUCK-GREEVEN, *Synopsis*, § 27-28, etc.

presumably the other three disciples) tracked him down (κατεδίωξεν) but according to Lk the people sought him out (οἱ ὄχλοι ἐπεζήτουν). The clause, people "would have kept him from leaving them" (differs par. Mk 1,36) shows a marked contrast to the attitude of the inhabitants of Nazareth (cf. 4,29). Lk replaces the Marcan κηρύσσειν with his favourite εὐαγγελίζεσθαι τὴν βασιλείαν [171]. Compared to Mk, Lk not only clarifies but also emphasizes the nature of Jesus' mission by adding δεῖ (connoting divine necessity) and by substituting ἀποστέλλειν, an apt verb to denote his mission, for the ambiguous ἐξέρχεσθαι. In 1,39 Mk mentions Jesus' ministry of preaching and of exorcism in the region of Galilee whereas the Lucan parallel (4,44) contains only one activity, namely, preaching in the synagogues of Judea.

3. Tradition and Redaction

The opinion of scholars regarding the traditional and redactional elements in 1,35-39 differs drastically [172]. A more precise analysis is therefore necessary. Despite the hapax legomenon ἔννυχα, there is ample evidence to consider v. 35 redactional. As previously mentioned, the multiplication of cognate verbs (ἐξῆλθεν ... ἀπῆλθεν) and double statements (πρωῒ ἔννυχα λίαν) are generally redactional in the second Gospel. Narrative and discourse (v. 35: ἀναστὰς ἐξῆλθεν ... v. 38: εἰς τοῦτο γὰρ ἐξῆλθον) frequently occur in redactional verses [173]. The verbs ἀνιστάναι, ἀπέρχεσθαι and ἐξέρχεσθαι and the nouns ἔρημος τόπος and πρωΐ are predominantly Marcan [174]. Finally, the motif of withdrawal from a crowd that considers Jesus primarily as a miracle worker also occurs in other redactional verses [175].

The occurrence of ὅτι recitativum [176] and the use of ζητεῖν in a hostile sense [177] argue for the Marcan hand in v. 37b. Mk 1,38cd may be considered

---

[171] In Lk thrice (4,43; 8,1; 16,16) and Acts once (8,12) but never in the rest of the NT.

[172] (1) GNILKA, I, 88; KOCH, Bedeutung, 161; and WICHELHAUS, "Am ersten Tage", 61, consider the whole of 1,35-39 redactional. (2) PRYKE, Redactional Style, 153, is of the view that v. 36 is from tradition but the rest redactional. (3) The following authors hold that 1,35-38 is from tradition but 1,39 is redactional: PESCH, "Ein Tag", 267; SCHMIDT, Rahmen, 58-62, 67, 76-77; TAYLOR, 182, 184. (4) GRUNDMANN, 65, and ERNST, 72, affirm that an exact distinction between tradition and redaction is difficult. The former considers v. 39 redactional while the latter considers vv. 38b-39 redactional.

[173] Cf. NEIRYNCK, Duality, 115-119.

[174] Cf. n. 180 below.

[175] See, for instance, Mk 3,9.

[176] See p. 82, n. 8.

[177] Cf. 3,32; 8,11.12; 11,18; 12,12; 14,1.11.55; 16,6.

redactional by virtue of the Marcan preferential verbs κηρύσσειν and ἐξέρχεσθαι [178] and γάρ explanatory [179]. Verse 39 is certainly redactional because, as observed before, double participial construction (κηρύσσων ... ἐκβάλλων) and double statements (synagogue ... the whole of Galilee) are typical of Mk. The verbs ἔρχεσθαι and κηρύσσειν, and the adjective ὅλος are Marcan preferential terms [180], and 'Galilee' is obviously redactional [181].

To sum up, vv. 35.37b.38cd.39 are redactional and the rest are from tradition. Not only the typically Marcan vocabulary, style, motifs, etc. are absent in the verses allotted to tradition but also three NT hapax legomena occur in them: καταδιώκειν in v. 36 and ἀλλαχοῦ and κωμόπολις in v. 38.

4. *Literary Division*

An analysis of the subject of the verbs in 1,35-39 is very revealing. In v. 35 the subject of the verbs (ἀναστὰς ἐξῆλθεν ... ἀπῆλθεν ... προσηύχετο) is exclusively Jesus while in vv. 36-37 it is Simon and those with him (κατεδίωξεν ... εὗρον ... λέγουσιν) or 'all' (ζητοῦσιν). And in vv. 38-39 the subject of the verbs is either Jesus (λέγει ... κηρύξω ... ἐξῆλθον ... ἦλθεν ... κηρύσσων ... ἐκβάλλων) or Jesus and his disciples (ἄγωμεν). Based on these literary observations, 1,35-39 may conveniently be divided into three parts: withdrawal (v. 35), quest (vv. 36-37) and answer (vv. 38-39).

---

[178] Cf. n. 180 below.

[179] Cf. PRYKE, *Redactional Style*, 126-127.

[180]	Mt	Mk	Lk	Jn	Acts	Paul	Rest		Total
ἀνιστάναι	4	17	26	8	45	5	2	=	107
ἀπέρχεσθαι	35	23	19	21	6	2	10	=	116
ἐξέρχεσθαι	43	39	44	29	29	8	24	=	216
ἔρημος τόπος	2	5	2	0	0	0	0	=	9
κηρύσσειν	9	14	9	0	8	19	2	=	61
ὅλος	22	18	16	6	19	14	13	=	108
παρακαλεῖν	9	9	7	0	22	54	8	=	109
πρωί	3	6	0	2	1	0	0	=	12

[181] Cf. p. 86, n. 24.

B. Interpretation

1. *Withdrawal (1,35)*

The narrative begins with a dual temporal reference, "in the early morning, when it was still quite dark". Here the second element specifies the first. Verse 35 narrates three events joined by the conjunction καί: Jesus' coming out from the house (at Capernaum), his departure to a lonely place, and his prayer there. As noted earlier, our evangelist employs ἔρημος in two ways: as a noun, used absolutely (1,3.4.12.13) and as an adjective (1,35.45; 6,31.32.35). We have said that the absolute use has a Messianic nuance [182] and the adjectival use of ἔρημος has a common characteristic: Jesus seeks separation from the crowds in a lonely place. In 1,35, however, there is not only a separation from the crowd but also a communing with God (προσηύχετο) [183]. The verb προσεύχεσθαι is predicated of Jesus only in three pericopes (1,35; 6,46; 14,32.35.39). In contrast to ἐξῆλθεν and ἀπῆλθεν in the aorist, προσηύχετο is in the imperfect, meaning a prolonged or repeated prayer. According to Mk, Jesus prays alone, at night, in a lonely place, and at decisively critical moments of his mission. The content of Jesus' prayer is not mentioned in 1,35 and 6,46, but it is distinctively emphasized in the Gethsemane scene. The prayer at Gethsemane reveals Jesus' unique relation to the Father (14,36: "Abba, Father") [184] and the Father's will for him as the suffering Messiah (14,36: "All things are possible to thee; remove this cup from me; yet not what I will, but what thou wilt"). "And again he went away and prayed, saying the same words" (14,39). It is very likely that in keeping with the structure of the Gospel our evangelist reveals the content of Jesus' prayer (i.e., his person and his mission) not in the first part but in the second. We are justified in affirming that Jesus' prayer in 1,35 also deals with his person and mission: more precisely, here it is a process of discerning the Father's will for him.

---

[182] Cf. p. 15.

[183] SWETE, 26: "Sunrise would bring fresh crowds, new wonders, increasing popularity. Was all this consistent with His mission? Guidance must be sought in prayer".

[184] Cf. MARCHEL, *Abba, Père*, 100-123.

2. Quest (1,36-37)

The subject of the verbs in vv. 36-37b is Σίμων καὶ οἱ μετ' αὐτοῦ. The phrase μετ' αὐτοῦ implies very close association (cf. 2,25; 5,40) and here it presumably stands for Andrew, James and John (cf. 1,16.19.29) [185]. The first action predicated of them is καταδιώκειν (the perfective of the verb διώκειν) which in light of the LXX (cf. Gen 14,14.15; 35,5, etc.) denotes an air of hostility. They find Jesus and tell him that all are searching for him (ζητεῖν). The verb ζητεῖν, as mentioned before, has a negative nuance in the second Gospel. For our evangelist, then, the disciples' pursuit of Jesus and the crowds' search for him are clear indications of their inadequate perceptions of Jesus.

3. Answer (1,38-39)

The wish in v. 38 commencing with ἄγωμεν has the destination εἰς τὰς ἐχομένας κωμοπόλεις. The present participle middle of ἔχειν is used in the sense of 'next', 'neighbouring' in the LXX [186] as well as in classical Greek [187]. And κωμόπολις denotes a small town having only the status of a village [188]. The purpose in going to the neighbouring villages is to preach (κηρύσσειν) which, as stated before, is a technical term used in the early Church for the proclamation of the Christian message [189]. The clause εἰς τοῦτο γὰρ ἐξῆλθον has two possible meanings: (1) Jesus had left Capernaum to exercise a wider preaching ministry in the neighbourhood [190]; (2) it was for the sake of this preaching ministry that he had come forth from God [191]. However, it should be noted that to describe Jesus' mission from God our evangelist generally uses not compound forms but the simple forms of the aorist of ἔρχεσθαι (cf. 1,24;2,17; 10,45). Yet the absolute use of ἐξῆλθον has not merely a local sense but also theological overtones elsewhere [192]. More-

---

[185] Against ARENS, ΗΛΘΟΝ-Sayings, 197: Simon "acted as spokesman for the crowds that were seeking Jesus".

[186] Cf. Num 2,5.12.20.27; 22,5; Deut 11,30; Judg 4,11; 19,14, etc.

[187] Cf. CRANFIELD, 89; TAYLOR, 184.

[188] Cf. CRANFIELD, 89; TAYLOR, 184.

[189] Cf. p. 90-91.

[190] Cf. GRUNDMANN, 65; PESCH, I, 138; RAWLISON, 19.

[191] Cf. LAGRANGE, 28; LOHMEYER, 43; SCHMIDT, Rahmen, 58.

[192] Cf. ARENS, ΗΛΘΟΝ-Sayings, 204-207.

over, ἐξῆλθον in our verse is preceded by a process of discerning God's will and followed by a ministry of preaching and exorcism throughout Galilee (v. 39), a prototype of the mission of the Twelve. Our evangelist then seems to be ambiguous: ἐξῆλθον in 1,38d denotes Jesus' coming out from Capernaum and at the same time it has a veiled reference to his coming from God [193].

The fulfilment of the wish (v. 39) exceeds the wish itself (v. 38) from two angles, namely, the geographical extension of Jesus' ministry and the content of his ministry. In v. 38 Jesus wanted to "go on to the next towns" while in v. 39 "he went throughout all Galilee". Again, according to v. 38 the purpose of his going to other towns is to preach but according to v. 39 he not only preaches but also casts out demons. Therefore, compared to v. 38, v. 39 clearly shows a progression.

C. Mk 1,35-39 in Context

The typical sabbath's activity concluded with a ministry of healings and exorcisms (1,32-34). But this apparently gave the people the impression that Jesus is a miracle worker. Moreover, the demons knew his identity (1.34d). Beset with these problems, Jesus withdraws to a lonely place for a prolonged process of discernment (1,35). As a result he decided to extend his ministry of proclamation and exorcism to the whole of Galilee.

V. Healing of the Leper (1,40-45)

A. Literary Analysis

1. *Textual Criticism*

There is only one disputed textual problem in this pericope [194]. Is σπλαγχνισθείς or ὀργισθείς the original reading in 1,41? The former reading is attested by diverse and widespread witnesses (ℵ A B K L W Δ Θ *al.*) [195]

---

[193] With CRANFIELD, 90; GNILKA, I, 89; LANE, 82; NINEHAM, 85; TAYLOR, 184.

[194] Regarding the variant readings in 1,40, it should be noted that, while it is difficult to account for the insertion of καὶ γονυπετῶν homoeteleuton could account for its accidental omission. And the variants in 1,45 consist merely of the transposition of words.

[195] GNT/NESTLE-ALAND, HUCK-GREEVEN, MERK, TISCHENDORF, TREGELLES, VON SODEN, WESTCOTT-HORT, etc. opt for this reading.

whereas the latter is found only in a few witnesses (D a ff² r¹) [196]. As Metzger observes, it is easier to see why ὀργισθείς ("being angry", too harsh and unnecessary to the context) would have prompted scrupulous copyists to change it to σπλαγχνισθείς ("being filled with compassion", more natural and suitable to context) than the contrary. Yet it should be noted that there are at least two other passages in Mk where Jesus is angry (3,5) or indignant (10,14) which have not been altered by scrupulous copyists. "It is possible that the reading ὀργισθείς either (a) was suggested by ἐμβριμησάμενος of v. 43, or (b) arose from confusion between similar words in Aramaic" [197]. Moreover, in the synoptic tradition, particularly in Mk, Jesus' feeling of compassion (σπλαγχνίζεσθαι) is followed by a miraculous deed to eradicate the suffering [198]. Therefore, we prefer σπλαγχνισθείς to ὀργισθείς.

2. Comparison with Mt 8,1-4 and Lk 5,12-16

a. Mk 1,40-45 and Mt 8,1-4

It is instructive to observe that not only Mt 8,1 has no parallel in Mk but also it is the redactional work of the first evangelist. He composed 8,1 to link the discourse on the mountain (5,1-7,29) with the narrative section of ten miracles (8,1-9,37):

4,25   And *great crowds followed* him from Galilee . . . from beyond Jordan.

5,1-2   *Seeing the crowds, he went up on the mountain* . . . opened his mouth and taught them.

7,28-29 The *crowds were astonished at his teaching* for he taught as one who had authority.

8,1   *When he had come down from the mountain, great crowds followed him.*

Thus the theme of Jesus coming down from the mountain and the crowds following him (8,1) logically flow from 4,23-7,29.

---

[196] TASKER; TAYLOR, 187; TURNER, "Commentary", 157; FUSCO, "Il segreto messianico", 246-247, etc. opt for this reading.

[197] METZGER, *Commentary*, 77.

[198] Cf. p. 166-167 below.

The clause in v. 2 where a leper "came to him and knelt before him" is a stereotypic Matthean phrase (cf. Mt 9,18; 15,25; 20,20) which probably had liturgical and cultic overtones [199]. The address Κύριε in v. 2 (absent in Mk 1,40) is not a mere courtesy title but one by which Mt presents the leper as a model for Christians who turn to Christ the Lord [200]. Jesus' emotional reactions (Mk 1,41a: σπλαγχνισθείς, 1,43: ἐμβριμησάμενος) are absent in the first Gospel. Of the Marcan synonymous expression in v. 42 ("and immediately the leprosy left him, and he was made clean") Mt retains the second element with slight modification ("and immediately his leprosy was cleansed"). Mk 1,43 is omitted by Mt because it is not only too strong but also superfluous. Mk 1,45 is totally absent in Mt because he probably wants to avoid the ex-leper's disobedience to Jesus' command to secrecy and because his theological perspective is different. After narrating three healings (leper, centurion's servant and Peter's mother-in-law) and a brief summary of his exorcisms and healings (8,16), the first evangelist proceeds to offer the theological significance of Jesus' healings in God's salvific plan by citing Is 53,4 in 8,17. Thus the theological import of 8,1-4 is brought to a finale only in 8,17 whereas in Mk the narrative climax is in 1,45. Furthermore, in Mt the miracle concludes with Jesus' own words on the observance of Mosaic Law which he had already stressed in 5,17-20.

b. Mk 1,40-45 and Lk 5,12-16

In order to effect a smooth transition from 5,1-11 to 5,12-16, Lk composed 5,12a. In the narration of the miracle, as in the Matthean parallel, Lk too has the leper address Jesus as Κύριε, and Jesus' emotional reactions are eliminated. Of the synonymous expression in Mk 1,42 Lk retains the first element. In 5,15-16, primarily a redactional composition, Lk highlights the impact of the miracle, viz., the spreading of the report concerning Jesus and the gathering of the multitudes to hear him and to be healed by him. All this leads Jesus to withdraw for prayer.

---

[199] Cf. Mt 2,2.8.11; 4,9.10; 14,33; 28,9.17.
[200] Cf. FABRIS, *Matteo*, 195; GRUNDMANN, *Matthäus*, 248.

3. *Tradition and Redaction*

The healing proper (the nucleus of the event) consists of vv. 40-42. In v. 40a redactional features are very prominent. As mentioned before, the following six features are typically Marcan: verbs of movement + πρός + αὐτόν (Jesus); historic present (ἔρχεται); double participial constructions; double statements, general and special; direct discourse preceded by a qualifying verb; and ὅτι recitativum. Among the synoptic Gospels παρακαλεῖν is relatively more frequent in the second Gospel [201]. Synonymous expressions ("the leprosy left him, and he was made clean" v. 42) is characteristic of Mk [202]. Of the two elements of the synonymous expression in v. 42, the first probably originated with our evangelist since, as previously observed, compound verbs followed by the same preposition (ἀπῆλθεν ἀπ') and the adverbial use of εὐθύς are typical of our evangelist. Moreover, according to the narrative sequence in vv. 40-42, the clause "the leprosy left him" in v. 42 is superfluous.

The events occurring after the healing (vv. 43-45) are also composed of traditional and redactional elements. In v. 43 except for εὐθύς there is no other compelling literary factor that would argue for its redactional character. However, a comparison of v. 43 with 5,40a; 7,33; 8,23a reveals that in the first part of the Gospel Jesus performs miracles of Messianic overtones not in public but in private. In 1,43 he demands privacy after performing the miracle but in 5,40a; 7,33; 8,23a before the performance of the miracle [203]. Mk 1,43 thus pertains to the theme of the Messianic secret. However, all passages dealing with the Messianic secret need not be redactional, some could easily have originated in the pre-Marcan tradition.

Verse 44a is redactional because the double negative and asyndetic construction are characteristic of Mk [204] and because the command to secrecy on the beneficiaries of miracles of Messianic implications is more frequent and more emphatic in Mk than in Mt and Lk [205]. In v. 45a there seems to be a fusion of redaction and tradition. Multiplication of cognate verbs (εἰσελθὼν . . . εἰς εἰσελθεῖν . . . ἤρχοντο πρός) [206] and ἄρχειν with infinitive [207] are charac-

---

[201] Cf. n. 180 above.

[202] Cf. p. 87, n. 30.

[203] Note that in 1,40-42 no one else is mentioned except the leper and Jesus whereas in 5,38-40a; 7,32 and 8,22 people were present.

[204] NEIRYNCK (*Duality*, 87-88) mentions 23 occurrences of double negative in Mk. Of these Mt follows Mk in 7 instances and Lk in 3; no parallel: Mt 3 and Lk 7; modifications: Mt 13 and Lk 13.

[205] Cf. p. 170-171.

[206] Cf. n. 21 above.

[207] Cf. PRYKE, *Redactional Style*, 79-87; LAGRANGE, LXIX.

teristically Marcan. Moreover, as noted before, κηρύσσειν and πολλά are typical of our evangelist. However, διαφημίζειν is hapax in the second Gospel and it occurs in combination with λόγος only twice in the whole NT (Mt 28,15; Mk 1,45). In v. 45b, as noted before, the construction ὥστε with infinitive indicating result, and compound verbs with the same preposition are distinct literary devices of Mk. Besides, double statements, negative and positive (μηκέτι . . . ἀλλ') are characteristic of Mk [208]. Furthermore, just as the adverb φανερῶς here, all three occurrences of the adjective φανερός in Mk are found in the context of the hiddenness and manifestation of Jesus (3,12; 4,22; 6,14). In v. 45c double statements, (ἔξω/ἔρημος τόπος) and the expression ἔρημος τόπος are typically Marcan. In v. 45d it should be noted that the construction, verbs of movement + πρός + αὐτόν (Jesus), is characteristic of Mk.

In conclusion, therefore, we hold that v. 40a is to a great extent redactional. The clause "the leprosy left him" in v. 42 most probably originates with Mk. Verses 44a and 45 (except the clause "and he spread the news") are redactional. The rest is pre-Marcan.

4. Literary Structure

40 A *Καὶ ἔρχεται πρὸς αὐτὸν λεπρὸς παρακαλῶν αὐτὸν καὶ γονυπετῶν καὶ λέγων αὐτῷ ὅτι Ἐὰν θέλῃς δύνασαί με καθαρίσαι.*

41 B *καὶ σπλαγχνισθεὶς ἐκτείνας τὴν χεῖρα αὐτοῦ ἥψατο καὶ λέγει αὐτῷ, Θέλω, καθαρίσθητι·*

42 C *καὶ εὐθὺς ἀπῆλθεν ἀπ' αὐτοῦ ἡ λέπρα, καὶ ἐκαθαρίσθη.*

43 B' *καὶ ἐμβριμησάμενος αὐτῷ εὐθὺς ἐξέβαλεν αὐτόν,*

44 *καὶ λέγει αὐτῷ, "Ορα μηδενὶ μηδὲν εἴπῃς, ἀλλὰ ὕπαγε σεαυτὸν δεῖξον τῷ ἱερεῖ καὶ προσένεγκε περὶ τοῦ καθαρισμοῦ σου ἃ προσέταξεν Μωϋσῆς, εἰς μαρτύριον αὐτοῖς.*

45 A' *ὁ δὲ ἐξελθὼν ἤρξατο κηρύσσειν πολλὰ καὶ διαφημίζειν τὸν λόγον, ὥστε μηκέτι αὐτὸν δύνασθαι φανερῶς εἰς πόλιν εἰσελθεῖν, ἀλλ' ἔξω ἐπ' ἐρήμοις τόποις ἦν· καὶ ἤρχοντο πρὸς αὐτὸν πάντοθεν.*

---

[208] NEIRYNCK (*Duality*, 89-94) mentions 106 occurrences of double statement: negative-positive. Of these Mt follows Mk in 46 instances while Lk does so in only 29 instances; no parallel: Mt 19 and Lk 42; modified: Mt 41 and Lk 35.

Just as the leper's entreaty to be cleansed (1,40: A) parallels his making the story known (1,45: A'), so too Jesus' curing him (1,41: B) parallels the prohibition to publicity (1,43-44: B'). His cure (1,42: C) is thus the core of the narrative [209].

This concentric structure, primarily based on parallelism, can also be reinforced by studying the text from the perspective of the dramatis personae and their actions:

A A *leper comes* to Jesus with the entreaty to cleanse him (1,40).

    B *Jesus* filled with compassion *touches* him and *cleanses* him (1,41).

        C The *leprosy left* him and he is cleansed (1,42).

    B' *Jesus prohibits* publicity and *sends* him to the priest (1,43-44).

A' The *ex-leper makes the story public* and its results (1,45).

B. Interpretation

1. *The Leper's Entreaty to Jesus (1,40)*

The coming of the leper to Jesus in 1,40 is striking because the situation of the sick is generally reported to Jesus by someone else (usually a close relative) with the implicit (1,29) or explicit request to heal (5,22-23; 7,24) or they are brought to him (2,3; 6,55; 7,32; 8,22; 9,20). In contrast, they approach Jesus on their own initiative in 1,40; 3,9-10; 5,27.33; 10,47-51. Of these four pericopes, in 1,40 the crowd is absent and the leper comes to Jesus all alone, probably because at that time a leper was sequestered from normal society. The leper's approach to Jesus is qualified by παρακαλῶν ... γονυπετῶν ... λέγων.

The verb παρακαλεῖν is used by Mk [210] only in the active voice with Jesus as its direct object, and exclusively in the context of miracles [211]. The second participle γονυπετῶν, a rare verb in the NT and used only in the participial form [212], denotes a posture of entreaty. The third participle (λέγων)

---

[209] PAUL, "La guérison", 597, proposes a structure in which 1,43 is the centre of the pericope. He has not taken into due consideration all of the literary elements of the pericope.

[210] Differ Mt (cf. 2,18; 5,4; 18,29.32; 26,53) and Lk (cf. 3,18; 15,28; 16,25).

[211] Mk 1,40; 5,10.12.17.18.23; 6,56; 7,32; 8,22.

[212] Only four occurrences in the NT: Mt 17,14; 27,29; Mk 1,40; 10,17.

introduces the direct discourse in which the leper expresses his earnest wish
to be healed (καθαρίσαι). The verb καθαρίζειν is used in the synoptic gospels
in the sense to heal from leprosy (Mt 8,2.3; 10,8; 11,5; Mk 1,40.41.42; Lk
4,27; 5,12.13; 7,22; 17,14.17) or to mean Levitical cleansing (Mt 23,25.26;
Mk 7,19; Lk 11,39). In Mk 1,40 the leper requests Jesus to heal him from
his leprosy. Therefore the whole dynamism of v. 40 concerns the leper's
earnest entreaty to Jesus to cleanse him: ἔρχεται ... παρακαλῶν ... γονυπετῶν
... λέγων ... 'Εὰν θέλῃς δύνασαί με καθαρίσαι.

2. Jesus' Response to the Leper (1,41)

Jesus' response to the leper perfectly corresponds to his entreaty:

Mk 1,40	Mk 1,41
Καὶ ἔρχεται πρὸς αὐτὸν λεπτός	καὶ σπλαγχνισθεὶς ἐκτείνας τὴν χεῖρα
παρακαλῶν αὐτὸν καὶ γονυπετῶν	αὐτοῦ ἥψατο
καὶ λέγων αὐτῷ ὅτι	καὶ λέγει αὐτῷ,
'Εὰν θέλῃς δύνασαί με καθαρίσαι	Θέλω, καθαρίσθητι·

Jesus' response to the leper is described in two stages: Jesus' healing
gesture, described by two participles followed by the main verb (v. 41a), and
his healing words (v.41b). Regarding the first participle (σπλαγχνισθείς) it is
instructive to note that various verbal forms of σπλαγχνίζεσθαι found in the
NT exclusively in the synoptic Gospels and used, whether in reference to
Jesus (Mt 9,36; 14,14; 15,32; 20,34; Mk 1,41; 6,34; 8,2; 9,22; Lk 7,13) or
others (Mt 18,27; Lk 10,33; 15,20), are followed by a benevolent act of Jesus
towards the person for whom he has compassion:

Cause for Feeling Compassion	Jesus Offers the Remedy
A leper's entreaty due to his deplorable state (Mk 1,40-41a)	Jesus heals him (1,41b-42).
People, like sheep without a shepherd and hungry (Mk 6,34-36)	Jesus miraculously feeds them (6,37-42).
People hungry (Mk 8,2-3)	Jesus satiates their hunger (8,4-8).
Request for pity and help (Mk 9,22)	Jesus liberates the boy from the possession of the evil spirit (9,25-27).

Thus, according to Mk, feeling of compassion is an attribute of Jesus which is followed by the eradication of the suffering.

The second participle predicated of Jesus is ἐκτείνας with the direct object τὴν χεῖρα. The verb ἐκτείνειν occurs in the NT always with the direct object τὴν (-ὰς) χεῖρ (-ας) except in Acts 27,30. In the OT ἐκτείνειν τὴν χεῖρα generally occurs in the context of the mighty deeds accomplished by God, particularly the wonders worked by God through Moses to liberate Israel from slavery in Egypt [213]. In the synoptic tradition Jesus stretches out his hand only in Mk 1,41 and its parallels (Mt 8,3; Lk 5,13). Therefore in the background of the wonders of exodus, Jesus' stretching out his hand in 1,41 has the nuance of liberation. As Yahweh liberated Israel from slavery in Egypt through Moses, so also Jesus liberates the leper from his solitude and religious slavery and reinstates him to the social and religious status of a person.

The main verb in v. 41 is ἥψατο. The verb ἅπτειν, occurring primarily in the synoptic Gospels, means "to light, to kindle", and in the middle voice it means "to touch, to take hold of". It is used in the sense to "light" only in the Lucan writings (Lk 8,16; 11,33; 15,8; 22,51; Acts 28,2). In the first and the second Gospels it is always used in the sense of "to touch" in the context of miracles, except in Mt 17,7 and Mk 10,13. Either Jesus touches the sick and the handicapped [214] or they touch him or his garments [215]. In Mk 1,41 Jesus' touch is accompanied by his assuring words: "I will; be clean".

3. *The Cure from Leprosy (1,42)*

Jesus' efficacious action and word had an immediate effect as the adverb εὐθύς and the aorist form of the verbs (ἀπῆλθεν ... ἐκαθαρίσθη) clearly express. In the NT, the compound verb ἀπέρχεσθαι followed by the preposition ἀπό (meaning to depart, go from) governs a personal subject (Mt 28,8; Mk 5,17; Lk 1,38; 2,15; 8,37; Acts 16,39) and an impersonal subject (Mk 1,42; Lk 5,13; Rev 18,14). By the use of the synonymous expression ("the leprosy left him, and he was made clean") Mk stresses the fact of the cure and the fact of being cleansed. Verse 42, therefore, emphasizes the suddenness and the wholeness of the cure.

---

[213] For instance, see Ex 3,20; 4,4; 7,5.19; 8,5.6.16.17; 9,22.23.33; 10,12.21.22; 14,16.21.26.27, etc.

[214] Mt 8,3.15; 9,29; 20,34; Mk 1,41; 7,33; 8,22.

[215] Mt 9,20.21; 14,36(bis); Mk 3,10; 5,27.28.30.31; 6,56 (bis).

Leprosy today is usually confined to Hansen's disease caused by a bacillus. In the Bible, however, it denotes various diseases of the skin and implies serious personal, social and religious repercussions (cf. Lev 13-14; Num 12,1-16; 2 Kings 5,3-14). The socio-religious status of lepers is underlined in the OT (cf. Num 12,9-15; 2 Chron 26, 16-21, etc.) and in the rabbinic tradition. Both view leprosy as God's punishment for committing grave sins and, as a consequence, lepers are considered equal to the dead and a cure from leprosy is judged to be as difficult as raising a dead person back to life [216]. Because of such theological conceptions about leprosy and its social and religious consequences, one can also understand why cleansing from leprosy was exclusively reserved to God and men authorized by Him. Furthermore, it was also believed that leprosy would no longer afflict men in the Messianic age [217]. The cleansing of the leper thus has Messianic implications: it shows the commencement of the Messianic age.

4. Jesus' Command to the Ex-Leper (1,43-44)

Just as Jesus' response to the leper in 1,41 consisted of a healing gesture and healing words so also vv. 43-44 are composed of Jesus' commanding action and commanding words. The main event in v. 43 is expressed by the verb ἐξέβαλεν on which depends the preceding participle ἐμβριμησάμενος.

The verb ἐμβριμᾶσθαι has the sense to snort, an expression of displeasure and probably of anger. Of the five instances of ἐμβριμᾶσθαι in the NT, four times it is predicated of Jesus (Mk 1,43; Mt 9,30; Jn 11,33.38). In Jn 11,33.38 ἐμβριμᾶσθαι is immediately followed by τῷ πνεύματι and ἐν ἑαυτῷ respectively. Therefore, it is obvious that the emotional reaction is within Jesus himself [218]. Regarding ἐμβριμησάμενος in Mk 1,43 there are different opinions [219]. In Mk 1,43 and Mt 9,30 it is followed by an indirect object: personal pronouns referring to the leper in the former and nouns referring to the two blind men in the latter. A comparison of Mk 1,43 with Mt 9,30 will clarify the meaning and function of this verb in our verse.

---

[216] Cf. JOSEPHUS, *Antiquities*, III,264. STR.-B., *Kommentar* IV, 745-763.

[217] Cf. STR.-B., *Kommentar* I, 593-596.

[218] RSV renders in both verses: "deeply moved"; NEB: "sighed heavily".

[219] Some hold that Jesus' emotional reaction is due to the leper's infringement of the Law. A few others see here a reference to Jesus' deep emotional feelings towards the leper. An appreciable number of authors connect the word with the injunction to silence. Cf. CRANFIELD, 93-94; FUSCO, "Il segreto messianico", 280-284, 297.

Mk 1,40-45	Mt 9,27-31
Jesus touched him (1,41a) and said to him, "I will; be clean" (1,41b).	Jesus touched their eyes (9,29a) saying, "According to your faith let it be done to you (9,29b).
And immediately the leprosy left him (1,42).	And their eyes were opened (9,30a).
καὶ ἐμβριμησάμενος αὐτῷ εὐθὺς ἐξέβαλεν αὐτόν (1,43)	καὶ ἐνεβριμήθη αὐτοῖς ὁ Ἰησοῦς (9,30b)
καὶ λέγει αὐτῷ, Ὅρα μηδενὶ μηδὲν εἴπῃς (1,44a).	λέγων, Ὁρᾶτε μηδεὶς γινωσκέτω (9,30c).
But he went out and began . . . to spread the news, so that Jesus could no longer openly enter a town (1,45ab).	But they went away and spread his fame through all that district (9,31).

The parallelism between these two healings is evident. However, what is relevant to us is the parallelism between Mk 1,43-44a and Mt 9,30bc. The verb ἐνεβριμήθη in Mt 9,30b is preceded by the opening of the eyes of two blind men, an event in which Jesus as the Messiah is revealed in a veiled manner (cf. Mt 11,2-6). In v. 30c the command to secrecy concerns the revelation of this event. Therefore, for Mt ἐνεβριμήθη αὐτοῖς in v. 30b has Messianic implications. In Mk 1,43, however, ἐμβριμησάμενος is followed by a commanding action (ἐξέβαλεν αὐτόν) and his injunction to secrecy. This is precisely so because, according to Mk, Jesus does not allow the crowd to see a miracle of Messianic implications (cf. 5,40; 7,33; 8,23) or hear about it (1,44a; 5,43a; 7,36a; 8,26). Therefore, the use of ἐμβριμησάμενος in 1,43 is founded on our evangelist's concern for the Messianic secret.

Regarding the clause εὐθὺς ἐξέβαλεν αὐτόν, it should be noted that ἐκβάλλειν here does not seem to be used in the sense to "drive out, expel, throw out", a rather widespread opinion among the German school of exegetes [220], but in the sense to "send out, dismiss", a view found in most of the translations [221]. To reinforce our opinion, ἐκβάλλειν is used in the latter sense in Mt 9,38 par. Lk 10,2; Jas 2,25, etc. There is not sufficient evidence

---

[220] ERNST, 75: "warf ihn sogleich hinaus"; GNILKA, I, 89: "drängte ihn sogleich hinaus"; SCHMITHALS, I, 135: "trieb ihn sogleich fort". Similarly, GRUNDMANN, SCHWEIZER, etc.

[221] Cf. RSV, BJ, NEB, TOB, etc. and the commentaries of JOHNSON, LANE, etc.

in the text that Jesus sent (threw) him out from a house or synagogue [222]. The adverb εὐθύς possibly emphasizes the immediacy in sending him away just after his being healed. Jesus did so because he did not want the public to see himself in the company of a person who was perfectly healed by him from his leprosy.

Jesus' dismissal of the man healed from leprosy is immediately followed by his command to secrecy (1,44a). Similar commands to secrecy occur in other miracles of Messianic character as well (cf. 5,43a; 7,36a; 8,26a).

The present imperative of ὁρᾶν followed asyndetically by a command or prohibition occurs elsewhere in the NT too (Mk 8,15; Mt 8,4; 9,30; 18,10; 24,6; 1 Thess 5,15, etc.). Moulton suggests that in Mk 1,44 ὅρα functions as a sort of participle adding emphasis [223]. Both negatives in ὅρα μηδενὶ μηδὲν εἴπῃς strengthen one another since the second negative is also compound. Therefore, Jesus' command to secrecy is severe both in intent and in manner.

The positive command (ἀλλὰ ὕπαγε... Μωϋσῆς) taken over from tradition, contains no terms or basic themes that are important for our study. Jesus' command to the leper to show himself to the priest (just as in Lk 17,14) and to make the offering for the ritual cleansing, both prescribed in Lev 14,1-32, indicate Jesus' respect for the Law, on the one hand, and the tension between revelation and secrecy, on the other. The phrase εἰς μαρτύ-ριον αὐτοῖς which probably originated in the early Christian preaching [224] has been variously interpreted [225]. In the NT εἰς + μαρτύριον + dative of persons occurs in Mk 1,44 (par. Mt 8,4; Lk 5,14); Mk 6,11 (par. Lk 9,5); Mk 13,9 (par. Mt 24,14; Lk 21,13); Mt 10,18; Jas 5,3. In our verse εἰς indicates purpose, μαρτύριον means a testimony or proof consisting of an action or circumstance that serves as a testimony, and αὐτοῖς is a personal pronoun. Whom does Mk mean by αὐτοῖς? In the Marcan parallels (6,11; 13,9) the context makes it clear: those who refuse to accept the apostles and their message (6,11), and governors and kings (13,9). However, the context in 1,44 is very ambiguous and so various views have been put forward [226]. The predominant opinions are these: (1) in v. 44 αὐτοῖς refers to people [227],

---

[222] TAYLOR, 189, mentions a number of authors who hold this view.

[223] MOULTON, *Grammar* I, 124.

[224] So FUSCO, "Il segreto messianico", 297; SCHENKE, *Wundererzählungen*, 139. But CAVE, "Leper" 250, considers it redactional.

[225] CRANFIELD, 95, lists seven possible interpretations.

[226] Cf. SCHENKE, *Wundererzählungen*, 139; PESCH, "Heilung eines Aussätzigen", 72-73.

[227] RSV. GRUNDMANN, 69-70: it is a testimony to the people so that they should accept him into the community. TAYLOR, 190, cites several authors who hold this view.

and (2) it refers to priests [228]. The first opinion does not seem to suit the context because Jesus explicitly forbids the ex-leper to have contact with people (vv. 43.44a). Regarding the second opinion, it should be noted that in v. 44b τῷ ἱερεῖ (singular) should be understood in the background of Lev 14,2-7.11-20.23-32 where only the singular form of ἱερεύς is employed; moreover, the agreement between τῷ ἱερεῖ in v. 44b and αὐτοῖς in v. 44d is ad sensum [229]. It is possible that what is meant by αὐτοῖς is not the priests only but the Jewish authorities as such [230]. The personal pronoun αὐτῶν in Mk 1,39 also seems to have such a generic sense.

What is the testimony or proof contained in 1,44? Fuller and Lohmeyer think that it is ultimately Moses who, bearing witness for the Messiah, stands as a testimony against the Jewish authorities. But this interpretation of Mk 1,44 is probably coloured by Jn 5,45 ("It is Moses who accuses you, on whom you set your hope") [231]. In Mk 6,11 the apostles' shaking off the dust from their feet functions as a testimony against them while in 13,9 the disciples' faith in Jesus Christ (implied in the context) bears testimony. Similarly, in 1,44 the information about healing from leprosy (understood as a miraculous healing by Jesus) and the implication that the one who healed is the Messiah stand as a testimony against the incredulity of the Jewish authorities [232]. The literary structure that we have proposed reinforces this interpretation: in 1,41 (B) Jesus by his action and words heals the leper, and in 1,43-44 (B') by his action and words he spells out the implications of his healing of the leper.

5. The Ex-Leper's Reaction and Its Result (1,45)

Regarding ἐξελθών in v. 45a there are two opinions: (1) there has been no indication of a change of subject since in v. 44a and so ὁ ἐξελθών should refer to Jesus [233]; and (2) ὁ ἐξελθών refers to the leper because ἐξελθών in v.

---

[228] Among others, ERNST, 77; KNABENBAUER, 66; LANE, 88; SWETE, 31; TAYLOR, 190.

[229] Cf. FUSCO, "Il segreto messianico", 294; SWETE, 31; TAYLOR, 190.

[230] Cf. FUSCO, "Il segreto messianico", 293-294; KERTELGE, Wunder, 69: "die Vertreter des Gesetzes".

[231] . So FULLER, Miracles, 49-50; LOHMEYER, 47-48. Both quote Jn 5,45 in this context.

[232] With FUSCO, "Il segreto messianico", 293; LANE, 88; SWETE, 31. Against BURKILL, "Injunctions", 604: it is a proof in a double sense — completeness of the cure and Jesus' respect for the Law.

[233] Cf. KLOSTERMANN, 21. In the recent past ELLIOTT has been advocating the view that the healing of the leper concludes with v. 44 and that v. 45, commencing with ὁ ἐξελθών referring to Jesus, pertains to what follows. See his articles in JTS 22 (1971) 153-157; 27 (1976) 402-405; ThZ 34 (1978) 175-176.

45a corresponds to ἐξέβαλεν in v. 43 and because v. 45a does not commence with the usual καί as in the previous verses but with δέ, indicating a contrast. The contrast is probably founded on the contrariety between Jesus' command to secrecy in v. 44a and the ex-leper's disobedience to it in v. 45a. We, therefore, opt for the second opinion, that is, ὁ ἐξελθών refers to the leper [234]. In v. 45a κηρύσσειν πολλά and διαφημίζειν τὸν λόγον are synonymously parallel. As a consequence, the second member explicates the first. The verb διαφημίζειν is found only thrice in the NT (Mt 9,31; 28,15; Mk 1,45). In the second and the third instances it occurs in combination with ὁ λόγος, in the former as the subject and in the latter as the object. In Mt 28,15 ὁ λόγος obviously means the story (namely, the disciples stole Jesus' body) and the term has the same meaning in Mk 1,45 too (namely, the story or the news of the cure from leprosy) [235]. Mk most probably understands τὸν λόγον in the sense of הַדָּבָר in the OT [236]. By implication, therefore, κηρύσσειν in the first member of the synonymous parallelism does not seem to have the technical meaning of preaching the Christian message [237] but to narrate his experience of the miraculous healing just as the man liberated from the demon tells his experience in Mk 5,20. This has a paradigmatic value for Christians inasmuch as they are to share their own experience of Christ with others [238].

What does Mk mean by the result clause ὥστε μηκέτι αὐτὸν δύνασθαι φανερῶς εἰς πόλιν εἰσελθεῖν? Was it because Jesus feared that the sick and the possessed would be brought to him as in 1,32; 3,7b-10; 6,53-56? Or was it because the ex-leper by narrating his experience of being healed by Jesus had somehow revealed Jesus' own identity? The text is not so clear as to offer a very precise answer. Therefore an adequate answer can be elicited only by a study of the context and the Marcan parallels. In Mk 1,35 and 3,9 the background of Jesus' withdrawal is that the sick thronged to him (1,32; 3,10) but these very pericopes explicitly mention also the demons' knowledge of his identity (1,34d; 3,11) and his stern command to secrecy (1,34c; 3,12). In the present context too, Jesus enjoins an injunction to silence (v. 44a) and the ex-leper's telling of his experience to others (v. 45a) implies Jesus'

---

[234] With CRANFIELD, 95; FUSCO, "Il segreto messianico", 294; GNILKA, I, 94; TAYLOR, 190.

[235] With RSV, NEB, BJ.

[236] A perusal of HATCH and REDPATH, *Concordance*, 881-887, shows that more than 90 percent of the occurrences of λόγος is a rendering of דָּבָר .

[237] Against GRUNDMANN, 70; KLOSTERMANN, 21.

[238] BEDA, 452: "evangelistae fructus officio mox egressus coepit praedicare et diffamare sermonem".

Messianic identity. Moreover, although the adverb φανερῶς occurs only here in Mk, the adjectival form (φανερός) is found in contexts where the key issue is Jesus' identity (3,12; 6,14). Therefore, we hold that the reason why Jesus could no longer openly enter a town is twofold: our evangelist's interest in the Messianic secrecy and the crowd's craving for miracles (cf. 1,45d). As a consequence, Jesus remained in a lonely place (1,45c). According to Mk 1,35 while Jesus was in a lonely place he prayed; according to 6,31-32 he wished to rest in the lonely place with his apostles; and according to 6,35 he taught and manifested himself there. In 1,45c, however, there is no mention about his activity in the lonely place; it seems that he was there just for the sake of being there. Despite Jesus' intention to be away from people, they were coming to him from every quarter (1,45d) [239]. Here our evangelist intentionally contrasts Jesus' strong desire to be hidden and the crowd's desire to flock to him (1,45d) as happens elsewhere (1,35-37; 2,1-2; 3,7-12.19b-20, etc.). The most striking parallel to 1,45cd is 6,31-34:

Mk 1,45cd	Mk 6,31-34
Jesus was out in a lonely place (1,45c)	Jesus with the disciples in a lonely place (6,31a.32)
but people were coming to him from every quarter (1,45d).	but a great throng gathered (6,33-34).

Yet one should recognize that Mk 1,44-45 has a uniqueness of its own. In 1,44-45, Mk, working up to a climax, has masterfully interwoven two contrasts, namely, the injunction to secrecy with its violation and Jesus' strong desire to be hidden with the people constantly flocking to him [240]. This is shown in the following scheme:

Command to secrecy (1,44a)   <——>   Its intentional violation (1,45a)

Jesus was purposely remaining   <——>   Yet people were coming to
hidden in a lonely place (1,45c).   him from every quarter (1,45d).

---

[239] Note the imperfect ἦν in 1,45c and the corresponding ἤρχοντο in 1,45d.

[240] Nowhere else in Mk are these two contrasts interwoven. The contrast between Jesus' stern injunction to secrecy and to its outright violation occurs also in 7,36-37 where the second motif, however, is absent.

C. Mk 1,40-45 in Context

Some consider Mk 1,40-45 a transitional pericope linking 1,21-39 with 2,1-3,6. In this view it simply functions as an introduction to 2,1-3,6. For unlike the other four pericopes in 1,21-39, it begins without any specified time or place and refers to the Mosaic law (1,44bcd) which is the key question in 2,1-3,6 [241]. The last point is not convincing because in v. 44 Jesus is presented as an observer of the Law while in 2,1-3,6 he is accused of violating it. Moreover, there do exist literary and thematic links between 1,40-45 and the preceding pericopes (1,21-39), particularly between 1,40-45 and 1,35-39. The literary links between these two pericopes are the following: κηρύσσειν (1,39.45), ἔρημος τόπος (1,35.45), Jesus' withdrawal (1,35.45c), people search for him(1,37b.45d). The key theme that connects 1,40-45 with the preceding pericopes is the Messianic secret (1,25.34cd.43.44a) which is totally absent in 2,1-3,6. Moreover, we have shown in chapter 3 that the five pericopes in 1,21-45 constitute a literary unit forming a concentric structure. Finally, 2,1 marks a new beginning with a specified time and place.

Mk 1,21-45 deals primarily with exorcisms and healings. In it our evangelist narrates a miracle with Messianic overtones as the climactic conclusion of the cycle of miracles in 1,21-45 just as he does in 4,35-5,43; 6,30-7,37; and 8,1-26. Furthermore, the theme of the people's flocking to Jesus (cf. 1,28.32.37) also reaches a climax in 1,45d. We are, therefore, of the opinion that 1,40-45 is the climactic conclusion of 1,21-45.

VI. Conclusion of Chapter Five

To place the main thrust and the salient points of 1,21-45 in proper perspective, we schematically conclude this chapter with the following observations.

First, the primary thrust of 1,21-45 is the mysterious revelation of Jesus' person and mission. Various events narrated in these five pericopes are channels of veiled revelation:

---

[241] Among others see CRANFIELD, 90; FUSCO, "Il segreto messianico", 285-286; KERTELGE, *Wunder*, 71.

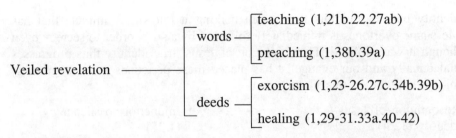

Veiled revelation
- words
  - teaching (1,21b.22.27ab)
  - preaching (1,38b.39a)
- deeds
  - exorcism (1,23-26.27c.34b.39b)
  - healing (1,29-31.33a.40-42)

Secondly, the response to the revelation is manifold. The response of Simon's mother-in-law to Jesus' revelatory deed is service (1,31c), a paradigm of Christian service [242]. In the case of the ex-leper, the response is the joyful narration of the experience of being healed from leprosy (1,45a), a paradigm of sharing one's encounter of Christ with others. But what interests us most here is not the response of the beneficiaries of Jesus' miraculous deeds — those who were, so to say, 'touched' by him — but that of a wider circle of people whose identity our evangelist does not reveal. Their positive attitude towards Jesus steadily grows with time and comes to a climax in 1,45d as the following scheme shows:

People were astonished at Jesus' authoritative teaching (1,22).

They were amazed at his qualitatively new teaching and his command over unclean spirits (1,27).

They brought to him all who were sick or possessed . . . the whole city was gathered together about the door (1,32-33).

They search for him (1,37b).

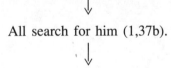

They came to him from every quarter (1,45d).

Lastly, even though people are enthusiastic about Jesus and appreciative of him, their knowledge of him is inadequate and incomplete for they view him primarily as a healer and exorcist. The demons, however, know his true

---

[242] Cf. p. 250-251.

identity but he prohibits them from making it known. A miracle that has Messianic overtones is immediately followed by a strict order to secrecy even though it was violated. The revelation of Jesus' true identity thus progresses dialectically and our evangelist has placed these pericopes at the beginning, middle and end of this literary unit:

Recognition of Jesus' identity (1,24)	<———>	Injunction to silence (1,25)
Demons' knowledge of Jesus' identity (1,34d)	<———>	Jesus prohibits them to speak (1,34c)
The command to secrecy (1,43.44a)	<———>	Its violation (1,45a).

CHAPTER SIX

MANIFESTATION OF JESUS' MESSIANIC AUTHORITY AND SCRIBAL AN PHARISAIC OPPOSITION (2,1-3,6)

I. Forgiveness and Healing of a Paralytic (2,1-12)

A. Literary Analysis [1]

1. *Synoptic Comparison*

a. *Mk 2,1-12 and Mt 9,1-8*

The Matthean parallel, the shortest among the three [2], is placed in the narrative section of the ten miracles (8,1-9,37) and it is immediately preceded by the exorcism of the two demoniacs of Gadara (8,28-34). Mt connects the healing of the paralytic (9,1-8) with the two preceding miracles (cf. 8,23-24.

---

[1] The reasons for our choice of the text in 2,1-12 are as follows. (a) In verse 1 ἐν οἴκῳ must be preferred to εἰς οἰκόν because on the one hand the MSS support is excellent and on the other hand εἰς (in the local sense) with the verb εἶναι occurs nowhere else in Mk whereas ἐν (in the local sense) with εἶναι does occur in Mk (cf. 1,13; 4,36; 5,5; 14,3; 15,41). (b) Of the four variant readings (cf. NESTLE-ALAND) in verse 3 the changes in the second and third variants consist only of transposition of words which suggests obvious attempts to improve upon the style and clarify the sense of the text. The addition and substitution in the fourth variant demonstrate the copyists' preoccupation with ameliorating the language and meaning of the text. (c) The absence of a direct object probably led to the substitution of προσεγγίσαι or προσελθεῖν for προσενέγκαι in verse 4. (d) Widespread and diversified MSS attestation supports καὶ ἰδών in verse 5. (e) In vv. 5 and 9 ἀφέωνται seems to be an assimilation to the Lucan parallel (5,20.23); therefore ἀφίενται is most probably the original text. (f) In v. 9 ἐγείρου is a grammatical correction for the intransitive ἔγειρε. (g) The difference among the three variants (cf. NESTLE-ALAND) in v. 10 is a matter of transposition of words only. "The text of B Θ represents the primitive, Aramaic order of words, which was rearranged, perhaps for subtle exegetical reasons, by copyists who produced the other readings" (METZGER, *Commentary*, 78). (h) The textual problem in v. 12 concerns the choice of a word: ἔμπροσθεν, ἐναντίον or ἐνώπιον. The MSS support for the first variant is excellent; moreover, ἐναντίον and ἐνώπιον occur nowhere else in Mk.

[2] Mt 9,1-8 = 126 words; Mk 2,1-12 = 196 words; Lk 5,17-26 = 213 words.

28.34) by means of verse 1 which is his own composition [3]. As a consequence no trace of the Marcan introduction (2,1-2) is found in Mt. Moreover, the first evangelist generally narrates only the essentials of miracles [4]. This probably explains why the lively details about the lowering of the paralytic through the roof (2,4) is absent in Mt. What seems to be redundant in Mk 2,7-8a is eliminated in the first Gospel (9,3b-4a) and Mk 2,9 is clarified by introducing γάρ in Mt 9,5. In the concluding verse there are two marked differences: (1) in Mk the crowds were amazed (2,12c) while in Mt they were afraid (9,8a: ἐφοβήθησαν) [5]; (2) according to Mk the reason why they glorified God is that they have never seen anything like this (2,12d) but according to Mt they glorified God because he has given such authority to men (9,8b).

b. *Mk 2,1-12 and Lk 5,17-26*

Although the immediate context of this pericope is similar both in Mk and Lk, the introduction to the miracle is strikingly different. The phrase καὶ ἐγένετο ἐν μιᾷ τῶν ἡμερῶν is a typical Lucan way of beginning a pericope [6] and the activity in which Jesus involves himself is teaching while according to Mk Jesus was preaching the word (2,2b). In the setting, Lk well prepares for the controversy and healing that follow by mentioning the Pharisees and teachers of the law [7] among Jesus' audience and by stating that the power of the Lord to heal was with him. In contrast, according to Mk it is πολλοί who constituted Jesus' audience and thronged to him. Finally, in Lk Jesus' accusers are scribes and Pharisees (5,21) while in Mk, the scribes only (2,6).

2. *Tradition and Redaction*

The redactional work of Mk is most conspicuous in the first two verses. Anacoluthon (εἰσελθών) is a sentence construction characteristic of Mk [8]. As stated before, the following two features are typical of our evangelist:

---

[3] SCHWEIZER, *Matthew*, 228.

[4] Compare the miracles in Mt 8-9 with the synoptic parallels.

[5] This the only instance in Mt where the crowds are afraid in the context of a healing. Note the variant reading ἐθαύμασαν in C L Θ, etc.

[6] Cf. Lk 1,5; 2,1; 6,1.6.12; 8,22; 9,37; 18,35; 20,1, etc.

[7] It is the first mention of 'Pharisees' and 'teachers of the law' in Lk. By stating their provenance ("from every village of Galilee and Judea and from Jerusalem") Lk highlights the strength and extension of their opposition.

[8] Cf. TAYLOR, 50; HAWKINS, *Horae Synopticae*, 135-137, etc.

compound verbs followed by the same preposition (εἰσελθών εἰς) and double statements, general and special. Moreover, εἰσέρχεσθαι is frequently found in redactional verses (1,21.45; 3,1; 7,24; 8,26). The adverb πάλιν, as mentioned in the third chapter, is editorial in Mk which primarily connects a pericope with a preceding one [9].

Concerning Καφαρναούμ there are two opinions: (1) because Mk's theological interest lies not in Capernaum but in Galilee, the former should be from tradition [10]; (2) the healing and forgiveness of the paralytic did not have a setting of time and place in tradition but it is Mk who gave it a geographical setting by situating it in Capernaum [11]. The first opinion appears to be an a priori deduction without studying the text in its context. As to the second view, if it is Mk who gave the geographical setting of Capernaum, what is his aim? The opinion that by providing this geographical setting in 2,1, Mk connects the 'house' in 2,1 with the 'house' in 1,29 is not fully convincing [12] since it is not explicitly mentioned. What our evangelist in fact does is to render a scenic connection between Jesus' first entry into Capernaum (1,21a) and his second entry there (2,1a).

Such scenic connections are typical of Mk [13]. Mk has a theological motif in connecting these two scenes. Mk 1,21a begins a series of five pericopes (1,21-45) where Jesus is accepted and appreciated by the public. Mk 2,1a also begins a series of five pericopes (2,1-3,6) but here he faces a steadily mounting opposition from the Jewish leaders. Therefore, by repeating 'Capernaum' at 2,1a our evangelist highlights the contrasting responses Jesus receives from the same place. The redactional insertion of δι' ἡμερῶν is necessitated by the situation created in 1,45, namely, people were flocking to Jesus with the result that he could no longer openly enter a town and so he was out in the country. As a consequence, a span of a few days was required to begin anew his ministry in Capernaum. The people's urge to come

---

[9] Compare 2,1 with 1,21a; 2,13 with 1,16; 3,1 with 1,21b; 4,1 with 2,13; 5,21 with 4,35 and 5,1; 7,14 with 6,45 and 6,54; 7,31 with 7,24; 8,1 with 7,17.33.36-37; 8,13 with 7,31 and 8,10; 8,25 with 8,23; 10,10 with 9,35; 11,27 with 11,15; 12,4 with 12,2; 14,39 with 14,35-36; 14,40 with 14,37; 14,61 with 14,60; 14,69 with 14,67; 14,70 with 14,68-69; 15,4 with 15,2; 15,12 with 15,9; 15,13 with 15,8.

Of these 23 instances of πάλιν connecting a pericope with a preceding one, Lk has only one parallel (8,4) and Mt five (19,24; 21,36; 26,42.43.72).

[10] MARXSEN, Evangelist, 62. See also GNILKA, I, 97; PESCH, I, 151.

[11] KLOSTERMANN, 22. See also KERTELGE, Wunder, 76; TAGAWA, Miracles, 21.

[12] So SCHMIDT, Rahmen, 79; J. WEIß, Das älteste Evangelium, 155.

[13] Compare 2,1a with 1,21a; 2,13a with 1,16a; 3,1a with 1,21b; 7,31a with 7,24a; 11,27a with 11,15a. These connections are absent both in the Matthean and Lucan parallels.

in contact with Jesus in 1,45 explains also the redactional use of ἠκούσθη in 2,1. Thus, in brief, we conclude that the whole of 2,1 is redactional.

The second verse is also fully redactional. Although συνάγειν occurs only five times in the second Gospel, it is always redactional (cf. 2,2; 4,1; 5,21; 6,30; 7,1) [14]; and πολλοί is frequently redactional (cf. 1,34; 2,15; 3,10; 6,33; 10,31, etc.). As mentioned in the fifth chapter, ὥστε with an infinitive indicating result is a typical style of Mk. Again, verbs with a cognate accusative or dative (ἐλάλει τὸν λόγον) is a distinctive literary feature of the second evangelist [15]. Besides, the expression, λαλεῖν τὸν λόγον, is redactional in the other two instances too (4,33; 8,32) [16]. The double negative (μηκέτι. . . μηδέ) is also a characteristic feature of Mk [17]. Among the synoptic Gospels θύρα, μηδείς and πολλά are Marcan editorial vocabulary [18]. And finally, the theme of preaching the word (cf. 4,33; 8,32) and people's gathering about the door (1,33) are theologically motivated [19]. Therefore, we conclude that verse 2 is a redactional composition of Mk.

As for the rest, πρὸς αὐτόν [20] in v. 3, διὰ τὸν ὄχλον [21] in v. 4 and τί οὗτος οὕτως λαλεῖ [22] in v. 7 are probably redactional. There are redactional touches also in verse 12. As noted before, ὥστε with an infinitive and λέγειν ὅτι occur frequently in redactional verses. The adverbial use of εὐθύς is almost always redactional. However, a precise distinction between tradition and redaction in v. 12 is extremely difficult.

----

[14] With GNILKA, I, 97, n. 12; SCHENKE, *Wundererzählungen*, 146-147 and THISSEN, *Erzählung*, 51, n. 28; but against MAISCH, *Heilung*, 13-14.

[15] Cf. p. 122, n. 29.

[16] Cf. GNILKA, I, 97, n. 10.

[17] Cf. p. 163, n. 204.

[18]

	Mt	Mk	Lk	Jn	Acts	Paul	Rest		Total
διαλογίζεσθαι	3	7	6	0	0	0	0	=	16
θύρα	4	6	4	7	10	3	5	=	39
λόγος	33	24	33	40	65	84	54	=	331
μηδείς	5	8	9	0	21	34	8	=	85
πάλιν	17	28	3	43	5	28	15	=	139
πολλά	4	16	1	3	1	4	3	=	32

[19] Cf. WOHLENBERG, 74; THISSEN, *Erzählung*, 51.

[20] Cf. p. 151, n. 151.

[21] Differing from Mt and Lk, Mk uses ὄχλος always in the singular except in 10,1.

[22] Verse 7 has two distinctive literary features typical of Mk: synonymous expressions (cf. p. 87, n. 30) and double questions (cf. p. 122, n. 28).

3. *Literary Structure*

1 ---- Καὶ εἰσελθὼν πάλιν εἰς Καφαρναοὺμ δι᾽ ἡμερῶν ἠκούσθη ὅτι ἐν
2 οἴκῳ ἐστίν. καὶ συνήχθησαν πολλοὶ ὥστε μηκέτι χωρεῖν μηδὲ τὰ πρὸς
τὴν θύραν, καὶ ἐλάλει αὐτοῖς τὸν λόγον.

3 A καὶ ἔρχονται φέροντες πρὸς αὐτὸν *παραλυτικὸν αἰρόμενον ὑπὸ*
4 *τεσσάρων.* καὶ μὴ δυνάμενοι προσενέγκαι αὐτῷ *διὰ τὸν ὄχλον*
ἀπεστέγασαν τὴν στέγην ὅπου ἦν, καὶ ἐξορύξαντες χαλῶσι τὸν
κράβαττον ὅπου ὁ παραλυτικὸς κατέκειτο.

5 B καὶ ἰδὼν ὁ Ἰησοῦς τὴν πίστιν αὐτῶν *λέγει τῷ παραλυτικῷ,*
Τέκνον *ἀφίενταί σου αἱ ἁμαρτίαι.*

6 C ἦσαν δέ τινες τῶν γραμματέων ἐκεῖ καθήμενοι *καὶ διαλογιζό-*
μενοι ἐν ταῖς καρδίαις αὐτῶν,

7 D Τί οὗτος οὕτως λαλεῖ; βλασφημεῖ· τίς δύναται ἀφιέναι
ἁμαρτίας εἰ μὴ εἷς ὁ θεός;

8 C᾽ καὶ εὐθὺς ἐπιγνοὺς ὁ Ἰησοῦς τῷ πνεύματι αὐτοῦ ὅτι οὕτως
διαλογίζονται ἐν ἑαυτοῖς λέγει αὐτοῖς, Τί ταῦτα *διαλογί-*
ζεσθε ἐν ταῖς καρδίαις ὑμῶν;

9 B᾽ τί ἐστιν εὐκοπώτερον, *εἰπεῖν τῷ παραλυτικῷ,* Ἀφίενταί σου αἱ
ἁμαρτίαι, ἢ εἰπεῖν, Ἔγειρε καὶ ἆρον τὸν κράβαττόν σου

10 καὶ περιπάτει; ἵνα δὲ εἰδῆτε ὅτι ἐξουσίαν ἔχει ὁ υἱὸς τοῦ
ἀνθρώπου ἀφιέναι ἁμαρτίας ἐπὶ τῆς γῆς -- *λέγει τῷ παραλυτικῷ,*

11 A᾽ Σοὶ λέγω, *ἔγειρε ἆρον τὸν κράβαττόν* σου καὶ ὕπαγε εἰς
12 τὸν οἶκόν σου. καὶ ἠγέρθη καὶ εὐθὺς ἄρας τὸν *πράβαττον ἐξῆλθεν*
ἔμπροσθεν πάντων,

---- ὥστε ἐξίστασθαι πάντας καὶ δοξάζειν τὸν θεὸν λέγοντας ὅτι Οὕτως
οὐδέποτε εἴδομεν.

Mk 2,1-12 is thus constituted of a clearly pronounced concentric structure (A B C D C᾽ B᾽ A᾽) with a narrative introduction (2,1-2) and a narrative conclusion (v. 12cd). Verses 3-6 (A B C) lead to v. 7 (D): a paralytic is brought to Jesus by four men whose painstaking effort to bring him near Jesus (A: action) is perceived by him as an expression of their faith. So with tenderness Jesus forgives the sins of the paralytic (B: Jesus' response). This triggers off an accusation against Jesus, the scribes first in a pensive way (C: problem in gestation) and then in a well-articulated manner ask, "Who can forgive sins but God alone?" (D: problem articulated). This question certainly

concerns the person and the mission of Jesus. Verses 8-12b (C' B' A') flow
from v. 7 (D). Jesus, perceiving the problem posed by the scribes (C': Jesus'
perception of the problem), responds to their question by arguing in a
juridico-exegetical manner and asserts his authority as the Son of Man to
forgive sins and so he commands the paralytic to take up his bed and go
home (B': Jesus' response to the problem). The paralytic immediately carries
out the command (A': implementation in action). Mk 2,1-12 is thus constituted of a literally balanced and thematically congruent concentric structure.
Its literary centre and thematic core is verse 7. One should note that verse 7
itself is also constituted of a concentric structure (a b a') whose central point
is the accusation of blasphemy.

B. Interpretation

1. *Narrative Introduction (2,1-2)*

The participle εἰσελθών, agreeing with ὁ Ἰησοῦς (understood from
preceding pericopes (cf. 1,25.17.14 or αὐτόν in 1,45), is an anacoluthon and
is used for the indicative [23]. The phrase δι᾽ ἡμερῶν like the classical διὰ
χρόνου means 'after some days' and it should be attached not to ἠκούσθη
but to εἰσελθών. With most of the translations and commentaries, ἠκούσθη
should be understood impersonally [24] rather than personally. In v. 2 we accept
the following syntactic structure for the clause (ὥστε μηκέτι χωρεῖν μηδὲ τὰ
πρὸς τὴν θύραν), namely, χωρεῖν is impersonal and τὰ πρὸς τὴν θύραν is
an accusative of respect [25]. And so, it ought to be translated: "so that there
was no longer room for them, not even about the door" (RSV) [26]. This
syntactic explanation suits the context better.

---

[23] Cf. MOULTON, *Grammar* I, 222-225.

[24] Cf. RSV, TOB, etc.; ERNST, 84; LOHMEYER, 49; SCHMITHALS, I, 148.

[25] Another possible syntactic explanation is that τὰ πρὸς τὴν θύραν is the subject of
χωρεῖν, in the accusative after ὥστε. Accordingly, the translation is: "that the space in front
of the door was not big enough to hold them" (NEB).

[26] Also BJ, TOB; GRUNDMANN, 72; S.E. JOHNSON, 54; LANE, 92; LOHMEYER, 49;
NINEHAM, 89; PESCH, I, 152; SCHWEIZER, 28.

Mk begins this pericope with the same geographical specification as at the beginning of Jesus' ministry on a typical sabbath (1,21-34):

καὶ εἰσπορεύονται εἰς Καφαρναούμ (1,21a)

καὶ εἰσελθὼν πάλιν εἰς Καφαρναοὺμ δι' ἡμερῶν (2,1a)

The temporal specification 'after some days' does not necessarily mean the interval between Jesus' first visit to Capernaum and the second but could refer to the days spent by him in the country as narrated in the immediately preceding verse (1,45cd) [27]. And the 'house' [28] presumably refers to the house of Simon and Andrew mentioned in 1,29 [29]. The news concerning Jesus' presence in the house causes the same reaction among people as in 1,33.

καὶ ἦν ὅλη ἡ πόλις ἐπισυνηγμένη πρὸς τὴν θύραν (1,33)

καὶ συνήχθησαν πολλοὶ ὥστε μηκέτι χωρεῖν μηδὲ τὰ πρὸς τὴν θύραν (2.2a) [30].

Just as in 1,33 so here too the gathering of the people to Jesus has an eschatological nuance [31]. In fact, it is clearer here since Jesus performed a miracle of Messianic implications in the immediately preceding pericope (1,40-45).

Jesus' response to the crowds consists of 'speaking the word' to them (2,2b). What does Mk mean by λαλεῖν τὸν λόγον? We shall examine this phrase first in a wider context and then more specifically in this context. It is characteristic of Mk that when Jesus is in an isolated place, crowds gather and he responds to them:

---

[27] Note that the verbs in 1,45c and 1,45d are in the imperfect tense.

[28] Cf. p. 144-145.

[29] Cf. KLOSTERMANN, 22; LANE, 93; NINEHAM, 92; RAWLINSON, 26, etc.

[30] It seems to have been a small Jewish house with the θύρα or house-door opening on to the street (cf. Mk 11,4); no προαύλιον (cf. 14,68) would intervene between the door and the street, nor would there be a θυρωρός (Jn 18,16) to exclude unwelcome visitors. The phrase τὰ πρὸς τὴν θύραν, then, would mean the neighbourhood of the door on the side of the street.

[31] Cf. p. 153.

Jesus in an isolated place	*crowds gather*	*Jesus' response*
Jesus at the home of Simon and Andrew (1,29)	the whole city (the sick and the possessed) gathered (1,32-33)	healing and exorcism (1,34ab)
Jesus at home (2,1b)	such a concourse as to choke the approaches to the house (2,2a)	speaking the word (2,2b)
Jesus beside the sea (2,13a)	crowds gathered (2,13b)	teaching (2,13c)
Jesus with his disciples beside the sea (3,7a)	great crowds came to him (3,7b-8)	healing (3,10)
Jesus beside the sea (4,1a)	crowds gathered (4,1b)	teaching in parables (4,2-9)
Jesus with the Twelve at a lonely place (6,31-32) (6,34b-44)	great throng gathered (6,33-34a)	teaching and feeding

From this scheme it is evident that when Jesus is in an isolated place and crowds gather to him, he heals the sick among them, exorcises the possessed, feeds the hungry, teaches and speaks the word to them. In brief, when crowds gather, Jesus responds to them through word and deed.

There are several authors who interpret λαλεῖν τὸν λόγον in the sense of the early Church's missionary preaching (= proclamation of the Gospel) [32]. It is true that not only λόγος is more frequent in Acts and Paul [33] but also it is frequently used for the missionary preaching, particularly when determined by τοῦ θεοῦ and τοῦ Κυρίου. But Mk uses τὸν λόγον absolutely, with the verb ἐλάλει (imperfect, thus denoting continuous activity), and predicated of Jesus in 2,2; 4,33; 8,32. Such a usage is found nowhere else in the NT.

---

[32] Cf. GRUNDMANN, 74; KLOSTERMANN, 22; NINEHAM, 92; SWETE, 33, etc.; THISSEN, *Erzählung*, 300-332.

[33] Cf. n. 18 above.

Therefore Mk may be using the phrase in a different sense than in the sense of missionary preaching of the early Church. The meaning of ἐλάλει τὸν λόγον is not clear in 2,2 and so we shall first determine its meaning in 4,33 and 8,32. Mk 4,33 is parallel to 4,2 [34]:

καὶ ἐδίδασκεν αὐτοὺς ἐν παραβολαῖς πολλά (4,2a)

καὶ τοιαύταις παραβολαῖς πολλαῖς ἐλάλει αὐτοῖς τὸν λόγον (4,33a)

Here ἐδίδασκεν is parallel to ἐλάλει, and πολλά is parallel to τὸν λόγον. Likewise 8,32a and 8,31a are synonymously parallel:

καὶ ἤρξατο διδάσκειν αὐτοὺς ὅτι δεῖ τὸν υἱὸν τοῦ ἀνθρώπου πολλὰ παθεῖν (8,31a)

καὶ παρρησίᾳ τὸν λόγον ἐλάλει (8,32a).

Here too ἤρξατο διδάσκειν is parallel to ἐλάλει and the content of Jesus' teaching (namely, the destiny of the Son of Man) is parallel to τὸν λόγον. By virtue of the synonymous parallelism, καὶ παρρησίᾳ τὸν λόγον ἐλάλει (8,32a) means the revelation of Jesus' destiny. In 4,33 ἐλάλει τὸν λόγον corresponds to the content of Jesus' parabolic teaching. Its primary content is the mystery of Jesus' person (cf. 4,10-12). Therefore, it is reasonable to conclude that ἐλάλει τὸν λόγον in 2,2b alludes to the mystery of Jesus' person. The object of λαλεῖν corresponds to the content of Jesus' teaching. This interpretation is reinforced by the fact that while narrating Jesus' didactic activity as well as his 'speaking the word', our evangelist consistently uses the imperfect tense [35]. Such a consistency in the use of the imperfect tense is lacking in the description of Jesus' other activities such as preaching and working miracles.

---

[34] Mk 4,1-2 and 4,33-34 constitute the introduction and conclusion respectively of Jesus' parabolic discourse which is concentrically structured. Cf. FUSCO, *Parola e regno*, 101-104; RADERMAKERS, 48-50;

[35] The imperfect of διδάσκειν in 1,21; 2,13; 4,2; 9,31; 10,1; 11,7 and constructions with the force of the imperfect in 1,22; 4,1; 6,2.6.34; 8,31; 12,35; 14,49. For the apostles' teaching activity the aorist is used (6,30). In reference to Jesus' speaking the word, only the imperfect of λαλεῖν is used (2,2; 4,33; 8,32).

2. The Action: Bringing a Paralytic to Jesus (2,3-4)

The narrative proper begins with the action of bringing a paralytic [36] to Jesus on a poor man's pallet or mattress (κράβαττος) [37] carried by four men. Their aim to bring him to Jesus is hindered by the large crowd present (2,4a), a theme already anticipated in 2,2a. So they mounted the roof (presumably by an external staircase) [38] and, having made an opening [39] on the roof [40], they lowered the pallet on which the paralytic lay to the place where Jesus was.

3. Jesus' Response (2,5)

Our evangelist portrays a vivid picture of the bold expedient of the four men in 2,3-4 not for its own sake but to stress, on the one hand, their strong conviction that Jesus had the power to heal this paralytic and, on the other, his recognition of it as an expression of their faith (2,5a). Although Mk uses the verb πιστεύειν in different contexts [41], the nouns πίστις (total 5 times) and ἀπιστία (total twice) are always found in the context of miracles. Jesus upbraids the disciples for their lack of faith (4,40), assures them that everything is possible if they have faith (11,22-24), and recognizes the faith of those healed (5,34; 10,52). In our verse, too, Jesus recognizes the faith both of those who carried the paralytic and of the paralytic himself [42]. Furthermore, Mk also states that ἀπιστία obstructs the working of miracles (cf. 6,5-6a; 9,22b-24). Thus Mk emphasizes the necessity of faith from the

---

[36] The term παραλυτικός is not used in classical Greek or LXX. It occurs 10 times in the NT (Mt 5; Mk 5, i.e., 2,3.4.5.9.10).

[37] Κράβαττος is a nonliterary word denoting a poor man's bed in contrast to κλίνη (cf. Lk 5,18).

[38] Cf. NINEHAM, 92; RAWLINSON, 26; SWETE, 33.

[39] BÖCHER (Christus Exorcista, 79) states that the hole in the roof is a device of the exorcist so that the demon can escape. This contention does not hold water because (1) there is no exorcism at all in 2,1-12; (2) the opening of the roof is mentioned elsewhere in the contemporary literature in a context not that of exorcism (cf. DAUBE, The New Testament, 385-387; VAN DER LOOS, Miracles, 440-442); (3) the evangelist underlines this bold expedient as an expression of their faith.

[40] TAYLOR, 19: "The roof was probably formed of beams and rafters across which matting, branches, and twigs, covered by earth trodden hard, were laid".

[41] Cf. p. 100-101.

[42] With CRANFIELD, 97; NINEHAM, 92; TAYLOR, 194.

petitioner (either implied in context or explicitly stated) so that a miracle can be worked, since a miracle is God's gift which can become operative only if the petitioner has a disposition of faith and trust.

Jesus' response to the paralytic goes beyond the expected, namely, instead of healing through gestures and words (cf. 1,41; 5,35-41; 7,33-35; 8,23-25) he says to the paralytic: "My child, your sins are forgiven". Here τέκνον is an affectionate form of address used of those with whom there is a personal relationship (cf. 10,24). The verb ἀφιέναι (present indicative passive) [43] has a punctiliar force ("aoristic present") [44], namely, the sins were forgiven at the very moment Jesus spoke those words. It is probably not a passivum divinum [45] but a declarative statement on Jesus' own authority. This is evident from the scribes' accusation of blasphemy (2,6-7) and Jesus' defence of it (2,10) [46]. By ἁμαρτίαι our evangelist does not seem to be referring to any personal sins or any particular sin as such but sin in general. Jesus' declaration of forgiveness of sins is intelligible against the background provided by the OT where sin and disease, forgiveness and healing are frequently interrelated concepts [47]:

Bless the Lord, O my soul . . .
who forgives all your iniquity,
who heals all your diseases (Ps 103,2-3).

In a number of texts healing and forgiveness are interchangeable terms:

As for me, I said, "O Lord, be gracious to me;
heal me, for I have sinned against thee!" (Ps 41,4).

"Return, O faithless sons,
I will heal your faithlessness" (Jer 3,22).

---

[43] On ἀφιέναι in Mk see p. 111-112.

[44] BLASS-DEBRUNNER, Grammar, § 320; MOULTON, Grammar I, 119.

[45] Against GNILKA, I, 99; GRUNDMANN, 73, 76; PESCH, I, 156, etc.

[46] The early Church associated forgiveness of sins with Jesus' Passion and Death (cf. Mk 10,45; 14,24; 1 Cor 15,3; Rom 3,23-25; 4,25, etc.) rather than with his earthly ministry. In the synoptic tradition, there are only two events (Mk 2,5-11 par; Lk 7,47-49) where there is an explicit mention of granting forgiveness of sins during Jesus' earthly ministry, even though in metaphors and parables this idea is expressed. These two pericopes possibly reflect the faith of the early Church in granting forgiveness in Jesus' name (cf. Acts 2,38; 5,31; 10,43; 13,38; 22,16; 26,18, etc.).

[47] See the OT texts and comments in BRONGERS, "Enkele opmerkingen", 129-142.

Therefore the connection between sin and sickness, forgiveness and healing in some of the texts of the OT and a few Talmudic and Rabbinic citations [48] clarifies the logic of Jesus' response in 2,5. However, the basis of Jesus' pronouncement on his own authority becomes clear only in v. 10.

4. The Problem in Gestation (2,6)

In 2,6 Mk rather abruptly mentions that some scribes, the principle opponents of Jesus in the second Gospel, were seated among the audience. They, perceiving the theological implication of Jesus' act of forgiving the sins of the paralytic, question in their hearts (διαλογιζόμενοι ἐν ταῖς καρδίαις αὐτῶν). It is worth noting that διακογίζεσθαι, a Marcan preferential verb [49], is predicated exclusively of Jesus' enemies (2,6.8; 11,31) or of his disciples (8,16.17; 9,33) in contexts where the latter fail to understand his person and mission [50]. The term καρδία occurs in the second Gospel in three contexts: (1) describing the disposition or attitude toward Jesus of his enemies — scribes (2,6.8) or Pharisees (3,5) — or of his disciples (6,52; 8,17); (2) the heart as the centre and source of moral life (7,19.21); (3) the centre and source of the whole inner life, particularly in the context of faith in God (11,22-24; 12,29-33) in contrast to unbelief. But the disciples' καρδία πεπωρωμένη is changed to faith in Jesus in 8,29. Therefore in light of the general use of καρδία in Mk, in 2,6.8 it not merely denotes the faculty of thought and understanding [51] but also the scribes' lack of faith in Jesus [52]. Thus, in brief, by mentioning the scribes, Jesus' chief opponents, in 2,6 and by stating their primary act as διαλογίζεσθαι ἐν ταῖς καρδίαις αὐτῶν our evangelist marks the beginning of an opposition rooted in incredulity.

5. The Problem Articulated (2,7)

The problem in gestation in 2,6 is clearly exposed in 2,7. Mk 2,7, consisting of a concentric structure, continues the theme of forgiveness of

---

[48] Cf. STR.-B., Kommentar I, 495-496.

[49] Cf. n. 18 above.

[50] In this respect Mt has no originality of his own since in all the three instances, he follows Mk. But the Lucan use of this verb differs (cf. 1,29; 3,15; 12,17; 20,14) except in two instances parallel to Mk (Lk 5,21.22).

[51] Cf. BAUER, Lexicon, 404.

[52] Cf. p. 131-132.

sins from 2,5b. Verse 7 is sandwiched between διαλογιζόμενοι ἐν ταῖς καρδίαις αὐτῶν (2,6b) and διαλογίζεσθε ἐν ταῖς καρδίαις ὑμῶν (2,8).

A διαλογιζόμενοι ἐν ταῖς καρδίαις αὐτῶν,

    a τί οὗτος οὕτως λαλεῖ;

B   b βλασφημεῖ·

    a' τίς δύναται ἀφιέναι ἁμαρτίας εἰ μὴ εἷς ὁ θεός;

A' διαλογίζεσθε ἐν ταῖς καρδίαις ὑμῶν;

In 2,7 οὗτος is probably used contemptuously in the sense of "this fellow" [53]. And οὕτως λαλεῖ refers to Jesus' declaration of forgiveness in 2,5b where its implication is precisely stated in the form of an accusation in the verb immediately following, βλασφημεῖ. In classical Greek this verb means to speak profanely of God or of sacred things, but it can also refer to the slandering of a human person [54]. In the LXX βλασφημεῖ (representing four Hebrew roots) is not at all frequent [55]. There are, however, other verbs, particularly ὀνειδίζειν (revile, reproach) and παροξύνεσθαι (stimulate, provoke to wrath) which do occur rather frequently. As distinct from these verbs, βλασφημεῖν primarily refers to something directed against God [56]. The punishment for blasphemy was death by stoning (cf. Lev 24,11-16; 1 Kings 21,13 etc.). In the NT, blasphemy, as in the OT, generally denotes an affront to the power and majesty of God [57]. In Mk βλασφημεῖν/βλασφημία occur in three contexts: (1) the catalogue of sins (7,22); (2) those passages in which Mk censures certain charges against Jesus as blasphemy (3,28-29; 15,29); (3) the accusations of Jesus' enemies against him of blasphemy — the scribes (2,7) and the high priest (14,64).

Verse 7c elucidates why the scribes consider Jesus' act of forgiving sins a blasphemy: τίς δύναται ἀφιέναι ἁμαρτίας εἰ μὴ εἷς ὁ θεός; Here εἷς ὁ θεός (cf. 10,18) is equal to μόνος ὁ θεός (Lk 5,21). The scribal contention has a very strong OT foundation because the forgiveness of sins is a prerogative of God (cf. Ex 34,7; Is 43,25; 44,22; Dan 9,9; Ps 103,3; 130,4, etc.). Moreover,

[53] Cf. CRANFIELD, 98; TAYLOR, 195.

[54] Cf. LIDDELL-SCOTT, Lexicon, 317-318.

[55] Both the verbal and the nominal forms are rare in the LXX: as a verb seven times (2 Kings 19,4.6.22; Is 52,5; Dan 3,29; 2 Mac 10,34; 12,14) and as a noun six times (Ezek 35,12; Dan 3,29; 1 Mac 2,6; 2 Mac 8,4; 10,35; 15,24).

[56] Cf. H.W. BEYER, TDNT I, 621-622; CRANFIELD, 98.

[57] Cf. H.W. BEYER, TDNT I, 622-623; CRANFIELD, 98; GNILKA, I, 100.

according to the belief of the time, the forgiveness of sins was entrusted not even to the Messiah [58]. Therefore, by placing the scribes' accusation of blasphemy against Jesus at the literary centre of the pericope, enclosed by the clasp διαλογίζεσθαι ἐν ταῖς καρδίαις in 2,6 and 2,8, Mk sharply focuses attention on the key issue of the pericope. The scribes affirm that by forgiving the sins of the paralytic Jesus has committed a sin of blasphemy. And by placing their accusation between διαλογίζεσθε ἐν ταῖς καρδίαις in 2,6 and in 2,8 Mk gives an inkling to his readers that the scribes' accusation is founded on their incredulity. In other words, by forgiving the sins of the paralytic the divinity of Jesus becomes manifest which the scribes are not prepared to accept. This attitude, according to the evangelist, expresses their incredulity.

6. Jesus' Perception of the Problem (2,8)

Verse 8 is composed of a synonymous parallelism:

ὅτι οὕτως διαλογίζονται ἐν ἑαυτοῖς λέγει αὐτοῖς,

Τί ταῦτα διαλογίζεσθε ἐν ταῖς καρδίαις ὑμῶν;

The second member of the parallelism marks a progression. Verse 8a is in indirect discourse while in 2,8b Jesus directly addresses the scribes. Verse 8 begins with καὶ εὐθὺς ἐπιγνοὺς ὁ 'Ιησοῦς τῷ πνεύματι αὐτοῦ. The verb ἐπιγινώσκειν has two meanings in the NT: (1) with the preposition ἐπί making its influence felt, it means to know exactly, completely, through and through; (2) with no emphasis on the preposition, it is equivalent to γινώσκειν. In the second Gospel ἐπιγινώσκειν occurs only four times: twice it is predicated of Jesus (2,8; 5,30) and twice predicated of the crowds (6,33.54). In the latter two instances it is equivalent to γινώσκειν and in the former two occurrences it is followed by τῷ πνεύματι αὐτοῦ and ἐν ἑαυτῷ respectively. This addition specifies the nature of the knowledge, namely, it is a knowledge from within, an inward awareness or perception. In our verse Jesus' discernment of the thoughts of the scribes has its basis not in the θεῖος-ἀνήρ concept as such [59] but in our evangelist's predilection to attribute the quality of discernment to Jesus in a pre-eminent degree (cf. 8,16-17;

---

[58] MOORE, *Judaism* I, 535: "Forgiveness of sin is a prerogative of God which he shares with no other and deputes to none". See also STR.-B., *Kommentar* I, 495, 1017.

[59] Against BUDESHEIM, "Jesus and the Disciples", 192, 198, 202; MAISCH, *Heilung*, 79-80, 121-124.

10,21; 12,15; 14,18.20.27.30) [60]. Mk is also convinced that God is the knower of men's hearts (καρδιογνώστης Acts 1,24; 15,8) [61]. Thus our evangelist gives an inkling of the transcendental aspect of Jesus' person in 2,8 too. Jerome aptly comments:

> Sed dominus videns cogitationes eorum, ostendit se Deum, qui possit cordis occulta cognoscere . . . . Eadem majestate et potentia qua cogitationes vestras intueor, possum et hominibus peccata dimittere [62].

7. Jesus' Response to the Problem (2,9-10)

Verse 10 constitutes a well-known crux in the interpretation of this pericope. Structurally there is an awkward change of address in the middle of the verse. Jesus appears to be addressing the scribes: "But that you may know that the Son of Man has authority on earth to forgive sins"; the text, however, proceeds with the abrupt transition, "he says to the paralytic, 'I say unto you . . .'" A more significant problem arises from the public use of "Son of Man" so early in Jesus' ministry. In the presence of the unbelieving scribes Jesus appears to make an open and unreserved claim to be the Son of Man with authority to forgive sins [63].

Therefore to ameliorate the syntactic structure of v. 10 and to clarify the difficulties, scholars suggest two remedies, one syntactic and the other interpretative. There are several authors who consider ἵνα εἰδῆτε a command [64]. In the second place, it is proposed that 2,10a (ἵνα δὲ εἰδῆτε . . . ἐπὶ τῆς γῆς) does not pertain to the direct discourse addressed to the scribes but is

---

[60] Jesus also predicts his own destiny (8,31; 9,31; 10,33-34) and future (14,28) and has prevision about situations (11,2-3; 14,13-15).

[61] See also 1 Sam 16,7; 1 Kings 8,39; 1 Chron 28,9; Jer 11,20; 17,10; Sir 42,18-20; Lk 16,15; 1 Thess 2,4; Rev 2,23.

[62] HIERONYMUS, In euangelium Matthaei, 56.

[63] LANE, 96. Similar opinions, even more elaborate, in several others, for instance, BOOBYER, "Mark II.10a", 115; CEROKE, "Mk 2,10", 369-370; DUPLACY, "Marc 2,10", 420-423; HAY, "The Son of Man", 71-72; MURPHY-O'CONNOR, "Peche et communauté", 182-183; SCHMITHALS, I, 151-152.

[64] On the use of ἵνα with subjunctive for commands see MOULTON, Grammar I, 178; MOULE, An Idiom Book, 144-146; SHARP, "Mark ii,10", 428-429, etc.

a comment of the evangelist to the Christian readers of the Gospel to indicate the significance of the miracle for them [65].

Prescinding from these opinions, we try to explain the syntactic structure of 2,9-10 in the context of verses 8-11. Verse 8a, taking up καὶ διαλογιζό-μενοι ἐν ταῖς καρδίαις αὐτῶν from 2,6b, introduces a direct discourse addressed to the scribes (λέγει αὐτοῖς). The direct discourse begins with a question in 2,8b (Τί ταῦτα διαλογίζεσθε ἐν ταῖς καρδίαις ὑμῶν) which literally repeats and thematically continues 2,6b as well as 2,8a. The scribes' question, at first pondered over in their hearts (2,6) and then forcefully expressed (2,7), is adequately answered in 2,9-11. Verse 9, again a question, is composed of a disjunctive proposition (τί ἐστιν εὐκοπώτερον, εἰπεῖν τῷ παραλυτικῷ, ᾽Αφίενταί σου αἱ ἁμαρτίαι, ἢ εἰπεῖν, ῎Εγειρε . . . περιπάτει) which explicates the implications of the scribes' question. The first member of the disjunctive proposition, namely, ᾽Αφίενταί σου αἱ ἁμαρτίαι (2,9b), is a verbatim repetition of Jesus' declaration to the paralytic in 2,5b (Τέλνον, ἀφίενταί σου αἱ ἁμαρτίαι) which provoked the scribes to charge Jesus of blasphemy in 2,7. In 2,10a Jesus answers this charge in the purpose clause (ἵνα δὲ εἰδῆτε . . . ἐπὶ τῆς γῆς). "This use of ἵνα with 'I will say this' to be supplied is also classical" [66]. Just as 2,8b is a direct address (διαλογίζεσθε) to the scribes, so also 2,10a is a direct address (εἰδῆτε) to them. Then the second member of the disjunctive proposition (2,9c: ῎Εγειρε . . . περιπάτει;) is taken up and answered by means of the command to the paralytic in 2,11. It is an apostrophe directed to the paralytic (ἔγειρε . . . τὸν οἶκόν σου) intro-duced by Σοὶ λέγω and prepared for by the insertion of λέγει τῷ παραλυτικῷ (2,10b). In light of our explanation, the syntactic structure of 2,10 is not so awkward as it appears but is rather coherently explicable in the context of 2,8-11 [67].

Moreover, according to the concentric structure we have proposed, the structural core and thematic centre of the pericope is 2,7 where the scribes question Jesus' authority to forgive sins and accuse him of blasphemy. Both their question and their serious accusation do require an adequate answer. The disjunctive proposition in 2,9 does not constitute an apt answer at all. On the contrary, the direct and solemn answer in 2,10a meets the demands in 2,7 [68].

---

[65] Besides the authors mentioned in n. 59, see also DIBELIUS, *Tradition*, 67.

[66] BLASS-DEBRUNNER, *Grammar*, § 470 (3).

[67] See the apt punctuations for Mk 2,8-11 in RSV and TOB.

[68] Those who consider v. 10 a comment of the evangelist to Christian readers do not do justice not only to verse 10 but also to verse 7. See, for instance, BOOBYER, "Mark II.10a", 117-120; CEROKE, "Mk 2,10", 379-383, 388; HAY, "Son of Man", 71-73; LANE, 95, 97.

Having clarified the syntactic structure of 2,9-10, we now proceed to interpret these verses. In 2,9 τί . . . ἤ is a popular variant for the classical πότερον . . . ἤ (whether-or). The adjective εὐκοπώτερος is the comparative of εὔκοπος, meaning, 'easy' (literally, with easy labour). In the NT εὐκοπώτερος is found only in the synoptic Gospels where it occurs exclusively in the expression εὐκοπώτερόν ἐστιν (= it is easier). This expression is followed by an infinitive in Mk 2,9 (par. Mt 9,5; Lk 5,23) and an accusative and infinitive in Mk 10, 25 (par. Mt 19,24; Lk 18,25) and Lk 16,17. As the rest of the terms in 2,9 were explained above, we proceed to explicate the argumentation of Jesus in this verse.

The method of reasoning in 2,9 resembles the first of the seven exegetical rules of Hillel. According to that rule one can argue from the easier to the more difficult [69]. At the surface level it is easier to declare the man's sins forgiven than to utter the word of healing since the latter involves the risk of ocular verification. However, at the deeper level it is harder to declare the man's sins forgiven because this deals with the invisible and supernatural order [70]. The content of Jesus' argumentation is based on the close connection between sin and sickness, forgiveness and healing on the one hand, and Jesus' authority to forgive sins, on the other. Verse 9 is preparatory to verse 10, the principal point of the answer. Just as with 2,7, 2,10, the main point of Jesus' answer to the scribes, is also sandwiched between Jesus' command to the paralytic in v. 9c and v. 11:

9   A   ἔγειρε καὶ ἆρον τὸν κράβαττόν σου καὶ περιπάτει

10   B   ἵνα δὲ εἰδῆτε ὅτι ἐξουσίαν ἔχει ὁ υἱὸς τοῦ ἀνθρώπου ἀφιέναι ἁμαρτίας ἐπὶ τῆς γῆς

11   A'   ἔγειρε ἆρον τὸν κράβαττόν σου καὶ ὕπαγε εἰς τὸν οἶκόν σου.

Because 2,10 constitutes the centre of the chiastic structure of 2,9-11 and because it is the focal point of Jesus' answer to the scribes, an indepth study of this verse is necessary. The meaning of ἐξουσία and οἶδα was explained in our exegesis of 1,22 and 1,24 respectively. And we have analysed ἀφιέναι and ἁμαρτίαι in our interpretation of 2,5 above. With regard to ὁ υἱὸς τοῦ ἀνθρώπου [71], one should note that it is unknown in secular

---

[69] Cf. STRACK, *Talmud und Midrash*, 96-97. See also BACHER, *Die exegetische Terminologie*, v.

[70] Cf. KLOSTERMANN, 23; LAGRANGE, 37; RAWLINSON, 26, etc.

[71] On the sources, philology and background of the title, the Son of Man, see COLPE, *TDNT*, VIII, 400-461; JEREMIAS, *Theology*, 257-272.

Greek but found 82 times in the Gospels. It occurs in all of the five strands of tradition (Mk, the source common to Mt and Lk, Mt proper, Lk proper and Jn). Unlike other titles such as the Son of God, Christ, the Son of David, etc., the title 'the Son of Man' is found exclusively on the lips of Jesus in all of the four Gospels. It does not occur in the Pauline writings. It is not found in the confessional formulae nor used attributively. This title is not employed in any prayers to Jesus nor is it used in statements about him. In fact, it is firmly anchored in the sayings of Jesus. The only logical explanation for this consistency is that the expression was rooted in tradition from the very beginning and the evangelists considered it so sacrosanct that no one dared to eliminate it [72].

What remains yet to be clarified is the relation between ἐξουσία and the Son of Man on the one hand, and the Son of Man and the forgiveness of sins, on the other. It is striking to note that in the Bible ἐξουσία, Son of Man and forgiveness of sins are found in close connection and in the same context only in Mk 2,10 and its parallels (Mt 9,6; Lk 5,24). However, forgiveness of sins was an essential aspect of the eschatological expectation of Israel (cf. Is 43,25; 44,22; Jer 31,34; Ezek 16,63; Mic 7,18-19; Dan 8,24; Ps 130,7-8, etc.). And in Dan 7,13-14 υἱὸς ἀνθρώπου is endowed with ἐξουσία (mentioned thrice in Dan 7,14) which is qualified as everlasting and imperishable. Later υἱὸς ἀνθρώπου of Dan 7,13 became a title for the redeemer in the apocalyptic literature [73]. Thus υἱὸς ἀνθρώπου of Dan 7,13 understood in the Messianic sense [74] became the foundation for the Son of Man sayings in the Gospels where this title is employed not only for his eschatological functions but also in reference to his Suffering, Death and Resurrection and to his earthly ministry. Therefore, the eschatological hope of the forgiveness of sins, the messianic interpretation of υἱὸς ἀνθρώπου of Dan 7,13 and his ἐξουσία in Dan 7,14 are merged and find fulfilment in Jesus' answer to the scribes in Mk 2,10.

Finally, what does ἐπὶ τῆς γῆς in 2,10 mean? [75] Is the contrast between heaven and earth the focal point of this phrase? In the Bible, depending on the context, the contrast between heaven and earth has different nuances. For instance, according to Mt 5,34-35, heaven is God's throne and earth his footstool. In Mt 6,19-20 and Heb 8,4-5, earth is imperfect and perishable while heaven is perfect and imperishable. In Mk 2,10, states Taylor, authority

---

[72] Cf. JEREMIAS, *Theology*, 266.

[73] See especially Similitudes of Ethiopian Enoch, chs. 37-71.

[74] Cf. FEUILLET, "Fils de l'homme", 171-174; JEREMIAS, *Theology*, 261, 269.

[75] CRANFIELD, 100-101, lists four opinions.

to remit sins on earth is set over against the divine prerogative exercised in heaven [76]. However, the real point of emphasis seems to be that the source of forgiveness is paradoxically transferred from heaven to earth inasmuch as the Son of Man is the one who exercises it [77].

To sum up, in verse 10, Jesus, identifying himself with the transcendental figure, the Son of Man (note the logical progression of the argumentation in 2,5b.7.10), asserts that he has authority to forgive sins. In this assertion the transcendental dimension of Jesus' person becomes manifest inasmuch as he affirms that he has authority to forgive sins, a prerogative reserved to God alone. In the words of Beda Venerabilis, "ergo idem ipse et Deus et filius hominis est ut et homo Christus per divinitatis suae potentiam peccata dimittere possit" [78]. The affirmation in 2,10 is enclasped by Jesus' command to the paralytic to rise, take up his pallet and go home (2,9.11). In this way the close connection between forgiveness and healing (as mentioned earlier) is emphasized.

8. *Implementation in Action (2,11-12b)*

There is a perfect correspondence between Jesus' command to the paralytic in 2,11 and its execution in 2,12ab:

ἔγειρε ἆρον τὸν κράβαττόν σου καὶ ὕπαγε εἰς τὸν οἶκόν σου

ἠγέρθη καὶ εὐθὺς ἄρας τὸν κράβαττον ἐξῆλθεν ἔμπροσθεν πάντων.

In 2,11 σοὶ λέγω is emphatic and the asyndetic construction gives the command a decisive tone. In 2,12 ἔμπροσθεν, an improper preposition with genitive, means 'before' or 'in the presence of'. By narrating the instantaneous execution of the command in 2,12ab ("and he rose, and immediately took up the pallet and went before them all") Mk emphasizes that Jesus' authority to forgive sins is demonstrably manifested in the perfect healing of the paralytic.

9. *Narrative Conclusion (2,12cd)*

The pericope concludes by narrating the reaction of the audience. Of the four occurrences of ἐξίστάναι in Mk, thrice it is employed to express

---

[76] Cf. TAYLOR, 198.
[77] Cf. FEUILLET, "Fils de l'homme", 174.
[78] BEDA, 456.

the reaction of amazement to Jesus' miracles (2,12; 5,42; 6,51) and once in the sense 'to be out of one's mind' (3,21). The verb δοξάζειν has in classical Greek two meanings: (a) to think, to have an opinion; (b) to praise, to value. In the LXX and NT, however, it is not used in the first meaning but in the second [79]. It occurs in Mk only in our verse where it expresses the idea of praising and glorifying, of ascribing to God the splendour due him. The words in Mk 2,12d οὕπως οὐδέποτε εἴδομεν, as Taylor notes, are colloquial and lifelike [80]. The pericope thus concludes on a very positive note — glorifying God for the marvels worked by Jesus [81].

C. Concluding Remarks

1. Just as in Mk 1,21-28, here too (2,1-12) Jesus' authority is manifested both in words and in deeds. Both the controversy and the healing form a single literary unit with a distinctive concentric structure (A B C D C' B' A'). The pivotal point of this literary unit is the scribes' questioning of Jesus' authority to forgive sins whereby their incredulity in his divinity is highlighted [82].

> Verum dicunt scribae quia nemo dimittere peccata nisi Deus potest qui per eos quoque dimittit quibus dimittendi tribuit potestatem, et ideo Christus vere Deus esse probatur quia dimittere peccata quasi Deus potest [83].

2. The scribes' failure to recognize Jesus' divinity is reiterated in the course of the Gospel (cf. 3,22.28-30). The chief priests and the elders also nurture the same conviction (cf. 11,27-33; 14,53-64).

3. Jesus' response that he has authority to forgive sins reveals his transcendental dimension. Jesus makes a similar assertion in 2,28 where he affirms his lordship over the sabbath. These two Son of Man sayings

---

[79] Cf. KITTEL, *TDNT* II, 253-254.

[80] Cf. TAYLOR, 198.

[81] By "all" in v. 12c Mk probably does not include the scribes mentioned in v. 6 since nowhere else in Mk they appreciate Jesus. So by using "the crowds" Mt (9,8) correctly interprets Mk's mind.

[82] FARRER (*Study*, 76-77) compares Mk 2,1-12 with Ex 4,1-9. Here, according to FARRER, one finds the first of several signs used to convince the elders that Moses had authority to deliver Israel from bondage.

[83] BEDA, 455.

emphasize Jesus' authority in his earthly ministry. But in the second part of the Gospel the Son of Man sayings bring to light two more aspects of his person and mission: he is destined to suffer, die and rise from the dead (8,31; 9,12.31; 10,33.45; 14,21.41) and he is also the eschatological judge (8,38; 13,26; 14,62). Thus by the use of the Son of Man sayings our evangelist projects a three-dimensional picture of Jesus: this title links Jesus' earthly ministry; his Passion, Death and Resurrection; and his eschatological functions.

II. Jesus' Call of Sinners (2,13-17)

A. Literary Analysis [84]

1. *Internal Coherence*

Several translations and commentaries divide Mk 2,13-17 into two literary units: 2,13-14 and 2,15-17 [85]. The unity of 2,13-17 is questioned also by form critics who offer different solutions [86]. Faced with such problems, we investigate whether there is literary coherence and thematic unity in the text.

The preposition παρά of 2,13a and its repetition in the compound verb παράγων in 2,14a form a connecting link between vv. 13 and 14. In 2,13a

---

[84] In 2,14 Λευὶν τὸν τοῦ 'Αλφαίου should be preferred, for the reading 'Ιάκωβον in the Western and the Caesarean texts shows the influence of 3,18 where 'Ιάκωβον τὸν τοῦ 'Αλφαίου is included among the Twelve. In 2,15-16 the reading of B must be preferred because the tendency of the copyists would have been to insert καί after οἱ γραμματεῖς under the influence of the common expression 'the scribes and the Pharisees'. Since in Mk the verb ἀκολουθεῖν is never predicated of those hostile to Jesus, a full stop should be placed after αὐτῷ. Unmindful of this usage, copyists transferred the stop after πολλοί and inserted καί before ἰδόντες. In 2,16 ἐσθίει is changed to ἐσθίετε because the question is addressed to the disciples. The addition of καὶ πίνει is a natural accretion inserted by copyists, perhaps under the influence of the Lucan parallel (5,30). And the addition of ὁ διδάσκαλος ὑμῶν appears to be an assimilation to the Matthean parallel (9,11). Therefore the reading of B D W is original.

[85] Cf. BJ, RSV, NEB; KLOSTERMANN, 24; LANE, 99, 102-103; LOHMEYER, 54-55; RAWLINSON, 27-28; SWETE, 39-40; TAYLOR, 201, 203, etc.

[86] Cf. BULTMANN, *Tradition*, 18, 39, 47-49, 54, 57, 62, 64, 244; DIBELIUS, *Tradition*, 43, 143, etc.

Jesus begins a movement which is carried on in 2,14a (παράγων) and it finds its culmination in Jesus' call of Levi. The clause καὶ ἠκολούθουν αὐτῷ in 2,15d recalls καὶ ἀναστὰς ἠκολούθησεν αὐτῷ of 2,14d. Τελώνιον in 2,14a and τελῶναι in 2,16(bis) connect these two verses. The combination of τελῶναι and ἁμαρτωλοί in verses 15-16 (which occurs only in this pericope in Mk) indicates the link between these two verses. The noun ἁμαρτωλοί in 2,15.16(bis).17 connects verses 15-17. The vocabulary on discipleship: ἀκολουθεῖν (2,14(bis).15), καλεῖν (2,17) and μαθηταῖς (2,15-16) imparts literary unity to 2,14-17.

Furthermore, a thematic unity and progression are discernible in 2,13-17. After the introduction (2,13), the pericope begins with Jesus' call of Levi, a tax collector, to be a disciple. Then Jesus dines with him. Thus far it was a relation between two individuals, Jesus and Levi. However, in 2,15b there is a growth: no more just two individuals but two groups (tax collectors and sinners, Jesus and his disciples). Jesus' personal association with tax collectors and sinners and his dining with them provoke the scribes of the Pharisees who question him. Jesus' response to them in 2,17 not only justifies his action but also clarifies the purpose of his mission. Two themes are thus intertwined in this pericope: (1) Jesus' meal with tax collectors and sinners; (2) his mission in calling them to discipleship.

Therefore, it is reasonable to hold that, although originally Mk 2,14 and 2,15-17 might have been two separate literary units, in the present form and context Mk 2,13-17 does contain literary coherence and thematic unity.

2. Synoptic Comparison

a. Mk 2,13-17 and Mt 9,9-13

The Marcan summary of Jesus' teaching the crowd (2,13), a redactional verse which functions as the introduction to the pericope, is absent in Mt. Instead, Mt connects this pericope with the preceding one by means of minor additions in 9,9a (ὁ Ἰησοῦς ἐκεῖθεν). According to the second evangelist, Jesus calls Levi, the son of Alphaeus, to be a disciple. His name, however, does not figure in the catalogue of the Twelve (3,16-19). In contrast, according to the first evangelist, the name of the disciple whom Jesus calls is not Levi, but Matthew, the tax collector, whose name does occur in the list of the twelve apostles (10,3). The clause in Mk 2,15c (ἦσαν γὰρ πολλοί, καὶ ἠκολούθουν αὐτῷ) is absent in Mt and in Lk probably because they found it superfluous. In Mk the opponents of Jesus are the scribes of the Pharisees but in Mt his interlocutors are the Pharisees themselves whose attitude Jesus censures frequently (cf. 5,20; 23,1-39). The key difference between Mk and Mt and the principal emphasis of the latter are indicated by the insertion of Hos 6,6 ("I desire mercy, and not sacrifice") between the proverb in 9,12 and the statement on Jesus' mission in 9,13c. By this citation not only does Mt picture Jesus as confronting the Pharisees that they should reflect on the meaning of the text but he also uses Hos 6,6 as the climactic statement of the pericope.

b. *Mk 2,13-17 and Lk 5,27-32*

Retaining ἐξῆλθεν and replacing πάλιν with μετὰ ταῦτα (cf. 10,1), Lk effects a smooth transition. Differing from the parallel in Mk, Lk employs θεᾶσθαι, a strong verb (cf. Lk 7,24; 23,35; Acts 1,11; 21,27; 22,9) which suggests that Jesus singled out Levi particularly. The Lucan phrase καταλιπὼν πάντα, even though in tension with the way in which Levi was able to hold a great feast in his house, does imply that for Levi discipleship meant forsaking everything in order to follow Jesus. In Mk 2,15 the meal functions only as a setting for the controversy whereas according to Lk Levi made a great feast for Jesus. The ambiguity of Mk 2,15, whether αὐτοῦ in the phrase ἐν τῇ οἰκίᾳ αὐτοῦ refers to the house of Levi or that of Jesus, is clarified in Lk 5,29: the feast took place in Levi's house. By substituting οἱ γραμματεῖς τῶν Φαρισαίων of Mk with οἱ Φαρισαῖοι καὶ οἱ γραμματεῖς αὐτῶν Lk not only clarifies but also correctly interprets Mk's mind. By adding ἐγόγγυζον (note the imperfect) at the beginning of 5,30, Lk emphasizes their displeasure towards the action of Jesus and his disciples. He reformulates the question so that it deals with the behaviour of the disciples rather than with that of Jesus. The addition of καὶ πίνετε accentuates the crime (cf. 5,33; 7,33-34). Instead of ἰσχύοντες (Mk 2,17) Lk employs ὑγιαίνοντες, a more accurate term. By using the perfect ἐλήλυθα in place of ἦλθον, Lk indicates that Jesus' mission was still in progress. And by the addition of εἰς μετάνοιαν in 5,32, he underlines the key concern of Jesus' mission to call sinners to repentance (cf. 15,7.10.20b-24, etc.). In brief, by careful modifications and distinctive additions, Lk places this pericope in line with others in his Gospel where the genuine conversion of sinners is considered not only a joyful event but also the main concern of Jesus' mission (cf. 7,36-50; 15,1-32; 18,9-14; 19,1-10; 23,40-43).

3. *Tradition and Redaction*

The redactional character is most conspicuous in 2,13. As previously mentioned, the verbs ἐξέρχεσθαι and διδάσκειν and the adverb πάλιν not only occur more frequently in Mk but also are generally found in redactional verses. It was also noted that verbs of movement + πρός + αὐτόν and the multiplication of cognate verbs are typical of Mk. Furthermore, the noun θάλασσα and the phrase πᾶς ὁ ὄχλος occur more often in the second Gospel [87]. Finally, the theme of the crowd gathering to Jesus and he in turn teaching them occurs elsewhere in redactional verses (cf. 4,1b-2; 6,34; 10,1, etc.). Verse 15c (ἦσαν γὰρ πολλοὶ καὶ ἠκολούθουν αὐτῷ) is also redactional for, as previously stated, γάρ explanatory is characteristic of Mk. The verb ἀκολουθεῖν and the adjective πολύς occur more often in Mk [88]. In conclusion, therefore, we hold that verses 13 and 15c are redactional and the rest is from tradition [89].

4. *Literary Structure*

13 ---- Καὶ ἐξῆλθεν πάλιν παρὰ τὴν θάλασσαν· καὶ πᾶς ὁ ὄχλος ἤρχετο πρὸς αὐτόν, καὶ ἐδίδασκεν αὐτούς.

14 A καὶ *παράγων εἶδεν* Δευὶν τὸν τοῦ 'Αλφαίου καθήμενον ἐπὶ τὸ τελώνιον, καὶ *λέγει αὐτῷ*, 'Ακολούθει μοι. καὶ ἀναστὰς ἠκολούθησεν αὐτῷ.

15 B Καὶ γίνεται κατακεῖσθαι αὐτὸν ἐν τῇ οἰκίᾳ αὐτοῦ, καὶ πολλοὶ τελῶναι καὶ ἁμαρτωλοὶ συνανέκειντο τῷ 'Ιησοῦ καὶ τοῖς μαθηταῖς αὐτοῦ · ἦσαν γὰρ πολλοὶ καὶ ἠκολούθουν αὐτῷ.

16   C καὶ οἱ γραμματεῖς τῶν Φαρισαίων ἰδόντες ὅτι ἐσθίει μετὰ τῶν ἁμαρτωλῶν καὶ τελωνῶν

   B' ἔλεγον τοῖς μαθηταῖς αὐτοῦ, Ὅτι μετὰ τῶν τελωνῶν καὶ ἁμαρτωλῶν ἐσθίει;

17 A' καὶ ἀκούσας ὁ 'Ιησοῦς λέγει αὐτοῖς (ὅτι) Οὐ χρείαν ἔχουσιν οἱ ἰσχύοντες ἰατροῦ ἀλλ' οἱ κακῶς ἔχοντες· οὐκ ἦλθον καλέσαι δικαίους ἀλλὰ ἁμαρτωλούς.

---

[87] Cf. n. 88 below.

[88]

	Mt	Mk	Lk	Jn	Acts	Paul	Rest		Total
θάλασσα	16	19	3	9	10	4	30	=	91
πᾶς ὁ ὄχλος	1	5	2	0	1	0	0	=	9
ἀκολουθεῖν	25	18	17	19	4	1	6	=	90
πολύς	50	57	51	36	46	82	31	=	353

[89] Several exegetes argue that Mk has redactionally composed 2,14 following the pattern of 1,16-18.19-20. Cf. PESCH, "Levi-Matthäus", 43,45; THISSEN, *Erzählung*, 56, 59, 317; TRAUTMANN, *Zeichenhafte Handlungen*, 136,138, etc. But there are not sufficient literary and thematic indications for such a claim.

ARENS (*ΗΛΘΟΝ-Sayings*, 28-30) holds that Mk 2,15a is redactional, but the evidence he has adduced is meagre.

As the display of the text demonstrates, Mk 2,13-17 consists of a concentric structure (A B C B' A'). Verse 13 serves as the introduction to the pericope. Verse 14 (A: call of Levi, a tax collector) is parallel to v. 17 (A': Jesus' answer to his opponents that he came to call sinners). In these two verses there is a thematic progression: the former deals with the call of a particular person to discipleship while the latter is a universal statement regarding Jesus' mission. Similarly, verse 15 (B: tax collectors and sinners dining with Jesus and his disciples) is parallel to verse 16bc (B': "Why does he eat with tax collectors and sinners?"). Compared to B, B' marks a clear shift of emphasis, namely, B narrates that tax collectors and sinners were dining with Jesus and his disciples whereas B' focuses attention on Jesus. And at the centre of the pericope the problem (C) is mentioned: the scribes of the Pharisees see Jesus eating with tax collectors and sinners (2,16a).

B. Interpretation

1. *Introduction (2,13)*

The verb ἐξέρχεσθαι in 2,13 has a transitional function as in other instances (cf. 1,29.35; 6,1; 8,11.27; 9,30). By means of πάλιν Mk connects the phrase παρὰ τὴν θάλασσαν in 2,13 with the same phrase in 1,16a. In 1,16-20 θάλασσα was the locus where Jesus encountered the first four disciples, while in 2,13 it is the locus where he encounters the crowd (cf. 3,7-10; 4,1-2; 5,21; 6,53-56). As previously noted, when Jesus is in a lonely place the crowds throng to him and he responds to them according to their needs. One can well note that in the first chapter Mk does not use the term ὄχλος. Instead, he employs either the impersonal plural (cf. 1,22.32.45) or πάντες, ἅπαντες or πολύς (cf. 1,27.32.34.37). The first occurrence of ὄχλος is at 2,4 and the second at 2,13. What role does ὄχλος have in the second Gospel? To determine the function of this term one must study it in its context and in relation to other dramatis personae.

In some instances ὄχλος has no specific role but functions as a backdrop for healings (5,21.24.30.31; 7,33; 10,46), exorcism (9,14.15.17.25), or manifestation to the disciples (4,36; 6,45). In a few other cases ὄχλος indicates the beneficiaries of miracles: healings (3,9-10) and feedings (6,39-42; 8,6-10). On two other occasions Jesus imparts special instructions to the crowd (7,14-23; 8,34-38). But in a number of instances, ὄχλος constitutes the audience of Jesus' teaching (2,13; 4,1-2; 6,33-34;10,1; 11,17-18) [90]. The

[90] See also Mk 2,2-4; 3,32-35; 8,1-2, etc.

crowd is astonished at his teaching (11,18; cf. 1,22.27). It is the positive
attitude of ὄχλος towards Jesus, particularly its astonishment at his teaching,
that prevented the Jewish authorities from destroying or arresting Jesus earlier
(cf. 11,18; 12,12). In the passion narrative, however, ὄχλος, persuaded by
the Jewish leaders (cf. 15,11), demands of Pilate to hand over Jesus for
crucifixion (cf. 15,8-15). In short, the ὄχλος on the whole had a positive
attitude towards and an appreciation of Jesus. Jesus' teaching of the crowd,
which started in 2,13 plays an important role for the beginning and growth
of its positive attitude towards him [91].

2. Call of Levi to Discipleship (2,14)

The call of Levi to discipleship follows the woodcut pattern of 1,16-
18.19-20 reduced to the essentials, as the following comparison demonstrates.

Mk 1,16-18	*Mk 2,14*
καὶ παράγων ... εἶδεν Σίμωνα	καὶ παράγων εἶδεν Λευὶν ...
ἀμφιβάλλοντας ἐν τῇ θαλάσσῃ	καθήμενον ἐπὶ τὸ τελώνιον
καὶ εἶπεν αὐτοῖς ...	καὶ λέγει αὐτῷ,
Δεῦτε ὀπίσω μου	Ἀκολούθει μοι
καὶ εὐθὺς ἀφέντες τὰ δίκτυα	--------------------
ἠκολούθησαν αὐτῷ	ἠκολούθησεν αὐτῷ

The fourth element, the renunciation of possessions, is absent in Mk 2,14
(but correctly supplied in the Lucan parallel) [92].

Compared to 1,16-20 there is a striking difference in 2,14. In the former
Mk narrates the call of two pairs, Simon and his brother Andrew, James and
his brother John. Making them apostles (cf. 3,13-19) Jesus commissions them
on a mission (6,7-13). But in 2,14 Mk narrates the call of a particular individual, Levi, whose name does not figure in the list of the Twelve nor is he
sent on a mission. Instead, the narration of Levi's call is followed by the
statement that he arranged a meal in his house where many tax collectors
and sinners dined with Jesus and his disciples. Mk thus presents Levi's
following of Jesus (2,14d) as a paradigm of discipleship in general (2,15d).

---

[91] Unlike Lk, Mk does not make a distinction between ὄχλος and λαός.
[92] For the exegesis of important terms in 2,14 see the interpretation of 1,16-20 in Ch. IV.

3. Action: Tax Collectors and Sinners Dining with Jesus
and His Disciples (2,15)

The construction in 2,15a is the impersonal use of γίνεσθαι followed by an accusative and infinitive. This construction occurs only once again in Mk (2,23). With an appreciable number of exegetes we hold that in 2,15a αὐτόν refers to Jesus (cf. 2,14d) and αὐτοῦ to Levi (cf. 2,14ab) [93]. According to Semitic parataxis, καί in 2,15d is most probably used in the sense of the relative pronoun οἵ [94]. Verse 15cd (ἦσαν γὰρ πολλοὶ καὶ ἠκολούθουν αὐτῷ) is a parenthesis which refers to τοῖς μαθηταῖς αὐτοῦ in 2,15b [95].

As mentioned in Ch. V, κατακεῖσθαι in 2,15a is used in the sense of 'to recline at table' and the noun οἰκία here means 'family'. Thus in 2,15a Mk narrates that Jesus is the guest in Levi's family. In 2,15b the term τελῶναι (= tax collectors, revenue officers) does not refer to the holders of tax farming contracts themselves but subordinates hired by them [96]. The prevailing system of tax collection afforded the collectors many opportunities to be unfair and rapacious in their dealings [97]. Hence they were generally hated by others [98]. The strict Jews were further offended because Jewish tax collectors had to maintain constant contact with Gentiles in the course of their work [99], thus rendering them ceremoniously unclean. A more serious reason for the Jewish animosity against Jewish tax collectors was that most of them ultimately served the unbelieving Romans, their very own oppressors. This might have been bitterly felt by the Jews in Jerusalem where the tax collectors did actually serve the Roman authorities and where the Jewish

---

[93] Among several others, see ARENS, *ΗΛΘΟΝ-Sayings*, 29; DONAHUE, "Tax Collectors", 56; HAENCHEN, 108-109; KLOSTERMANN, 25; TRAUTMANN, *Zeichenhafte Handlungen*, 138. ABRAHAMS (*Pharisaism* I, 56) notes that the Pharisees would not have been scandalized at eating with sinners if it could be done in one's own house where the ritual prescriptions could be observed; scandal would arise from eating at the house of sinners.

MALBON ("Mark 2,15 in Context", 282-292) argues that τῇ οἰκίᾳ αὐτοῦ in Mk 2,15 refers not to Levi's but Jesus' house. Her arguments are not well-founded.

[94] Correctly translated in RSV, NEB, BJ, but TOB connects v. 15d with v. 16.

[95] With most of the translations and authors but against TOB and authors such as BARTSCH, "Problematik", 91-96; TRAUTMANN, *Zeichenhafte Handlungen*, 140, 143; VÖLKEL, "Freund der Zöllner", 6, etc.

[96] Cf. JEREMIAS, *Theology*, 110-111 and DONAHUE, "Tax Collectors" 42, 45, 49-50.

[97] Cf. MICHEL, *TDNT* VIII, 89-99; JEREMIAS, *Jerusalem*, 124-126.

[98] Pagan writers mention them together with adulterers, brothel-keepers, robbers, etc. Cf. MICHEL, *TDNT* VIII, 99-101, particularly n. 133.

[99] Rabbinic literature lists them among those engaged in despised trades. Cf. JEREMIAS, *Jerusalem*, 303-312; STR.-B., *Kommentar* I, 377-380.

resistance to Rome was especially strong and persistent [100]. In Mk the noun
τελῶναι does not occur by itself but only in conjunction with ἁμαρτωλοί.

The term ἁμαρτωλός by nature is an adjective (= sinful) but is often
used, as here, as a noun (= sinner). Of its six occurrences in Mk, only once
is it used as an adjective (8,38) and all the other times as a substantive: twice
absolute use (2,17; 14,41) and thrice with the noun τελῶναι (2,15.16(bis)).
What does ἁμαρτωλοί mean in the formula τελῶναι καὶ ἁμαρτωλοί? This
formula occurs only in the synoptic Gospels and the critical opinion is sharply
divided over the identification of ἁμαρτωλοί. The crux of the discussion is
whether by ἁμαρτωλοί is meant sinners according to the Pharisaic
understanding or sinners according to the popular view. The Pharisees viewed
sinners as those guilty of ritual failing, particularly of contamination through
contact with pagans, while the common people understood sin as immorality
and did not consider ritual sin as the main sin.

Depending on the choice one makes between these two alternatives and
the modifications one would make, a wide range of opinions prevails in the
present exegetical discussion. (1) Some identify ἁμαρτωλοί as עַם הָאָרֶץ viz..
those who do not keep the Law in its fullest sense [101]; (2) a few others hold
that this term primarily denotes 'the people of the land', and, in the second
place, those who lead an immoral life [102]. Perrin paraphrases the term as "other
Jews who made themselves as Gentiles" [103]. (4) Gnilka: "Als Sünder galten
insbesondere die Heiden, aber auch jene, die wie die Heiden die
Reinheitsvorschriften nicht beachteten" [104]. (5) Still another group of authors
consider that by ἁμαρτωλοί is primarily meant those who are immoral, and.
in the second place, it may signify 'the people of the land' [105] (6) Finally.
spearheaded by Jeremias, some authors reject the Pharisaic conception of
sinners and assert that 'sinners' refers to those who by their immoral mode
of life and/or dishonourable vocation were despised and carried a social
stigma in public life [106].

---

[100] Cf. DONAHUE, "Tax Collectors", 42-49, 59-61.

[101] For instance ARENS, *HΛΘON-Sayings*, 30; FABRIS. *Matteo*. 217-218; LOHSE.
Environment, 80; OPPENHEIMER, *Social History*. 61-62, etc.

[102] Cf. MONTEFIORE, *Gospels* I, 54.

[103] PERRIN, *Rediscovering*, 93-94, 106. Similarly. FARMER. "Tax Collectors". 169. 171.

[104] GNILKA, I, 106.

[105] Cf. CRANFIELD, 103; GRUNDMANN. 82; NINEHAM. 100. See also ABRAHAMS.
Pharisaism, 55; RENGSTORF, *TDNT* 1. 327: "ἁμαρτωλοί partly means those who live a flagrant-
ly immoral life . . . and partly those who follow a dishonourable vocation or one which inclines
them strongly to dishonesty".

[106] Cf. JEREMIAS. "Zöllner". 295. 300; id.. *Jerusalem*. 303-312.

In assessing these opinions, it is worth mentioning the following observations of Jeremias. At the time of Jesus' ministry the Pharisees numbered only about 6,000. Hence it would be unlikely that the concept of ritual sin would be so widespread as to be found in the Gospels in the same sense. Secondly, according to the Pharisees, virtually all the עַם הָאָרֶץ would be sinners, and in a place like Capernaum, the whole population, mixed as it was with Gentiles, would be so considered. Therefore, Jesus' association with sinners, Jeremias asserts, could not be censured since, according to the Pharisees, Jesus himself is a member of the עַם הָאָרֶץ [107]. Based on these reasons one should be cautious to identify ἁμαρτωλοί as עַם הָאָרֶץ. Regarding Perrin's contention, Donahue, a former doctoral student of Perrin, making the necessary distinctions observes that the latter's view is not valid for Galilee during Jesus' ministry [108]. Gnilka's view is applicable to texts such as Mt 5,46-47; 18,17 where the correlated expression 'tax collector(s) . . . Gentile(s)' occurs or Gal 2,15; Mk 14,41 par., etc. where ἁμαρτωλοί means Gentiles. However, his view is not applicable to Mk 2,15.

With regard to Jeremias' opinion two critical observations are due. The formula τελῶναι καὶ ἁμαρτωλοί occurs in the common synoptic tradition (Mk 2,15-16 par.), in the tradition common to the first and the third Gospels (Mt 11,19 par. Lk 7,34) and in the material proper to Lk (15,1-2). But in Mk 2,15-16 par. and Lk 15,1-2 those who question or complain about Jesus are primarily the Pharisees. In 7,29-30 Lk contrasts the religiosity of the common people and tax collectors with that of the Pharisees and the lawyers. In all the three strands of tradition the accusation against Jesus that he associates and eats with tax collectors and sinners presupposes a Pharisaic contention. And their contention is primarily concerned with, not the neglect or violation of the rules of piety (as for instance in Mk 7,1-4), but Jesus' association with immoral people or the followers of degrading occupations [109]. Just as Jesus' Death on the cross was a scandal, so also his eating with tax

[107] Cf. JEREMIAS, "Zöllner", 293-300.

[108] Cf. DONAHUE, "Tax Collectors", 42-61, particularly 59-61. But FARMER ("Tax Collectors", 172-173) notes that the situation in Galilee was not very different from that of Judea and Samaria.

[109] ABRAHAMS, *Pharisaism*, 55: "Sinners were not those who neglected the rules of ritual piety, but were persons of proven dishonesty and followers of suspected or degrading occupations". According to MONTEFIORE (*Gospels* I, 54) sinners are those "who knowingly violated or were believed to have violated some precept of the law, whether ceremonial or moral".

collectors and sinners was a scandal during Jesus' ministry [110] which cannot be caused by the neglect or violation of the ritual regulations. In the second place, even though a whole series of trades were generally despised and those who practised them might have been exposed to social degradation [111], there seems to have been exceptions. For instance, according to Josephus, a certain tax collector named John was one of the leading citizens of the Jewish community in Caesarea. When certain anti-Semitic elements defiled the synagogue, this tax collector acted as the spokesman for the elders of the Jews there and sought the help of the Roman authorities to normalize the situation [112].

To sum up, we are of the opinion that in the formula τελῶναι καὶ ἁμαρτωλοί, the latter term primarily denotes immoral people, but it also denotes those who follow a dishonourable vocation or one which inclines them strongly to dishonesty. There seems to have been some respectable individuals among those who practised 'despised trades'. Regarding the correlation between τελῶναι and ἁμαρτωλοί it is evident that 'sinners' is not a class as 'tax collectors'. Therefore, as it is clear from our foregoing explanation, 'sinners' is inclusive of 'tax collectors'.

After the detailed discussion on tax collectors and sinners, we proceed to interpret the rest of the verse. In the NT the verb συνανακεῖσθαι (= recline at table with; eat with) occurs only in the synoptic Gospels [113]. In Mk 2,15 (par. Mt 9,10) it is used in the imperfect tense and in other instances it is in the participial form, in the sense of 'guests' [114]. All the five occurrences of the participial use are found in the context of a banquet. Such a nuance is implied in 2,15 too [115]. However, what is important in verse 15 is the significance of the meal: "in the ancient world tablefellowship was regarded as a sign and pledge of real intimacy" [116]. And "in the east, even today, to invite a man to a meal was an honour. It was an offer of peace, trust, brotherhood and forgiveness; in short, sharing at table meant sharing life" [117].

---

[110] Cf. JEREMIAS, *Theology*, 121; PERRIN, *Rediscovering*, 102-108. The argument of WALKER ("Tax Collectors", 221-238) questioning the historicity of Jesus' meal with tax collectors and sinners is not convincing. A number of scholars affirm the historicity of this event. Cf. VÖLKEL, "Freund der Zöllner", 1-10; BRAUN, "Nonkonformisten", 97-101; TRAUTMANN, *Zeichenhafte Handlungen*, 154-164.

[111] JEREMIAS, *Jerusalem*, 303-312.

[112] JOSEPHUS, *Jewish Wars*, II,284-292.

[113] Mt 2, Mk 2, Lk 3.

[114] Cf. Mk 6,22 (par. Mt 14,9); Lk 7,49; 14,10.15.

[115] Cf. JEREMIAS, *Theology*, 115, n. 2.

[116] NINEHAM, 95.

[117] JEREMIAS, *Theology*, 115.

By the redactional inclusion of 2,15cd — there were many who followed (ἠκολούθουν) him — Mk has achieved various motifs: (1) by using the imperfect plural (ἠκολούθουν) in 2,15d in contrast to the ingressive aorist singular (ἠκολούθησεν) in 2.14d Mk presumably underscores the point that an appreciable number of disciples were permanently accompanying him. (2) The note that a permanent body of disciples were with him legitimizes the question addressed to the disciples concerning the behaviour of their master in 2,16 and justifies the questions addressed to Jesus about his disciples' behaviour in 2,18.24. (3) This prepares for Jesus' choice of the Twelve (3,14-19) from his many disciples (3,13).

4. Problem: Jesus Dining with Tax Collectors and Sinners (2,16a)

According to the structure we have proposed, 2,16a is the centre of the concentric structure. This verse is also the centre of the double chiasm of 2,15-16:

tax collectors . . . sinners . . . dining	a	b	c
dining . . . sinners . . . tax collectors	c'	b'	a'
tax collectors . . . sinners . . . dining	a''	b''	c''

By the phrase οἱ γραμματεῖς τῶν Φαρισαίων (partitive genitive) is meant the scribes who belonged to the party of the Pharisees (cf. Acts 23,9) [118], viz., the scribes who kept the Law and taught it according to the strict Pharisaic tradition. Their attention is directed towards one person, Jesus, and his action of eating with sinners and tax collectors. The reference to τῶν ἁμαρτωλῶν καὶ τελωνῶν (in the inverted order) perhaps prepares for the final answer in 2,17 where not the tax collectors but only sinners are mentioned [119].

5. Question: Why Dining with Tax Collectors and Sinners? (2,16bc)

The question of the scribes is perfectly valid since in Judaism table-fellowship means fellowship before God: "eating of a piece of broken bread

---

[118] Cf. JEREMIAS, Jerusalem, 236-237, 243.
[119] Against ARENS, ΗΛΘΟΝ-Sayings, 35, n. 37: "The inversion may have no real significance but be the product of carelessness on the part of RMK".

by everyone who shares in the meal brings out the fact that they all have a share in the blessings which the master of the house had spoken over the unbroken bread" [120]. A meal with such a religious significance could not be shared with sinners; in fact, the supreme duty of a pious Jew was to keep away from sinners. In Qumran too a banquet was only for the pure, the full members of the community [121]. In such a socio-religious milieu, Jesus' eating with tax collectors and sinners would have been scandalous. A most striking expression is found in the mocking and contemptuous description of Jesus as "a glutton and a drunkard, a friend of tax collectors and sinners" (Mt 11,19 par. Lk 9,34).

6. Jesus' Answer (2,17)

Jesus' answer to his opponents consists of both a proverb about the physician and the sick which has analogies in the Greek literature [122] and a saying on the purpose of his coming [123]. The proverb and the saying are synonymously parallel:

Οὐ χρείαν ἔχουσιν οἱ ἰσχύοντες ἰατροῦ ἀλλ᾽ οἱ κακῶς ἔχοντες·
οὐκ ἦλθον καλέσαι δικαίους ἀλλὰ ἁμαρτωλούς.

The noun χρεία occurs in Mk only as the object of the verb ἔχειν: thrice χρείαν ἔχειν τινός (2,17; 11,3; 14,63) and once the absolute use (2,25). The verb ἰσχύειν occurs in Mk two ways: as a finite verb (5,4; 9,18; 14,37) and in the participial form (2,17). The noun ἰατρός (= physician), a rare word in the NT [124], occurs in the second Gospel twice: once in the singular form (2,17) and the other in the plural (5,26). In 2,17 Jesus answers his opponents by citing a proverb to justify his tablefellowship with tax collectors and sinners: just as it is a physician' duty to be with the sick, so also it is Jesus' responsibility to eat with tax collectors and sinners. The central point in 2,17 is neither the doctor nor the healthy but the sick (οἱ κακῶς ἔχοντες) and their need.

---

[120] JEREMIAS, *Theology*, 115.

[121] Cf. BETZ, *Jesus*, 74; JEREMIAS, *Theology*, 118.

[122] Cf. LANE, 104, n. 43; LOHMEYER, 56, n. 2.

[123] ARENS *ΗΛΘΟΝ-Sayings*, 40-42, argues that the proverb (v. 17a) was the original answer whereas the saying (v. 17b) was added later. TRAUTMANN, *Zeichenhafte Handlungen*, 153, 157, holds the contrary opinion.

[124] Mt 1, Mk 2, Lk 2, Paul 1 = total 6.

The second member of the parallelism (2,17b) clarifies the proverb and brings the narrative to a climactic conclusion. As previously mentioned, the verb ἦλθον/ἦλθεν predicated of Jesus and followed by an infinitive underlines Jesus' soteriologically intended career on behalf of mankind (10,45), on behalf of sinners (2,17). It was also stated in Ch. IV that the absolute use of καλεῖν is very likely a technical term (frequent in Paul) to signify God's offer of salvation. In Mk 1,20 καλεῖν connotes Jesus' fundamental call to discipleship. The immediate context of 2,17 dos not permit an interpretation of this verb as a call to discipleship. By the addition of εἰς μετάνοιαν the Lucan parallel makes the purpose of Jesus' call crystal clear. In Mk, however, it is not explicit. Some authors hold that it is an invitation to tablefellowship, an anticipation of the heavenly banquet or an eschatological meal in the kingdom of God [125]. Such an interpretation is acceptable if the expression 'tablefellowship' or 'eschatological meal' is symbolically understood, viz., Jesus' call to sinners to share in God's offer of salvation, since the absolute use of καλεῖν has this significance and since at a deeper level the participants of a common meal become partakers of the divine blessings.

In the NT the adjective δίκαιος (= righteous, upright, just) is used of God, of Jesus, of human beings and of things. Compared to the first and the third Gospels, it occurs very seldom in the second (Mt 17, Mk 2, Lk 11) where it is used of human beings exclusively (2,17; 6,20). It is widely disputed whether δίκαιος in 2,17b is ironically used in reference to the Pharisees. The opinions may be grouped as follows. (1) Jesus recognized the true zeal of the Pharisees for righteousness and he shared the common conviction of Judaism that the sins of the righteous did not seriously jeopardize their relationship with God [126]. (2) "Righteous" is used ironically in reference to the Pharisees who were incapable of perceiving Jesus' call because of their self-righteous attitude [127]. (3) The negative statement in 2,17b is not a categorical, all-exclusive negative but a Semitic way of strengthening the positive. Hence it is not said that the righteous are excluded; in fact, the decisive point is that the call is directed towards sinners [128]. The first opinion is not consonant

---

[125] ARENS, ΗΛΘΟΝ-Sayings, 55; BULTMANN, Tradition, 18; GRUNDMANN, 84; LOHMEYER, 56; GNILKA, I, 109; NINEHAM, 96; TRAUTMANN, Zeichenhafte Handlungen, 162.

[126] See the authors cited in LANE, 105, n. 45.

[127] See the authors mentioned in LANE, 105, n. 44; JEREMIAS, Theology, 116: "It should be noticed that 'the righteous' seems to have been a self-designation of the Pharisees, cf. Ps. Sol. 13,11; 15,6f".

[128] Cf. ARENS, ΗΛΘΟΝ-Sayings, 44, 54; GNILKA, I, 109; GRUNDMANN, 84; PESCH, "Zöllnergastmahl", 74; TRAUTMANN, Zeichenhafte Handlungen, 162.

with Jesus' strongly critical sayings against the Pharisees' attitude towards the Law (cf. 2,25-28; 3,2-5; 7,1-15). Regarding the second and the third opinions, there are no satisfactory reasons to opt for one to the exclusion of the other. For, on the one hand, there is an implied contrast between righteous and sinners in 2,17b and, on the other hand, there are clear statements in Mk that Jesus' mission is oriented to all (cf. 10,45; 14,24).

C. Mk 2,13-17 in Context

1. A story in which Jesus' authority to forgive sins has been demonstrated in words (2,1-12) is fittingly followed by the present narrative in which he is shown calling a tax collector to discipleship, welcoming sinners and implicitly bestowing upon them a forgiveness expressed symbolically in action (tablefellowship). Jesus' tablefellowship with tax collectors and sinners marks a distinctive feature of his mission whereby his attitude and approach to the despised section of human society are distinguished from those of his Jewish contemporaries.

2. By the inversion of 'tax collectors and sinners' in 2,16a and by placing 'sinners' at the centre of the double chiasm, Mk emphasizes the nature of the relation between Jesus and sinners as the key point of the controversy. And the climactic close (2,17b) highlights the fact that Jesus' mission is oriented towards sinners. This orientation to sinners was already contained in Jesus' summons to repentance in 1,15c and it is further developed in the soteriologically pregnant statements in 10,45 and 14,42. Thus Mk brings to light the soteriological significance of Jesus' earthly ministry, a significance which Paul primarily attaches to Jesus' Death.

III. The Question of Fasting, and the Old and the New (2,18-22)

A. Literary Analysis [129]

1. *Comparison with Mt 9,14-17 and Lk 5,33-39*

a. *Mk 2,18-22 and Mt 9,14-17*

The substance of the Matthean narrative corresponds to that of Mk, but one notices the following differences in perspectives. In Mk the literary link between 2,18-22 and 2,13-17 is vague, but Mt does it better by means of τότε as he does elsewhere [130]. Jesus' interlocutors in Mk 2,18 are unidentified but in Mt they are identified as the disciples of John the Baptist. Despite John's strong condemnation of the Pharisees in 3,7-11, here his disciples are one with the Pharisees in the practice of fasting contrary to the practice of Jesus' disciples. Furthermore, by using πενθεῖν in 9,15a, Mt considers fasting as an expression of sorrow (cf. 5,4) even though Jesus himself recommends it in 6,16-18. Finally, in Mt as in Lk, the tautological statement of Mk 2,19b is absent. Within the frame of the remote context, however, the Matthean narrative has a different orientation. While Mk places it as the central pericope in the literary unit of five controversies (2,1-3,6), Mt has integrated it within the narrative section of ten miracles (8,1-9,38).

b. *Mk 2,18-22 and Lk 5,33-39*

Lk has not only rendered linguistic improvements upon the Marcan text but also modified the content too to some extent. Unlike in the Marcan parallel, the questioners in Lk 5,33 are probably the Pharisees and their scribes mentioned in 5,30 [131]. Differing from Mk, in Lk the accusation contains a reference to Jesus' prayer also which, however, is not taken up in Jesus' reply. By the mention of ἐσθίουσιν καὶ πίνουσιν in the place of the οὐ νηστεύουσιν of Mk, Lk links better this pericope with the preceding one (cf. 5,30) and also intensifies the accusation. He describes the second part of

---

[129] With regard to the two textual problems in v. 22, the variant preserved in B best explains the origin of others (cf. METZGER, *Commentary*, 79).

[130] Cf. Mt 2,16; 3,13; 4,1; 11,20; 12,22.38; 13,36; 15,1; 18,21; 19,13; 20,20; 22,15; 23,1; 25,1; 26,14.31.36; 27,3.27.

[131] Cf. GRUNDMANN, *Lukas*, 133; MARSHALL, *Luke*, 222.

Jesus' answer (vv. 36-39) as a parable (cf. v. 36a) but the use of δὲ καί indicates that the preceding saying (5,34-35) is also parabolic (cf. 6,39; 18,9). The wording of the saying about the patch is brought into closer parallelism with the saying about the wine by stressing that the new garment from which the patch is taken is spoilt in the process. The final saying, obviously added on the principle of catch word by Lk, ironically comments on the attitude of the Pharisees who preferred the old wine of Judaism to the new wine of the gospel.

2. *Literary Division*

The pericope commences with the question about fasting (νηστεύειν). All the six occurrences of this verb in Mk are found in this pericope but limited to 2,18-20 exclusively. On the other hand, παλαιός, καινός and νέος are the key words which provide literary cohesion to 2,21-22, but these terms do not occur in 2, 18-20 at all. Hence it is logical to divide the pericope into two units, vv. 18-20 and 21-22. Furthermore, within 2,18-20 there are literary indications for a division between verse 18 and verses 19-20. In verse 18 the subject is μαθηταί (thrice), whether of John, of the Pharisees or of Jesus, while in 2,19-20 the subject is either οἱ υἱοὶ τοῦ νυμφῶνος or ὁ νυμφίος. Therefore Mk 2,18-22 may be divided as follows: the question (2,18); Jesus' answer: the first step (2,19-20); Jesus' answer: the second step (2,21-22).

B. Interpretation

1. *The Question (2,18)*

Verse 18 consists of three parallel clauses, the first two synonymously parallel and the third antithetically:

Καὶ ἦσαν οἱ μαθηταὶ 'Ιωάννου καὶ οἱ Φαρισαῖοι νηστεύοντες . . .

Διὰ τί οἱ μαθηταὶ 'Ιωάννου καὶ οἱ μαθηταὶ τῶν Φαρισαίων νηστεύουσιν, οἱ δὲ σοὶ μαθηταὶ οὐ νηστεύουσιν;

Without any specification of time or place, Mk begins the narrative with the statement that the disciples of John and the Pharisees were fasting (2,18a) [132].

---

[132] GNILKA, I, 112; KLOSTERMANN, 27; PERRIN, *Rediscovering*, 79; and W. WEIß, *Eine neue Lehre* (*ad loc.*) argue that Mk 2,18a is redactional. The only evidence for its redactional character is the periphrastic construction.

That John the Baptist had disciples is attested to by multiple NT sources [133]. Although the OT stipulated fasting only on the Day of Atonement, designated as a day of cleansing from sin and affliction of the soul (cf. Lev 16,29; 23,26-32), voluntary fasting was undertaken by various Jewish groups, including the disciples of John the Baptist, following the austere life of their master (cf. Mk 1,6 par; Mt 11,18 par.) and the Pharisees [134]. Jesus' disciples, did not fast; and so, people [135] question him about their failure to fast. The direct question, introduced by διὰ τί (cf. 7,5; 11,31), contrasts the disciples of John and those of the Pharisees [136] who fast with Jesus' disciples who do not fast.

2. Jesus' Answer: The First Step (2,19-20)

In the first stage of the answer Jesus distinguishes between a present time when it is impossible for the disciples to fast (2,19) and a future time when they will fast (2,20). Verse 19 consists of a synonymous parallelism enclosed by a twofold negation: μὴ δύνανται and οὐ δύνανται.

Μὴ δύνανται οἱ υἱοὶ τοῦ νυμφῶνος ἐν ᾧ ὁ νυμφίος μετ' αὐτῶν ἐστιν νηστεύειν;

ὅσον χρόνον ἔχουσιν τὸν νυμφίον μετ' αὐτῶν οὐ δύνανται νηστεύειν·

Even though from the point of view of the content, 2,19b adds nothing to 2,19a, there is an additional emphasis introduced by the repetition. In 2,19b the particle μή followed by the indicative suggests a negative answer. The expression οἱ υἱοὶ τοῦ νυμφῶνος (literal meaning = the sons of the bride chamber or wedding hall) is differently translated: "wedding guests" (RSV); "les compagnons de l'époux" (BJ); "the bridegroom's friends" (NEB); "les invités à la noce" (TOB). According to Bauer, they are "that group of the wedding guests who stood closest to the groom and played an essential part in the wedding ceremony" [137]. The use of υἱός (or τέκνον) with the genitive

---

[133] Mk 2,18 par.; 6,29 par.; Mt 11,2 par. Lk 7,18; 11,1; Jn 1,35.37; 3,25.

[134] Lk 18,12: "I fast twice a week".

[135] In v. 18b ἔρχονται and λέγουσιν are impersonal plural, meaning "people'. So RSV, NEB, BJ, etc.

[136] The scribes of the Pharisees had disciples but not the Pharisees themselves. Hence by οἱ μαθηταὶ τῶν Φαρισαίων is probably meant those who were influenced by Pharisaic ideals and practices.

[137] BAUER, Lexicon, 547.

in a metaphorical expression is Semitic and so it is best regarded as translation Greek [138]. By ἐν ᾧ (understood χρόνῳ) is meant 'while' or 'during' [139]. In 2, 19b ὅσον χρόνον (accusative of time) means 'as long as'.

What is the significance of the question, "Can the wedding guests fast while the bridegroom is with them?" A wedding is a joyful and festive event whereas fasting is an expression of mourning (cf. 1 Sam 31,13; Jud 8,6; 1 Mac 1,25-28). The wedding guests were free from the obligation of fasting during the seven days of the wedding celebrations [140]. Hence it is incompatible for the wedding guests to fast during the wedding. This every day experience has a deeper religious significance in our verse. In the OT Yahweh is portrayed as the husband of his covenant people (cf. Hos 2,19; Is 54,4-8; 62,4-5; Ezek 16,6-63) and the same image is applied to Christ in the NT (cf. Jn 3,29; 2 Cor 11,2; Eph 5,21-33; Rev 19,7; 21,2). Although neither in the OT nor in Judaism was 'bridegroom' a Messianic title [141], a wedding was a common symbol of the time of salvation, the day of the Messiah [142]. Hence Jesus' saying in 2,19a has Messianic overtones and it underlines the immense joy the disciples have in being with their master.

Verse 20 also consists of a synonymous parallelism enclosed by a twofold time factor: ἐλεύσονται δὲ ἡμέραι and ἐν ἐκείνῃ τῇ ἡμέρᾳ.

ἐλεύσονται δὲ ἡμέραι ὅταν ἀπαρθῇ ἀπ᾽ αὐτῶν ὁ νυμφίος,

καὶ τότε νηστεύσουσιν ἐν ἐκείνῃ τῇ ἡμέρᾳ

In this verse, only ὅταν ἀπαρθῇ requires a detailed analysis since the rest of the words are clear. The temporal particle ὅταν (ὅτε + ἄν meaning 'when', 'whenever', etc.) is used with the indicative or with the subjunctive. When used with the aorist subjunctive, the action of the subordinate clause precedes that of the main clause. In our verse, therefore, ἀπαρθῇ precedes ἐλεύσονται. Hence verse 20 may be translated: the days will come when the bridegroom will be taken away from them, and then, on that day, they will fast [143].

[138] Cf. CRANFIELD, 109; KLOSTERMANN, 28.

[139] Most of the translations render ἐν ᾧ as 'while' but JEREMIAS (Parables, 52, n. 14), probably rightly, prefers 'during'.

[140] Cf. STR.-B., Kommentar I, 506-517,

[141] Cf. GNILKA, "Bräutigam", 298-301; JEREMIAS, TDNT IV, 1101-1103; LANE, 110; PESCH, I, 173, etc.

[142] JEREMIAS, Parables, 117; PERRIN, Rediscovering, 80.

[143] With most of the translations and commentaries but against the rendering in RSV, NINEHAM, etc.

What is the significance of ἀπαρθῇ? The verb ἀπαίρεσθαι occurs in the NT only thrice : Mk 2,20 and the parallels. In these instances it is used with the preposition ἀπό. In the LXX, the same verb occurs about 122 times, more frequent with the preposition ἐκ than with ἀπό. Of the 13 occurrences of ἀπαίρεσθαι with ἀπό in the LXX, only once ἀπό governs a genitive of person (Gen 13,11) and in the other 12 instances it governs genitive of place. None of these 13 instances provides a contextual affinity to Mk 2,20. The closest parallel to Mk 2,20, however, is found in Is 53,8 where αἴρειν occurs twice:

ὅτι αἴρεται ἀπό τῆς γῆς ἡ ζωὴ αὐτοῦ

ἀπὸ τῶν ἀνομιῶν τοῦ λαοῦ μου ἤχθη εἰς θάνατον.

Is 53,8 obviously deals with the suffering and death of the servant. Likewise, Mk 2,20 also contains an allusion to Jesus' Passion and Death, the first hint on the lips of Jesus [144]. It is evidently not a prediction of the Passion as Mk 8,31; 9,31; 10,32-34 but a real allusion to it [145].

To sum up, in Mk 2,19 Jesus answers that his presence with his disciples is like a wedding, a time of joy and festivity when fasting is totally out of place. On the contrary, in verse 20 he says that when he will be taken away from their midst by death, it will be a time of sorrow and then fasting will be fitting and proper. The contrast in 2,19-20, then, lies not merely in not fasting and fasting but also in Jesus' presence and absence [146]. The focal point, therefore, seems to be the joy that the disciples have in Jesus' personal presence, because in him the time of salvation has definitely been ushered in.

3. Jesus' Answer: The Second Step (2,21-22)

The second stage of Jesus' answer is composed of twin metaphors: the new garment (2,21) and the new wine (2,22). Both metaphors have the same structure: each begins with a negative statement introduced by the indefinite pronoun οὐδείς with the verb in the present indicative (ἐπιράπτει in 2,21 and

---

[144] Form critics hold that Mk 2,20 attempts to offer rationale for the Church's practice of fasting in the light of the Passion (cf. BULTMANN, *Tradition*, 18-19 et passim; DIBELIUS, *Tradition*, 65-66). But our concern is to find the meaning and the function of 2,20 in Mk (cf. CREMER, *Fastenansage*, 7-36, 49-51, 112-125; DUNKERLY, "Bridegroom", 303-304).

[145] We do not find convincing BRAUMANN's arguments ("Mk II, 20") that 2,20 refers to the Parousia.

[146] Cf. O'HARA, "Mk 2,18-22", 188-195; SCHÄFER, "Mk 2,20", 140-147.

βάλλει in 2,22) and continues the narrative with a conditional clause. In the conditional clause, the protasis is constituted by the expression εἰ δὲ μή (without a verb) and the apodosis consists of two clauses joined by the conjunction καί with the verbs in the indicative (αἴρει and γίνεται in 2,21; ῥήξει and ἀπόλλυται in 2,22). The last clause in 2,22 (ἀλλὰ οἶνον νέον εἰς ἀσκοὺς καινούς) presumably functions as the climax of both verses 21 and 22 [147]. The meaning of all the terms and expressions in these two verses are clear except εἰ δὲ μή and καινός. The expression εἰ δὲ μή (= otherwise) is a classical usage found also in the papyri. And we have already mentioned in Ch. V that καινός, distinct from νέος, has an eschatological content.

Like other parables, similes and metaphors, these two metaphors are also founded on the practical wisdom gained from daily experiences. It is folly to mend a tattered garment with a valuable new piece of linen; it is equally foolish to pour fermenting new wine into worn-out, damaged wineskins. Although the meaning of these two metaphors appears clear at the surface level of interpretation, they do contain a deep theological significance. There are numerous references in the history of religions where the cosmos is compared to the world garment [148]. In the Bible too, the term 'garment' is used not merely in a literal sense but also in a symbolic sense, meaning cosmos. In Heb 1,10-12, following Ps 102,25-27, the author describes how at the Parousia Christ rolls up the cosmos like an old garment and unfolds the new cosmos. In Acts 10,11-16 and 11,5-11, "Peter, in the symbol of a sheet tied at the four corners and containing every kind of living creature, beholds the new cosmos, restored and declared clean by God" [149]. Mk 2,21 must be understood in the context of this symbolic meaning: the old world order has run out and the new world order has begun in Jesus' person and mission [150].

There are many references in the Bible where the term 'wine' has a symbolic meaning. In an extensive study on the symbolism of wine, Serra states that there are three aspects: covenant, eschatology and the word of God [151]. Wine, by its very nature, is a source of joy; and so, when the prophets

---

[147] Verses 21 and 22 are connected both literally and thematically. Note οὐδείς at the beginning of v. 21 and καὶ οὐδείς at the beginning of v. 22. Similar to the last clause of v. 22 (but new wine into new wineskins) a clause (a piece of unshrunk cloth on a new garment) is understood at the end of v. 21.

[148] Cf. EISLER, *Weltenmantel*, passim; STARK, *Erlösererwartung*, 18-20.

[149] JEREMIAS, *Parables*, 118.

[150] Cf. HAULOTTE, *Symbolique du vêtement*, 320-324.

[151] Cf. SERRA, *Contributi*, 229-257.

describe the prosperity and happiness of the people after their suffering in exile, they speak of the abundance of the best wine (cf. Is 25,6; 55,1; 62,8; Jer 31,12; Zech 9,17; Amos 9,13-14, etc.). These texts, at least indirectly, allude to the eschatological, Messianic era. In the targums there are texts where the eschatological, Messianic motif is closely associated with wine [152]. In tune with the prophets, the rabbis, using the metaphor of wine, speak of the joy of the eschatological, Messianic era [153]. In the eschatological meal of the Qumran community and in the paschal supper of the Jews, wine and the Messianic era stand in close association [154]. In Mk 2,22, then, the mention of new wine symbolizes the eschatological, Messianic era, the time of salvation, inaugurated in the person and mission of Jesus. It is worth noting that at the last supper Jesus says, "I shall not drink again of the fruit of the vine until that day when I drink it new in the kingdom of God" (Mk 14,25).

In short, the metaphors of a new piece of cloth on an old garment (2,21) and of new wine in old wineskins (2,22) tell us that Jesus regarded his ministry as marking a new point of departure quite incompatible with the existing categories of Judaism. Compared to the first metaphor, the second marks a clear progression: the first implies a partial destruction whereas the second presupposes a total destruction. The newness is underlined not only by means of the symbolic meaning of garment and wine but also by the use of the adjective καινός twice in these two verses.

C. Mk 2,18-22 in Context

1. Jesus' answer in verses 19-22 goes beyond the question posed in v. 18. Using the symbols of wedding, garment, and wine and the term καινός, Mk emphasizes that the eschatological, Messianic hopes are being realized in Jesus' person and ministry. The new way of life inaugurated by Jesus and proclaimed by the early Church cannot be linked with the old ways of Judaism (the practice of the Pharisees and the asceticism of John the Baptist's disciples); on the contrary, the new way of life must be allowed to develop without being fettered by the old ways.

2. In verses 21-22 Mk has particularly accentuated the newness wrought by Jesus. This accentuation is significant in the context of the structure of 2,1-3,6 at the centre of which occurs 2,18-22. The newness consists in the

---

[152] *Ibid.*, 244-246.
[153] *Ibid.*, 246-247.
[154] *Ibid.*, 247-248.

fact that just as Yahweh in the OT, so also Jesus in the NT enjoys the divine prerogative to forgive sins (2,1-12). And his mission is oriented to call sinners to personal relation with him and ultimately to enter into communion with God (2,13-17). Furthermore, Jesus enjoys lordship over the sabbath (2,23-28) and by curing a man with a withered hand on the sabbath, he reinstates the original meaning of the sabbath. The scribes and the Pharisees fail to recognize the newness ushered in through Jesus' person and mission.

IV. Plucking Grain and Sabbatical Observance (Mk 2,23-28)

A. Literary Analysis

1. *Textual Criticism*

In this pericope there is only one textual problem [155] where the critical editions differ among themselves. And it conerns verse 23 which has the following four variant readings:

1) παραπορεύεσθαι (p⁸⁸ ℵ Θ 700. 892) [156]
2) διαπορεύεσθαι (B D it) [157]
3) παραπορεύμενον (565)
4) πορεύεσθαι (W)

The question is whether παραπορεύεσθαι or διαπορεύεσθαι is the original text. Although the MSS support for the first reading is relatively better, there are two reasons why the second reading is to be preferred. Compound verbs followed by the same preposition (as noted often before) is a characteristic feature of Mk's style. In the second place, reading four, avoids the confusion caused by the compound verb since the idea is conveyed

---

[155] The evidence for λέγει αὐτοῖς in verse 25 is solid. The rendering ἔλεγεν in B is perhaps an emendation for narrative elegance (cf. ἔλεγον in 2,24). Similarly, the MSS support for ἐπὶ ᾿Αβιαθὰρ ἀρχιερέως in v. 26 is excellent. The omission of the phrase in D W *al.* is to avoid the historical difficulty, namely, the event narrated in v. 26 took place during the high priesthood of Ahimelech, not Abiathar (cf. 1 Sam 21,1-6 and n. 170 below).

[156] GNT/NESTLE-ALAND, HUCK-GREEVEN, MERK, TASKER, TISCHENDORF, VOGELS, VON SODEN, etc. and commentaries of LAGRANGE, TAYLOR, etc.

[157] TREGELLES, WESTCOTT-HORT, etc. and SWETE, 47.

by the preposition διά. The first reading probably originated in the scribal attempt to improve upon the sense since going through the grainfields is unlikely whereas passing by the grain fields is very likely.

2. *Synoptic Comparison*

a. *Mk 2,23-28 and Mt 12,1-8*

The content of Mt 12,1-8 differs considerably from that of Mk. By mentioning that Jesus' disciples were hungry in 12,1 (differs Mk 2,23) and that David and his followers were also hungry in 12,3, Mt emphasizes perfect correspondence between the two situations. To justify the action of Jesus' disciples Mt employs two scriptural arguments both of which are introduced in the same way (12,3.5: οὐκ ἀνέγνωτε). The first is a haggadic example (12,3-4), parallel to Mk 2,25-26, illustrating how David and his followers ate the showbread which only the priests were permitted to eat. The second is a halachic example (absent in Mk) showing how the priests profane the sabbath by their temple service and yet they are guiltless. This is followed by a saying, with a solemn introduction (12,6a: "but I say to you") which seems to prepare for the Son of Man saying in verse 8, and which emphasizes the surpassing superiority of acts of mercy over sabbatical laws [158]. The saying concludes with a citation from Hos 6,6 in verse 7 (= Mt 9,13). The finale, just as in Mk, is a Son of Man saying in v. 8 where the Christological emphasis is evident.

b. *Mk 2,23-28 and Lk 6,1-5*

Lk closely follows Mk in context as well as in content, but he obviously improves upon the Marcan style. He also adds the details, "ate some heads of grain, rubbing them in their hands" (6,1). Again, differing from Mk, the Pharisees question the disciples, and Jesus steps in only to defend them. To avoid a historical error Lk (also Mt) cancels the clause, "when Abiathar was high priest". By the omission of Mk 2,27, the statement that the Son of Man is the lord of the sabbath stands in direct juxtaposition to the allusion to David, thereby forcefully expressing Jesus' right to interpret the law.

---

[158] GRUNDMANN, *Matthäus*, 322.

3. *Literary Coherence and Literary Structure*

A number of authors divide Mk 2,23-28 into two literary units: 2,23-26 and 2,27-28 [159]. Is their claim valid? Or can one find literary coherence and a thematic unity in 2,23-28? Verse 23 narrates a situation where Jesus' disciples pluck ears of grain on the sabbath. This triggers a question from the Pharisees. They ask Jesus: Ἴδε τί ποιοῦσιν τοῖς σάββασιν ὃ οὐκ ἔξεστιν; (2,24). Jesus answers their question in two steps: 2,25-26 and 2,27-28. Both steps have similar introductions: καὶ λέγει αὐτοῖς (2,25a) and καὶ ἔλεγεν αὐτοῖς (2,27a). The key phrases τί ποιοῦσιν and ὃ οὐκ ἔξεστιν of the question (2,24) are repeated only in the first stage of the answer (2,25-26). The noun τοῖς σάββασιν recurs only in the second phase of the answer (2,27-28). Furthermore, by the haggadic argument in 2,25-26 Jesus establishes not the legitimacy to violate sabbatical laws as such — which is the question at issue in v. 24 — but the right to break a law in specific circumstances. And it is in verses 27-28 that Jesus offers the theological basis for breaking sabbatical laws. Both phases of the answer complement each other, and the question posed in verse 24 is not adequately answered without both of them. Therefore, there are sufficient literary and thematic indices to conclude that Mk 2,23-28 is a coherent pericope.

These literary observations offer clues regarding the literary structure of the pericope as demonstrated below:

23 ----   Καὶ ἐγένετο αὐτὸν ἐν τοῖς σάββασιν διαπορεύεσθαι διὰ τῶν σπορίμων, καὶ οἱ μαθηταὶ αὐτοῦ ἤρξαντο ὁδὸν ποιεῖν τίλλοντες τοὺς στάχυας.

24 A   καὶ οἱ Φαρισαῖοι ἔλεγον αὐτῷ,
    a   Ἴδε τί ποιοῦσιν τοῖς σάββασιν
    b   ὃ οὐκ ἔξεστιν;

25 B b' καὶ λέγει αὐτοῖς, Οὐδέποτε ἀνέγνωτε τί ἐποίησεν Δαυίδ, ὅτε χρείαν ἔσχεν καὶ ἐπείνασεν αὐτὸς καὶ οἱ μετ' αὐτοῦ;
26   πῶς εἰσῆλθεν εἰς τὸν οἶκον τοῦ θεοῦ ἐπὶ 'Αβιαθὰρ ἀρχιερέως καὶ τοὺς ἄρτους τῆς προθέσεως ἔφαγεν, οὓς οὐκ ἔξεστιν φαγεῖν εἰ μὴ τοὺς ἱερεῖς, καὶ ἔδωκεν καὶ τοῖς σὺν αὐτῷ οὖσιν;

27 a'   καὶ ἔλεγεν αὐτοῖς, Τὸ σάββατον διὰ τὸν ἄνθρωπον ἐγένετο καὶ
28   οὐχ ὁ ἄνθρωπος διὰ τὸ σάββατον · ὥστε κύριός ἐστιν ὁ υἱὸς τοῦ ἀνθρώπου καὶ τοῦ σαββάτου.

---

[159] See the division in BJ, NEB; Pesch, I, 179; Taylor, 214, 218, etc.

Plucking ears of grain on the sabbath (2,23) sparks off the questioning of Jesus by the Pharisees in 2,24. The question (A) is made up of two parts, one of which concerns the sabbath as such and the other, the lawfulness of doing what they did on the sabbath. Jesus' answer (B) to this question, however, is given in reversed order. He first answers the question of the lawfulness (b': 2,25-26) and then the question of the sabbath (a': 2,27-28).

B. Interpretation

1. The Situation (2,23)

The narrative in 2,23-28, unlike that in the preceding one, contains a reference to time (sabbath) and place (grainfields). The construction in 2,23a γίνεσθαι used impersonally with the following accusative and infinitive is found fairly often in the NT as well as in the papyri [160]. The noun σπόριμος (standing grain) occurs in the NT only here and in the parallels. The expression ὁδὸν ποιεῖν (= ὁδοποιεῖν) probably a Latinism (iter facere) [161], occurs in the NT only here. The verb τίλλειν is found in the NT only thrice (2,23 and par.) and its complement στάχυς occurs only five times in the NT: Mk 2,23 par. and 4,28 (bis). It would be possible to translate the Greek in 2,23b in the sense of, 'they began to make their way by plucking the ears of corn' or 'they began to advance by plucking the ears of corn'. From the sequel, however, it is clear that the disciples' offence is not that of ὁδὸν ποιεῖν but of plucking the ears of grain. In other words, the main idea is expressed by the participle, the infinitive being subordinate in force. The key term, as evident from the controversy that follows, is the 'sabbath'.

2. The Pharisees' Question (2,24)

The imperfect ἔλεγον in the introductory clause (2,24a) appears to be used loosely for the aorist, as correctly interpreted by Mt and Lk. The Pharisees [162] question Jesus for the action of his disciples since the master

---

[160] Cf. CRANFIELD, 102; TAYLOR, 215.

[161] It is generally considered a Latinism. Yet see the reservations in CRANFIELD, 114; LOHMEYER, 62-63; RAWLINSON, 33.

[162] In Mk the Pharisees are Jesus' opponents. They are scandalized at the violation of the sabbatical observance whether by the disciples (2,24) or by Jesus himself (3,2). They are also scandalized at the neglect of ritual ablutions (7,1-5). They seek from Jesus a sign from

was responsible for his disciples [163]. The disciples' action of plucking ears of corn on the sabbath constituted a violation of the sabbatical law. In fact, plucking ears of grain was in itself not forbidden [164] but doing it on the sabbath was tantamount to reaping, and reaping was formally prohibited by the Mosaic Law. Of the 39 key activities explicitly forbidden on the sabbath, reaping ranked third [165]. The theological reason for prohibiting reaping is the need for rest on the sabbath which is rooted in the decalogue (Ex 20,8-11; Deut 5,12-15). The Pharisees raise a question of halakha, of what is legally permitted or prohibited [166], perhaps with the intention of satisfying the legal requirement of a warning prior to prosecution for violating the sabbath [167].

3. Jesus' Answer: The First Phase (2,25-26)

Jesus' answer to the Pharisees, a counterquestion with an appeal to the Scriptures, is characteristic of rabbinical arguments [168]. Mk employs this method also elsewhere (cf. 12,10.26). The adverb οὐδέποτε is found in Mk only twice (2,12.25). The verb ἀναγινώσκειν has two meanings in the NT: (1) to read; (2) to read aloud in public. Of its four occurrences in Mk, thrice it is used in the verbal form in Jesus' arguments with his opponents where he refers to a particular passage (12,10-11 = Ps 118,22-23) or to a particular incident (2,25-26 = 1 Sam 21,1-6; 12,26 = Ex 3,6) of the OT. In 2,26 by ὁ οἶκος τοῦ θεοῦ is meant the tent or shrine in which the sacred ark was kept (cf. LXX Judg 18,31; 1 Sam 1,7.24, etc.). As regards the phrase ἐπὶ Ἀβιαθὰρ ἀρχιερέως, ἐπί with the genitive, when referring to time, implies contemporaneity. Here it means 'in the days of' or 'in the time of' [169]. When an anarthrous title is added to the personal name, the period is limited to the term

---

heaven (8,11), ask questions to test him (10,2-9), try to trap him into a wrong answer (12,13-17), and plot against his life (3,6). Jesus considers the Pharisees' rigour of the law intolerable (2,25-27), a device to evade its obligations (7,6-13). He is grieved at their hardness of hearts (3,5). He also warns his disciples against the leaven of the Pharisees (8,15).

[163] Cf. Daube, "Responsibilities of Master", 1-15.

[164] Deut 23,25: "When you go into your neighbour's standing grain, you may pluck the ears with your hand, but you shall not put a sickle to your neighbour's standing grain".

[165] The Jerusalem Talmud *Shabbath* VII, 2.9c (plucking of grain is an act of reaping). Schürer, *History* II, 468 lists the 39 activities.

[166] Οὐκ ἔξεστιν (= not permitted) is legal terminology. Cf. Lohse, "Jesu Worte", 86, n. 27.

[167] Cf. The Mishnah *Sanhedrin* VII, 8.

[168] Cf. Fiebig, *Der Erzählungsstil*, 107-112; Str.-B., *Kommentar* I, 618-619.

[169] Cf. Blass-Debrunner, *Grammar*, § 234 (8).

of office (cf. 1 Mac 13,42; Lk 3,2; Acts 11,28). Therefore, the whole phrase, then means, "in the time of Abiathar, the High Priest" (NEB) [170]. The expression οἱ ἄρτοι τῆς προθέσεως (genitive of purpose) stands for the Hebrew לֶחֶם הַפָּנִים which has different renderings in the LXX [171]. It describes the twelve newly baked loaves, the 'showbread', placed every sabbath in two rows on a table in front of the Tabernacle, and later eaten by the priests (cf. Lev 24,5-9). In 2,26b ἔξεστιν is followed by the accusative with infinitive (found also in classical Greek) even though the dative with infinitive is more frequent.

Having given the philological and grammatical explanations of some of the terms and phrases in 2,25-26, we proceed to interpret these two verses from the Marcan perspective. There are only very few literal similarities between the narrative in Mk 2,25-26 and the event it alludes to in 1 Sam 21,1-6: the main similarity is the expression τοὺς ἄρτους τῆς προθέσεως (Mk 2,26b; 1 Sam 21,7). The key point that Mk underlines is the similarity between the action of David and his men and that of Jesus and his disciples. If David, a man of God and the very model of piety, when pressed by hunger and hardship, had transgressed the Law by eating the 'showbread' which only priests were allowed to eat, then, Jesus is also entitled to grant freedom from the Law to his disciples in certain circumstances. In brief, 2,25-26 implies that in exceptional cases the Law might rightly be regarded as subordinate to human needs, and the tradition of the Pharisees is unduly stringent, going beyond the intention of the Law.

4. Jesus' Answer: The Second Phase (2,27-28)

The second phase of Jesus' answer to the Pharisees begins with the phrase καὶ ἔλεγεν αὐτοῖς which is used in Mk not so much to indicate the beginning of a discourse (cf. 4,2; 6,10) as to show a step or a turning point in the course of a discourse (cf. 2,27; 4,11.21.24; 7,9; 8,21; 9,1). Διά with the accusative indicates the reason: 'because of', 'for the sake of'. The conjunction ὥστε introduces either a dependent or an independent clause. In the latter, it is followed by the indicative (as in 2,28) or the imperative in

---

[170] According to 1 Sam 21,1-6, it was not Abiathar but his father Ahimelech who gave David the holy bread. Abiathar appears in record for the first time almost two chapters later (22,20). Because Abiathar was better known in association with David than his father, it is commonly assumed that a primitive error entered the tradition before it came into Mk's hands.

[171] ἄρτοι προκειμένοι   (Ex 39,17)
   ἄρτοι τοῦ προσώπου   (1 Sam 21,7)
   ἄτροι τῆς προσφορᾶς   (1 Kings 7,34)
   ἄρτοι ἐνώπιοι   (Ex 25,30).

which case it means 'for this reason', 'therefore'. The noun κύριος occurs in the NT either in a general sense ('owner', 'master', 'lord') or in a religious sense. In 2,28 it is probably used in the general sense.

In 2,25-26 Jesus' answer was based on the example of David while in 2,27-28 Jesus' response has a different orientation. Verse 27, a universal statement, has gnomic content and v. 28, a theological assertion, has Christological content. The saying in 2,27 consists of a chiastic structure:

Τὸ σάββατον διὰ τὸν ἄνθρωπον ἐγένετο   a   b   c

καὶ οὐκ ὁ ἄνθρωπος διὰ τὸ σάββατον   c'   b'   a'

In this verse Jesus reaffirms the original intention [172] of the sabbath, namely, the sabbath is subservient to the needs of man. Although this saying appears excessively radical, there is a similar adage of Rabbi Simeon ben Menasya (c. 180 AD): "the sabbath is delivered over for your sake, but you are not delivered over to the sabbath" (Mekilta 109b on Ex 31,14).

Without entering into the details of the question about the literary cohesion [173] between verses 27 and 28, we hold that ὥστε introduces an independent proposition which is best translated as "therefore" or "so" [174]. By ὁ υἱὸς τοῦ ἀνθρώπου is meant not "man" in general but "the Son of Man" [175] which is used here as a self-designation for Jesus. It underlines the transcendental dimension of his person. The expression κύριος τοῦ σαββάτου describes one who exercises authority over the use of the sabbath. In the OT it was God himself (cf. Ex 20,8-11; 23,12; 31,12-17; 34,21; 35,1-3; Lev 19,3; 23,1-3; 26,2; Deut 5,12-15, etc.). Therefore, by affirming Jesus' lordship over the sabbath, Mk implies that Jesus has the same authority as God himself. In other words, verse 28 affirms Jesus' divinity. It also functions as the climactic statement of the whole pericope in which Mk expresses the conviction that Jesus is the Lord of all that belongs to man, including the sabbath [176].

---

[172] In 7,9-13 and 10,6-9 too, Jesus displays his concern for the original intention.

[173] The main literary problem arises from the initial ὥστε in verse 28. Although ὥστε can introduce an absolute proposition, more frequently it establishes a link of consequence between two propositions. It is this more usual function of ὥστε that seems awkward since in v. 27 "man" is in view and in v. 28 "the Son of Man". Exegetes have proposed different solutions to this problem. For a summary, see GILS, "Le sabbat", 509-513. In the second place, what is the relation between "man" and "the Son of Man" in v. 28? See the discussion in: BEARE, "Sabbath", 130-136; HULTGREN, "Mark 2,23-28", 38-40.

[174] Cf. NEB, RSV, BJ, TOB, etc.

[175] Against JEREMIAS, *Theology*, 261; COLPE, *TDNT* VIII, 405.

[176] Among several others, see GNILKA, I, 124; NINEHAM, 106; TAYLOR, 220.

C. Concluding Remarks

The following scheme reveals a constant progression in Jesus' answer to the Pharisees:

If David and his men, faced with dire need, could violate the Law,
then Jesus is also empowered to dispense his disciples
from the Law's observance (2,25-26).

The sabbath is subservient to man (2,27)

Jesus, the Son of Man, is lord over the sabbath (2,28).

Thus from a simple event Mk progressively leads the reader to the mystery of Jesus' person in 2,28: Jesus is the transcendental Son of Man who he is lord over the sabbath. He is God himself.

V. Healing on the Sabbath (3,1-6)

A. Literary Analysis

1. *Textual Criticism*

There are two textual problems to be clarified in this pericope [177]: the first in 3,3 and the second in 3,4.

---

[177] In verse 2 the addition of ἐν, perhaps under the influence of Lk 6,7, is an intentional clarification since dative denotes only point of time but ἐν with dative implies both point and duration of time (cf. BLASS-DEBRUNNER, *Grammar*, § 200). It is very likely that in verse 5 σου was added following the parallels in Mt 12,13 and Lk 6,10. In verse 6 the substitution of ἐδίδουν with ποιεῖν is an attempt to improve upon the text, perhaps under the influence of Mk 15,1 where the latter verb is used with συμβούλιον.

In 3,3 there are four alternative readings:

1) τὴν ξηρὰν χεῖρα ἔχοντι (ℵ Δ Θ) [178]

2) τὴν χεῖρα ἔχοντι ξηρὰν (B *al*.) [179]

3) ἔχοντι τὴν χεῖρα ξηράν (W lat *al*.)

4) ἐξηραμμένην ἔχοντι τὴν χεῖρα (A *al*.)

The substitution of ξηράν with ἐξηραμμένην (repeated from 3,1) in the fourth variant is an intentional change. The difference among the other three variants is a matter of transposition of words: in the third variant the participle ἔχοντι is brought nearer to the noun which it qualifies, and the MSS support for this variant is weak. Although the MSS evidence is almost equally good for both the first and the second readings, from a grammatical point of view the predicative use of the adjective ξηράν is better. Consequently, the second reading should be preferred.

In Mk 3,4 there are three variant readings:

1) ἀγαθὸν ποιῆσαι (ℵ W) [180]

2) ἀγαθοποιῆσαι (A B C L Θ *al*.) [181]

3) τὶ ἀγαθὸν ποιῆσαι (D b e)

In the third variant τί is intentionally added and its MSS support is very weak. The MSS support, however, for the first and the second variants is almost equally strong, perhaps the second slightly better. Yet there is no convincing reason why ἀγαθοποιεῖν was changed into ἀγαθόν ποιεῖν. On the contrary, ἀγαθοποιεῖν in 3,4 is probably an amelioration of the text, perhaps under the influence of the Lucan parallel (6,9), and in imitation of κακοποιεῖν in 3,4. Therefore, the first variant is possibly to be preferred.

---

[178] GNT/NESTLE-ALAND, HUCK-GREEVEN, TISCHENDORF, VOGELS, etc.

[179] MERK, TASKER, TREGELLES, WESTCOTT-HORT, etc. and the commentaries of LAGRANGE, SWETE, TAYLOR, etc.

[180] GNT/NESTLE-ALAND, MERK, TASKER, TISCHENDORF, etc.

[181] HUCK-GREEVEN, TREGELLES, VOGELS, VON SODEN, WESTCOTT-HORT, etc. and the commentaries of LAGRANGE, SWETE, TAYLOR, etc.

2. Synoptic Comparison

a. Mk 3,1-6 and Mt 12,9-14

Both in Mk and in Mt the principal literary connection with the immediately preceding pericope is the term 'sabbath'. However, Mk 3,1a seems to refer back to 1,21b while by means of καὶ μεταβὰς ἐκεῖθεν Mt links 12,9-14 with 12,1-8. According to Mk 3,2 Jesus' opponents silently watch him to see whether he would break sabbatical laws while according to Mt 12,10b they ask him a direct question, "Is it lawful to heal on the sabbath?" The interesting comparison of a sheep that has fallen into a pit [182] and a man in need in 12,11 are proper to Mt. Absent from Mt are the two sets of alternatives (to do good or to do harm; to save life or to kill), the mention of the opponents' silence in Mk 3,4, the note of Jesus' anger and grief regarding their hardness of heart in 3,5, and the reference to the Herodians in 3,6. These changes indicate that the focal point of Mt's narrative is man in need (cf. 12,11-12), a theme he had already initiated in the preceding verses (cf. 11,28-30; 12,7).

b. Mk 3,1-6 and Lk 6,6-11

The opening statement (6,6a) is reshaped by Lk and brought into closer parallelism with 6,1. The insertion of a note about Jesus' teaching in 6,6b is in tune with the Lucan presentation of Jesus' ministry in the synagogue (cf. 4,15.31; 13,10). By mentioning that it was the right hand of the man that was afflicted, Lk accentuates the hardship involved. The use of ξηρός in place of the Marcan ἐξηραμμένος in 6,6 and the addition of εὑρίσκειν in 6,7 are for the sake of clarification. Lk has also brought forward the presence of the Pharisees from Mk 3,6 and added scribes, their normal companions. In 6,8 Lk mentions that Jesus intuitively knew his adversaries' thoughts, adds the clarifying καὶ στῆθι and explicitly states that his command was obeyed. In 6,10 he omits the references to Jesus' anger and his grief at the hardness of their heart. The closing verse is to a great extent rewritten by Lk where he omits the mention of Herodians although he notes Herod's own threat against Jesus in 13,31 and plays down the Pharisees' hostile reaction to Jesus. This is probably because of Jesus friendly relationship with some of them (cf. Lk 7,36; 11,37; 13,31; 14,1; 17,20). The main thrust of Lk 6,11 is very

---

[182] For Mt, the expression "lost sheep" represents man whom Jesus searches for with love, compassion and mercy (cf. Mt 10,6; 15,24).

different from that of Mk. In Lk the impression given is that Jesus' opponents are at their wits' end and do not know what to do. For the moment no further action is taken, and Jesus continues his task unhindered. On the contrary, in Mk the Pharisees hold counsel with the Herodians against Jesus to destroy him. But Jesus withdraws from the scene (3,7).

3. *Tradition and Redaction*

There are ample redactional features in 3,1a. As mentioned before, compound verbs followed by the same preposition (εἰσῆλθεν εἰς) is characteristically Marcan and by means of Jesus' entry and exit our evangelist redactionally links various pericopes. Furthermore, the adverb πάλιν almost always and the noun συναγωγή often occur in redactional verses. Besides 3,1a is a literal repetition of Mk 1,21b, a redactional verse.

The last clause in 3,4, οἱ δὲ ἐσιώπων, is very likely redactional not only because the verb σιωπᾶν is more frequent in Mk [183] but also because this clause is not necessary for the narrative as such. There is clear redactional activity in 3,5a. Two or more participles before or after the main verb is a Marcan stylistic feature [184]. The use of μετά with genitive is preferred by Mk [185]. Again, of the seven occurrences of περιβλέπεσθαι in the NT, six are in Mk.

Furthermore, the expression, hardness of heart, whether with the noun πώρωσις (3,5) or the verb πωροῦν (6,52 and 8,17, both predicated of the disciples in redactional verses), is exclusive to Mk [186]. Finally, as stated before, ἐπί causative is generally redactional in Mk. However, the noun ὀργή occurs in Mk only here and the verb συλλυπεῖσθαι is hapax in the NT. Further, it would be linguistically better if λέγει, the main verb in 3,5a, were preceded by a participial phrase as in the Lucan parallel. In 3,3 and 3,4, however, λέγει is not preceded by a participial phrase, but a direct discourse follows immediately in 3,5. Hence, we are of the opinion that περιβλεψά-

---

[183] Cf. n. 186 below.
[184] Cf. PRYKE, *Redactional Style*, 119-126.
[185] Cf. ALAND, *Konkordanz* I/2, 774-779.

[186]	Mt	Mk	Lk	Jn	Acts	Paul	Rest		Total
σιωπᾶν	2	5	2	0	1	0	0	=	10
hardness of heart......	0	3	0	1	0	1	0	=	5
ξηραίνειν	3	6	1	1	0	0	4	=	15

μενος αὐτοὺς μετ᾽ ὀργῆς, συλλυπούμενος ἐπὶ τῇ πωρώσει τῆς καρδίας αὐτῶν is redactional [187].

The main arguments put forward against the redactional character of 3,6 are the following. First of all, συμβούλιον διδόναι and ὅπως occur only in this verse in Mk [188]. Secondly, the reference to Jesus' Passion occurs too early [189]. And thirdly, the mention of the Pharisees with the Herodians in a redactional verse is strange [190].

The noun συμβούλιον occurs in the NT only eight times (Mt 5, Mk 2, Acts 1). In Acts 25,12 it is found in combination with the verb συλλαλεῖν, in Mt invariably with λαμβάνειν (12,14; 22,15; 27,1.7; 28,12) and in Mk with διδόναι (3,6) and ποιεῖν (15,1). By the use of two different verbs with συμβούλιον in 3,6 and in 15,1, Mk seems to intend subtly different nuances in these two verses [191]. Regarding the hapax ὅπως, it is instructive to note the similarity between 3,6 and 11,18:

ὅπως αὐτὸν ἀπολέσωσιν (3,6)

πῶς αὐτὸν ἀπολέσωσιν (11,18)

Moreover, as noted above, hapax legomena occur in other redactional verses as well. The second point, the early reference to the Passion, is comprehensible in the light of the structure of the Gospel and the programmatic character of 1,14-3,6 [192]. Finally, the mention of the Pharisees with the Herodians may be explicable on philological bases [193].

Having critically evaluated the arguments against the redactional character of 3,6, we proceed to establish the literary and thematic evidence in favour of its redactional nature. As noted in Ch. V, the verb ἐξέρχεσθαι occurs relatively more often in Mk than in Mt and Lk, and καί + ἐξέρχεσθαι is used redactionally in other instances too [194]. The adverb εὐθύς is obviously redactional. Furthermore, the coupling of 'Pharisees' with 'Herodians' found

---

[187] In light of multiple literary indications for redaction, the occurrence of two hapax legomena is not a convincing counterargument since hapax legomena are found also in other redactional verses (cf. 3,9; 4,1; 6,30, etc.).

[188] Cf. THISSEN, Erzählung, 86; SCHENKE, Wundererzählungen, 185-186.

[189] Already ALBERTZ, Streitgespräche, 5-16.

[190] Cf. KERTELGE, Wunder, 83; SCHENKE, Wundererzählungen, 164.

[191] Cf. p. 237-238 below.

[192] Cf. p. 37-60, 260-265.

[193] Cf. immediately below.

[194] Cf. Mk 1,28; 2,13; 6,1.12.34.54; 7,31; 8,11.27, etc.

also in 12,13, is absent in the parallel verses in Mt and Lk. And lastly, the preposition μετά followed by genitive, particularly genitive of person, is characteristic of Mk [195].

From the thematic perspective, the following two arguments are of utmost importance. Mk 3,1-6 is a combination of a healing and a controversy. In both of them Jesus finally emerges victorious. But the negative perspective of 3,6 contradicts the main thrust of 3,1-5 where Jesus is depicted as the winner over his enemies. In the second place, one of the key interests of Mk is Jesus' Passion. Mk 3,6 gives a direct hint about it without specific details; "it raises the question of the further progress and outcome of the plot against Jesus." [196]. The linear development of the plot in 3,6; 11,18; 12,12 and 14,1 is particularly striking, especially the increasing hostility of the Jewish authorities towards Jesus and their calculatively cautious measures to destroy him [197]. A verse that has such a programmatic and vital importance in the development of the theme of Jesus' Passion does not appear to be the ending of a source.

In conclusion, we believe that the arguments against the redactional nature of Mk 3,6 are not as strong as they appear. The literary evidence and in particular the thematic motifs argue in favour of the redactional character of 3,6.

Once the redactional character of 3,6 is established, it is logical to ask whether 3,2b is redactional or not. Some authors hold that Mk 2,23-28 and 3,1-6 belonged together in tradition and that there existed a logical connection between the Pharisees' warning (2,24), their watching to arrest him (3,2) and holding counsel to destroy him (3,6) [198]. But we have established that 3,1a is redactional. As a consequence 2,23-28 and 3,1-6 most probably did not exist together in tradition. We have also established that 3,6 is the redactional work of Mk. The logical connection between 3,2b and 3,6 is, then, the work of the evangelist. Therefore, by implication, it appears that 3,2b (ἵνα κατηγορήσωσιν αὐτοῦ) is redactional [199].

---

[195] In the following instances μετά followed by the genitive is absent in the synoptic parallels: μετά with genitive of persons (1,20.29.36; 2,16.19b; 3,6.14; 4,36; 5,18.24.37.40; 6,50; 8,10.14; 9,8; 11,11; 14,33; 15,1.7); μετά with genitive of things (3,5; 6,25; 10,30; 14,62).

[196] DEWEY, *Markan Public Debate*, 47.

[197] See folder in Ch. II, and p. 258-259.

[198] Cf. JEREMIAS, *Theology*, 38, 279; PESCH, I, 187-188.

[199] Our findings on the redactional contribution of Mk in 3,1-6 seriously question the view of KERTELGE, *Wunder*, 82-84; PESCH, I, 188; THISSEN, *Erzählung*, 74-89 who attribute the whole of this pericope, except πάλιν in 3,1a, to tradition and confirm the opinion of GNILKA, I, 126; SAUFER, "Mk 3,1-6", 185-196 and W. WEIB, *Eine neue Lehre*, 108-114.

4. *Literary Structure*

1 ---- Καὶ εἰσῆλθεν πάλιν εἰς τὴν συναγωγήν. καὶ ἦν ἐκεῖ ἄνθρωπος
ἐξηραμμένην ἔχων τὴν χεῖρα·

2 A καὶ παρετήρουν αὐτὸν εἰ τοῖς σάββασιν θεραπεύσει αὐτόν, *ἵνα*
κατηγορήσωσιν αὐτοῦ.

3 B a καὶ *λέγει τῷ ἀνθρώπῳ τῷ τὴν χεῖρα ἔχοντι ξηράν,* Ἔγειρε
εἰςτὸ μέσον.

4   b *καὶ λέγει αὐτοῖς,* Ἔξεστιν τοῖς σάββασιν ἀγαθὸν
ποιῆσαι ἢ κακοποιῆσαι, ψυχὴν σῶσαι ἢ ἀποκτεῖναι;

C οἱ δὲ ἐσιώπων.

5 B' b' *καὶ περιβλεψάμενος αὐτοὺς μετ' ὀργῆς, συλλυπούμενος*
ἐπὶ τῇ πωρώσει τῆς καρδίας αὐτῶν,

a' *λέγει τῷ ἀνθρώπῳ,* Ἔκτεινον τὴν χεῖρα. καὶ ἐξέτεινεν,
καὶ ἀπεκατεστάθη ἡ χεὶρ αὐτοῦ.

6 A' καὶ ἐξελθόντες οἱ Φαρισαῖοι εὐθὺς μετὰ τῶν Ἡρῳδι ανῶν
συμβούλιον ἐδίδουν κατ' αὐτοῦ *ὅπως αὐτὸν ἀπολέσωσιν.*

Verse 1 is the setting for the narrative. Verse 2 (A) and verse 6 (A')
are parallel: in the former the Pharisees spy on Jesus and in the latter they
plot to destroy him. Verses 3-4b (B) are parallel to verse 5 (B'). And both
B and B' are composed of Jesus' command to the man with a withered hand
(Ba B'a') and his question to the Pharisees (Bb) and his strong emotional
reaction against them (B'b'). At the centre is placed the silence of the
Pharisees (C). A and B lead to C: the Pharisees' spying on Jesus and Jesus'
questioning them evoke no reaction from them; they are diplomatically silent.
Likewise, B' and A' flow from C: their diplomatic silence provokes strong
reaction in Jesus who then heals the man with a withered hand. The Pharisees,
in turn, begin plotting against Jesus.

The same structure emerges by studying the text from the point of view
of dramatis personae and their actions .

---- Narrative introduction

A   The *Pharisees watch* Jesus to *accuse* him.

	B *Jesus' action*	a	command to the *man with a withered hand*
		b	questions the *Pharisees*

      C *Pharisees silent*

	B' *Jesus' reaction*	b'	emotional reaction against the *Pharisees*
		a'	command to *the man with a withered hand*

A'   The *Pharisees plot against Jesus to destroy him.*

B. Interpretation

1. *Introduction to the Narrative (3,1)*

The narrative begins with a statement that Jesus entered again into the synagogue, which recalls his first entry into the synagogue in 1,21b. In the synagogue there was a man who had a withered hand. Here the participle ἔχων is not periphrastic but descriptive. The verb ξηραίνειν (= dry up, wither), relatively more frequent in Mk [200], is used in reference to human beings (3,1; 5,29; 9,18) and plants/trees (4,6; 11,20.21). In our verse it denotes paralysis; and the perfect participle seems to imply that the paralysis was not from birth.

2. *Pharisees Spy on Jesus (3,2)*

The main verb in 3,2 παρατηρεῖν (= watch closely, observe carefully), a hapax in Mk, can mean to watch maliciously. In 3,2 it has such a nuance.

---

[200] Cf. n. 186 above.

The subject of παρετήρουν is the Pharisees (cf. 2,24; 3,6). The imperfect tense implies a continuous or a repeated action [201]. They were watching Jesus to see whether he would perform a healing on the sabbath so that they could bring a charge against him. The verb κατηγορεῖν (= to accuse) is nearly always used in a legal sense to bring charges against someone. In the synoptic tradition this verb occurs in two contexts: in the Passion narrative and in our pericope. In the Passion narrative it occurs in Jesus' trial before Pilate (Mk 15,1-15 par.) where the members of the Sanhedrin accuse Jesus (15,3) and in the scene of Jesus before Herod (Lk 23,6-12) where the chief priests and the scribes vehemently accuse (23,10) him. In Mk 3,2 those who are bent on accusing Jesus are the Pharisees.

3. *Jesus Commands the Man (3,3)*

In 3,3 the adjective ξηρός is used figuratively of a diseased state. The phrase ἔγειρε εἰς τὸ μέσον is a pregnant construction, meaning, 'arise (and come) into the midst'.

4. *Jesus' Questioning the Pharisees (3,4ab)*

Jesus' question in 3,4ab is composed of two synonymously parallel statements, each in the form of an antithesis:

ἔξεστιν τοῖς σάββασιν   ἀγαθὸν ποιῆσαι ἢ κακοποιῆσαι
                         ψυχὴν σῶσαι ἢ ἀποκτεῖναι

The phrase ἀγαθὸν ποιεῖν (= ἀγαθοποιεῖν), meaning to do good, is equivalent to the classical εὖ ποιεῖν. The verb κακοποιεῖν has two meanings: (1) to do wrong, to be a criminal; (2) to harm, injure. On the basis of the parallelism between κακοποιῆσαι and ἀποκτεῖναι, it is better to translate this verb in the sense of "to do evil" as in BJ and NEB [202]. One should note that all the four occurrences of κακοποιεῖν in the NT are contrasted with

---

[201] The translation, 'were watching to see' (BJ, NEB) is to be preferred to 'watched to see' (RSV).

[202] The rendering in RSV ('to do harm') is weak.

ἀγαθόν ποιεῖν/ἀγαθοποιεῖν (cf. Mk 3,4; Lk 6,9; 1 Pet 3,17; 3 Jn 11). The noun ψυχή (= soul, life) has various nuances in the NT [203]. And here it probably corresponds to the Hebrew נֶפֶשׁ meaning, life, self, person. In Mk ψυχή is the object of σώζειν in 3,4 and 8,35 and of ἀπολλύναι/ζημιοῦν in 8,35.36. But it is the object of διδόναι only in reference to Jesus (10,45).

There are various opinions on the meaning of 3,4, which can be grouped as follows: (1) Jesus implicitly contrasts his own act of healing, which is 'doing good' and 'saving life',with the hostile activity of his opponents who are doing evil in trying to kill him [204]. (2) Many scholars consider 3,4 as expressing a general principle that failure to do a good deed on the sabbath is tantamount to doing evil [205]. (3) Evaluating German scholarship on 3,4, Dietzfelbinger proposes a psychologico-theological explanation. From the time of the exile sabbatical observance was considered the sign of Israel's election. It was held that not only the fulfilment of God's salvific promises depended on it but also Israel's deplorable state was attributed to the failure to observe the first sabbath. This theological thinking provided the religious motivation for sabbatical observance and the failure to observe it could be penalyzed by the death penalty. But forceful, coercive observance of a law is rooted in fear. Therefore, to reestablish the original meaning of the sabbath as a source of joy, to liberate man from any sort of alienation, and to experience God's love, Jesus violated the sabbatical laws [206].

The first opinion, as Nineham rightly observes, is attractive in some ways, but it involves reading a good deal into the text. And if it is correct, "the argument is purely ad hominem and Jesus offers no real justification for his breach of the sabbath law" [207]. The second opinion is also not fully convincing, for how could Jesus explicitly violate the sabbath observance, God's own commandment [208]. From another point of view, the Pharisaic law did allow healing on the sabbath in case of mortal danger [209]. But the paralysis in question was neither mortal nor immediately urgent. Dietzfelbinger's

---

[203] Cf. BAUER, *Lexicon*, 901-902; ZORELL, *Lexicon*, 1473-1477.

[204] Cf. RAWLINSON, 35-36; Swete, 53.

[205] Among others, see TAYLOR, 222; NINEHAM, 109.

[206] Cf. DIETZFELBINGER, "Sabbatheilungen", 290-298.

[207] NINEHAM, 109.

[208] Ex 31,14: "You shall keep the sabbath, because it is holy for you; every one who profanes it shall be put to death; whoever does any work on it, that soul shall be cut off from among his people". See also Ex 20,8; 23,12; 35,2; Deut 5,12-15, etc.

[209] *Yoma* 8,6; *Shabbath* 18,3; 19,2, etc. For details see STR.-B, *Kommentar* I, 623-629; LOHSE, *TDNT* VII, 14-15.

interpretation applies modern psychology to the text. His opinion does not pay sufficient attention to the context and the literary unit (2,1-3,6) in which the saying is placed. In 2,18-22, the structural core of 2,1-3,6, Mk has stated that Jesus' coming inaugurated a new situation so urgent and unprecedented (cf. 1,15) that the laws applicable to the 'old age' are no longer relevant, and in 2,28 he asserted that Jesus is lord even of the sabbath. The Pharisees fail to recognize this unique character of Jesus' mission. On the contrary, they view him solely from a human perspective and set their mind to accuse him if he were to heal on the sabbath (3,2). But Jesus' question in 3,4ab has a deeper dimension. From a general principle of doing good or doing evil on the sabbath (the content of the first member of the synonymous parallelism), Jesus focuses attention on a soteriological point — that of saving life or killing (the content of the second member of the synonymous parallelism). For Jesus the basic issue is not that of healing on the sabbath but of leading man to salvation (in both the physical and spiritual sense) [210]. This interpretation can be reinforced from the following considerations. First of all, the verb θεραπεύειν occurs in 3,2 but not in Jesus' question in 3,4ab nor in the actual healing in 3,5bc. In the second place, Jesus' looking around with anger in 3,5a is caused by the hardening of the Pharisees' hearts, an expression stressing their incredulity (cf. exegesis of 3,5a). Finally, in the Gospels the phrase σώζειν (τὴν) ψυχήν occurs only in combination with ἀπολλύναι (or a similar verb) τὴν ψυχήν in a soteriological context. Jesus' question in 3,4ab is thus profoundly soteriological.

5. Pharisees' Silence (3,4c)

Jesus' question, however, evoked no reaction or response from the Pharisees. Instead, they remained silent. The verb σιωπᾶν is used in Mk in two ways: (1) to silence those who cry out or make noise (10,48; 4,39); (2) to keep silence when a question is asked (3,4; 9,34; 14,61). In 14,61 Jesus remained silent when he was questioned about the destruction of the temple made with hands and the construction of another not made with hands. In 9,34 the disciples kept silent when Jesus questioned them regarding the subject of their discussion on the way. They had, in fact, been discussing who was the greatest, something diametrically opposed to Jesus' understanding of his mission (cf. 10,45) and the true nature of discipleship (cf. 8,35-38; 9,35-37; 10,42-44). In 3,4c the Pharisees were silent when Jesus

---

[210] Cf. BEDA, 465-466.

asked them, "Is it lawful on the sabbath to do good, or to do harm, to save life or to kill?" Their silence is primarily founded not so much in their legalistic attitude and hatred towards Jesus as in their incredulity. This is evident from Jesus' reaction in 3, 5a. Verse 4, then, ends on a note where Mk emphasizes the basic difference between Jesus and the Pharisees.

6. *Jesus' Reaction to the Pharisees (3,5a)*

Jesus' reaction to the silent Pharisees is narrated in 3, 5a. He looks around challengingly at them all and then commands the man to stretch out his hand. The verb περιβλέπεσθαι used only in the middle voice and predicated of Jesus in 3,4.34; 5,32; 10,23; 11,11 denotes the swift searching glance of Jesus upon his friends or enemies. The noun ὀργή expresses not so much an emotional outburst as a reaction against evil. And the cause of Jesus' grief is the hardening of the Pharisees' hearts. The verb πωροῦν and the noun πώρωσις are always used in the NT figuratively. It refers to the hardening of the Jews (Jn 12,40; Rom 11,7.25; 2 Cor 3,14) or of the Gentiles (Eph 4,18). Mk uses the verb (6,52; 8,17) as well as the noun (3,5) as a quality of the heart.

Mk 6,52 is a comment of Mk, underscoring the disciples' incomprehension and the hardening of their hearts even though Jesus revealed himself to them in the multiplication of the loaves (6,34-44) and manifested himself to them by walking over the waters and calming the raging sea (6,45-51). Yet they continued to remain blind. In 6,52 incomprehension and hardness of heart are correlated as they are synonymously parallel:

οὐ γὰρ συνῆκαν ἐπὶ τοῖς ἄρτοις,

ἀλλ' ἦν αὐτῶν ἡ καρδία πεπωρωμένη,

Likewise, 8,17 is found at a strategic place in Mk: it occurs at the end of the bread section (6,34-8,21) where Mk very strongly emphasizes the incomprehension of the disciples, their blindness and deafness, and their hardness of heart (cf. 8,17-18. 21). This reprimand to the disciples is immediately followed by the narration of the blind man at Bethsaida (8,22-26) which symbolizes the gradual insight of the disciples into the person of Jesus. And this, in turn, is immediately followed by the acknowledgement and confession of Jesus' Messiahship by Peter in his capacity as the spokesman for the disciples.

Therefore, in brief, hardness of heart in 6,52 and 8,17 expresses the disbelief of the disciples. So in Mk 3,5 too, 'hardness of heart' has the same meaning, namely, Mk considers hardness of the heart, the seat of faith, as the highest expression of disbelief and an utter insensitivity to man's needs and problems. He has put the expression 'hardness of the heart' at 3,5 because each of the first three sections of the first part of his Gospel ends on a note of incredulity (3,5-6; 6,1-6a; 8,14-21).

7. Jesus Heals the Man (3,5b)

Jesus asks the man to stretch out his hand. He stretches it out and it was immediately restored. The verb ἀποκαθιστάναι became a technical one for the restoration of Israel to its own land by Yahweh (cf. Jer 16,15; 23,8; 24,6; Ezek 16,55, etc.). This verb was "increasingly understood in a Messianic and eschatological sense" [211]. Mk uses it in 3,5 for the restoration of the man's withered hand and in 8,25 for the restoration of sight to the blind man. This verb is used to refer to Jesus' activities not in the second part but only in the first part of Mk where the predominant theme is the progressive revelation of the mystery of Jesus' identity. Therefore, Mk's usage of this verb in 3,5 and 8,25 possibly has Messianic overtones.

8. Pharisees' Plotting against Jesus (3,6)

In 3,6 Mk narrates the Pharisees' reaction. They go out to plot with the Herodians how to destroy Jesus. The noun συμβούλιον occurs in Mk only twice (3,6; 15,1). In 15,1 the Sanhedrin held a consultation (συμβούλιον ποιήσαντες) and as a result they handed Jesus over to Pilate. Their holding a consultation had an official character. In 3,6, συμβούλιον ἐδίδουν (= began plotting) [212] does not have an official character. The Pharisees are not only antagonistic towards Jesus, but, together with the Herodians, they act as the agents of the chief priests and the scribes to entrap Jesus by asking politically intricate questions of him (12,13-17). So the plot that began in 3,6, was reiterated in 11,18; 12,12 and 14,1-2.43-50 and was finally executed in 15,1-15. As for the identity of the Herodians, there is no unanimous opinion. Daniel identifies them with the Essenes [213] while Bennett thinks that the term 'Herodians' is a theological construction of Mk to mean the enemies of John

---

[211] Cf. OEPKE, *TDNT* I, 388.
[212] Cf. NEB, BJ.
[213] Cf. DANIEL, "Les Hérodiens", 31-53; id., "Nouveaux arguments", 397-402.

the Baptist and Jesus [214]. A majority of scholars, however, think that most probably they are the friends and political supporters of Herod Antipas [215].

One should note the progression in the action of the Pharisees. First, they were watching Jesus (παρετήρουν imperfect tense) with a view to arrest him if he violated the laws of the sabbath. Next, when questioned by Jesus, they remained silent (ἐσιώπων imperfect tense). And finally they plot (ἐδίδουν imperfect tense) to destroy him. By using the imperfect tense to describe the actions of the Pharisees, Mk emphasizes the continuity of their actions, an expression of the constancy of their hatred towards Jesus and of their disbelief in him. Thus a dark cloud of death hangs over the further course of his ministry. Jesus' immediate reaction was simply to withdraw from there (3,7).

C. Mk 3,1-6 in Context

The assertion that Jesus as the Son of Man is lord of the sabbath (2,28) is fittingly followed by the present story in which Jesus demonstrates his lordship over sabbath, thereby confounding his opponents. Unlike previous controversies, however, this one resulted in his opponents plotting against his very life. Jesus quits the synagogue for ever, except the one in his own hometown (6,2) where he also faces disbelief in him. Thus 3,6 marks the definitive break in Jesus' relationship with official Judaism.

VI. Chapter Six: Concluding Remarks

The primary thrust of 2,1-3,6, as in 1,21-45, is the mysterious revelation of Jesus' person and mission in words and deeds. In contrast to the appreciation and acceptance that Jesus received from people in 1,21-45, in 2,1-3,6, Jesus faces steadily mounting opposition from the Jewish leaders. These two aspects, the mysterious revelation and the consistent opposition, can be schematically demonstrated as below.

---

[214] Cf. BENNETT, "Herodians", 9-14.

[215] Among several others, see GNILKA, I, 128; GRUNDMANN, 97; NINEHAM, 111; PESCH, I, 195.

Jesus as the Son of Man has authority to forgive sins.	Jesus as the Son of Man is the lord even of the sabbath.

↓   ↓

Demonstration of this authority in forgiving sins through the symbolic action of table fellowship with taxcollectors and sinners	Exercise of this lordship in healing a man with a withered hand on the sabbath

In Jesus' person and mission
the NEW has overtaken and
absolved the OLD.

It is precisely the newness of the kingdom, ushered in through Jesus' person and mission, that his adversaries refuse to recognize. As a result, they consistently oppose him by questioning him and finally by plotting his destruction. This opposition can be visualized as demonstrated below:

Scribes question Jesus' authority to forgive sins (2,6).

Scribes of the Pharisees question: "Why does he eat with
tax collectors and sinners?" (2,16b)

Jesus is questioned because his disciples do not fast (2,18b).

Pharisees question Jesus because his disciples
break sabbatical laws (2,24).

They watch Jesus to see whether he would heal on the sabbath
so that they might accuse him (3,2).

Pharisees plot with the Herodians to destroy Jesus (3,6).

FUNCTION OF MK 1,14-3,6 IN THE WHOLE OF THE GOSPEL

Having determined the place of 1,14-3,6 in Mk (part one) and having clarified the meaning of this section (part two), in the third part we pose the question: What is the role of 1,14-3,6 in Mk? The answer to this question will be developed in two steps: (1) in chapter seven an attempt is made to discover the literary relation and thematic progression of the twelve pericopes in 1,14-3,6 in the frame of Mk as a whole; (2) and in chapter eight, based on the literary and thematic indices, we propose that Mk 1,14-3,6 has a programmatic character.

CHAPTER SEVEN

MK 1,14-3,6 IN THE FRAME OF THE GOSPEL

I. Mk 1,14-20 from the Gospel Perspective

A. Mk 1,14-15 in the Frame of the Whole Gospel

As stated in Chs. I and II, the main thrust of the first part of Mk (1,14-8,30) is the progressive revelation of the mystery of Jesus' Messiahship. Mk develops it in three successive sections (1,14-3,6; 3,7-6,6a; 6,6b-8,30) showing clearly the marked progression in unveiling this mystery. Each section begins with a summary on Jesus' ministry immediately followed by a pericope on discipleship or apostleship, indicating the development of Jesus' ministry and the increasing role of the disciples or apostles in it.

According to this scheme, Mk 1,14-15 constitutes the introduction to the first section (1,14-3,6). In addition to this, because of the progressive character of the first part of Mk and because the second part presupposes the first, 1,14-15 is linked to 3,7-16,8 as well. Furthermore, as established in Ch. IV, both τὸ εὐαγγέλιον and ἡ βασιλεία τοῦ θεοῦ have a Christological content — they are almost identifiable with the person of Jesus Christ. Thus by virtue of these two key terms, 1,14-15 is thematically connected with the mystery of Jesus' person, the main concern of Mk.

B. Mk 1,16-20 in the Plan of the Gospel

1. *Mk 1,16-20 and the Theme of Discipleship*

A key emphasis in the first part of Mk, as mentioned in Ch. II, is Jesus' self-revelation to his disciples in a very personal way (cf. 4,35-41; 6,38-51; 8,1-10, etc.) although they fail to understand him (cf. 6,52; 8,14-21). Continuously following after Jesus, they function as intermediaries between

him and the crowd (cf. 3,9; 5,31; 6,35-37.41; 8,4-5, etc.). In the second part
Mk narrates other aspects of discipleship. A predominant theme is the necessity for a disciple to suffer. This is first stated in 8,34-38 (a pericope parallel
to 1,16-20 in many respects) [1] immediately after the first prediction of Jesus'
Passion in 8,31. Jesus unequivocally says, "If any man would come after me,
let him deny himself and take up his cross and follow me" (8,34). This is a
universal statement applicable to all. Jesus, Mk affirms, is a suffering Messiah
(cf. 8,31; 9,31; 10,32-34.45) whose disciples must tread the path of suffering
(cf. 8,35-38; 9,33-38; 10,35-44). In fact, suffering is an essential condition for
the disciples not only during Jesus' earthly life but also in the time after his
death (cf. 13,9-13). Jesus, the suffering Messiah goes ahead (προάγειν) and
his disciples follow (ἀκολουθεῖν) him (cf. Mk 10,32; 14,28; 16,7).

2. *Mk 1,16-20 and Apostleship*

The saying in Mk 1,17 ("I will make you become fishers of men") is
oriented towards the institution and mission of the Twelve [2]. The disciples
are called (καλεῖν 1,20a; cf. 1,17a; 2,14b) but for the call of the apostles
Mk uses another verb (προσκαλεῖσθαι 3,13b). By using this verb Mk seems
to underscore the closeness of the apostles to Jesus on whom he bestows a
specific mission. The double mention of ἐποίησεν δώδεκα (3,14.16) seems
to emphasize this point [3]. The call of the Twelve is directed to the twelve
tribes by which is meant all of mankind.

To be with Jesus, to be sent out to preach, and to have authority to cast
out demons (3,14-15) are characteristics typical of the apostles. Jesus calls
his disciples two by two (1,16.19) and he sends his apostles out on mission
two by two (6,7b). By this Mk probably emphasizes that the message they
deliver is a communitarian sharing in the person and mission of Jesus himself.

3. *The Four Disciples in the Frame of the Gospel*

The names of the four disciples occur according to the sequence of the
call narrative (1,16a.19a) only once again (1,29) in Mk. Later on there is a
noticeable difference both in importance and in the sequence of their names.

---

[1] Cf. p. 109, n. 127.
[2] Cf. p. 109-111.
[3] Cf. K. STOCK, *Boten*, 16-17; SCHMAHL, *Zwölf*, 49-50.

In the catalogue of the Twelve, the rank of Andrew is not only lowered to the fourth position, but also among the first called he alone does not receive a new name (cf. 3,16-18) [4]. To the private circle of the disciples to whom Jesus delivers the eschatological discourse, Andrew ranks fourth (cf. 13,3). Furthermore, there are three important occasions (raising of Jairus' daughter to life, the transfiguration, and the agony in Gethsemane) when Jesus on his own initiative takes Peter, James and John (5,37; 9,2; 14,33) but not Andrew. The pre-eminence of Peter, James, and John and the depreciation of Andrew could presumably be explained by the key roles that Peter, James and John played in the early church and the decisive functions they held [5], whereas Andrew seems to have faded away from the mainstream of the early life of the church [6].

Among the three (Peter, James, and John) Peter has a unique role. This is obvious from two considerations. (1) Up to the bestowal of a new name by Jesus the first disciple is mentioned only as Simon (six times) but after giving the new name, he is invariably called by his new name, Peter (19 times) except in 14,37. It is instructive to note that although James and John too were surnamed "Boanerges, that is, sons of thunder" (3,17), such a name is never used of them later. Instead, they are always called James and John. This extraordinary consistency in distinguishing the first apostle's name (and his alone) in the period prior to his naming and appointment (3,16) and after it indicates a specific role (indeed, a unique role) the first apostle has to fulfil in his capacity as Peter. This unique role consists of being the first among the apostles and being closest (i.e., personal relationship) to Jesus. This brings us to the second consideration, correlated with the first. (2) Peter is the leader and spokesman of the apostles and closest to Jesus. He is the first called (1,16a) and the first named (3,16). His name is mentioned first when Jesus takes the three apostles on three extraordinarily important occasions (5,37; 9,2; 14,33). He speaks as the representative of the apostles (cf. 8,32b; 9,5; 10,28) and he is recognized as such (16,7). To crown it all, he is the first human being to confess Jesus' Messiahship (8,29). This confession he makes not as Simon but precisely as Peter. His closeness to Jesus is also implied in his paradoxically contrasting attitudes: he confesses Jesus' Messiahship

---

[4] But according to the catalogue of Mt and Lk, Andrew has the second place, and James and John also do not receive a new name (cf. Mt 10,2; Lk 6,14).

[5] Cf. Acts 3,1-16; 4,13-22; 8,14-24; 12,2-5; Gal 2,9, etc.

[6] Excluding the Gospels, the name Andrew figures only once in the rest of the NT, namely, in the catalogue of the Eleven in Acts 1,13. Here he does not have the second place but the fourth.

(8,29) but he does not want him to be a suffering Messiah (8,32b); he pledges his loyalty to Jesus even at the cost of his life (14,29.31) but he disowns him (14,67-71), after which, nonetheless, "he broke down and wept" (14,72d). Mk thus portrays a dramatically unique portrait of Peter: his primacy among the apostles, his exceptionally personal closeness to Jesus and yet his failure to integrate personally the demands of following a suffering Messiah.

II. Mk 1,21-45 in the Gospel Scheme

A. Mk 1,21-28 in the Gospel Perspective

1. *Jesus' Teaching: A Key Emphasis*

It is crystal clear that Mk underlines Jesus' teaching in 1,21-28. Not only that the didactic vocabulary occurs in redactional verses but also that it is used very intensely. In no other pericope in the second Gospel does didactic vocabulary occur four times as in 1,21-28: διδάσκειν (1,21.22) and διδαχή (1,22.27). Nowhere else in Mk is διδάσκειν modified by the phrase ὡς ἐξουσίαν ἔχων and διδαχή qualified by καινὴ κατ' ἐξουσίαν. Such a frequent use of didactic vocabulary and its attributive qualification cannot be fortuitous but intentional.

In the exegesis of 1,21-22.27 we have established that the primary content of Jesus' teaching is his person and mission. It is precisely the Messianic overtones that distinguish his teaching from that of the scribes and create intense emotional reactions of amazement and dread among the listeners. By redactionally enclosing Jesus' first miracle, an exorcism (1,23-26), with references to his teaching (1,22.27), Mk gives an inkling about the person and mission of Jesus.

2. *Messianic Overtones of the Exorcism*

We have pointed out that the original story was about Jesus performing an exorcism upon a possessed man but it is Mk who has supplemented it with elements of plurality (1,24: ἡμῖν . . . ἡμᾶς and has probably introduced the motif of the Messianic secret (cf. 1,24-25). By these modifications Mk depicts a picture of Jesus' first exorcism as a struggle between the Messiah and the spokesman of the evil spirits in which the evil spirits are defeated and subdued. This narrative is strikingly parallel to 4,35-41 where Jesus calms the raging sea, a force hostile to God:

Mk 1,21-28	Mk 4,35-41
A man possessed by an evil spirit cried out (1,23-24).	A great storm arose, and the waves lashed against the boat (4,37).
Jesus rebuked (ἐπετίμησεν) him (1,25a)	Jesus rebuked (ἐπετίμησεν) the wind (4,39a)
saying, "Be silent, and come out of him" (1,25b).	and said to the sea, "Peace! Be still!" (4,39b).
And the unclean spirit . . . came out of him (1,26).	And the wind ceased and there was great calm (4,39c).
And they were all amazed (1,27a)	And they were filled with awe (4,41a)
so that they questioned among themselves (1,27b)	and said to one another (4,41b)
"What is this? . . . He commands even unclean spirits and they obey (ὑπακούσιν) him?" (1,27cd)	"Who then is this, that even wind and sea obey (ὑπακούει) him?" (4,41c)

By liberating the possessed man from the domain of the evil spirits and by calming the raging sea, Jesus subdues forces hostile to God and exercises his sovereignty over them. In and through these events, therefore, his Messianic identity becomes translucent. It is true that compared to 1,27 ("What is this? . . . even the unclean spirits . . . obey him?") Mk has more sharply posed the question of Jesus' identity in 4,41 ("Who then is this, that even wind and sea obey him?"). Nonetheless, the concentric structure we have proposed for 1,21-28 makes it crystal clear that the main thrust of this pericope is Jesus' Messianic identity, particularly accentuated in 1,24-25.

3. Teaching and Exorcism: Vehicles of Revelation

Both Jesus' teaching and his exorcism in 1,21-28 have one and the same scope, viz., the mysterious revelation of Jesus' identity and his Messianic mission. His teaching and miracles evoke questions concerning his identity in 6,2-3 as well, a pericope parallel to 1,21-27 in many respects:

Mk 1,21-27	*Mk 6,1-3*
Coming to Capernaum with the disciples (1,21a)	Coming to his own country, followed by his disciples (6,1)
On the sabbath teaching in the synagogue (1,21b)	On the sabbath teaching in the synagogue (6,2a)
Astonishment of the audience (1,22a)	Astonishment of the audience (6,2b)
Reason for the astonishment (1,22b)	Reason for the astonishment (6,2cd)
Exorcism (1,23-26)	Reference to miracles (6,2e)
Question: "What is this?" (1,27)	Question: "Is not this the carpenter?" (6,3)

Again, it is primarily Jesus' teaching and the activity of cleansing the temple that provoked the chief priests, scribes and elders to ask him questions about the source of his authority (11,15-18.28). It is impressive to observe that Mk 1,21-27 and 11,15-18.28 are also comparable from various aspects:

Mk 1,21-27	*Mk 11,15-18.28*
Coming to Capernaum with the disciples and entering the synagogue (1,21a)	Coming to Jerusalem with the disciples and entering the temple (11,15a)
--------------------	Cleansing the temple (11,15b-16)
Teaching (1,21b)	Teaching (11,17)
Astonishment of the audience (1,22)	Astonishment of the audience (11,18c)
Casting out the evil spirit (1,23-26)	--------------------
Question: "What is this?" (1,27)	Question: "By what authority are you doing these things?" (11,28)

The similarity in these three pericopes (1,21-27; 6,1-3; 11, 15-18.28) is remarkably impressive. Despite the manifold similarities of these pericopes at the surface level, the underlying fundamental structure may be presented according to the following scheme:

Jesus' Activity	*Questions Posed*
Teaching (1,21-22)	Question: "What is this?"
Exorcism (1,23-26)	(1,27)
Teaching (6,2ab)	Question: "Is not this the
Miracles (6,2e)	carpenter?" (6,3)
Teaching (11,17)	Question: "By what authority are
Cleansing the	you doing these things?" (11,28)
temple (11,15b-16)	

This scheme distinctively demonstrates that Jesus' teaching and his deeds of exorcism, miracles and cleansing the temple are geared to a single question. And that question concerns the identity of Jesus' person and his Messianic mission. In other words, Jesus' teaching and his deeds are vehicles of his revelation.

B. The Role of 1,29-31 in the Gospel

On the basis of our exegesis of 1,29-31, we focus attention on two aspects that emerge from the text: (1) the similarity between the healing of Peter's mother-in-law and the resuscitation of Jairus' daughter; (2) her service to Jesus and his disciples as a paradigm of ecclesial function of Christians.

1. *Mk 1,29-31 and 5,22-24.35-43*

1,29-31	*5,22-24.35-43*
They left the synagogue (1,29a).	Jairus, a ruler of the synagogue came to Jesus (5,22a).
Jesus entered the house of Simon and Andrew with James and John (1,29b).	He besought Jesus to make his daughter well (5,22b-23a).
Peter's mother-in-law lay sick with fever (1,30a).	She is at the point of death (5,23b).
They told him of her (1,30b).	Jesus, accompanied by Peter, James and John, entered the house of Jairus (5,37.39).

Jesus action (1,31a):	Jesus' action (5,40-41):
— he came	— he went in where the child was
— took her by the hand	— taking her by the hand said to her
— lifted (ἤγειρεν) her up.	— "Little girl, I say to you, arise (ἔγειρε 5,41b).
Cure: the fever left her (1,31b).	Resuscitation: she got up and walked (5,42ab).
And she served them (1,31c).	And he told them to give her something to eat (5,43c).

Our evangelist narrates various healings (1,40-45; 2,1-12; 3,1-6; 5,25-34; 7,31-37; 8,22-26; 10,46-52) and mentions different summaries of healings (1,32-34; 3,10; 6,55-56). Nevertheless, the cure of Simon's mother-in-law is not modelled on any of these healings but on the resuscitation of Jairus' daughter, the only resuscitation in the second Gospel. Do these parallel features enable the reader to view 1,29-31 as a resurrection type of miracle?

2. A Paradigm for Christian Διακονία

According to Mk, people from Galilee accompanied Jesus in his ministry and followed him on his way to Jerusalem. It is only in 15,40-41 that our evangelist identifies the names of some of them and specifies their function. The following scheme graphically shows the progressive role of those who accompanied Jesus:

A great multitude from Galilee followed (3,7b differ par. Mt + Lk).

And they were on the road, going up to Jerusalem, . . . and
they were amazed, and those who followed were
afraid (10,32 differ par. Mt + Lk).

And those who went before and those who followed cried out,
"Hosanna! . . . Blessed is the kingdom of our father David
that is coming! Hosanna in the highest!" (11,9-10).

There were also women looking on from afar, among whom were Mary
Magdalene, and Mary the mother of James the younger and of

Joses, and Salome, who, when he was in Galilee, followed
(ἠκολούθουν) him, and ministered (διηκόνουν) to
him; and also many other women who came up
with him to Jerusalem (15,40-41
differ par. Mt + Lk).

Women participate in Jesus' burial, they visit his tomb to
anoint his body, and they are the official emissaries of
the glad tidings of his resurrection (15,47-16,7).

Thus according to Mk 15,41 some women were following (note the imperfect ἠκολούθουν) Jesus from the beginning of his ministry and they were
ministering (again note the imperfect διηκόνουν) to him. Mk 15,47-16,7 gives
concrete examples of their service (διακονία) to him. Thus (διακονεῖν) is the
characteristic activity of the women followers of Jesus [7]. But, according to Mk,
Jesus came not to be served (διακονηθῆναι) but to serve (διακονῆσαι) [8]
and to give his life as a ransom for many (10,45); this is the epitome of
Jesus' ministry and death [9]. Again, according to Mk there is but one path to
true greatness: becoming διάκονος πάντων (9,35; 10,43). This is an unconditional demand to be Jesus' true apostles. This typically Christic and apostolic
quality is being predicated of the women followers of Jesus in 15,41 and of
Peter's mother-in-law in 1,31c. Therefore, the service rendered by Peter's
mother-in-law to Jesus and to his disciples is a paradigm for Christian
διακονία.

C. Mk 1,32-34 in the Frame of the Gospel

The following scheme shows a steady progression in the knowledge of
Jesus' identity by the demons and the force with which he commands them
to secrecy:

---

[7] Service of women followers of Jesus is complementary to the ministry of preaching,
exorcism and healing of Jesus and of his apostles.

[8] The ministry of the women followers is thus a personal participation in Jesus' own
ministry.

[9] Note the contrasting attitudes of the Twelve (cf. 9,33-37; 10,35-44; 14,45.50.54.66-
72) and of the women disciples (cf. 15,40-16,8).

Demons' Knowledge	*Jesus' Reaction*
An unclean spirit recognizes Jesus' true identity (1,24).	Jesus imposes silence (1,25).
They knew (ἤδεισαν) him (1,34d).	Jesus would not permit (οὐκ ἤφιεν) them to speak (1,34c).
They confess Jesus' identity (3,11).	He strictly ordered (ἐπετίμα) them not to make him known (3,12).

The summary statements on Jesus' healings indicate a clear progression in his healing power.

He *healed* many who were sick with various diseases (1,34).

He had healed many so that all who had diseases pressed upon him to *touch him* (3,10).

They laid the sick in the market places, and besought him that they might *touch even the fringe of his garment* (6,56).

D. Mk 1,35-39 in the Frame of the Gospel

1. Mk 1,32-39 and 3,9-15

1,32-39	*3,9-15*
The sick and the possessed flocking to Jesus (1,32-33)	The sick and the possessed flock to Jesus (3,9b.10b).
Jesus' healing of the sick (1,34a)	Jesus heals the sick (3,10a).
Jesus' casting out the demons (1,34b)	--------------------
Demons' knowledge of Jesus' identity (1,34d)	Demons confess Jesus' identity (3,11).
Jesus' prohibition (1,34c)	Jesus orders them to secrecy (3,12).
Jesus' withdrawal to a lonely place (1,35ab)	Jesus withdraws to the hills (3,13a).

Jesus' prayer (1,35c)   Jesus appoints the Twelve
                                         (3,13b-14a).

Jesus' mission (1,39):   Jesus sends the Twelve on
                                         a mission (3,14c.15a):
— preaching (1,39a)   — preaching (3,14c cf. 6,12a)
— casting out demons   — casting out demons
   (1,39b)   (3,15a cf. 6,7c.13a)

This scheme sheds light on 1,35-39 from two angles. First, the reason why Jesus withdrew to a lonely place is primarily not because the sick and the possessed flocked to him but because the demons knew his true identity (cf. 1,34c-35b; 3,12-13a). And secondly, Jesus' ministry of preaching and casting out demons (1,39) is paradigmatic for the ministry of preaching and exorcism of the Twelve (3,14c.15a; 6,7c.12a.13a).

2. Three Passages on Jesus' Prayer

In Mk the three passages on Jesus' prayer, occurring almost at the beginning, in the middle, and at the end of the Gospel, have common features:

	1,35	*6,46*	*14,32-39*
Time	in the early morning when it was still quite dark	evening	night
Place	a lonely place	hills	the garden of Gethsemane
Mode	alone	alone	alone
Preceding Event	healing and exorcism, demon's knowledge of Jesus' identity and his command to secrecy	multiplication of loaves	last supper, the defection of the disciples and the denial of Peter foretold
Following Event	ministry of preaching and exorcism throughout Galilee	walking on the water	arrest of Jesus
Content	----------------	----------------	Jesus' person and mission

Jesus prays all alone, in a place naturally conducive to prayer, and at a time appropriate to deep contemplation. In fact, communing with his Father is the only activity in which he is found all by himself. Jesus prays at critical moments of his mission. When people consider him merely as a miracle worker, he withdraws from them to immerse himself in prolonged prayer. And it is only after praying that he extends his ministry to the whole of Galilee. After the multiplication of the loaves, the crowds and the disciples fail to understand him (cf. 6,52). He then withdraws to pray. Finally, it is in the process of a repeated and prolonged prayer that he discerns his Father's will and submits himself to it (14,32-39). Thus Jesus' prayer is closely linked with his person and mission.

E. Mk 1,40-45 in the Plan of the Gospel

In the course of our interpretation of Mk 1,40-45 we have mentioned that healing the leper has features parallel to the miracles narrated in 5,21-24b.35-43; 7,31-37 and 8,22-26. It was also noted that these miracles are placed at the end of a series of miracles (1,21-45; 4,35-5,43; 6,31-7,37; 8,1-22). Here we schematically present these parallel elements:

	Leper cleansed (1,40-45)	Dead raised to life (5,21-24b. 35-43)	Deaf hear, dumb speak (7,31-37)	Blind see (8,22-26)
REQUEST	to be cleansed (1,40)	to touch his daughter (5,22-23)	to lay hands upon a deaf and dumb man (7,32)	to touch him (8,22)
PRIVACY	Nobody else present	puts out the crowd (5,39-40)	takes him aside from the multitude(7,33a)	takes him out of the village (8,23a)
RESPONSE — Action	touch	taking her by the hand	puts fingers into his ears, spits and touches his tongue	spits on his eyes, lays hands upon him. . . again lays hands on his eyes

— Word	"I will; be clean" (1,41)	"Little girl, I say to you, arise" (5,41)	"be opened" (7,33b-34)	asks him questions (8,23b-25c)
IMMEDIATE RESULT	leprosy left him (1,42)	she got up and walked (5,42a)	his ears were opened and tongue released, and he spoke plainly (7,35)	he saw everything clearly (8,25d)
COMMAND to SECRECY	"See that you say nothing to anyone" (1,43-44a).	no one should know this (5,43a).	tell no one (7,36a).	"Do not even enter the village" (8,26).

One should note that Mk places these four miracles as climactic events of chains of miracles in 1,21-45; 4,35-5,43; 6,31-7,37 and 8,1-26. Each series contains a question regarding Jesus' identity either directly posed (1,27; 4,41) or framed by such a question (6,14-15; 8,27-29). It is worth recalling in Mk that only these four miracles are enjoined by an injunction to secrecy (1,43-44a; 5,43a; 7,36a; 8,26).

In interpreting 1,40-45, we have affirmed that these four miracles have Messianic nuances. Therefore, while Mt in 11,5 has Jesus respond to John's question about his Messiahship by saying, "The blind receive their sight and the lame walk, lepers are cleansed and the deaf hear, and the dead are raised up", Mk gives the same answer but in a different way:

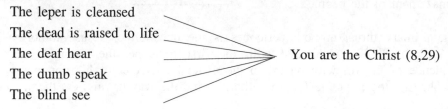

The leper is cleansed
The dead is raised to life
The deaf hear   You are the Christ (8,29)
The dumb speak
The blind see

In this scheme the healing of the leper is important inasmuch as it is the first miracle with Messianic overtones and it also sets the stage for the three other miracles with the same Messianic emphasis.

III. Mk 2,1-3,6 from the Gospel Perspective

A. Mk 2,1-12 in the Gospel Perspective

1. *Mk 2,1-12 and 11,15-18.27-33*

2,1-12	*11,15-18.27-33*
Coming to Capernaum and entering the house (2,1)	Coming to Jerusalem and entering the temple (11,15a)
Speaking the word (2,2b)	Cleansing the temple (11,15b-16)
Healing the paralytic (2,5)	Teaching (11,17)
--------------------	Astonishment at Jesus' teaching
The scribes question Jesus: — Why does this man speak thus? (2,7a) — Who can forgive sins but God alone? (2,7b)	The Sanhedrin question Jesus: — By what authority are you doing these things? (11,28a) — Who gave you this authority to do them? (11,28b)
Jesus' answer (2,8-11): — comment — counterquestion — final answer: Jesus has authority as the Son of Man	Jesus' answer (11,29-33): — comment — counterquestion — Jesus refuses to give the final answer concerning the source of his authority
Amazement of the people	--------------------

The primary thrust in both pericopes is the question of Jesus' authority (2,7.10; 11,28.33). Compared with the first pericope, the second gives evidence of growth with regard to the official character of his opponents (Sanhedrin, the Supreme Jewish authority) and the way he answers them.

2. *Mk 2,1-12 and 14,53.60-65*

2,1-12	*14,53.60-65*
Opponents: scribes (2,6)	Opponents: the chief priests, elders and scribes (14,53)

Charge: blasphemy (2,7)

Revelation: Jesus as the
Son of Man has authority
to forgive sins (2,10).

Charge: blasphemy (14,64a)

Revelation: Jesus is the Christ
. . . the Son of Man sitting at
the right hand of Power, and coming
with the clouds of heaven (14,61-62).

Response: Jesus' authority
verified in action (2,11-12a).

Response: Jesus is condemned as
deserving death (14,64b).

Reaction: amazement and
glorifying God (2,12cd)

Reaction: mockery and maltreatment
(14,65)

In the first pericope, Jesus' mysterious revelation is followed by a verifying action and the crowds' appreciative reaction to it whereas, in the second, Jesus' revelation is followed by the consensus of the Sanhedrin that he deserves death (14,64b). Furthermore, one must recall that from the narrative point of view, Jesus' trial before the Sanhedrin (14,55-65) constitutes the core of the Passion narrative (cf. Ch. II). The parallelism between 2,1-12 and 14,53.60-65 sheds light on how the conflict between Jesus and the Jewish authority led step by step to his crucifixion.

B. Mk 2,13-17 in the Plan of the Whole Gospel

Mk 2,15-17	*Mk 3,20-35*	*Mk 14,3-9*
Jesus in the house of Levi (2,15a)	Jesus' going home (3,20a)	Jesus in the house of Simon, the leper (14,3)
Meal in the company of tax collectors and sinners (2,16)	Crowds' gathering (3,20bc)	Meal in Simon's house and a woman's anointing Jesus (14,3)
Question: "Why does he eat with tax collectors and sinners?" (2,16)	Comment: Jesus is beside himself . . . possessed by Beelzebul (3,22).	Question: "Why was the ointment wasted?" (14,4-5)
Jesus' response: he came not to call the righteous but sinners (2,17).	Jesus' answer: he casts out demons by the power of the Holy Spirit (3,23-30); he states the nature of his true family (3,31-35).	Jesus' answer: she has anointed his body beforehand for burying (14,7-9).

A comparison of these three narratives indicates how the behaviour of Jesus becomes the subject of the critical scrutiny of the scribes (2,16; 3,22), of his friends (3,22) and of some others (14,4-6). In this way Mk depicts the growing opposition to Jesus from various quarters. Jesus defends himself by pointing out to his opponents the true nature of his person and mission.

C. Mk 2,23-28 in the Frame of the Gospel

2,23-28	*12,35-37*
Jesus' going through the grain field (2,23a)	Jesus' teaching in the temple (12,35a)
Pharisees' questioning Jesus about the violation of sabbath by his disciples (2,24)	Scribes' saying that the Christ is the son of David (12,35b)
Jesus' answer: — reference to scripture (2,25-26; cf. 1 Sam 21,1-6) — a saying on Jesus' identity (2,28)	Jesus' answer: — reference to scripture (12,36; cf. Ps 110,1) — a question on Jesus' identity (12,37a)

These parallel elements reveal the contrasting views of Jesus and his opponents. Such views led to the crucifixion of Jesus.

D. Mk 3,1-6 from Gospel the Perspective

The Pharisees with the Herodians held counsel how to destroy Jesus (3,6).

The chief priests and the scribes sought a way to destroy Jesus (11,18).

The chief priests and the scribes tried to arrest him (12,12).

The chief priests and the scribes were seeking how to arrest him
by stealth and kill him (14,2).

The chief priests, scribes and elders arrest him by stealth (14,43-50).

The chief priests, scribes and elders (presided over by the high priest)
condemned him as deserving death (14,55-65).

This scheme distinctively indicates the progression in two ways: (1) the
rank of Jesus' opponents gradually becomes more and more specific and at
the last phase Jesus is confronted by the highest Jewish authority; (2) there
is a consistent growth in the intensity of the actions against Jesus and at last
they condemn him to death.

IV. Concluding Observations

Our comparative study of Mk 1,14-3,6 in the frame of the whole Gospel
has shown that these twelve pericopes are not mere isolated literary units but
are literally and thematically related to one or more pericopes of Mk.
Although 1,14-3,6 is the first section of the first part of Mk where the progressive revelation of the mystery of Jesus' identity is the main thrust, our study
has shown that Mk 1,14-3,6, especially 2,1-3,6, is also related to the second
part (particularly chs. 11-12, 14-15) where the mystery of the suffering Son
of Man is the primary thrust.

CHAPTER EIGHT

THE PROGRAMMATIC CHARACTER OF MK 1,14-3,6

Based on the literary and thematic indices, we propose in the eighth and last chapter of our investigation that Mk 1,14-3,6 has a programmatic character in the context of the whole Gospel. This we will do in five stages: (1) Mk 1,14-3,6 in the frame of the whole Gospel; (2) vocabulary and themes in 1,14-3,6; (3) Jesus' ministry to the Jews in 1,14-3,6; (4) special features in the following chapters; and (5) conclusion.

I. Mk 1,14-3,6 in the Gospel Frame

We stated in Ch. II that Mk's main concern in the first part of his Gospel is the gradual revelation of the mystery of Jesus' identity. And in our interpretation of 1,14-3,6 it became clear that the basic question behind Jesus' ministry of preaching and teaching, prayer and controversies, call to discipleship and injunction to secrecy, and exorcisms and healings is his identity. In the course of our exegesis we also noticed that there are veiled allusions to Jesus' Passion in 1,14-3,6. We will now take a closer look at these references to the Passion to spell out their implications.

There are some specific terms that occur in 1,14-3,6 which have particular relevance for Jesus' Passion:

Occurrence in 1,14-3,6	*Later occurrences*
The absolute use of παραδιδόναι in 1,14.	Other occurrences of παραδιδόναι (absolute use) in the predictions of the Passion (9,31; 10,33) and in the Passion narrative proper (14,21.41).
Jesus' authority (ἐξουσία) in teaching (1,22.27) and in forgiving sins (2,10).	The chief priests, the scribes and the elders question Jesus' authority (11,28(bis).29.33) with a view to destroy him (cf. 11,18).

The scribes accuse Jesus of blasphemy (2,7).	The high priest in an official session of the Sanhedrin accuses Jesus of blasphemy (14,64).
The Pharisees seek a chance to accuse (a legal term) Jesus (3,2).	The chief priests accuse Jesus of many things before Pilate (15,3.4).
The Pharisees plot with the Herodians how to destroy Jesus (3,6).	Its gradual progression in chapters 11-12, 14-15 (particularly 11,18; 12,12; 14,1-2.43-65; 15,1-39).

One must duly consider the following points. First of all, the terms mentioned above occur in 1,14-3,6 and in the second part of Mk (8,27-16,8) but never in the second and the third sections (3,7-6,6a; 6,6b-8,30) of the first part. In the second place, they are found in those passages in the second part where Jesus' Passion is greatly stressed or important decisions to put him to death are being taken. And in the third place, κατηγορειν is a legal term (= to summon someone to court), συμβούλιον can have legal nuances, and βλασφημία is the criminal charge made against Jesus by the high priest in an official session of the Sanhedrin where they all condemned him to death.

Again, in the course of our exegesis of 1,14-3,6, we observed that some terms and phrases have allusions to the Passion. There is a possibility that on the basis of Mk 14,67 and 16,6 the appellation Ναζαρηνός in 1,24 may allude to the cross. As mentioned earlier, the clause, "the days will come when the bridegroom is taken away from them" (2,20a), contains an allusion to Jesus' Passion and Death, the first hint on Jesus' lips. By placing the Son of Man sayings pertaining to Jesus' earthly ministry in the literary unit 2,1-3,6, where there are many direct or indirect references to the Passion, does not Mk closely associate these two sayings with those on the Suffering and the Death of the Son of Man (8,31; 9,9.12.31; 10,33.45; 14,21.41) frequent in the second part? Among various opponents of Jesus the scribes constitute his archenemies [1]. By mentioning them thrice (1,22; 2,6.16) in the beginning

---

[1] The term γραμματεύς occurs relatively more frequently in Mk (Mt 22, Mk 21, Lk 14). Among the hostile groups, they figure the first (1,22) and the last (15,31). They accuse Jesus of blasphemy (2,7) and of possession by Beelzebul. They figure in key events in Jesus' Passion: the predictions of the Passion (8,31; 10,33), the plan to destroy him (11,18), arrest him (12,12), arrest and kill him (14,1), actual arrest (14,43), official involvement in his trial (14,53-65), handing over Jesus to Pilate (15,1) and mockery (15,31).

of Jesus' ministry [2], does not Mk give a hint about the strong opposition that Jesus will be facing from them in the second part of the Gospel?

Furthermore, we stated in Chs. II and VI that in 2,1-3,6 Jesus faces a steadily mounting opposition, working up to a climax in 3,6 where the Pharisees together with the Herodians plot to destroy him. This opposition to Jesus is not so consistent in the synoptic parallels. For, Mt has broken the continuity by placing 9,1-17 (= Mk 2,1-22) in the section of ten miracles (8,1-9,37) and 12,1-14 (= Mk 2,23-3,6) in the section on the incredulity and hostility of the Jews (11,1-12,50). Although Lk follows the Marcan sequence, the climax of the opposition in 3,6 is less intense in Lk 6,11. And, in the second place, even though Jesus faces opposition from the Jews in his ministry at Jerusalem (11,15-12,34), it is neither steady nor continuous (cf. 11,20-26). Moreover, in it Jesus always emerges victorious. In fact, the series of the controversies in 11,15-12,34, unlike those in 2,1-3,6, concludes on a positive note for Jesus: "And after that no one dared to ask him any question" (12,34).

Finally, we have established in Ch. VI, that the logical connection between 2,24 and 3,2 is probably the redactional work of Mk and the link between 3,2 and 3,6 obviously comes from Mk. The progression of these three passages is schematically shown below:

The Pharisees warn Jesus (2,24).

↓

They were watching him (3,2)
and obtained evidence (3,5).

↓

They decide to destroy Jesus (3,6).

This three step progression corresponds to the requirements of the Jewish law to accuse someone of capital crime and bring him to judgment: demonstrable warning before witnesses, willful violation of the law and judgment [3].

In conclusion, therefore, we hold that the primary thrust of Mk 1,14-3,6, just as the second and the third sections (3,7-6,6a; 6,6b-8,30) of the first

---

[2] In 3,7-8,30 they are mentioned only thrice (3,22; 7,1.5) but in the second part 16 times.

[3] Cf. *Sanhedrin*, 5,1; 8,4; 12,8-9, etc.

part, is the progressive revelation of the mystery of Jesus' identity. However, in contrast to 3,7-6,6a and 6,6b-8,30 [4] in 1,14-3,6 there are literary and thematic evidences alluding to Jesus' Passion, the main thrust of the second part of Mk.

II. Vocabulary and Themes in Mk 1,14-3,6

Mk 1,14-3,6 introduces the reader or listener to a number of themes dear to our evangelist. Jesus comes to Galilee primarily as a herald: all the occurrences of κηρύσσειν predicated of Jesus are found in our section (1,14.38.39). The object of Jesus' preaching, τὸ εὐαγγέλιον, already mentioned in the title (1,1), is further specified in 1,14-15. The main content of the gospel is the kingdom of God which occurs in the very first utterance of Jesus (1,15). The whole of verse 15, both in content and in tone, orients the reader to what follows. Galilee, the privileged place where Jesus himself proclaimed the gospel, occurs in 1,14.28.39. Again, the call of the disciples (1,16-20; 2,14) and their close association with Jesus (cf. 1,21.29; 2,15-16.18.23-24) are dear to our evangelist. It is also characteristic of Mk that he depicts Jesus as a teacher, a theme found from the beginning of Jesus' ministry (1,21-22.27; 2,2.13). The theme, Messianic secret, more emphasized by Mk than by Mt and Lk and initiated in 1,25, is further highlighted in 1,34 and 1,44-45. Exorcisms (1,23-26.34), healings (1,29-31.34.40-44; 2,3-5.10-11; 3,1-5) and the amazement of the audience (1,27-28; 2,12) are also dear to Mk.

Furthermore, as stated in Chs. V and VI, Jesus' ministry in this section is characterized by an authority that is extraordinary and unique (cf. 1,22.27; 2,7.28) and a sense of his mission that is conscious and deliberate (1,38; 2,17). As mentioned in Chs. II, V and VI, this section marks a contrast between appreciation and acceptance of Jesus by the common people, although their knowledge of him continues to remain incomplete and inadequate, and Jesus faces a steadily mounting opposition from the Jewish authorities. These contrasting attitudes emphasized in 1,14-3,6 continue in varying degrees in the rest of Jesus' ministry. In the Passion narrative, however, they are wooed and won over by the Jewish authorities (cf. 15,11-15). Finally, the theology of the cross, a theme particularly stressed by Mk, is initiated in 1,14-3,6.

---

[4] Mk 6,14-29 primarily and per se deals with John the Baptist's beheading. It concerns Jesus only insofar as there is parallelism between John's fate and that of Jesus.

In brief, Mk 1,14-3,6 is characterized by typically Marcan vocabularies and themes. It is, then, logical to ask: Why does Mk intensify his characteristic vocabulary and themes in 1,14-3,6?

III. Jesus' Ministry to the Jews in 1,14-3,6

It is evident that in 1,14-3,6 Jesus devotes his ministry to Jews. The nouns συναγωγή (1,21.23.29.39; 3,1) and σάββατον (1,21; 2,23.24.27(bis). 28; 3,2.4) occur predominantly in this section. Later they are found only once again in the course of Jesus' ministry, in his own town (6,2) where he faces disbelief from his own countrymen (cf. 6,3-6a). The adversaries whom Jesus encounters in this section are either the scribes (2,6.16) or the Pharisees (2,18.24; 3,2.6). Finally, the controversies in 2,1-3,6 are typically of Jewish character and the climax of these controversies marks a definitive break between Jesus and official Judaism. Negatively, in 1,14-3,6 Mk does not give any hint about Jesus' ministry to the Gentiles.

IV. Special Features in the Following Chapters

The definitive break with the Jewish leaders, expressed by the withdrawal (3,7) from the scene of opposition, marks a turning point in Jesus' ministry. His ministry now develops in two new directions: on the one hand, he begins to intensify his relationship with his disciples whereby a new community is born and, on the other, he extends his ministry to the Gentiles too.

As mentioned in Ch. II, the theme of the formation of a new community and its various dimensions are found in diverse pericopes of 3,7-16,8. The decisive event, however, is the institution of the Twelve, a new and unique act. The expression 'the Twelve' symbolizes the twelve tribes of Israel, the whole of Israel, but in the Marcan redaction 'the Twelve' transcends the boundaries of Israel [5]. They participate in Jesus' person by means of intimate association with him and are privileged to receive private instructions on the mystery of his person and its suffering character. They are sent out as his ambassadors to carry on his own mission. People gather around them and the new community grows both intensively and extensively.

---

[5] K. STOCK, *Boten*, 41: "Nach der Darstellung des Mk ist die 12-Gruppe von Anfang an so ausgerichtet, daß sie nicht nur Israel bei Jesus vergegenwärtigt und daß sie nicht nur für Israel eine Sendung hat; sie hat eine unbegrenzte Sendung und sie vertritt alle".

From 3,8 onwards Mk shows an orientation to the Gentiles. Jesus' withdrawal from the scene of opposition and plotting to another scene — the sea — is marked by the presence of innumerable crowds. One should note the order in which the names of the places are mentioned. It begins with the people of Israel, continues with the marginal groups that are also religiously suspect (Idumea and beyond Jordan), and concludes with the pagan territory (Tyre and Sidon). In the subsequent chapters Jesus extends his ministry to the Gentile territory (5,1-20; 7,24-30). As the narrative progresses the emphasis on universalism becomes more and more prominent. The rights of the Gentiles should be respected (11,17) and the barrier of separation is rent asunder (15,38). Jesus gives his life as a ransom for many (10,45) and he establishes a new covenant with a universal orientation (14,24). And finally, the mission of the Church, the preaching of the Gospel, embraces the Gentiles too (13,10; 14,9).

V. Conclusion

Why does Mk introduce the reader in 1,14-3,6 to a number of themes which are further developed in the course of the Gospel? In contrast to 3,7-8,30, why does 1,14-3,6 not only develop the theme of the mystery of Jesus' person (the predominant theme of the first part) but also allude to Jesus' Passion (the prime concern of the second part) by direct references and indirect allusions? Why is the ministry in 1,14-3,6 exclusively devoted to the Jews whereas from 3,7 onwards there is an orientation to the Gentiles? Why is the definite break between Jesus and the Jewish leaders in 3,6 immediately followed by the birth of a new community, the true family of Jesus? The answers to all of these questions converge on one point — *Mk 1,14-3,6 has a programmatic character.*

CONCLUSION

We started our investigation by asking pertinent questions regarding Mk 1,14-3,6 from three angles: organization of the text, tradition and redaction, and the role of this section in Mk. In the course of our study we have answered these questions. Now we bring its results to a systematic conclusion.

1. The first question we asked was about the extent of the introduction to Mk. After critically evaluating the arguments of those who hold that the introduction consists of 1,1-15, we showed that the introduction actually consists of 1,1-13. We then proceeded to the next question regarding the extent of the first section. We critically examined the view of those who hold that the first section begins with 1,16-20 and concludes with 3,7-12 and found it inadequate. We argued that both literary and thematic indicators support the opinion that the first section begins with 1,14-15 and ends at 3,5-6.

The next task was to situate 1,14-3,6 in the frame of Mk. Having critically assessed the contrasting opinions on the structure of Mk, on the bases of literary and theological indices we affirmed that the structure proposed by Léon-Dufour, de la Potterie, etc. correspond to the texture of the text and the theological intention of the evangelist. According to this structure 1,14-3,6 constitutes the first section of the first part of Mk.

Having located 1,14-3,6 in the structural frame of Mk, in the third chapter we focused attention on its internal cohesion and literary division. We found that by means of key words, basic themes, and geographical and scenic connections various pericopes in 1,14-3,6 are closely linked. Nevertheless, one can discover three literary units in 1,14-3,6: 1,14-20; 1,21-45; 2,1-3,6. The second and the third literary units have a concentric structure. In the course of the literary analysis we clarified the problems dealing with the organization of specific pericopes: 1,21-28; 1,35-39; 2,1-12; 2,13-17, etc.

2. The second problem in the introduction was the distinction between tradition and redaction in 1,14-3,6. In our indepth and precise distinction between tradition and redaction we established that, contrary to the opinion of a number of exegetes, there is considerable redactional activity of the evangelist in 1,21-34(39). In 2,1-3,6 too, Marcan redaction is conspicuous, particularly in 2,1-12; 2,13-17; and 3,1-6.

3. The third problem concerned the function of 1,14-3,6 in Mk. We noted that in addition to the theme of the mystery of Jesus' Messiahship, a theme common with the second and third sections (3,7-6,6a; 6,6b-8,30) of the first part, 1,14-3,6 also contains direct references and indirect allusions to Jesus' Passion, the predominant thrust of the second part. This enabled us to affirm that 1,14-3,6 has a programmatic character.

BIBLIOGRAPHY

I. Texts

ALAND, K. et al. (eds.), *The Greek New Testament*, Münster ³1975.
HUCK, A. and GREEVEN, H., *Synopsis of the First Three Gospels*, Tübingen ¹³1981.
KITTEL, R. (ed.), *Biblia Hebraica*, Stuttgart ¹⁵1968.
MERK, A. (ed.), *Novum Testamentum Graece et Latine*, Romae ⁹1964.
NESTLE, E. and ALAND, K. (eds.), *Novum Testamentum Graece*, Stuttgart ²⁶1979.
RAHLFS, A. (ed.), *Septuaginta*, Stuttgart ⁹1971.
SODEN, H. F. VON (ed.), *Die Schriften des Neuen Testaments*, Göttingen 1913.
TASKER, R. V. G. (ed.), *The Greek New Testament*, Oxford 1964.
TISCHENDORF, C. (ed.), *Novum Testamentum Graece*, Editio octava critica major, I, (Bib VI 34 5), Lipsiae 1869.
VOGELS, H. J. (ed.), *Novum Testamentum Graece et Latine*, Friburghi Brisgoviae 1949.
WESTCOTT, F. and HORT, J. A. (eds.), *The New Testament in the Original Greek*, New York 1963.

II. Commentaries on Mark

ANDERSON, H., *The Gospel of Mark* (New Century Bible), London 1976.
BEDA VENERABILIS, *In Marci Evangelium Expositio*, (ed. D. Hurst; CChrSL 120), Turnholti 1960, 427-648; = Migne PL 92, 131-302.
BELO, F., *Lecture matérialiste de l'évangile de Marc*, Paris ²1975.
BOLKESTEIN, M. H., *Het verborgen rijk. Het evangelie naar Marcus*, Nijkerk 1954.
BRANSCOMB, B. H., *The Gospel of Mark* (The Moffat New Testament Commentary 2), London ⁷1964.
CARRINGTON, P., *According to Mark. A Running Commentary on the Oldest Gospel*, Cambridge 1960.
CRANFIELD, C. E. B., *The Gospel according to St. Mark* (Cambridge Greek Testament Commentary), Cambridge ²1963.
DEHN, G., *Der Gottessohn. Eine Einführung in das Evangelium des Markus*, Hamburg ⁶1953.
DELORME, J., *Lecture de l'Évangile selon Saint Marc* (Cahiers Évangile I/2), Paris 1972.
DERRETT, J. D. M., *The Making of Mark. The Scriptural Bases of the Earliest Gospel*, Warwickshire 1985.

ERNST, J., *Das Evangelium nach Markus* (RNT 2), Regensburg 1981.

GNILKA, J., *Das Evangelium nach Markus* (EKK II/1-2), Zürich - Köln - Neukirchen-Vluyn 1978-1979.

GOULD, E. P., *A Critical and Exegetical Commentary on the Gospel according to St. Mark*, Edinburgh ¹¹1975.

GRANT, F. C., *The Gospel according to St. Mark* (IB 7), New York 1951.

GRUNDMANN, W., *Das Evangelium nach Markus* (THKNT 2), Berlin ⁷1977.

HAENCHEN, E., *Der Weg Jesu. Eine Erklärung des Markus-Evangeliums und der kanonischen Parallelen*, Berlin 1966.

HARRINGTON, W., *Mark* (New Testament Message 4), Dublin 1979.

HAUCK, F., *Das Evangelium des Markus* (THNT 2), Leipzig 1931.

HERMANN, I., *Das Markusevangelium* I-II, Düsseldorf 1965, 1967.

HIERONYMUS, *Opera II. Tractatus sive homiliae in Psalmos, in Marci Evangelium, aliaque varia argumenta* (ed. G. Morin; CChrSL 78), Turnholti ²1968, 451-500.

HUBY, J., *L'Évangile selon Saint Marc*, Paris ³1961.

JOHNSON, S. E., *A Commentary on the Gospel according to St. Mark* (Black's New Testament Commentaries), London ³1977.

KLOSTERMANN, E., *Das Markusevangelium* (HNT 3), Tübingen ⁴1950.

KNABENBAUER, J., *Evangelium secundum S. Marcum*, Parisiis 1894.

LAGRANGE, M.-J., *Évangile selon Saint Marc*, Paris ⁴1929.

LANE, W. L., *The Gospel according to Mark*, Grand Rapids 1974.

LOHMEYER, E., *Das Evangelium des Markus*, Göttingen ¹⁷1967.

LOISY, A., *L'Évangile selon Marc*, Paris 1912.

MALLY, E. J., "The Gospel according to Mark", in: *JBC* II (eds. R. E. Brown et al.), Bangalore 1972, 21-61.

NINEHAM, D. E., *The Gospel of St Mark* (The Pelican New Testament Commentaries), Harmondsworth 1976 = ²1969.

PESCH, R., *Das Markusevangelium* (HTKNT II/1-2), Freiburg - Basel - Wien ³1980, ²1980.

RADERMAKERS, J., *La bonne nouvelle de Jésus selon saint Marc* (I. Texte, II. Lecture continue), Bruxelles 1974 = *Lettura pastorale del vangelo di Marco* (trans. G. Bernabei), Bologna ²1981.

RAWLINSON, A. E. J., *The Gospel according to St. Mark* (West Minister Commentaries), London ⁷1949.

SANNER, A. E., *Mark* (Beacon Bible Expositions 2), Kansas City 1978.

SCHMID, J., *Das Evangelium nach Markus* (RNT 2), Regensburg ⁴1958.

SCHMITHALS, W., *Das Evangelium nach Markus* (ÖTKNT 2/1-2), Gütersloh - Würzburg 1979.

SCHNACKENBURG, R., *Das Evangelium nach Markus* (Geistliche Schriftlesung II/1-2), Düsseldorf 1966, 1971.

SCHNIEWIND, J., *Das Evangelium nach Markus*, Göttingen 1952.

SCHWEIZER, E., *Das Evangelium nach Markus* (NTD 1), Göttingen ⁶1983.

SISTI, A., *Marco* (Nuovissima versione della Bibbia 34), Roma ³1980.

STANDAERT, B., *L'évangile selon Marc. Commentaire* (lire la Bible 61), Paris 1983.

SWETE, H. B., *The Gospel according to St Mark. The Greek Text with Introduction, Notes and Indices*, London ²1908.
TAYLOR, V., *The Gospel according to St. Mark*, London ²1966.
URICCHIO, F. M. and STANO G. M., *Vangelo secondo san Marco* (La Sacra Bibbia), Roma - Torino 1966.
WELLHAUSEN, J., *Das Evangelium Marci*, Berlin ²1909.
WOHLENBERG, G., *Das Evangelium des Markus*, Leipzig ³1930.

III. Other Literature

ABRAHAMS, I., *Studies in Pharisaism and the Gospels*, Cambridge 1917 = New York 1967.
ACHTEMEIER, P. J., "Person and Deed. Jesus and the Storm-Tossed Sea", *Int* 16 (1962) 169-176.
AERTS, T., *À la suite de Jésus. Le verbe ἀκολουθεῖν dans la tradition synoptique* (ALBO IV/37), Paris 1967.
AGNEW, F. "Vocatio primorum discipulorum in traditione synoptica", *VD* 46 (1968) 129-147.
AICHINGER, H., "Quellenkritische Untersuchung der Perikope vom Ährenraufen am Sabbat Mk 2,23-28 Par.", in: *Jesus in der Verkündigung der Kirche* (Hrsg. A Fuchs; SNTU 1) 1976, 110-153.
ALAND, K., *Synopsis Quattuor Evangeliorum*, Stuttgart ⁸1973.
——, *Vollständige Konkordanz zum griechischen Neuen Testament*, Berlin - New York 1983.
ALBERTZ, M., *Die synoptischen Streitgespräche. Ein Beitrag zur Formgeschichte des Urchristentums*, Berlin 1921.
AMBROZIC, A. M., "New Teaching with Power (Mk 1,27)", in: *Word and Spirit*, (FS. D. M. Stanley; ed. J. Plevnik) Willowdale, Ontario 1975, 113-149.
——, *The Hidden Kingdom. A Redaction-Critical Study of the References to the Kingdom of God in Mark's Gospel* (CBQMS 2), Washington 1972.
ANNEN, F., *Heil für die Heiden. Zur Bedeutung und Geschichte der Tradition vom besessenen Gerasaner* (Mk 5,1-20 parr) (FTS 20), Frankfurt am Main 1976.
ARENS, E., *The ΗΛΘΟΝ-Sayings in the Synoptic Tradition: A Historico-Critical Investigation* (OBO 10), Fribourg - Göttingen 1976.
ARGYLE, A. W., "The Meaning of ἐξουσία in Mark 1,22.27", *ExpTim* 80 (1969) 343.
ATKINSON, C. W., "The New Patch on an Old Garment", *ExpTim* 30 (1918-19) 233-234.
AUERBACH, E., *Mimesis. Dargestellte Wirklichkeit in der abendländischen Literatur*, Bern 1946.
BAARLINK, H., *Anfängliches Evangelium. Ein Beitrag zur nährenen Bestimmung der theologischen Motive im Markusevangelium*, Kampen 1977.
BACHER, W., *Die exegetische Terminologie der jüdischen Traditionliteratur*, Leipzig 1905.

BARRETT, C. K., *The Gospel according to St John*, London ²1978.

BARTINA, S.,"La red esparavel del Evangelio (Mt 4,18; Mc 1,15)", *EstB* 19 (1960) 215-227.

BARTSCH, H.-W., "Zur Problematik eines Monopoltextes des Neuen Testaments. Das Beispiel Markus 2, Vers 15 und 16", *TLZ* 105 (1980) 91-96.

BAUER, W., *A Greek-English Lexicon of the New Testament and Other Early Christian Literature* (trans. W. F. Arndt and F. W. Gingrich), London 1957.

BAUERNFEIND, O., *Die Worte der Dämonen im Markusevagelium* (BWANT 44), Stuttgart 1927.

BEARE, W., "The Sabbath was Made for Man", *JBL* 79 (1960) 130-136.

BECKER, J., *Das Heil Gottes. Heils- und Sündenbegriffe in den Qumrantexten und im Neuen Testament* (SUNT 3), Göttingen 1964.

BEHM, J. and WÜRTHWEIN, E. "Μετανοέω, μετάνοια", *TDNT* IV, 975-980.

——, "Καινός, καινότης", *TDNT* III, 447-454.

——, "Νεός", *TDNT* IV, 896-901.

BELO, F., "Lecture matérialiste de l'évangile de Marc et de la grande séquence des pains", *FV* 77 (1978) 19-33.

BENNETT, W. J., "The Herodians of Mark's Gospel", *NT* 17 (1975) 9-14.

BENOIT, P., "Les épis arrachés (Mt 12,1-8 et par.)", *SBF* 13 (1962-63) 76-92.

BENOIT, P. and BOISMARD, M.-E., *Synopse des quatre évangiles* II, Paris 1980.

BERKEY, R. F., "ΕΓΓΙΖΕΙΝ, ΦΘΑΝΕΙΝ, and Realized Eschatology", *JBL* 82 (1963) 177-187.

BEST, E., "Mark II.1-12", *BibTh* 3 (1953) 41-46.

BETZ, O., *What Do We Know about Jesus?* (trans. M. Kohl), London 1968.

BEVAN, E., "Note on Mark 1,41 and John 11,33.38", *JTS* 33 (1932) 186-188.

BEYER, H. W., "Βλασφημέω, βλασφημία", *TDNT* I, 621-625.

BEYER, K., *Semitische Syntax im Neuen Testament* (SUNT 1), Göttingen 1962.

BIGUZZI, G., *"Io distruggerò questo tempio". Il tempio e il giudaismo nel vangelo di Marco*, Roma 1987.

BILEZIKIAN, G. G., *The Liberated Gospel. A Comparison of the Gospel of Mark and Greek Tragedy*, Grand Rapids 1977.

BLACK, M., "The Kingdom of God Has Come", *ExpTim* 63 (1951-52) 289-290.

BLASS, F. and DEBRUNNER, A., *A Greek Grammar of the New Testament and Other Early Christian Literature* (trans. R. W. Funk), London 1961.

BLATHERWICK, D., "The Markan Silhouette?", *NTS* 17 (1970-71) 184-192.

BLENKER, A., "Tilgivelse i Jesu forkyndelse (Mk 2,1-12)", *DTT* 34 (1971) 105-109.

BÖCHER, O., *Christus Exorcista. Dämonismus und Taufe im Neuen Testament* (BWANT 96), Stuttgart 1972.

BOISMARD, M.-E., "La guérison du lépreux (Mc 1,40-45 et par.)", *Salm* 28 (1981) 283-291.

BOOBYER, G. H., "Galilee and Galileans in St. Mark's Gospel", *BJRL* 35 (1953) 334-348.

——, "Mark II.10a and the Interpretation of the Healing of the Paralytic", *HTR* 47 (1954) 115-120.

BORNHAUSER, K., "Zur Perikope vom Bruch des Sabbats", *NKZ* 33 (1922) 325-334.

BOUMAN, W. R., "Reflections on Mark from a Confessional Theologian", *CurTM* 2 (1975) 326-331.

BOVER, J. M., "Critica textuelle de Mc 1,41", *EE* 23 (1944) 355-357.

——, "La parabola del remicendo (Mt. 9,15; Mc. 2,21; Lc. 5,36)", *StAns* 27 (1951) 327-339.

BRANSCOMB, H., "Mark 2,5: Son, Thy Sins Are Forgiven", *JBL* 53 (1934) 53-60.

BRAUMANN, G., "An jenem Tag (Mk 2,20)", *NT* 6 (1963) 264-267.

BRAUN, H., "Gott, die Eröffnung des Lebens für die Nonkonformisten. Erwägungen zu Markus 2, 15-17", in: *Festschrift für E. Fuchs* (Hrsg. G. Ebeling et al.), Tübingen 1973, 97-101.

——, "Erwägungen zu Markus 2,23-28 Par.", in: *Entscheidung und Solidarität* (FS. J. Harder), Wuppertal 1973, 53-56.

BRIERE, J., "Jésus agit par ses disciples. Mc 1,16-20", *ASeign* 34 (1973) 32-46.

BRONGERS, H. A., "Enkele opmerkingen over het verband tussen zonde en ziekte enerzijds en vergeving en genezing anderzijds in het Oude Testament", *NTT* 6 (1952) 129-142.

BRUN, L., "Die Berufung der ersten Jünger Jesu in der evangelischen Tradition", *SO* 11 (1932) 35-54.

BUDESHEIM, T. L., "Jesus and the Disciples in Conflict with Judaism", *ZNW* 62 (1971) 190-209.

BUETUBELA, B., *Jean-Baptiste dans l'Évangile de Marc. Analyse littéraire et interprétation christologique* (Dissertation PBI), Rome 1983 (unpublished).

BULTMANN, R., *Die Geschichte der synoptischen Tradition*, Göttingen ⁷1967.

——, *The History of the Synoptic Tradition* (trans. J. Marsch), Oxford 1972.

BURKILL, T. A., "The Injunctions to Silence in St. Mark's Gospel", *ThZ* 12 (1956) 585-604.

——, "Strain on the Secret: An Examination of Mark 11,1-13,37", *ZNW* 51 (1960) 31-46.

——, *Mysterious Revelation. An Examination of the Philosophy of St. Mark's Gospel*, Ithaca 1963.

——, "Mark 3,7-12 and the Alleged Dualism in the Evangelist's Miracle Material", *JBL* 87 (1968) 409-417.

——, "Should Wedding Guests Fast? A Consideration of Mark 2,18-20", in: *New Light on the Earliest Gospel*, London 1972, 39-47.

BURKITT, F. C., "Levi, Son of Alphaeus", *JTS* 28 (1926-27) 273-274.

BURROWS, M. et al., (eds.), *The Dead Sea Scrolls of St. Mark's Monastery* I-II, New Haven 1950-51.

BUTTERWORTH, R., "The Composition of Mark 1-12", *HeyJ* 13 (1972) 5-26.

BUTTERWORTH, R. and SMITH, M., *A Reading of Mark's Gospel*, London 1982.

CABANISS, A., "A Fresh Exegesis of Mark 2,1-12", *Int* 11 (1957) 324-327.

CANGH, J.-M. VAN, "La Galilée dans l'Évangile de Marc: un lieu théologique?", *RB* 79 (1972) 59-76.

CALLOUD, J., "Towards a Structural Analysis of the Gospel of Mark", *Semeia* 16 (1979) 133-165.

CAMPBELL, J. Y., "The Kingdom of God Has Come", *ExpTim* 48 (1936-37) 91-94.

CAMPONOVO, O., *Königtum, Königsherrschaft und Reich Gottes in den Frühjüdischen Schriften*, (OBO 58) Freiburg - Göttingen 1984.

CANCIK, H. (ed.), *Markus-Philologie. Historische, literargeschichtliche und stilitische Untersuchungen zum zweiten Evangelium* (WUNT 33), Tübingen 1984.

CARMIGNAC, J. et al., *Les Textes de Qumran: traduits et annotés* I-II, Paris 1961, 1963.

CASEY, P. M., "Culture and History: The Plucking of the Grain (Mark 2.23-28)", *NTS* 34 (1988) 1-23.

CAVE. C. H., "The Leper: Mark 1,40-45", *NTS* 25 (1978-79) 245-250.

CERFAUX, L., *La voix vivante de l'évangile au début de l'église*, Tournai - Paris ²1958.

CEROKE, C. P., "Is Mk 2,10 a Saying of Jesus?", *CBQ* 22 (1960) 369-390.

CHARLES, R. H. (ed.), *The Apocrypha and Pseudoepigrapha of the Old Testament* I-II, Oxford 1913.

CHILTON, B. D., *God in Strength. Jesus' Announcement of the Kingdom*, Freistadt 1979.

CLARK, K. W., "Realized Eschatology", *JBL* 59 (1940) 367-383.

COHN-SHERBOK, D. M., "An Analysis of Jesus' Arguments concerning the Plucking of Grain on the Sabbath", *JSNT* 2 (1979) 31-41.

COLPE, C., "ὁ υἱὸς τοῦ ἀνθρώπου", *TDNT* VIII, 400-477.

CONZELMANN, H., *Grundriß der Theologie des Neuen Testaments*, München 1967.

CONZELMANN, H. and LINDEMANN, A., *Arbeitsbuch zum Neuen Testament*, Tübingen ²1976.

COOK, M. J., *Mark's Treatment of the Jewish Leaders* (SupplNT 51), Leiden 1978.

CREMER, F. G., *Die Fastenansage Jesu* (BBB 23), Bonn 1965.

——, "'Die Söhne des Brautgemachs' (Mk 2,19 Parr) in der griechischen und lateinischen Schrifterklärung", *BZ* 11 (1967) 246-253.

CULLMANN, O., *The Christology of the New Testament* (trans. S. C. Guthrie and C. A. M. Hall), London ²1963.

——, *Christ and Time: The Primitive Conception of Time and History* (trans. F. V. Filson), London 1967.

CZAJKOWSKI, M., *De paralytico a Jesu absoluto et sanato. Analysis litteraria et nuntius theologicus Marci 2,1-12 par.*, Wratislaviae 1976.

DANIEL, C., "Les 'Hérodiens' du Nouveau Testament sont-ils des Esséniens?" *RevQ* 6 (1967) 31-53.

——, "Nouveaux arguments en faveur de l'identification des Hérodiens et des Esséniens", *RevQ* 7 (1970) 397-402.

DANKER, F. W., "Mark 1:45 and the Secrecy Motif", *CTM* 37 (1966) 492-499.

DAUBE, D., "'Εξουσία in Mark 1,22 and 27", *JTS* 39 (1938) 45-59.

——, *The New Testament and Rabbinic Judaism*, London 1965.

——, "Responsibilities of Master and Disciples in the Gospels", *NTS* 19 (1972-73) 1-15.

DAUTZENBERG, G., "Die Zeit des Evangeliums. Mk 1,1-15 und die Konzeption des Markusevangeliums", *BZ* 21 (1977) 219-234; 22 (1978) 76-91.

DE LA CALLE, F., *Situación al servicio del Kerigma. Cuadro geográfico del Evangelio de Marcos*, Salamanca - Madrid 1975.

De Maat, P., "Hoe krijgt Mc 2,15-17 betekenis? Analyse van de narratieve syntaxis van het oppervlakte-niveau", *Bijdr* 43 (1983) 194-206.

Delling, G., "Καιρός, ἄκαιρος", *TDNT* III, 455-464.

——, "Πλήρης, πληρόω, πλήρωμα", *TDNT* VI, 283-311.

Derett, J. D. M., "Contributions to the Study of the Gerasene Demoniac (Mc 5,1-20)", *JSNT* 3 (1979) 2-17.

——, "'Ησαν γὰρ ἁλιεῖς (Mk 1,16). Jesus' Fishermen and the Parable of the Net", *NT* 22 (1980) 108-137.

——, "Christ and the Power of Choice (Mark 3,1-6)", *Bib* 65 (1984) 168-188.

Dewey, J., "The Literary Structure of the Controversy Stories in Mark 2,1-3,6", *JBL* 92 (1973) 394-401.

——, *Markan Public Debate: Literary Technique, Concentric Structure, and Theology in Mark 2:1-3:6* (SBLDS 48), Chico 1980.

Dibelius, M., *From Tradition to Gospel* (trans. B. L. Woolf), London 1971.

Dideberg, D. and Mourlon Beernaert, P., "Jésus vint en Galilee. Essai sur la structure de Marc 1,21-45", *NRT* 98 (1976) 306-323.

Dietzfelbinger, O. L., "Vom Sinn der Sabbatheilungen Jesu", *EvTh* 38 (1978) 281-298.

Diez Macho, A., "Jesús 'Ho Nazoraios'", in: *Quaere Paulum* (FS. L. Turrado), Salamanca 1981, 9-26.

Dodd, C. H., "The Kingdom of God Has Come", *ExpTim* 48 (1936-37) 138-142.

——, *The Parables of the Kingdom*, London ³1961.

Donahue, J. R., "Tax Collectors and Sinners. An Attempt at Identification", *CBQ* 33 (1971) 39-61.

——, *Are You the Christ? The Trial Narrative in the Gospel of Mark* (SBLDS 10), Missoula 1973.

Dormeyer, D., "Narrative Analyse von Mk 2,1-12", *LingBib* 31 (1974) 68-88.

——, "Die Kompositionsmetapher 'Evangelium Jesu Christi, des Sohnes Gottes' Mk 1.1. Ihre theologische und literarische Aufgabe in der Jesus-Biographie des Markus", *NTS* 33 (1987) 452-468.

Doudna, J. C., *The Greek of the Gospel of Mark*, Philadelphia 1961.

Doughty, D. J., "The Authority of the Son of Man (Mark 2,1-3,6)", *ZNW* 74 (1983) 161-181.

Dschulnigg, P., *Sprache, Redaktion und Intention des Markus-Evangeliums* (SBB 11), Stuttgart 1984.

Dunkerley, R., "The Bridegroom Passage", *ExpTim* 64 (1952-53) 303-304.

Dunn, J. D. G., "Mark 2,1-3,6: A Bridge between Jesus and Paul on the Question of the Law", *NTS* 30 (1984) 395-415.

Duplacy, J., "Mc 2,10. Note de syntaxe", in: *Mélanges A. Robert*, Paris 1957, 420-427.

Dupont, J., "Vin vieux, vin nouveaux", *CBQ* 15 (1953) 268-304.

——, "Il Cieco di Gerico riacquista la vista e segue Gesù (Mc 10,46-52)", in: *Seguimi!* (ParSpV II), Roma 1980, 105-123.

EGGER, W., "Die Verborgenheit Jesu in Mk 3,7-12", *Bib* 50 (1969) 466-490.
——, *Frohbotschaft und Lehre. Die Sammelberichte des Wirkens Jesu im Markus-evangelium* (FTS 19), Frankfurt am Main 1976.
EISLER, R., *Weltenmantel und Himmelszelt*, München 1910.
ELLIOTT, J. K., "The Conclusion of the Pericope of the Healing of the Leper and Mark 1,45", *JTS* 22 (1971) 153-157.
——, "Is ὁ ἐξελθών a Title for Jesus in Mark 1,45?", *JTS* 27 (1976) 402-405.
——, "The Healing of the Leper in the Synoptic Parallels", *ThZ* 34 (1978) 175-176.
ELLIS, P. F., "Patterns and Structures in Mark's Gospel", in: *Biblical Studies in Contemporary Thought* (ed. M. Ward), Somerville 1975, 88-103.
FABRIS, R., *Matteo*, Roma 1982.
FARMER, W. R., "Who Are the 'Tax Collectors and Sinners' in the Synoptic Tradition?", in: *From Faith to Faith* (FS. D. G. Miller; ed. D. Y. Hadidian), Pittsburgh 1979, 167-174.
FARRER, A. M., *A Study of Mark*, Westminster 1951.
FAW, C. E., "The Outline of Mark", *JBR* 25 (1957) 19-23.
FELDMEIER, R., *Die Krisis des Gottes Sohnes. Die Gethsemaneerzählung als Schlüssel zur Markuspassion* (WUNT II/21), Tübingen 1987.
FENEBERG, W., *Der Markusprolog. Studien zur Formbestimmung des Evangeliums* (SANT 36), München 1974.
FEUILLET, A., "L'ἐξουσία du Fils de l'homme d'après Marc 2,10-28 et par.", *RSR* 42 (1954) 161-192.
——, "La controverse sur le jeûne (Mc 2,18-22; Mt 9,14-15; Lc 5,33-35)", *NRT* 90 (1968) 113-136, 252-277.
FIEBIG, P., *Der Erzählungsstil der Evangelien*, Leipzig 1925.
FLOWERS, H. J., "'Ὡς ἐξουσίαν ἔχων (Mk 1,22)", *ExpTim* 66 (1955) 254.
FOERSTER, W., "Διαβάλλω, διάβολος", *TDNT* II, 71-81.
——, "Ἔξεστιν, ἐξουσία", *TDNT* II, 560-575.
——, "Σατανᾶς", *TDNT* VII, 151-161.
FONCK, L., "Zum Abdecken des Daches (Mk 2,4; Lk 5,19)", *Bib* 6 (1926) 450-454.
FOWLER, R. M., *Loaves and Fishes. The Function of Feeding Stories in the Gospel of Mark* (SBLDS 54), Chico 1981.
FRIEDRICH, G., "Beobachtungen zur messianischen Hohenpriestererwartung in den Synoptikern", *ZTh* 53 (1956) 265-311.
FRIEDRICH, H., "Εὐαγγελίζομαι, εὐαγγέλιον", *TDNT* II, 707-737.
——, "Κῆρυξ, κηρύσσω, κήρυγμα", *TDNT* III, 683-718.
FULLER, R. H., *The Mission and Achievement of Jesus* (SBT 12), London 1954.
——, *The Foundations of New Testament Christology*, New York 1965.
——, *Interpreting the Miracles*, London 1966.
FUSCO, V., *Parola e Regno. La Sezione delle parabole (Mc 4,1-34) nella prospettiva Marciana* (Aloisiana 13), Brescia 1980.
——, "Il segreto messianico nell'episodio del lebbroso (Mc. 1,40-45)", *RivB* 29 (1981) 273-313.
——, "L'économie de la révélation dans l'évangile de Marc", *NRT* 104 (1982) 532-554.

GAIDE, G., "Le paralytique pardonné et guéri (Mc 2,1-12)", *ASeign* 38 (1970) 79-88.
———, "Question sur le jeûne. Mc 2,18-22", *ASeign* 39 (1972) 44-54.
GALIZZI, M., "Inizio del vangelo di Gesù il Cristo il Figlio di Dio (Mc 1,1-15)", *ParVi* 26 (1981) 4-18.
GAMBA, G. G., "Considerazioni in margine alla redazione di Mc 2,13-17", *DT(P)* 72 (1969) 201-226.
GASTON, L., *Horae Synopticae Electronicae. Word Statistics of the Synoptic Gospels* (SBLSBS 3), Missoula 1973.
GIBBS, J. M., "Mark 1,1-15, Matthew 1,1-4,16, Luke 1,1-4,30, John 1,1-51. The Gospel Prologues and Their Function", *StEv* VI (1973 = TU 112) 154-188.
GILS, F., "'Le sabbat a été fait pour l'homme et non l'homme pour le sabbat' (Mc II,27)", *RB* 69 (1962) 506-523.
GNILKA, J., "'Bräutigam' — spätjüdisches Messiaspredikat?", *TTZ* 69 (1960) 298-301.
———, *Die Verstockung Israels: Isaias 6,9-10 in der Theologie der Synoptiker*, München 1961.
———, "Das Martyrium Johannes des Täufers (Mk 6,17-29)", in: *Orientierung an Jesus. Zur Theologie der Synoptiker* (FS. J. Schmid; Hrsg. P. Hoffmann et al.), Freiburg - Basel - Wien 1973, 78-92.
———, "Das Elend vor dem Menschensohn (Mk 2,1-12)", in: *Jesus und der Menschensohn* (FS. A. Vögtle; Hrsg. R. Pesch et al.), Freiburg 1975, 196-209.
GOODENOUGH, E. R., *Jewish Symbols in the Greco-Roman Period I-XIII*, New York 1953-68.
GRÄSSER, E., "Jesus in Nazareth (Mark VI. 1-6a). Notes on the Redaction and Theology of St. Mark", *NTS* 16 (1969-70) 1-23.
GRASSI, J. A., "The Five Loaves of the High Priest", *NT* 7 (1964) 119-122.
GRELOT, P., *L'espérance juive à l'heure de Jésus*, Paris 1978.
GROB, R., *Einführung in das Markus-Evangelium*, Zürich 1965.
GRUNDMANN, W., *Das Evangelium nach Lukas*, Berlin ⁷1974.
———, *Das Evangelium nach Matthäus*, Berlin ⁴1975.
GUELICH, R. A., "'The Beginning of the Gospel' — Mark 1:1-15", *BR* 27 (1982) 5-15.
GUILLEMETTE, P., "Mc 1,24 est-il une formule de défense magique?", *ScEs* 30 (1978) 81-96.
———, "Un enseignement nouveau, plein d'autorité", *NT* 22 (1980) 222-247.
HAENCHEN, E., "Die Komposition vom Mk VII [sic] 27-IX 1 und Par.", *NT* 6 (1963) 81-109.
HAHN, F., *Christologische Hoheitstitel. Ihre Geschichte im frühen Christentum* (FRLANT 83), Göttingen ²1964.
———, "Die Bildworte vom neuen Flicken und vom jungen Wein (Mk. 2,21f parr)", *EvTh* 31 (1971) 357-375.
HALLBÄCK, G., "Materialistische Exegese und strukturale Analyse. Ein methodologischer Vergleich an Hand von Markus 2,1-12", *LingBib* 50 (1982) 7-32.
HATCH, E. and REDPATH, H. A., *A Concordance to the Septuagint*, Graz, Austria 1975.
HAWKINS, J. C., *Horae Synopticae. Contributions to the Study of the Synoptic Problem*, Oxford ²1909 (1968).

HAY, S., "The Son of Man in Mark 2,10 and 2,28", *JBL* 89 (1970) 69-75.

HAULOTTE, E., *Symbolique du vêtement selon la Bible*, Paris 1966.

HEDRICK, C. W., "The Role of 'Summary Statements' in the Composition of the Gospel of Mark: A Dialog with Karl Schmidt and Norman Perrin", *NT* 26 (1984) 289-311.

HEIL, J. , *Jesus Walking on the Sea. Meaning and Gospel Functions of Matt 14,22-33, Mark 6,45-52 and John 6,15b-21* (AnBib 87), Rome 1981.

HELFMEYER, F. J., *Die Nachfolge Gottes im Alten Testament* (BBB 29), Bonn 1968.

———, "'Gott Nachfolgen' in den Qumrantexten", *RevQ* 7 (1969-71) 81-104.

HENGEL, M., *The Charismatic Leader and His Followers* (trans. J. C. G. Greig), Edinburgh 1981.

HERRANZ MARCO, M., "Las espigas arrancadas en sábado (Mt 12,1-8 par.)", *EstB* 28 (1969) 313-348.

———, "La curación de un leproso según San Marcos (Mc 1,40-45)", *EstB* 31 (1972) 399-433.

HERRENBRÜCK, F., "Wer waren die 'Zöllner'?", *ZNW* 72 (1981) 178-194.

HIERONYMUS, *Commentarium in euangelium Matthaei* (Migne PL 26), col. 15-232.

HILGERT, E., *The Ship and Related Symbols in the New Testament*, Assen 1962.

HINZ, C., "Jesus und der Sabbat", *KD* 19 (1973) 91-108.

HORSTMANN, M., *Studien zur markinischen Christologie. Mk 8,27-9,13 als Zugang zum Christusbild des zweiten Evangeliums*, Münster in W. 1969.

HULTGREN, A. J., "The Formation of the Sabbath Pericope in Mark 2,23-28", *JBL* 91 (1972) 38-43.

———, *Jesus and His Adversaries. The Form and Function of the Conflict Stories in the Synoptic Tradition*, Minneapolis 1979.

HUTTON, W. R., "The Kingdom of God Has Come", *ExpTim* 64 (1952-53) 89-91.

IERSEL, B. M. F. VAN, "La vocation de Lévi (Mc., II, 13-17 par.). Traditions et rédactions", in: *De Jésus aux Évangiles. Tradition et rédaction dans les évangiles synoptiques* (ed. I. de la Potterie; BETL 25), Gembloux 1967, 212-232.

———, "'Aanvang van de Verkondiging over Jezus Christus'. Traditie en redactie in Mc. 1:1-15", *VoxTh* 39 (1969) 169-179.

———, "De betekenis van Marcus vanuit zijn topografische structuur", *TTh* 22 (1982) 117-138.

———, "Locality, Structure, and Meaning in Mark", *LingBib* 53 (1983) 45-54.

JAHNOW, H., "Das Abdecken des Daches Mc 2,4; Lc 5,19", *ZNW* 24 (1925) 155-158.

JAY, B., "Jésus et le sabbat. Simples notes à propos de Marc 2,23-28", *ETR* 50 (1975) 65-68.

JEREMIAS, J., "Zöllner und Sünder", *ZNW* 30 (1931) 293-300.

———, *The Parables of Jesus*, London 1963.

———, *The Eucharistic Words of Jesus* (trans. N. Perrin), London 1966.

———, *Jerusalem in the Time of Jesus* (trans. F. H. and C. H. Cave), London 1969.

———, *New Testament Theology* I (trans. J. Bowden), London 1971.

———, "Γραμματεύς", *TDNT* I, 740-742.

———, "Νύμφη, νυμφίος", *TDNT* IV, 1099-1106.

JOHNSON, E. S., "Mark 10:46-52: Blind Bartimaeus", *CBQ* 40 (1978) 191-204.

KAHMANN, J. J. A., "Marc 1,14-15 en hun plaats in het geheel van het Marcus-Evangelie", *Bijdr* 38 (1977) 84-98.

KARNETZKI, M., "Die galiläische Redaktion im Markusevagelium", *ZNW* 52 (1961) 238-272.

KÄSEMANN, E., *Commentary on Romans* (trans. G. M. Bromiley), London 1980.

KATO, Z., *Die Völkermission im Markusevangelium. Eine redaktionsgeschichtliche Untersuchung* (EurHS XXIII/252), Frankfurt - Bern - New York 1986.

KECK, L. E., "Mark 3,7-12 and Mark's Christology", *JBL* 84 (1965) 341-358.

——, "The Introduction to Mark's Gospel", *NTS* 12 (1965-66) 352-370.

KEE, A., "The Question about Fasting", *NT* 11 (1969) 161-173.

——, "The Old Coat and the New Wine. A Parable of Repentance", *NT* 12 (1970) 13-21.

KEE, H. C., "The Terminology of Mark's Exorcism Stories", *NTS* 14 (1967-68) 232-246.

——, *Community of the New Age: Studies in Mark's Gospel*, London 1977.

KELBER, W. H., *The Kingdom in Mark. A New Place and a New Time*, Philadelphia 1974.

KERNAGHAN, R., "History and Redaction in the Controversy Stories in Mark 2:1-3:6", *StBT* 9 (1979) 23-47.

KERTELGE, K., *Die Wunder Jesu im Markusevagelium. Eine redaktionsgeschichtliche Untersuchung*, München 1970.

——, "Die Vollmacht des Menschensohnes zur Sündenvergebung (Mk 2,10)", in: *Orientierung an Jesus. Zur Theologie der Synoptiker* (FS. J. Schmid; Hrsg. P. Hoffmann et al.), Freiburg - Basel - Wien 1973, 205-213.

KILPATRICK, G. D., "Mark 1,45 and the Meaning of λόγος", *JTS* 40 (1939) 389-390.

——, "Mark 1,45", *JTS* 42 (1941) 67-68.

KIRCHSCHLÄGER, W., "Jesu Gebetsverhalten als Paradigma zu Mk 1,35", *Kairos* 20 (1978) 303-310.

KITTEL, G., "Δοκέω, δόξα, δοξάζω", *TDNT* II, 232-255.

——, "Ἔρημος, ἐρημία", *TDNT* II, 654-660.

KLAUCK, H.-J., "Die Frage der Sündenvergebung in der Perikope von der Heilung des Gelähmten (Mk 2,1-12 parr)", *BZ* 25 (1981) 223-248.

KLEIN, G., "Die Berufung des Petrus", *ZNW* 58 (1967) 1-44.

KOCH, D.-A., *Die Bedeutung der Wundererzählung für die Christologie des Markusevangeliums* (BZNW 42), Berlin 1975.

——, "Zum Verhältnis von Christologie und Eschatologie im Markusevangelium. Beobachtungen aufgrund vom Mk 8,27-9,1", in: *Jesus Christus in Historie und Theologie* (FS. H. Conzelmann; Hrsg. G. Strecker), Tübingen 1975, 395-408.

——, "Inhaltliche Gliederung und geographischer Aufriss im Markusevangelium", *NTS* 29 (1983) 145-166.

KOWALSKI, T. W., "Les sources présynoptiques de Marc 1,32-34 et parallèles", *RSR* 60 (1972) 541-573.

KRAUSS, S., "Das Abdecken des Daches, Mc 2,4; Lc 5,19", *ZNW* 25 (1926) 307-310.

KRUSE, H., "Das Reich Satans", *Bib* 58 (1977) 29-61.

KUBY, A., "Zur Konzeption des Markus-Evangeliums", *ZNW* 49 (1958) 52-64.

KUHN, H. W., *Ältere Sammlungen im Markusevagelium* (SUNT 8), Göttingen 1971.

KÜMMEL, W. G., *Promise and Fulfilment. The Eschatological Message of Jesus* (trans. D. M. Barton), London 1957.

——, *Introduction to the New Testament* (trans. H. C. Kee), London 1975.

——, *Theology of the New Testament* (trans. J. E. Steely), London 1980.

LAKE, K., "'Εμβριμησάμενος and ὀργισθείς (Mark 1,40-43)", *HTR* 16 (1923) 197-198.

LAMARCHE, P., "La guérison de la belle-mère de Pierre et le genre littéraire des évangiles", *NRT* 87 (1965) 515-526.

——, "Le possédé de Gérasa (Mt 8,28-34; 5,1-20; Lc 8,26-39)", *NRT* 90 (1968) 581-597.

——, "L'appel à la conversion et à la foi. La vocation de Lévi (Mc., 2,13-17)", *LV* 25 (1970) 125-136.

——, "L'appel de Lévi. Marc 2,13-17", *Christus* 23 (1976) 106-118.

LA POTTERIE, I. DE, "Οἶδα et γινώσκω. Les deux modes de la connaissance dans le quatrième évangile", *Bib* 40 (1959) 709-725.

——, "De compositione evangelii Marci", *VD* 44 (1966) 135-141.

——, "Mors Johannis Baptistae (Mc 6,17-29)", *VD* 44 (1966) 142-151.

——, "La confessione messianica di Pietro in Marco 8,27-33", in: *San Pietro* (ASB XIX), Brescia 1967, 59-77.

——, "Le sens primitif de la multiplication des pains", in: *Jésus aux origines de la christologie* (éd. J. Dupont; BETL 40), Gembloux 1975, 303-329.

——, *La Vérité dans Saint Jean* I-II (AnBib 73-74), Rome 1977.

——, *Exegesis quarti evangelii. De matre Jesu in quarto evangelio*, Romae ²1982-1983.

LAMPE, G. W. H., *A Patristic Greek Lexicon*, Oxford 1961.

LANG, F. G., "Kompositionsanalyse des Markusevangeliums", *ZTK* 74 (1977) 1-24.

LEE, G. M., "They That Are Whole Need not a Physician", *ExpTim* 76 (1964-65) 254.

LÉGASSE, S., "Scribes et disciples de Jésus", *RB* 68 (1961) 497-502.

LEITCH, J. W., "Lord also of the Sabbath", *SJTh* 19 (1966) 426-433.

LÉON-DUFOUR, X., "La guérison de la belle-mère de Simon-Pierre", *Études* 24 (1965) 125-148.

——, *Résurrection de Jésus et message pascal*, Paris 1971.

——, *Introduzione al Nuovo Testamento, 2. l'annuncio del vangelo* (trans. A. Mastrandrea and B. Liverrani), Roma 1980.

LEROY, H., "Vergebung als Heilung. Zur jesuanischen Sicht der Vergebung", *Diak* 14 (1983) 79-84.

LEWIS, R. R., "'Επίβλημα ῥάκους ἀγνάφου (Mk 2,21)", *ExpTim* 45 (1933-34) 185.

LIDDELL, H. G. and SCOTT, R., *A Greek-English Lexicon*, Oxford ⁹1977.

LIGHTFOOT, R. H., *The Gospel Message of St. Mark*, Oxford 1950.

LINDEMANN, A., "'Der Sabbat ist um des Menschen willen geworden. . .' Historische und theologische Erwägungen zur Traditionsgeschichte der Sabbatpericope Mk 2,23-28 parr.", *WuD* 15 (1979) 79-105.

LOHMEYER, E., *Galiläa und Jerusalem* (FRLANT 34), Göttingen 1936.
——, *Gottesknecht und Davidssohn* (FELANT 61), Göttingen ²1953.
LOHSE, E., "Σάββατον", *TDNT* VII, 1-35.
——, "Υἱὸς Δαυίδ", *TDNT* VIII, 478-488.
——, "Jesu Worte über den Sabbat", in: *Judentum - Urchristentum - Kirche* (FS. J. Jeremias; Hrsg. W. Eltester), Berlin 1960, 79-89.
——, *The New Testament Environment* (trans. J. E. Steely), London 1976.
LOOS, H. VAN DER, *The Miracles of Jesus*, Leiden 1965.
LOSADA, D. A., "El Relato de la Pesca Milagrosa", *RevistB* 40 (1978) 17-26.
LÜHRMANN, D. *Das Markusevangelium* (HNT 3), Tübingen 1987.
LUZ, U., "Das Geheimnismotiv und die markinische Christologie", *ZNW* 56 (1965) 9-30 = in: *Das Markus-Evangelium* (Hrsg. R. Pesch; WdF 411), Darmstadt 1979, 211-237.
MAISCH, I., *Die Heilung des Gelähmten. Eine exegetischtraditionsgeschichtliche Untersuchung zu Mk 2,1-12* (SBS 52), Stuttgart 1971.
MALBON, E. S., "Elements of an Exegesis of the Gospel of Mark according to Lévi-Strauss' Methodology", in: *SBL Seminar Papers* 11 (ed. P. J. Achtemeier), 1977, 155-170.
——, "Mythic Structure and Meaning in Mark: Elements of a Lévi-Straussian Analysis", *Semeia* 16 (1979) 97-132.
——, "Galilee and Jerusalem: History and Literature in Marcan Interpretation", *CBQ* 44 (1982) 242-255.
——, "Τῇ οἰκίᾳ αὐτοῦ: Mark 2,15 in Context", *NTS* 31 (1985) 282-292.
——, *Narrative Space and Mythic Meaning in Mark*, San Francisco 1986.
MÁNEK, J., "Fishers of Men", *NT* 2 (1957) 138-141.
MANGATT, G., *The Disciples of Jesus and the Way of the Passion: Mk 8,27-10,52* (Dissertation PBI), Rome 1971 (unpublished).
MANICARDI, E., *Il cammino di Gesù nel Vangelo di Marco. Schema narrativo e tema cristologico* (AnBib 96), Roma 1981.
MANSON, T. W., "Mark II.27f.", *CNT* 11 (1947) 138-146.
MARCHEL, W., *Abba, Père! La prière du Christ et des chrétiens* (AnBib 19), Rome 1971.
MARCHESELLI, C., "La ricerca di Dio nei segni dei tempi. La struttura tematico letteraria di Mc 1,21-3,6 par.", in: *Quaerere Deum* (ed. G. Danieli; ASB XXV), Brescia 1980, 289-313.
MARSHALL, I. H., *The Gospel of Luke*, Exeter, Devon 1979.
MARXSEN, W., *Einleitung in das NT. Eine Einführung in ihre Probleme*, Gütersloh ³1964.
——, *Introduction to the New Testament* (trans. G. Buswell), Philadelphia 1968.
——, *Mark the Evangelist. Studies on the Redaction History of the Gospel* (trans. J. Boyer et al.), New York 1969.
MASSON, C., "La péricope du lépreux (Marc 1,40-45)", *RTP* 26 (1938) 287-295.
MAYER, B., "Überlieferungs- und redaktionsgeschichtliche Überlegungen zu Mk 6,1-6a", *BZ* 22 (1978) 187-198.
MEAD, R. T., "The Healing of the Paralytic — A Unit?", *JBL* 80 (1961) 348-354.

MERCURIO, R., "And Then They Will Fast", *Worship* 35 (1961) 150-154.

MERKLEIN, H., "Die Umkehrpredigt bei Johannes dem Täufer und Jesus von Nazaret", *BZ* 25 (1981) 29-46.

METZGER, B. M., *A Textual Commentary on the Greek New Testament*, London 1971.

MICHAELIS, W., "Die Davidssohnschaft Jesu als historisches und kerygmatisches Problem", in: *Der historische Jesus und der kerygmatische Christus* (Hrsg. H. Ristow and K. Matthiae), Berlin 1960, 317-330.

MICHEL, O., "Τελώνης", *TDNT* VIII, 88-105.

MINETTE DE TILLESSE, M., *Le secret messianique dans l'évangile de Marc* (LD 47), Paris 1968.

MONTEFIORE, C. G., *The Synoptic Gospels*, vol. I, London ²1927 = New York 1968.

MOORE, G. F., *Judaism in the First Centuries of the Christian Era. The Age of the Tannaim*, Cambridge vol. I-II 1927; vol. III 1930.

MORGEN, C. S., "When Abiathar was High Priest (Mk 2;26)", *JBL* 98 (1979) 409-410.

MORGENTHALER, R., *Statistik des neutestamentlichen Wortschatzes*, Zürich - Frankfurt am Main ³1982.

MOULE, C. F. D., *An Idiom Book of New Testament Greek*, Cambridge 1953.

MOULTON, J. H., *A Grammar of New Testament Greek*. vol. I: *Prolegomena*, Edinburgh 1908.
    vol. II: (with W. F. HOWARD) *Accidence and Word Formation*, Edinburgh 1928.
    vol. III: (with N. TURNER) *Syntax*, Edinburgh 1963.
    vol. IV: (with N. TURNER) *Style*, Edinburgh 1976.

MOULTON, W. F., *A Concordance to the Greek Testament*, Edinburgh ⁵1978.

MOURLON BEERNAERT, P., "Jésus controversé. Structure et théologie de Marc 2,1-3,6", *NRT* 95 (1973) 129-149.

MURMELSTEIN, B., "Jesu Gang durch die Staatfelder", *Angelos* 3 (1930) 111-120.

MURPHY-O'CONNOR, J., "Péché et communauté dans le Nouveau Testament", *RB* 74 (1967) 161-193.

MUßNER, F., "Die Bedeutung von Mk 1,14f für die Reichsgottesverkündigung Jesu", *TTZ* 66 (1957) 257-275.

——, "Ein Wortspiel in Mk 1,24?", *BZ* 4 (1960) 285-286.

——, "Gottesherrschaft und Sendung Jesu nach Mk 1,14f. Zugleich ein Beitrag über die innere Struktur des Markusevangeliums", in: *Praesentia Salutis. Gesammelte Studien zu Fragen und Themen des Neuen Testaments*, Düsseldorf 1967, 81-98.

——, "Jesu Ansage der Nähe der eschatologischen Gottesherrschaft nach Markus 1,14.15. Ein Beitrag der modernen Sprachwissenschaft zur Exegese", in: *Gottesherrschaft-Weltherrschaft* (FS. R. Graber), Regensburg 1980, 33-49.

NAGEL, W., "Neuer Wein in alten Schläuchen (Mt 9,17)", *VigChr* 14 (1960) 1-8.

NEIRYNCK, F., *Duality in Mark. Contributions to the Study of the Markan Redaction* (BETL 31), Leuven 1972.

——, "Les accords mineurs et la rédaction des évangiles. (Mc., II,1-12)", *ETL* 50 (1974) 215-230.

——, "Jesus and the Sabbath. Some Observations on Mark II,27", in: *Jésus aux origines de la christologie* (ed. J. Dupont; BETL 40), Gembloux 1975, 227-270.

——, "Papyrus Egerton 2 and the Healing of the Leper", *ETL* 61 (1985) 153-160.
NEUHÄUSLER, E., "Jesu Stellung zum Sabbat. Versuch einer Interpretation", *BibLeb* 12 (1971) 1-16.
——, *Anspruch und Antwort Gottes. Zur Lehre von den Weisungen innerhalb der synoptischen Jesusverkündigung*, Düsseldorf 1962.
NICKLIN, T., "Mark 1,45", *ExpTim* 51 (1939-40) 252.
NIESE, B. (ed.), *Flavii Josephi Opera* I-VII, Berlin 1877-1904, Neudruck 1955.
NOLLI, G., *Evangelo secondo Marco*, Roma 1978.
NORDEN, E., *Agnostos Theos. Untersuchungen zur Formengeschichte religiöser Rede*, Darmstadt ⁵1971.
——, *Die antike Kunstprosa vom VI. Jahrhundert v. Chr. bis in die Zeit der Renaissance* I-II, Stuttgart ⁸1981.
OEPKE, A., "'Αποκαθίστημι", *TDNT* I, 387-393.
O'HARA, J., "Christian Fasting. Mk. 2,18-22", *ScrB* 19 (1967) 82-95.
OPPENHEIMER, A., *The 'Am Ha-Aretz'. A Study in the Social History of the Jewish People in the Hellenistic-Roman Period*, Leiden 1977.
OSBORNE, B. A. E., "Peter: Stumbling-Block and Satan", *NT* 15 (1973) 187-190.
OSTEN-SACKEN, P. VON DER, "Streitgespräch und Parabel als Formen markinischer Christologie", in: *Jesus Christus in Histotie und Theologie* (FS. H. Conzelmann; Hrsg. G. Strecker), Tübingen 1975, 375-394.
PALMER, R. E., *Hermeneutics: Interpretation Theory of Schleiermacher, Dilthy, Heidegger, and Gadamer*, Evanston 1969.
PANIMOLLE, S. A., *Lettura pastorale del vangelo di Giovanni* I-III, Bologna 1978, 1980, 1984.
PAUL, A., "La guérison d'un lépreux. Approche d'un récit de Marc (1,40-45)", *NRT* 92 (1970) 592-604.
PEABODY, D. B., *The Redactional Features of the Author of Mark: A Method Focusing on Recurrent Phraseology and its Application*, Michigan 1986.
PERELS, O., *Die Wunderüberlieferung der Synoptiker in ihrem Verhältnis zur Wortüberlieferung* (BWANT IV/12), Stuttgart 1934.
PERRIN, N., *Rediscovering the Teaching of Jesus*, London - New York 1967.
——, "Towards an Interpretation of the Gospel of Mark", in: *Christology and a Modern Pilgrimage — A Discussion with N. Perrin* (ed. H. D. Betz), Missoula, Montana 1971, 1-78.
——, *The New Testament: An Introduction*, New York 1974.
——, "The Interpretation of a Biblical Symbol", *JR* 55 (1975) 348-370.
——, *Jesus and the Language of the Kingdom: Symbol and Metaphor in New Testament Interpretation*, Philadelphia 1976.
PESCH, R., "Levi—Matthäus (Mc 2,14/Mt 9,9; 10,3). Ein Beitrag zur Lösung eines alten Problems", *ZNW* 59 (1968) 40-56.
——, "'Eine neue Lehre aus Macht'. Eine Studie zu Mk 1,21-28", in: *Evangelienforschung* (Hrsg. J. B. Bauer), Graz - Wien - Köln 1968, 241-276.
——, "Ein Tag vollmächtigen Wirkens Jesu in Kapharnaum (Mk 1,21-34.35-39)", *BibLeb* 9 (1968) 114-128, 177-195, 261-277.
——, *Naherwartungen. Tradition und Redaktion in Mk 13*, Düsseldorf 1968.

——, "Berufung und Sendung, Nachfolge und Mission. Eine Studie zu Mk 1,16-20", *ZKT* 91 (1969) 1-31.
——, "Anfang des Evangeliums Jesu Christi. Eine Studie zum Prolog des Markusevangeliums", in: *Die Zeit Jesu* (FS. H. Schlier; Hrsg. G. Bornkamm and K. Rahner), Freiburg - Basel - Wien 1970, 108-144.
——, "Das Zöllnergastmahl (Mk 2,15-17)", in: *Mélanges bibliques en hommage au R. P. Beda Rigaux*, Gembloux 1970, 63-87.
——, "Die Erzählung von der Heilung eines Aussätzigen", in: *Jesu ureigene Taten? Ein Beitrag zur Wunderfrage*, Freiburg 1970, 52-87.
——, *Der Besessene von Gerasa. Entstehung und Überlieferung einer Wundergeschichte* (SBS 56), Stuttgart 1972.
——, "Die Heilung der Schwiegermutter des Simon-Petrus", in: *Neuere Exegese — Verlust oder Gewinn?*, Freiburg 1978, 143-175.
PETERSEN, N. R., "'Point of View' in Mark's Narrative", *Semeia* 12 (1978) 97-121.
POPKES, W., *Christus traditus. Eine Untersuchung zum Begriff der Dahingabe im Neuen Testament* (ATANT 19), Zürich - Stuttgart 1967.
PREISKER, H., "Ἐγγύς, ἐγγίζω", *TDNT* II, 330-332.
PRYKE, E. J., *Redactional Style in the Marcan Gospel* (SNTSMS 33), Cambridge 1978.
QUESNELL, Q., *The Mind of Mark. Interpretation and Method through the Exegesis of Mark 6,52* (AnBib 38), Rome 1969.
RAITT, T. M., "The Prophetic Summons to Repentance", *ZAW* (1971) 30-49.
RAMAROSON, L., "Le plan du second Évangile", *ScEs* 27 (1975) 219-233.
RENGSTORF, K. H., "Ἁμαρτωλός", *TDNT* I, 317-335.
——, "Μανθάνω, καταμανθάνω, μαθητής", *TDNT* IV, 390-461.
REPLOH, K.-G., *Markus-Lehrer der Gemeinde. Eine redaktionsgeschichtliche Studie zu den Jüngerperikopen des Markus-Evangeliums* (SBM 9), Stuttgart 1969.
——, "'Evangelium' bei Markus. Das Evangelium des Markus als Anruf an die Gemeinde zu Umkehr und Glaube (1,14-15)", *BiKi* 27 (1972) 110-114.
REUMANN, J., "Mark 1,14-20", *Int* 32 (1978) 405-410.
RIGATO. M. L., "Tradizione e redazione in Mc 1,29-31 (e paralleli). La guarigione della suocera di Simon Pietro", *RivB* 17 (1969) 139-174.
RIGAUX, B., *Témoignage de l'évangile de Marc*, Bruges 1965.
ROBBINS, V. K., "Summons and Outline in Mark: The Three Step Progression", *NT* 23 (1981) 97-114.
——, "Mark 1,4-20: An Interpretation at the Intersection of Jewish and Graeco-Roman Traditions", *NTS* 28 (1982) 220-236.
ROBINSON, J. M., *The Problem of History in Mark*, London 1957.
ROLLAND. P., "Les prédécesseurs de Marc. Les sources présynoptiques de Mc 2,18-22 et parallèles", *RB* 89 (1982) 370-405.
RÜGER, H. P., "ΝΑΖΑΡΕΘ/ΝΑΖΑΡΑ, ΝΑΖΑΡΗΝΟΣ/ΝΑΖΩΡΑΙΟΣ", *ZNW* 72 (1981) 257-263.
RUSSELL. E. A., "Mark 2,23-3,6 — A Judean Setting?" *StEv* VI (1973 = TU 112), 466-472.
RYRIE. C. C., "The Cleansing of the Leper", *BS* 113 (1956) 262-267.

SANTRAM, P. B., "Jesus Christ and the Kingdom of God: A New Testament Perspective", *IJT* 29 (1980) 81-91.

SAUFER, J., "Traditionsgeschichtliche Überlegungen zu Mk 3,1-6", *ZNW* 73 (1982) 183-203.

SCHÄFER, K. T., "'Und dann werden sie fasten an jenem Tage' (Mk 2,20 und Par.)", in: *Synoptische Studien* (FS. A. Wikenhauser), München 1953, 124-147.

SCHENKE, L., *Studien zur Passionsgeschichte des Markus. Tradition und Redaktion in Markus 14,1-42* (FzB 4), Würzburg 1971.

——, *Die Wundererzählungen des Markusevangeliums*, Stuttgart 1974.

——, "Der Aufbau des Markusevangeliums — Ein hermeneutischer Schlüssel?", *BibNot* 32 (1986) 54-82.

SCHILLE, G., "Die Topographie des Markusevangeliums, ihre Hintergründe und ihre Einordnung", *ZDPV* 73 (1957) 133-166.

——, "Bemerkungen zur Formgeschichte des Evangeliums. Rahmen und Aufbau des Markus-Evangeliums", *NTS* 4 (1957-58) 1-24.

——, *Offen für alle Menschen*, Berlin 1973.

SCHLOSSER, J., *Le règne de Dieu dans les dits de Jésus* I-II, Paris 1980.

SCHMAHL, G., *Die Zwölf im Markusevangelium. Eine redaktionsgeschichtliche Untersuchung* (TTS 30), Trier 1974.

SCHMIDT, K. L., *Der Rahmen der Geschichte Jesu*, Darmstadt 1969.

——, "Καλέω, κλῆσις, κλητός", *TDNT* III, 487-536.

SCHNACKENBURG, R., "'Das Evangelium' im Verständnis des ältesten Evangelisten", in: *Orientierung an Jesus. Zur Theologie der Synoptiker* (FS. J. Schmid; Hrsg. P. Hoffmann), Frieburg 1973, 309-324.

SCHNEIDER, J., "Ἔρχομαι, ἔλευσις", *TDNT* II, 666-684.

SCHREIBER, J., "Die Christologie des Markusevangeliums. Beobachtungen zur Theologie und Komposition des zweiten Evangeliums", *ZTK* 58 (1961) 154-183.

——, *Theologie des Vertrauens. Eine redaktionsgeschichtliche Untersuchung des Markusevangeliums*, Hamburg 1967.

SCHULZ, A., *Nachfolgen und Nachahmen* (SANT 6), München 1962.

SCHULZ, S., *Die Stunde der Botschaft*, Hamburg - Zürich ²1970.

SCHÜRER, E., *The History of the Jewish People in the Age of Jesus Christ* I-II (ed. and trans. G. Vermes), Edinburgh 1979.

SCHÜRMANN, H., *Das Lukasevangelium. Kommentar zur Kap. 1,1-9,50* (HTKNT III/1), Freiburg - Basel - Wien 1969.

SCHWEIZER, E., "'Er wird Nazoräer Heißen', (Mc 1,24, Mt 2,23)", in: *Judentum - Urchristentum - Kirche* (FS. J. Jeremias; Hrsg. W. Eltester), Berlin 1960, 90-93.

——, "Anmerkungen zur Theologie des Markus", in: *Neotestamentica et Patristica* (FS. O. Cullmann; SupplNT 6), Leiden 1962, 35-46; = *Neotestamentica. Deutsche und englische Aufsätze 1951-1963*, Zürich - Stuttgart 1963, 93-104.

——, "Die theologische Leistung des Markus", *EvTh* 24 (1964) 337-355; = *Beiträge zur Theologie des Neuen Testaments*, Zürich 1970, 21-42; = *Das Markus-Evangelium* (Hrsg. R. Pesch; WdF 411), Darmstadt 1979, 163-189.

——, "The Portrayal of the Life of Faith in the Gospel of Mark", *Int* 32 (1978) 387-399.

——, *The Good News according to Matthew*, London 1980.

SEITZ, O. J. F., "Praeparatio evangelica in the Markan Prologue", *JBL* 82 (1963) 201-206.

——, "Gospel Prologues: A Common Pattern?", *JBL* 83 (1964) 262-268.

SERRA, A., *Contributi dell'antica letteratura gudaica per l'esegesi di Giovanni 2,1-12 e 19,25-27*, Roma 1977.

SHAE, G. S., "The Question on the Authority of Jesus", *NT* 16 (1974) 1-29.

SHARP, D. S., "Mark 2,10", *ExpTim* 38 (1927-28) 428-429.

SIBINGA, J. S., "Text and Literary Art in Mark 3,1-6", in: *Studies in New Testament Language and Text* (FS. G. D. Kilpatrick; SupplNT 44), Leiden 1976, 357-365.

SIMPSON, P., "Reconciliation in the Making: A Reading of Mark 1,14-3,6", *AfER* 17 (1975) 194-203.

SMITH, C. W. F., "Fishers of Men. Footnotes on a Gospel Figure", *HTR* 52 (1959) 187-203.

SMITH, M., *Tannaitic Parallels to the Gospels* (JBLMS 6), Philadelphia 1951.

——, "The Composition of Mark 11-16", *HeyJ* 22 (1981) 363-377.

SMITH, S. H., "The Literary Structure of Mark 11:1-12:40", *NT* 31 (1989) 104-124.

SNOY, T., "Les miracles dans l'évangile de Marc. Examen de quelques études récentes", *RTL* 3 (1972) 449-464; 4 (1973) 58-101.

SOARES PRABHU, G. M., *The Formula Quotations in the Infancy Narrative of Matthew. An Enquiry into the Tradition History of Mt 1-2* (AnBib 63), Rome 1976.

SÖDING, T., *Glaube bei Markus. Glaube an das Evangelium, Gebetsglaube und Wunderglaube im Kontext der markinischen Basileiatheologie und Christologie* (SBB 12), Stuttgart 1987.

SOUBIGOU, L., "O Plano do Evangelho segundo São Marcos", *RCB* 12 (1975) 84-96.

STAERK, W., *Die Erlösererwartung in den östlichen Religionen*, Stuttgart 1938.

STANDAERT, B., *L'évangile selon Marc. Composition et genre litteraire*, Zevenkerken - Brugge, 1978.

STARR, J., "The Meaning of 'Authority' in Mark 1,22", *HTR* 23 (1930) 302-305.

STEIN, R. H., "The 'Redaktionsgeschichtlich' Investigation of a Markan Seam (Mc 1,21f.)", *ZNW* 61 (1970) 70-94.

STEINHAUSER, G., "Neuer Wein braucht neue Schläuche. Zur Exegese von Mk 2, 21f par.", in: *Biblische Randbemerkungen* (FS. R. Schnackenburg; Hrsg H. Merklein and J. Lange), Würzburg 1974, 113-123.

STOCK, A., "Literary Criticism and Mark's Mystery Play", *BiTod* 100 (1979) 1909-1915.

——, *Call to Discipleship. A Literary Study of Mark's Gospel*, Wilmington, Delaware 1982.

STOCK, K., *Boten aus dem Mit-Ihm-Sein. Das Verhältnis zwischen Jesus und den Zwölf nach Markus* (AnBib 70), Rom 1975.

——, "Gesù è il Cristo, il Figlio di Dio, nel Vangelo di Marco", *RasT* 17 (1976) 242-253.

STRACK, H. L., *Einleitung in Talmud und Midrasch*, München ⁵1921.

STRACK, H. L. and BILLERBECK, P., *Kommentar zum Neuen Testament aus Talmud und Midrasch* I-VI, München 1978-79.

STRECKER, G., "Literarkritische Überlegungen zum εὐαγγέλιον-Begriff im Markusevangelium", in: *Neues Testament und Geschichte. Historisches Geschehen und Deutung im Neuen Testament* (FS. O. Cullmann; Hrsg. H. Baltensweiler and B. Bricke), Zürich - Tübingen 1972, 91-104.

SUHL, A., "Überlegungen zur Hermeneutik an Hand von Mk 1,21-28", *Kairos* 26 (1984) 28-38.

SUNDWALL, J., *Die Zusammensetzung des Markusevangeliums*, Abo 1934.

SWETNAM, J., "Some Remarks on the Meaning of ὁ δὲ ἐξελθών in Mark 1,45", *Bib* 68 (1987) 245-249.

TAGAWA, K., *Miracles et Évangile. La Pensée personnelle de l'Évangeliste Marc*, Paris 1966.

TAYLOR, V., *Formation of the Gospel Tradition*, London ²1964.

THEIßEN, G., *Urchristliche Wundergeschichten* (SNT 8), Gütersloh 1974.

——, "Die aretalogische Evangelienkomposition des Markus", in: *Das Markus-Evangelium* (Hrsg. R. Pesch; WdF 411), Darmstadt 1979, 377-389.

THEOBALD, M., "Der Primat der Synchronie vor der Diachronie als Grundaxiom der Literarkritik. Methodische Erwägungen an Hand von Mk 2,13-17/Mt 9,9-13", *BZ* 22 (1978) 161-186.

THISSEN, W., *Erzählung der Befreiung. Eine exegetische Untersuchung zu Mk 2,1-3,6* (FzB 21), Würzburg 1976.

TRAUTMANN, M., *Zeichenhafte Handlungen Jesu. Ein Beitrag zur Frage nach dem geschichtlichen Jesus* (FzB 37), Würzburg 1980.

TREVIJANO ETCHEVERRIA, R., "El trasfondo apocalyptico de Mc. 1,24.25; 5,7.8 y par.", *Burg* 11 (1970) 117-133.

——, *Comienzo del Evangelio. Estudio sobre el Prólogo de San Marcos*, Burgos 1971.

TRILLING, W., "Die Botschaft vom Reiche Gottes (Mk 1,14-15)", in: *Christusverkündigung in den synoptischen Evangelien*, München 1969, 40-63.

TROADEC, H., "Le Fils de l'homme est maître même du sabbat (Marc 2,23-3,6)", *BVC* 21 (1958) 73-83.

TROCMÉ, É., *La formation de l'Évangile selon Marc*, Paris 1963.

TROSSEN, C., "Das Ährenpflücken der Apostel", *ThGl* 6 (1914) 466-475.

TRUDINGER, P., "The Word on the Generation Gap. Reflections on a Gospel Metaphor", *BTB* 5 (1975) 311-315.

TURNER, C. H., "Marcan Usage: Notes, Critical and Exegetical, on the Second Gospel", *JTS* 25 (1924) 377-386; 26 (1925) 12-20, 145-156, 225-240; 27 (1926) 58-62; 28 (1927) 9-30, 349-362; 29 (1928) 275-289, 346-361.

——, "Notes and Studies. A Textual Commentary on Mark", *JTS* 28 (1927) 145-158.

VAGANAY, L., "Marc 1,41. Essai de critique textuelle", in: *Mélanges E. Podechard*, Lyon 1945, 238-252.

VIA, D. O., *Kerygma and Comedy in the New Testament. A Structuralist Approach to Hermeneutics*, Philadelphia 1975.

288 BIBLIOGRAPHY

VIELHAUER, P., *Geschichte der urchristlichen Literatur. Einleitung in das Neue Testament, die Apokryphen und die Apostolischen Väter*, Berlin - New York 1975.

VÖGTLE, A., "Messiasbekenntnis und Petrusverheißung. Zur Komposition Mt 16,13-23 Par.", *BZ* 1 (1957) 252-272; 2 (1958) 85-103.

VÖLKEL, M., "Freund der Zöllner und Sünder", *ZNW* 69 (1978) 1-10.

VOLZ, P., *Die Eschatologie in der jüdischen Gemeinde im neutestamentlichen Zeitalter*, Tübingen ²1934 = Hildesheim 1966.

WAIBEL, M., "Die Auseinandersetzung mit der Fasten- und Sabbatpraxis Jesu in der urchristlichen Gemeinde", in: *Zur Geschichte des Urchristentums* (QD 87), Freiburg - Basel - Wien 1979, 63-96.

WALKER, W. O., "Jesus and the Tax Collectors", *JBL* 97 (1978) 221-238.

WEEDEN, T. J., *Mark—Tradition in Conflict*, Philadelphia 1971.

WEGENAST, K., "Das Ährenrupfen am Sabbat (Mk 2,23-28)", in: *Streitgespräche* (eds. H. Stock et al.), Gütersloh 1968, 27-37.

WEIß, J., *Das Älteste Evangelium. Ein Beitrag zum Verständnis des Markusevangeliums und der ältesten evangelischen Überlieferung*, Göttingen 1903.

WEIß, K., "Ekklesiologie, Tradition und Geschichte in der Jüngerunterweisung Markus 8,27-10,52", in: *Der historische Jesus und der kerygmatische Christus*, (Hrsg. H. Ristow and K. Matthiae), Berlin 1960, 414-438.

WEIß, W. *"Eine neue Lehre in Vollmacht". Die Streit- und Schulgespräche des Markus-Evangeliums* (BZNW 53), Berlin - New York 1989.

WIBBING, S., "Das Zöllnergastmahl (Mk 2,13-17; vgl. Mt 9,9-13; Lk 5,27-32)", in: *Streitgespräche* (eds. H. Stock et al.), Gütersloh 1968, 84-107.

————, "Die Heilung eines Gelähmten", in: *Wundergeschichten* (eds. U. Becker et al.), Gütersloh 1965, 12-33.

WICHELHAUS, M., "Am ersten Tage der Woche. Mk. 1,35-39 und die didaktischen Absichten des Markus-Evangelisten", *NT* 11 (1969) 45-70.

WIKENHAUSER, A., *Einleitung in das Neue Testament*, Freiburg - Basel - Wien ³1959.

WIKGREN, A., "'Ἀρχὴ τοῦ εὐαγγελίου [Mc 1,1]", *JBL* 61 (1942) 11-20.

WOLFF, H. W., "Das Thema 'Umkehr' in der alttestamentlichen Prophetie", *ZTK* 48 (1951) 129-148.

————, "Das Kerygma des deuteronomistischen Geschichtswerks", *ZAW* 73 (1961) 171-186.

WREDE, W., *Das Messiasgeheimnis in den Evangelien. Zugleich ein Beitrag zum Verständnis des Markusevangeliums*, Göttingen 1901.

————, "Zur Heilung des Gelähmten (Mc 2,1ff.)", *ZNW* 5 (1904) 354-358.

WRETLIND, D. O., "Jesus' Philosophy of Ministry: A Study of a Figure of Speech in Mark 1,38", *JETS* 20 (1977) 321-323.

WUELLNER, W. H., *The Meaning of 'Fishers of Men'*, Philadelphia 1967.

ZELLER, D., "Die Heilung des Aussätzigen (Mk, 40-45). Ein Beispiel bekennender und werbender Erzählung", *TTZ* 93 (1984) 138-146.

ZERWICK, M., *Untersuchungen zum Markus-Stil*, Rom 1937.

————, *Biblical Greek* (trans. J. Smith), Rome 1963.

ZIESLER, J. A., "The Removal of the Bridegroom: A Note on Mark II.18-22 and parallels", *NTS* 19 (1972-73) 190-194.

ZORELL, F., *Lexicon graecum novi testamenti*, Romae ³1978.

INDEX OF BIBLICAL REFERENCES
(Selective)

INDEX OF AUTHORS

TIPOGRAFIA POLIGLOTTA DELLA PONTIFICIA UNIVERSITÀ GREGORIANA
PIAZZA DELLA PILOTTA, 4 - ROMA